THE STRANGE WORLD OF HUMAN SACRIFICE

STUDIES IN THE HISTORY AND ANTHROPOLOGY OF RELIGION

Editor: Jan N. BREMMER

In recent years, especially after the tragic events of 9/11, religion has increasingly drawn the attention of scholars. Whereas, traditionally, religion was studied by historians, anthropologists and students of the main religious traditions, today religion can be seen as a major factor on the contemporary political stage and is omnipresent in the media. Yet modern developments can rarely be well understood without proper anthropological and historical analyses. That is why we are pleased to announce a new series, *Studies in the History and Anthropology of Religion*. The editor welcomes contributions on specific aspects of religion from a historical and/or anthropological perspective, be it proceedings of conferences or monographs.

1. *The Strange World of Human Sacrifice*, J.N. Bremmer (ed.), Leuven, 2007

2. *What is Religion? What is the Secular?*, J.N. Bremmer and A.L. Molendijk (eds.), Leuven, 2007

The Strange World of Human Sacrifice

EDITED BY

Jan N. Bremmer

PEETERS
LEUVEN – PARIS – DUDLEY, MA
2007

Library of Congress Cataloging-in-Publication Data

The strange world of human sacrifice / edited by Jan N. Bremmer.
   p. cm. -- (Studies in the history and anthropology of religion ; 1)
   Proceedings of a conference held in winter 2004 at the Rijksuniversiteit Groningen
   Includes bibliographical references and index.
   Contents: Aztec human sacrifice as expiation / M. Graulich -- Human sacrifice in
medieval Irish literature / J. Borsje -- Myth and ritual in Greek human sacrifice: Lykaon,
Polyxena, and the case of the Rhodian criminal / J.N. Bremmer -- The early Christians
and human sacrifice / L. Roig Lanzillotta -- Child sacrifice in ancient Israel: the status
quaestionis / E. Noort -- Human sacrifice in ancient Egypt / H. te Velde -- Retainer
sacrifice in Egypte and in Nubia / J. van Dijk -- Human sacrifice in India in Vedic times
and before / A. Parpola -- Human sacrifice (purusamedha), construction sacrifice, and the
origin of the idea of the "man of the homestead" (vastupurusa) / H.T. Bakker -- Human
sacrifice among the Konds / L.P. van den Bosch -- Human sacrifice in Japan / K.
Harimoto -- Human sacrifice and self-sacrifice in China: a century of revelations / T.H. Barrett.
   ISBN 978-90-429-1843-6 (alk. paper)
   1. Human sacrifice--Congresses. I. Bremmer, Jan N.

BL570.S433 2006
203'.42--dc22
                                                                          2006050881

Cover illustration:
The cover depicts a human sacrifice, in a morai (temple), in Otaheite (Tahiti) by
John Webber (1751-1793). It was witnessed by Captain Cook, who is standing on
the right, on 1 September 1777.

© 2007, Peeters – Bondgenotenlaan 153 – B-3000 Leuven – Belgium
ISBN   978-90-429-1843-6
D. 2006/0602/128

CONTENTS

PREFACE

In recent years, religion has increasingly drawn the attention of scholars. Whereas, traditionally, it was studied by historians, anthropologists and students of the main religious traditions, today religion can be seen as a major factor on the contemporary political stage and is omnipresent in the media. Yet modern developments can rarely be well understood without proper anthropological and historical analyses. That is why we are pleased to announce a new series, *Studies in the History and Anthropology of Religion*. The editor welcomes contributions on specific aspects of religion from a historical and/or anthropological perspective, be it proceedings of conferences or monographs.

The present volume presents the proceedings of a conference on human sacrifice, one of the most gruesome and intriguing aspects of religion. The volume starts with a brief introduction to the subject, which is followed by studies of Aztec human sacrifice and the literary motif of human sacrifice in medieval Irish literature. Turning to ancient Greece, three cases of human sacrifice are analysed: a ritual example, a mythical case, and one in which myth and ritual are interrelated. The early Christians were the victims of accusations of human sacrifice, but in turn imputed the crime to heterodox Christians, just as the Jews imputed the crime to their neighbours. The ancient Egyptians rarely seem to have practised human sacrifice, but buried the pharaoh's servants with him in order to serve him in the afterlife, albeit only for a brief period at the very beginning of pharaonic civilization. In ancient India we can follow the traditions of human sacrifice from the earliest texts up to modern times, where especially in eastern India goddesses, such as Kali, were long worshipped with human victims. In Japanese tales human sacrifice often takes the form of self-sacrifice, and there may well be a line from these early sacrifices to modern *kamikaze*. The last study throws a surprising light on human sacrifice in China. The volume is concluded with a detailed index.

The international conference that formed the basis of this book was organised by the research group *Religious Symbols* and took place at the Faculty of Theology and Religious Studies of the Rijksuniversiteit Groningen in the winter of 2004. We would like to thank both the Faculty of Theology and Religious Studies of the Rijksuniversiteit Groningen and the Groningen Research School for the Humanities for their financial support towards the conference. The University of Chicago Press kindly permitted us to reprint the study by Michel Graulich on Aztec human sacrifice. Last but not least, Kristina Meinking was a great help in reading the proofs and making the index.

Jan N. BREMMER   Groningen, Summer 2006

NOTES ON CONTRIBUTORS

Hans Bakker (1948) is Gonda Professor of Hinduism in the Sanskrit Tradition &Indian Philosophy at the Rijksuniversiteit Groningen. He is the author of i.a., *Ayodhya* (1986), *The Vakatakas* (1996), and co-editor of The *Skandapurana*, Vols. I, IIA (1998–2004). He is co-editor-in-chief of *Indo-Iranian Journal* and editor-in-chief of the *Groningen Oriental Studies*.

Tim H. Barrett (1949) is Professor of East Asian History at the School of Oriental and African Studies, the University of London. He is the author of *Singular Listlessness: A Short History of Chinese Books and British Scholars* (1989), *Li Ao: Buddhist, taoist, or Neo-Confucian?* (1992), *Taoism under the T'ang* (1996), and second author with Zhou Xun, *The Wisdom of the Confucians* (2001) and Peter Hobson, *Poems of Hanshan* (2003).

Jacqueline Borsje (1961) is researcher in Celtic Studies and Religious Studies at Utrecht University. She is the author of *From Chaos to Enemy: Encounters with Monsters in Early Irish Texts. An investigation related to the process of christianization and the concept of evil* (1996). She has published widely on medieval Irish mythology, religion and literature, including J. Borsje & Fergus Kelly, '"The evil eye" in early Irish literature and law', *Celtica* 24 (2003) 1-39), which is also on line: http://www.celt.dias.ie/publications/celtica/c24.html.

Lourens van den Bosch (1944) is Associate Professor emeritus of Religious Studies at the Rijksuniversiteit Groningen. He is the author of *Atharvaveda-parisista, chapters 21-29* (1978) and *Friedrich Max Müller: a life devoted to the humanities* (2002). He is the co-editor of *Between Poverty and the Pyre. Moments in the history of widowhood* (1995).

Jan N. Bremmer (1944) is Professor of Religious Studies at the Rijksuniversiteit Groningen. He is the author of *The Early Greek Concept* *of the Soul* (1983), *Greek Religion* (1999²), *The Rise and Fall of the After-life* (2002) and *Van zendelingen, zuilen en zapreligie* (2006²); co-author of *Roman Myth and Mythography* (1987); editor of *Interpretations of Greek Mythology* (1987) and *From Sappho to De Sade* (1989); co-editor of *A Cultural History of Gesture* (1991), *Between Poverty and the Pyre. Moments in the history of widowhood* (1995), *A Cultural History of Humour* (1997), *The Metamorphosis of Magic from Antiquity to the Middle Ages* (2003), *Cultures of Conversions* (2006) and *Paradigms, Poetics and Politics of Conversion* (2006). He is also editor-in-chief of the series *Studies on Early Christian Apocrypha*.

Jacobus van Dijk (1953) is Associate Professor of Egyptology at the Rijksuniversiteit Groningen. He is the author of *The New Kingdom Necropolis of Memphis: Historical and Iconographical Studies* (1993); co-author of *The Tomb of Tia and Tia* (1997) and *The Tombs of Three Memphite Officials* (2001); editor of *Essays on Ancient Egypt in Honour of Herman te Velde* (1997), and co-editor of *Objects for Eternity: Egyptian Antiquities from the W. Arnold Meijer Collection* (2006). He is also editor-in-chief of the series *Egyptological Memoirs*.

Michel Graulich (1944) is Professor at the Université Libre de Bruxelles and Directeur d'études, l'Ecole Pratique des Hautes Etudes, Section des sciences religieuses, Sorbonne, Paris (Religions de l'Amérique précolombienne). He is the author of *Montezuma ou l'apogée et la chute de l'empire aztèque* (1994), *Myths of Ancient Mexico* (1997), *Rituales aztecas: las fiestas de las veintenas* (1999) and *Le sacrifice humain chez les Aztèques* (2005).

Kengo Harimoto (1964) has been educated at Kyushu University, Japan, and took his PhD from Asian and Middle Eastern Studies at the University of Pennsylvania. He has been an assistant professor at Temple University, a visiting scholar at the University of Hamburg, a research fellow at the Rijksuniversiteit Groningen, and is currently a Gonda Fellow at the International Institute of Asian Studies, Leiden University. His research interest includes cultures and religions in Japan and South Asia.

Ed Noort (1944) is Professor of Ancient Hebrew Literature, Old Testament Interpretation and the History of Israelite Religion at the Rijksuniversiteit Groningen. He is the author of *Die Seevölker in*

Palästina (1994) and *Das Buch Josua* (1998), and co-editor of *The Sacrifice of Isaac: The Aqedah (Genesis 22) and its Interpretations* (2002) and *Sodom's Sin: Genesis 18-19 and its Interpretations* (2004). He has widely published in the fields of material culture and its relations to textual traditions.

Lautaro Roig Lanzillotta (1967) is Lecturer and Research Fellow at the Department of Antiquities (Greek Philology) of the Faculty of Arts of the University of Córdoba (Spain). In addition to numerous articles on Greek philosophy and literature as well as Christian apocrypha, he is the author of *La envidia en el pensamiento griego* (Diss. Madrid 1997), *The Acts of Andrew. A New Approach to the Character, Thought and Meaning of the Primitive Text* (Diss. Groningen 2004) and of *Acta Andreae. An Inquiry into the Greek Original* (2006).

Asko Parpola (1941) is Professor Emeritus of Indology at the University of Helsinki. He is the author of *The Srautasutras of Latyayana and Drahyayana and their commentaries*, 2 vols (1968-69), *The literature and study of the Jaiminiya Samaveda* (1973), *The Sky Garment* (1985), *Deciphering the Indus Script* (1994) and 'The Nasatyas, the chariot and Proto-Aryan religion' (2005, in the *Journal of Indological Studies* 16-17); editor-in-chief of the *Corpus of Indus Seals and Inscriptions* (so far 2 vols., 1987, 1991); co-editor of *South Asian Archaeology 1993*, 2 vols (1994), *Changing Patterns of Family and Kinship in South Asia* (1998) and *Early Contacts between Uralic and Indo-European: Linguistic and Archaeological Considerations* (2001).

Herman te Velde (1932) is Professor Emeritus of Egyptology at the Rijksuniversiteit Groningen. He is the author of *Seth, God of Confusion* (1977[2]) and of numerous articles on Egyptian religion, including studies on the gods Heka (1970) and Shu (1982) and the goddess Mut (1980, 1982, 1988).

HUMAN SACRIFICE: A BRIEF INTRODUCTION

Jan N. Bremmer

After the dramatic attack on the Twin Towers on 9/11, reports admiringly related how firemen 'sacrificed' their lives in order to save people, and how many people had become 'victims' of this atrocious crime. Both English terms, 'sacrifice' and 'victim', eventually derive, via the French, from Latin sacrificial language.[1] Even though most of us no longer condone or practice animal sacrifice, let alone human sacrifice, these metaphors are a powerful reminder of the practice of offering animals or humans as gifts to gods and goddesses, a practice that once was near universal, but nowadays becomes increasingly abandoned. Undoubtedly, the most fascinating and horrifying variety of sacrifice remains human sacrifice, and a new collection of studies hardly needs an apology.[2] Serious studies are rare in this area where sensation often rules supreme. New approaches to the sources (below), new anthropological insights and new archaeological discoveries, for instance those in ancient India to which Hans Bakker draws our attention in Ch. IX, all enable us to take a fresh look at old problems, but also to start thinking about areas that have long been neglected in this connection, such as ancient China, as Tim Barrett reminds us (Ch. XII).

Human sacrifice was sometimes combined with cannibalism. This was the case among the ancient Celts,[3] the ancient Chinese (Ch. XII)

---

[1] For Roman sacrifice see most recently Bremmer, 'Opfer 3: Römische Religion', in *Religion in Geschichte und Gegenwart*, fourth edition, vol. 6 (Tübingen, 2003) 578-80; J. Scheid, *Quand faire, c'est croire – Les rites sacrificiels des Romains* (Paris, 2005).

[2] The more so as the most recent overview by K. Read, 'Human sacrifice', in the authoritative *Encyclopedia of Religion*, second edition, vol. 6 (New York, 2005) 4182-85 is wholly unsatisfactory. Much better, I Taloş, 'Menschenopfer', in *Enzyklopädie des Märchens*, vol. 9 (Berlin and New York, 1999) 578-82.

[3] K. Strobel, 'Menschenopfer und Kannibalismus. Neue Erkenntnisse zur Kultpraxis und Kultur der Keltenvölker in Kleinasien', *Antike Welt* 33 (2002) 487-91.

and the ancient Greeks, as Jan Bremmer (Ch. III.3) argues in his discussion of the secret initiatory rites of the Arcadians, where a novice
had to taste the entrails of a slaughtered boy. Although recent
decades have recognised that cannibalism is far more often the subject of myths and stories than of real practices,[4] the one-time existence of human sacrifice is beyond any doubt, even though here too
we regularly find the practice ascribed to innocent peoples, tribes or
groups, as we will see presently.

The ideal analysis should always pay attention to the question of
who sacrifices what to whom, where, when, why and with what kind
of rhetoric. To begin with the sacrificers, it is clear that human sacrifice was already practised in the Stone Age,[5] and it is therefore not
surprising that it occurs in one of our oldest surviving religious texts,
the Indian Vedas, as Asko Parpola demonstrates (Ch. VIII). This
volume can only present a selection of important cases, but the literature shows that human sacrifice was once widespread. It was practised not only among the ancient Germans, whose practices are the
subject of one of the earliest books on the subject,[6] and other early
European peoples,[7] but also in the Ancient Near East,[8] among the
Arabs,[9] the Turks,[10] Indonesia,[11] West Africa,[12] native Americans,[13]

---

[4] For the most recent reviews of the debates around the reality of cannibalism see
P. Hulme, 'Introduction: The Cannibal Scene', and W. Arens, 'Rethinking Anthropophagy', in F. Barker et al. (eds), *Cannibalism and the Colonial World* (Cambridge,
1998) 1-38, 39-62, respectively.

[5] R. Thurnwald, 'Menschenopfer (C. Allgemein)', in M. Ebert (ed.), *Reallexikon der
Vorgeschichte* VIII (Berlin, 1927) 145-154; J. Maringer, 'Menschenopfer im Bestattungs-
brauch Alteuropas. Eine Untersuchung über die Doppel- und Mehrbestattungen im
vor- und frühgeschichtlichen Europa, insbesondere Mitteleuropa', *Anthropos* 37-40
(1942-1945) 1-112.

[6] G. Schütze, *De cruentis Germanorum gentilium victimis humanis liber unus* (Leipzig,
1743); see most recently A. Hultgård, 'Menschenopfer', in *Reallexikon der Germanischen
Altertumskunde*, Vol. 19 (Berlin and New York, 2001) 533-46.

[7] K. Dowden, *European Paganism* (London and New York, 2000) 179-88, 280-90.

[8] A.R.W. Green, *The role of human sacrifice in the Ancient Near East* (Missoula, 1975).

[9] J. Henninger, 'Menschenopfer bei den Arabern', *Anthropos* 53 (1958) 721-805.

[10] S. Vryonis Jr, 'Evidence on human sacrifice among the early Ottoman Turks',
Journal of Asian History 5 (1971) 140-46.

[11] R. Jordaan and R. Wessing, 'Human Sacrifice at Prambanan', *Bijdragen tot de
taal-, land- en volkenkunde* 152 (1996) 45-73.

[12] C. Wright, *Superstitions of the Ashantees, especially those which lead them to sacrifice
on certain occasions, thousands of human victims* (Troy, NY, 1848); J.D. Graham, 'The
Slave Trade, Depopulation and Human Sacrifice in Benin History', *Cahiers d'Études
Africaines* 6 (1965) 317-34; R. Law, 'Human sacrifice in Pre-Colonial West Africa',
African Affairs 84 (1985) 53-87.

[13] S.B. Ross, *Das Menschenopfer der Skidi-Pawnee* (Bonn, 1989).

and Polynesia[14] – just to mention more recent investigations. In many of these cases we have only scattered notices that need to be carefully sifted and analysed before we can reconstruct an outline of the rituals involved. Unfortunately, a 'thick description' of the practice, as we would expect from modern anthropologists, can be given only rarely, and the analysis of the Konds by Lourens van den Bosch (Ch. X) is a welcome exception to this rule.

These cases and those that are analysed in this volume have made increasingly clear that human sacrifice is not something that is typical of marginal and minor tribes. On the contrary, as a regular practice on a grander scale, human sacrifice seems to belong to agrarian societies and larger empires that could happily dispose of criminals or prisoners of war without the community suffering a disastrous loss of members, as was the case among the ancient Aztecs, whose sacrifices are illuminated by Michel Graulich (Ch. I). The connection of human sacrifice with more developed cultures was already seen by one of the pioneers of anthropological fieldwork, the Finnish sociologist, anthropologist and moral philosopher, Edward Westermarck (1862-1939). In the language of a century ago he observed that human sacrifice 'is found much more frequently among barbarians and semi-civilised peoples than among genuine savages (!), and at the lowest stages of culture known to us it is hardly heard'.[15] In a similar vein, the later Regius Professor of Hebrew at Cambridge, Stanley Arthur Cook (1873-1949), noted that 'human sacrifice stamps relatively advanced and especially decadent peoples'.[16] It is not surprising, then, that cultures that practise human sacrifice usually have a strong government.[17]

Given that human sacrifice is a nasty business, it is perhaps not surprising that people often tried to minimise its emotional and financial costs. That is why the victim was often very young or old,[18]

---

[14] A. Schoch, *Rituelle Menschentötungen in Polynesien* (Ulm, 1954); G. Obeyesekere, *Cannibal talk: the man-eating myth and human sacrifice in the South Seas* (Berkeley, Los Angeles, London, 2005).

[15] E. Westermarck, *The Origin and Development of Moral Ideas*, 2 vols (London, 1908-1912) I².436f.

[16] S.A. Cook *apud* W.R. Smith, *Lectures on the Religion of the Semites* (London, 1927³) 631.

[17] As was already observed by E.M. Loeb, *The Blood Sacrifice Complex* (Menasha, 1923) 8f.

[18] For old people see S. Silva, 'Traces of Human Sacrifice in Kanara', *Anthropos* 50 (1955) 577-92 at 586.

a criminal, a stranger, a slave, or a prisoner of war. Modern biological research has now also shown that the Moche, the dominant culture on the North Coast of Peru (200 BC – AD 750) and avid human
sacrificers, sacrificed not their own members but those of a number
of competing Moche polities.[19] In other cases, such as among the
nineteenth-century Indian Konds, the victims were always treated
with great kindness before being sacrificed. In turn, the Konds
expected them to offer themselves voluntarily for their well-being
(Ch. X). The Swiss historian of religion and folklorist Karl Meuli
(1891-1968) has termed such behaviour of the sacrificers a 'comedy
of innocence'.[20] He showed that the idea of voluntariness goes back
to the world of the early hunters, who pretended that their game
had offered itself voluntarily so that they would not be guilty of
their deaths. The idea lasted a long time and could also be found in
Greek representations of human sacrifice (Ch. III).

As the victims of human sacrifice were often strangers to, or marginal members of, the community, the practice seems rarely to have
been challenged internally. Two brief notices from the Pacific suggest, though, that not every participant was happy with the ritual.
When in eighteenth-century Tonga '[the ruler] Tuku'aho was killed
at Mu'a the people came to Hihifo where there was a very beautiful
girl, the daughter of Tuku'aho's tu'asina [maternal uncle]. She was
at the beach washing her hair. When she heard the news she went
on with her washing, then she straightened herself up, tossed back
her hair and went forward to meet the men. One of the men who
was to strangle her could not do it, so Ulakai [son of Tuku'aho] took
both ends of the rope in his hands and finished her himself'. And
when the Tahitian ruler Pomare I (1742-1803) placed excessive
demands for human victims upon the commoners of Tahiti in the
early 19th century, they fought back: 'Some time previous to the
death of Pomarrie he had ordered a human sacrifice from the next
district: the people were so exasperated against him on this account,

---

[19] R.C. Sutter and R.J. Cortez, 'The Nature of Moche Human Sacrifice: A Bio-
Archaeological Perspective', *Current Anthropology* 46 (2005) 521-49. For Moche
human sacrifice see also C.P. Popson, 'Grim rites of the Moche', *Archaeology* 55 (2002)
30-35; P. Gwin, 'Peruvian Temple of Doom', *National Geographic* 206.1 (2004) 102-17;
E.K. de Bock, *Human sacrifices for cosmic order and regeneration: structure and meaning
in Moche iconography, Peru, AD 100-800* (Oxford, 2005).

[20] K. Meuli, 'Griechische Opferbrauche', in his *Gesammelte Schriften*, 2 vols (Basel
and Stuttgart, 1975) II.907-1021 at 982-3, 995-7. His views have been much debated,
see Bremmer, *Greek Religion* (Oxford, 2003³) 41-3.

that they suddenly rose upon him one night, and he escaped with difficulty to Matavai'.[21] Yet these cases are rare exceptions, and the lack of details and the regular secrecy of the rites makes that we rarely get a glimpse of what those concerned really thought.

The receiving gods or other supernatural beings can be of quite varying status. Sometimes they are left anonymous, as in ancient Greece, where our texts are sometimes extremely vague in specifying the gods to whom the human sacrifice is offered. Yet at the same time, it is not the case that the receiving divinity is always marginal or terrifying. On the contrary, divine recipients in ancient Greece could be found among the most important gods and goddesses, such as Zeus, Apollo and Artemis;[22] the ancient Irish sacrificed humans to their 'chief idol' Crom Crúaich, as Jacqueline Borsje well illustrates (Ch. II.1), and among the Indian Konds the receiving goddess was the earth goddess, who was also often thought to be the founding goddess of the village and the first female ancestor – clearly, the most important divinity of the community (Ch. X). Whatever people may have said, it is clear that human sacrifice is often connected with the most important gods of ancient and modern religions.

In West Africa, on the other hand, the recipients usually were the more prominent recently deceased, whose retinue in the afterlife apparently was in need of enlarging;[23] for a similar reason, retainers were sacrificed in ancient Egypt and Sudan, as Jaap van Dijk demonstrates (Ch. VII). Arab travellers also noted that female slaves were sacrificed at the funerals of wealthy men in ancient Ghana.[24] In fact, the great Dutch 'armchair anthropologist' Olfert Dapper (1635-1689) already noted that in West Africa 'nobody important dies without it costing blood'.[25] Such sacrifices may have even become 'secularised' into the suicide attacks of the Japanese *kamikaze*, as Kengo Harimoto suggests (Ch. XI).

---

[21] Both examples are taken from M. Filihia, 'Rituals of sacrifice in early post-European contact Tonga and Tahiti', *Journal of Pacific History* 34 (1999) 5-22.

[22] See S. Georgoudi, 'À propos du sacrifice humain en Grèce ancienne: remarques critiques', *Archiv f. Religionsgeschichte* 1 (1999) 61-82.

[23] Law, 'Human sacrifice', 57.

[24] N. Levtzion and J. Hopkins (eds), *Corpus of Early Arabic Sources for West African History* (Cambridge, 1981) 52.

[25] O Dapper, *Naukeurige beschrijvinge der Afrikaensche gewesten* (Amsterdam, 1676²) second part, 125.

Where were the victims sacrificed? The spatial aspect of human sacrifice has not always received the attention it deserves. Was such an emotionally loaded sacrifice performed in the heart of the community or did people do it outside? In Greece, a criminal could be sacrificed to Kronos before the city gate (Ch. III.1), but among the Konds human sacrifices took place in the centre of the village (Ch. X.6), and in the case of construction sacrifices, they were commonly performed for public and communal structures, such as dykes, city gates, palaces and waterworks.[26] Each case, then, has to be judged on its own merits.

The occasions for human sacrifice varied widely, but certain moments clearly stand out. The aftermath of war was already the stage for human sacrifice among the ancient Germans, as Tacitus knew,[27] and prisoners of war were often favourite victims, from the Aztecs to the ancient Arabs. Secondly, the sacrifices often took place during exceptional circumstances, as was the case in Roman history in periods of crisis, like the wars against Carthage;[28] in Egypt, too, human sacrifice seems to have been rather rare, as Herman te Velde shows (Ch. VI), and limited to certain festivals or the well being of an extremely ill pharaoh. In other cases, for example in Tonga, a child was sacrificed in order to avert the wrath of the gods or when the yam crops threatened to fail.[29] In other words, human sacrifice was often resorted to when the life of the community was in great danger: extreme situations clearly required extreme measures. A third important category seems to have been the construction sacrifice, which is also the type of human sacrifice that has left the most traces in European folklore. It is attested all the way from Russia to

---

[26] For example, see R. Wessing and R. Jordaan, 'Death at the Building Site: Construction Sacrifice in Southeast Asia', *History of Religions* 37 (1997) 101-21.

[27] Tacitus, *Annales* 13.57; Jordanes, *Getica* 41.

[28] See most recently B. Twyman, 'Metus Gallicus. The Celts and Roman human sacrifice', *Ancient History Bulletin* 11.1 (1997) 1-11; C. Grottanelli, 'Ideologie del sacrificio umano: Roma e Cartagine', *Archiv f. Religionsgeschichte* 1 (1999) 41-59; I. Gradel, 'Jupiter Latiaris and human blood: fact or fiction?', *Classica & Medievalia* 53 (2002) 235-54; V. Rosenberger, 'Metus und Menschenopfer: Überlegungen zur Gallierfurcht und zur zweiten Gründung Roms', in A. Kneppe and D. Metzler (eds), *Die emotionale Dimension antiker Religiösität* (Münster, 2003) 47-64. In the nineteenth century, the problem was even discussed in the highest English circles, cf. Ph. Stanhope, *Were human sacrifices in use among the Romans? Correspondence on the question between Mr. Macaulay, Sir Robert Peel, and Lord Mahon, in December 1847* (London, 1860).

[29] Filihia, 'Rituals of sacrifice', 10, 12.

France and from Scandinavia to Greece, even if it was especially popular in the Balkans.[30]

However, we are still at the beginning of a discussion of the deeper-lying reasons for human sacrifice. To what extent can we isolate social, economic and political factors that favoured human sacrifice? Is there a correlation between the violent character of a society and the practice of human sacrifice? Was there an ecological basis? Several scholars have argued that the Aztecs practised human sacrifice in order to combat protein scarcity, but this approach is certainly not generally accepted and no scholarly consensus has yet been reached.[31] In fact, human sacrifice is often analysed in isolation from the larger issues of a society, and in this respect much work still remains to be done.

Finally, the heated debate around the reality of cannibalism has made scholars much more careful in their handling of the sources for human sacrifice than used to be the case in earlier times. We now realise that we have to be attentive to the discourse of our texts. Do they report 'facts' or is human sacrifice used 'to think with'. In other words, is human sacrifice used as, for example, a means to stigmatise others? The latter usage can already be found in the Old Testament, where it is always the others who are accused of this abominable practice, whereas, as Ed Noort (Ch. V) argues, it now seems probable that at a certain stage and under certain circumstances child sacrifice did indeed belong to the belief system and praxis of Ancient Israel. On the other hand, although the early Christians were, undoubtedly wrongly, accused of child sacrifice, orthodox Christians did not hesitate to use the same charges against numerous splinter groups in their crusade against heresy and, later on, with catastrophic effects, against the Jews, as Lautaro Roig Lanzillotta (Ch. IV) shows. The examples from Israel and early Christianity are comfortably removed in time, but we come much closer when we look at the entertainment scene of contemporary Nigeria. Here the Igbo people of the south-eastern part of the country turn out home videos in high numbers. These frequently portray human sacrifice as a means to fabulous wealth and success. In the

---

[30] For an extensive bibliography see M. Eliade, *Zalmoxis, the Vanishing God* (Chicago, 1972) 164-90.

[31] See most recently M. Winkelman, 'Aztec Human Sacrifice: Cross-Cultural Assessments of the Ecological Hypothesis', *Ethnology* 37 (1998) 285-98.

end, the success is often only temporary, but the perpetrators are certainly not always punished: actually, their crimes do regularly pay.[32]

The ritual of human sacrifice that started in the dark prehistory of *homo sapiens* is hardly practised any longer, but its occurrence in home videos and contemporary horror movies still shows something of the fascination that the practice holds over the minds of many peoples.[33] Its religious significance may have disappeared, but its emotional power still grips us and makes us shiver. Human sacrifice will probably stay with us for a long time still.[34]

---

[32] J.Z. Okwori, 'A dramatized society: representing rituals of human sacrifice as efficacious action in Nigerian home-video movies', *Journal of African Cultural Studies* 16 (2003) 7-24; see also *Christianity Today* 48.12 (2004) 22.

[33] Many examples of movies with the theme of human sacrifice can be found on the Web; see also M. Pizzato, *Theatres of Human Sacrifice: from ancient ritual to screen violence* (Albany NY, 2005).

[34] I am most grateful to Yme Kuiper for comments and to Ken Dowden for kindly correcting my English.

I. AZTEC HUMAN SACRIFICE AS EXPIATION

Michel Graulich

Although the ideology of Aztec human sacrifice has drawn attention from the scholarly world for more than a century, the proposed interpretations mostly restrict themselves to what is explicitly stated in the sources: the hearts of the victims nourished the gods and more in particular the sun; certain victims embodied gods. Sir James Frazer (1854-1941) especially gained many adherents, first with his insistence on the 'killing of the god', 'nowhere... carried out so systematically and on so extensive a scale' and intended 'as a means of perpetuating the divine energies in the fulness of youthful vigour', that is, to revivify the gods; second, by establishing a link with the deities called, later on, 'dema'; and, finally, by his 'energetic' theory which sees the sun as the source of all energy that [= the sun] must be fed with lives.[1]

These ideas return constantly later on, for example in the works of Eduard Seler (1849-1922) and Konrad Preuss (1869-1938) around the turn of the century, or of Mircea Eliade (1907-1986) who explains that the regeneration rituals 'obviously' repeat primordial acts, which is sometimes true. In France, Frazer's, Seler's and Preuss' interpretations were diffused by Jacques Soustelle (1912-1990), who added the dubious thesis that nomads with a solar cult would have superimposed their human sacrifice on the agrarian rituals of Central Mexico's autochthons. More recently, Christian Duverger and Yólotl González Torres proposed again the energetic theory, the first author explaining in his essay that feeding the diurnal and nocturnal sun is

---

[1] J. Frazer, *The Magic Art*, 2 vols (London, 1911) 1.314-5, *Spirits of the Corn and of the Wild*, 2 vols (London, 1912) 2.88, *The Scapegoat* (London, 1913) 275-305 and *Adonis, Attis, Osiris: studies in the history of oriental religion*, 2 vols (London, 1914) 2.107. Dema deities: L. Lévy-Bruhl, *La mythologie primitive. Le monde mythique des Australiens et des Papous* (Paris, 1935) 27-34; A.E. Jensen, *Myth and cult among primitive peoples*, transl. M.T. Choldin and W. Weissleder (Chicago, 1963).

the ultimate rationale for all Aztec human sacrifices, while Gónzalez adds the other Frazerian interpretations. In her new and controversial book on *Time and Sacrifice in the Aztec Cosmos*, Kay A. Read also stresses mainly the energetic-alimentary aspect, as did Inga Clendinnen before her.[2]

It thus appears that recent research on sacrifice tends to neglect its exceptional variety and its rich scope of meaning and to concentrate on a few arbitrarily privileged sources. Humans were put to death not only by excision of the heart (usually followed by decapitation), but also by decapitation (sometimes followed by heart extraction), cutting the throat, throwing into fire (mostly followed by heart extraction), scratching (followed by heart extraction) and flaying in the so-called 'gladiatorial' sacrifice, arrows (usually followed by heart extraction), drowning, burying alive and hurling down from the top of a pole or a pyramid. Less common were deaths by bludgeon strokes, stoning, impaling, tearing out the entrails, having the roof of a house falling down on victims or squeezing them in a net.[3]

For most of these types of immolation, the prototypical, mythical act reactualized in ritual is clearly recognizable; for others, information is lacking. Reenacted myths help us to understand the rationale and the hidden or overt ends of those sacrifices which, together with the consecutive cannibalistic meals, constituted the culminating points of the great sacred dramas that were the Aztec festivals.[4] These rituals helped the universe function by reenacting the creation of the world and the birth of Venus-Maize, then the creation of the sun that vanquished the forces of darkness in the underworld and rose, bringing the day and the rainy season assimilated to it; by

---

[2] E. Seler, *Gesammelte Abhandlungen zur Amerikanischen Sprach- und Altertumskunde*, 5 vols (Berlin, 1902-23) 1.442, 2.800, 4.57 and 448; K.Th. Preuss, 'Phallische Fruchtbarkeitsdämonen als Träger des altmexikanischen Dramas', *Arch. f. Anthrop.* 1 (1903) 130-88, and 'Der Ursprung der Menschenopfer in Mexico', *Globus* 86 (1904) 105-19; M. Eliade, *Traité d'histoire des religions* (Paris, 1949) 292; J. Soustelle, *La pensée cosmologique des anciens Mexicains* (Paris, 1940); C. Duverger, *La fleur létale. Economie du sacrifice aztèque* (Paris, 1979); Y. Gónzalez Torres, *El sacrificio humano entre los mexicas* (Mexico City, 1985); I. Clendinnen, *Aztecs: an interpretation* (Cambridge, 1991); K.A. Read, *Time and Sacrifice in the Aztec Cosmos* (Bloomington and Indianapolis, 1998).

[3] Some of these types of sacrifices are enumerated in Fray Bernardino de Sahagún, *Florentine Codex. General History of the Things of New Spain*, 13 vols, transl. and ed. C.E. Dibble and A.J.O. Anderson (Salt Lake City, 1950-82) bk. 4, ch. 27, p. 93.

[4] Used with no other meaning than the common one of '1. consecrated to a god, 2. having to do with religion' (Webster's).

erecting trees that supported the sky, by nourishing the gods and in particular Sun and Earth, by making offerings to propitiate the earth and rain deities, the Tlaloques, etc. Reenacting the founding myths implied the ritual killing of victims impersonating dema and other deities whose death in primeval times had made earth, sun and moon, stars, maize and other useful plants appear. Helping the universe to function sometimes called for sacrifices in which deities were rejuvenated or revitalized through their own death (via impersonators) or through oblations of human blood.

The multifarious Aztec sacrifice seems to revolve around two poles: the ritual killing of the deity and the alimentary sacrifice to nourish the gods. The two main categories of victims, bathed (that is, purified) slaves who impersonated deities and prisoners of war, do substantiate this division in some degree, but there were many intermediate situations. For instance, killed deities could also feed other gods, and the prisoners of war actually represented lesser and rather impersonal spirits or deities called Mimixcoas. A victim could impersonate or represent a deity, a mythical hero, food, game, fecundating fruit or seed, maize, a heavenly body, or several of these simultaneously, or more simply play the part of a messenger, a companion to a deceased or a base, or a 'litter' for more important sacrificial victims. Obviously a single sacrifice could have several layers of meanings: e.g., reactualizing mythical killings, rejuvenating deities or revitalizing them and nourishing other deities.[5] But apart from these cosmic ends, sacrifices could at the same time pursue the whole range of more usual intentions, such as placating or conciliating deities in order to obtain something, transmitting messages to the other worlds; accompanying the deceased to the hereafter, consecrating or strengthening certain places, altars, buildings, persons, and expiating transgressions or sins to win a

---

[5] When a woman impersonating Toci-Tlalteotl, the Earth deity, was killed in Ochpaniztli, the myth reactualized was that of the creation of the earth by the tearing apart of Tlalteotl from whose body the useful plants were born. Her ritual killing was like a wedding; the impersonator was killed and skinned, and a new, vigourous impersonator henceforth played her part, mimicking a hierogamy and the delivery of maize. So here we have the themes of reenacting myth in order to reproduce and re-actualize the primeval event (but in a different, actualized version); of the rejuvenation of the earth deity who is to give birth to maize once again. Other victims killed represented water and maize. Their deaths rejuvenated what the deities stood for, but at the same time their hearts were offered to the sun to nourish it. And, as we shall se, there was also the expiation aspect.

glorious or happy afterlife.[6] My purpose in this contribution is to demonstrate that the more fundamental meaning and ends of Aztec sacrifice was expiation of sins and transgressions in order to deserve a worthy afterlife, and that the alimentary or energetic interpretation is only a late and derived one that never managed to relegate the other meanings.

The centrality of expiation has been emphasized before. More than a century ago, in his book on ancient Mexican civilization and history, Manuel Orozco y Berra outlines an at that time current theory and evolution of sacrifice and insists that its core is expiation (atonement?) and that the victim serves as a substitute for the sinner. Unfortunately, he neglects to apply this theory to the Aztecs. In the fifties and sixties of last century, Laurette Séjourné laboured to defend the idea that through penance and sacrifice the ancient Mexicans sought to expiate their sins, thus liberating their soul or spirit, imprisoned in the human body (more precisely, the heart) since conception, but she neglected to stave her intuitions with solid evidence.[7]

That the alimentary aspect is neither primordial nor essential is demonstrated by an interesting Mixtec myth, the only one we have on the origins of offerings and sacrifice. At the beginning the supreme creator couple created a paradise and begot two sons who honored their parents by offering them incense of powdered tobacco. After this first offering, the sons created a garden for their pleasure and a beautiful meadow full of things necessary for their 'offerings and sacrifices'. Later on, 'to oblige them [their parents] more' so that they would create the sky and the earth, they drew blood from their ears and tongues and scattered it on trees and plants, 'and they always showed submission to the gods their parents and attributed them more power and divinity than they had between themselves'. We here have an evolution from 'immaterial'

---

[6] See J. Haekel, 'Menschenopfer', in *Lexikon für Theologie und Kirche*, vol. 7 (1962). I do not hesitate to use the word 'sin', first, because its general sense can be 'any offense or fault' (*Webster*'s), second, because even in the Christian sense, it encompasses transgressions without any knowledge of good or evil – the original sin–, and, third, because Mesoamerican mythology presents several transgressions that very much resemble the Biblical ones (*Genesis*), as Spanish friars immediately realized.

[7] M. Orozco y Berra, *Historia antigua y de la conquista de México*, 4 vols (Mexico City, 1960, [1880¹]) 1.160-6; A. Elisabeth del Río, *Bases psicodinámicas de la cultura azteca* (Mexico City, 1973) 257; L. Séjourné, *Pensamiento y religión en el México antiguo* (Mexico City, 1957).

offerings (incense) to products of the meadow (flowers and plants, possibly also animals), and finally blood.[8] Apparently the offering by the creatures of their own blood rather than flowers or animals only signifies their recognition that they owe their life to their creators and are ready to give it back. What appears very clearly in this myth is that the mechanism of offerings and sacrifices is not to feed the creators – who existed before without anybody feeding them – but to humble one's self, thus acknowledging one's inferiority. Only by behaving in this way may the creatures expect to obtain something from their parents.[9]

A few words about the sources at our disposal are necessary before we examine the prototypical myth of human sacrifice. Not only are they scarce and fragmentary – all the myths put together would fill only a small volume – but most often they are deprived of any context: only two sources, the *Leyenda de los Soles* (in Nahuatl) and the *Historia de los Mexicanos por sus pinturas* offer a complete connected cosmogony, and both are late products of Motecuhzoma II's program of religious reforms.[10] More important still, our information on myth and ritual has never been provided by priests or other specialists who speculated on the matter. The few existing explanations rather appear to be disputable popular ones – as though we tried to fathom the mysteries of Christianity only by interrogating the person on the street – or are comments made by the Spanish monks who recorded the myths.

---

[8] A similar evolution from offerings of incense, then of animals and finally of humans is mentioned in the part of the *Popol Vuh* dedicated to the migrations of the Quichés: *Popol Vuh: the Mayan book of the dawn of life*, transl. D. Tedlock (New York, 1985) 185-7. In this source with strong Nahua influence, the humans are said to have been created to 'provide and nurture' the gods (163). On this influence, see M. Graulich, 'El Popol Vuh en el Altiplano mexicano', in *Memorias del segundo Congreso Internacional de Mayistas* (Mexico City, 1995) 117-30.

[9] Fray Gregorio García, *Origen de los Indios del Nuevo Mundo e Indias Occidentales* (Madrid, 1729). In a Maya myth the creator had thirteen children of which the older ones sought to create humans without their parents' permission, ('they became proud') but could produce only common household vessels and were thrown into hell. But the the younger ones humbled themselves and therefore were able to create. Graulich, *Autosacrifice in Postclassic Ancient Mexico*, presents other myths of autosacrifice (e.g., Quetzalcoatl in Tollan), in which there is no question of feeding the gods.

[10] M. Graulich, *Montezuma ou l'apogée et la chute de l'empire aztèque* (Paris, 1994) 97-126.

The 'creation of the sun and the moon'

The well-known myth of 'the creation of the sun and the moon' at Teotihuacan is illustrative in this respect because its main subject is very different from the one indicated by the Aztec informants. According to Fray Bernardino de Sahagún's version, when everything was still in darkness, the gods gathered in Teotihuacan and asked themselves who would make the sun and dawn appear. Tecciztecatl, 'He of the conch-shell', volunteered and the gods chose Nanahuatl, 'the one with buboes', who accepted the task happily. A great fire was lit, and Tecciztecatl and Nanahuatl did penance for five days. Everything Tecciztecatl had was luxurious – his 'bloody thorns', for instance, were coral – while Nanahuatl made only humble but true offerings: instead of coral he offered his own blood, while his incense was the scabs from his pustules. After doing penance they put on their sacrificial adornments, Tecciztecatl those of a bathed slave and Nanahuatl those of a warrior. At midnight, Tecciztecatl tried to jump into the fire but was forced to back off from the intensity of the heat four times. Then Nanahuatl jumped into the brazier, followed later on by Tecciztecatl, and both were consumed.[11] Then he emerged as the sun.[12] Tecciztecatl-Moon also rose, shining with equal brilliance, but one of the gods dimmed the moon's face by striking it with a rabbit.[13]

The sun and the moon remained motionless and the anxious gods asked, 'How will we live? The sun does not move! Shall we live among the commoners? But all right, may he be vivified by us, may we all die.' Ehecatl-Wind sacrificed them by extracting their hearts to feed the sun, but still the sun did not move until Ehecatl blew him into motion.[14]

The myth certainly explains how the sun and the moon came into being, but it is immediately evident that the central theme is death, victory over death, and a return to a more glorious, celestial life.

---

[11] The *Histoyre du Méchique* indicates that Nanahuatl went down to the underworld, from where he returned with rich spoils.

[12] In the *Leyenda*, when he reaches the sky, the supreme creators solemnly enthrone him.

[13] According to the *Leyenda*, Tecciztecatl was derisively enthroned in the west by demons of darkness, the Tzitzimime.

[14] In the *Leyenda*, the Sun treats the gods as though he had vanquished them and exacts their blood.

It also presents the first human or, rather, divine sacrifices, those of Nanahuatl and Tecciztecatl, who willingly jump into the fire, followed by the quite different immolations of the gods. Strangely enough, the latter ones are more readily considered to be *the* prototypical sacrifices, and these are the ones on which the 'energizing-feeding' theory is based. However, the prototypical sacrifices are and must be those of Nanahuatl and Tecciztecatl, first, because most of the independent versions of the myth do not mention a slaying of the gods[15]; second, because Nanahuatl and Tecciztecatl ostensibly represent the two great categories of victims, ritually bathed slaves and captured warriors; and, third, because the logic of the complete story implies it, as will be seen further on.

If we examine the myth of Teotihuacan as narrated above, obscurities and inconsistencies appear that apparently have left the investigators mostly untroubled. What are the gods doing on earth and in darkness? Why are they material and why is one of them bubonous, like a human punished by a god for having sinned?[16] How and why have they become mortal? Why do they have to die, in a fire that destroys the body, or under the sacrificial knife? Why do they fear to have to live among humans, on earth, when the sun does not move? And what about that erratic necessity to feed the sun? To answer these questions we need to turn to the context of the myth, a context absent in all but one version and absent in all the versions used by current research. This version was copied by Mendieta and Torquemada from Fray Andrés the Olmos' lost *Antigüedades*, one of our most ancient sources, based on enquiries made in cities like Mexico, Texcoco, Tlaxcala, Huexotzinco, Cholula, Tepeaca and Tlalmanalco. The author mentions the diversity of beliefs in the different cities,

---

[15] The killing of the gods is reported in Sahagún, *Leyenda de los Soles*, in *History and Mythology of the Aztecs. The Codex Chimalpopoca*, 2 vols, transl. J. Bierhorst (Tucson, 1992) and Fray Gerónimo de Mendieta, *Historia Eclesiástica Indiana*, 4 vols (Mexico City, 1945). It is not mentioned in the *Historia de los Mexicanos por sus pinturas*, in J. García Icazbalceta (ed.), *Nueva colección de documentos para la historia de México* (Mexico City, 1941); the *Histoyre du Méchique*, ed. E. de Jonghe, *Journal de la Société des Américanistes de Paris* NS 2 (1905) 1-41); H. Ruiz de Alarcón, 'Tratado de las supersticiones y costumbres gentílicas que hoy viven entre los indios naturales de esta Nueva España', *Anales del Museo Nacional de Historia* 6 (1892) 123-224 and D. Muñoz Camargo, 'Descripción de la ciudad y provincia de Tlaxcala', in R. Acuña (ed.), *Relaciones geográficas del siglo XVI: Tlaxcala*, vol. 1 (Mexico City, 1984).

[16] E.g., Fray Diego Durán, *Historia de los indios de Nueva España e Islas de la Tierra Firme*, 2 vols, ed. A. M. Garibay (Mexico City, 1984) ch.16, v.1 p.156; Sahagún, *Florentine Codex*, bk. 3, ch. 2, p. 11.

but he insists that most of them were in agreement on the following myth.

The heavenly city

In heaven there was a marvelous city where the gods lived with their parents, the supreme creators, Ometecuhli and Omecihuatl ('Lord' and 'Lady Two'). Once upon a time, Omecihuatl gave birth to a flint knife that the frightened gods threw from the heaven, and it fell in Chicomoztoc, 'Seven Caves'. Sixteen hundred gods sprang forth from it. Seeing that they were 'fallen and banished' (*caídos y desterrados*) on earth, they implored their mother, who had 'rejected and exiled them' (*desechado de sí y desterrado*) for permission to create people who would serve them. She answered that, if they had behaved properly they would still be with her, but they did not deserve it; and if they wanted servants, they would have to go to the underworld and ask the lord of the dead for bones or ashes of previous humans. Then follows the myth of the creation of humankind and next that of the birth of the sun and the moon in Teotihuacan.[17]

The flint knife containing fire to which Omecihuatl gives birth symbolizes one of the fertilizing sparks that the supreme couple drills in the highest heaven in order to send them to women when they conceive.[18] The flint falls in Chicomoztoc, 'Seven Caves', a reference to the seven openings of the human body,[19] and, in this case, the body of the earth. Thus impregnated, the earth gives birth to the sixteen hundred children expelled from the celestial city. The myth is then about the illicit descent to earth of the first one of the sparks and the resulting illicit fecundation.

The theme of the primeval transgression that brings exile on earth, in darkness, and death, is one of the most fundamental ones of Mesoamerican mythology. The sins may vary: a goddess plucking

[17] Mendieta, *Historia*, v. 1.83-84; Fray Juan de Torquemada, *Monarquía Indiana*, 3 vols (Mexico City, 1969) 2. 37-38, 76-770.

[18] In the Codex Vaticanus A (3738) or *Ríos*, in *Antigüedades de México*, ed. J. Corona Núñez, 4 vols (Mexico City, 1964-67) 3.7-313, the first human couple is shown wrapped in a mantle, that is to say, having sex. The spark from Omeyocan that impregnates the woman is symbolized by a flint knife. In the *Ritual of the Bacabs*, transl. and ed. R.L. Roys (Norman, 1965) 61-2, flint is called 'genitals' and '1 Ahau', i.e., 1 Xochitl among the Aztecs, the name of Cinteotl-Venus, born from the first transgression in other myths.

[19] Ruiz de Alarcón, *Tratado*, 208-9, 218-9.

the flower of a forbidden tree (codices *Telleriano-Remensis* fol. 13r, *Ríos, Borgia* p. 11, 66; Sahagún, *Primeros Memoriales* fol. 254r) or fruit (*Codex Telleriano-Remensis, Popol Vuh*), having intercourse (*Histoyre du Méchique* fol. 86; *Anales de Cuauhtitlan* p. 6; *Chilam Balam of Chumayel* p. 20), or playing ball (*Popol Vuh*), making fire (*Leyenda de los Soles* p. 75), tearing a monster into pieces (*Histoyre du Méchique* fol. 84), expelling from heaven an unusual flint-brother, and so forth; but fundamentally, the common element is that the culprits assert themselves as equal to their creators by creating (the to and fro movement of the fire sticks and of the ball in the ballgame are also acts of creation), procreating (plucking a flower or a fruit symbolizes having sex), or taking one's life without asking permission to do so. They are proud, and pride, that is, failing to recognize the authority of superiors, fathers, elders and rulers, is the main transgression creatures may commit.[20] It is one of the main themes of Mesoamerican thought, the other being the opposite, the 'first will be the last' theme: the valorous younger one, the newcomer, the warrior, the nomad who overtakes or vanquishes his abusive parents, elders or superiors, often characterized as autochthons (Nanahuatl overtaking Tecciztecatl, the Twins of the *Popol Vuh* defeating their elders and their great-uncles, Quetzalcoatl defeating his uncles, Huitzilopochtli his elder brothers, the Mexica newcomers the autochthons of Central Mexico, etc.).[21]

It is in the myth recorded by Olmos and its variants that we have to seek the explanation for the events that follow, at Teotihuacan: the gods' presence on earth – for the gods who sprang forth from the flint knife are obviously the ones who had been expelled from heaven ('if they had behaved properly they would still be with her') –, and their mortality. They are exiled on earth, where they henceforth live like (more) material mortals, for having committed a transgression. Nanahuatl's buboes avow his guilt,

[20] On the first transgression, see M. Graulich, 'Myths of Paradise Lost in Pre-Hispanic Central Mexico', *Current Anthropology* 24 (1983) 575-88 and Graulich, *Myths of Ancient Mexico* (Norman, 1997) 49-59, 91-95, 99-109, 160, 192-201, 210-19; A. López Austin, *Los mitos del tlacuache. Caminos de la mitología mesoamericana* (Mexico City, 1990) 97-100, 475-78, and *Tamoanchan y Tlalocan* (Mexico City, 1994) 73-7, 93-101 (with interpretations of the myth I cannot always agree with); G. Olivier, *Moqueries et métamorphoses d'un dieu aztèque. Tezcatlipoca, le 'Seigneur au miroir fumant'* (Paris, 1997).

[21] M. Graulich, *Autóctonos y recién llegados en el pensamiento mesoamericano. Pensar América. Cosmovisión mesoamericana y andina*, ed. A. Garrido Aranda (Cordoba, 1997).

while Tecciztecatl's pride conceals it, but both are willing to expiate to regain paradise lost. The gods are banished to earth, in darkness, and are condemned to die: their only wish can only be to try and recuperate their lost paradise and return to heaven. Hence their sacrifice, their voluntary death, the accepted destruction of their material body that binds them here below. They die, go to the underworld, conquer death and leave the land of the deceased in a more or less glorified form in accordance with their merit. They ascend to heaven, where Nanahuatl is enthroned by the creators, which proves that he managed to reestablish contact. Their sacrifice is exemplary. Warriors who follow their example and die voluntarily on the battlefield or the sacrificial stone (or who die symbolically through a victim they offer) shall also descend to Mictlan and emerge to accompany the sun in its glorious ascent. Other deserving humans will go to the paradise of Tlaloc. That is, humans will go to the two hereafters established by, and almost identical to, Nanahuatl and Tecciztecatl: the sun and the paradise of Tlaloc located on the moon which is equated with a cave.[22]

In the myth of the creation of the sun and the moon – but indeed about much more than that –, after the self-immolation of the Nanahuatl and Tecciztecatl, the gods ask themselves if they will have to live with the humans, which means on earth. It would seem that they expected to benefit from the sacrifice of the two heroes, in the same manner as, in ritual, sacrifiers (those who offer the victim) do benefit from the death of their victims by dying symbolically through them. This interpretation is suggested by Ruiz de Alarcón's version of the myth, in which the other gods do penance during the immolation and expect to metamorphose according to their merit.[23]

---

[22] Codex Vaticanus A (3738) (1964-1967: pl. 2, 11); Graulich, *Myths of Ancient Mexico*, 123. On the hereafter, see also Graulich, 'Afterlife in Ancient Mexican Thought', in B. Illius and M. Laubscher (eds), *Circumpacifica, Festschrift für Thomas S. Barthel*, 2 vols (Frankfurt, 1990) 2.165-87; N. Ragot, *Les au-delàs aztèques. Approche des conceptions sur la mort et le devenir des morts (Mexique)* (Diss. Paris, 1999). Sahagún, *Florentine Codex*, bk. 6, ch. 7, pp. 30-32 contains an interesting speech addressed by a soothsayer or 'confessor' to a penitent, in which the sinner is described as one whom the gods send into death in the underworld but who, thanks to his rite of purification, is born again as a child or as the rising sun. The adventures of the Twins in Xibalbá, in the *Popol Vuh*, are constructed on the same model.

[23] Ruiz de Alarcón, *Tratado*, 150-1, 221-3. We give the name 'sacrifier' to the subject to whom the benefits of sacrifice thus accrue, or who undergoes its effects: H. Hubert and M. Mauss, *Sacrifice: its nature and function* (London, 1964).

The gods' expectation is in vain: all of them must die to feed the sun. It has already been said that most versions omit this episode of the killing of the gods. The very idea that the sun needs their blood and hearts to go on its way is rather odd: it did not need them to ascend to the zenith, and the moon and stars appear to be able to travel all the time without such fuel. Moreover, the efficiency and, therefore, the necessity of feeding the sun in this way is frankly negated in one of the two major sources (both in nahuatl) that mention it. According to Sahagún's informants (who possibly were not from Mexico-Tenochtitlan), in spite of the general immolation of the gods, the sun did not move until Ehecatl's breath (the breath of life, for Ehecatl is also the deity who endows the recently born children with this breath) animated it.

As a justification for their constant war waging, the Mexicas probably urged the idea that the sun had to be constantly nourished in this peculiar way. They only had to manipulate somewhat the myth to introduce it. I have shown elsewhere that many Aztec myths are fragments of a great cycle of which the adventures of the Twins of the *Popol Vuh* are a variant.[24] In this Maya-Quiche myth the Twins die in Xibalbá, the underworld, by jumping in a fire, then are born again, conquer the lords of Xibalbá and sacrifice them before they emerge as sun and moon, with the spoils alluded to in the *Histoyre du Méchique*.[25] The Mexicas transformed the defeat of the lords into the death of the gods to nourish the sun. Let us remember that in the *Leyenda* the gods are also treated as enemies.

The first war to nourish the sun and earth

The gods had to die to expiate their sin and recover their lost paradise. But what about the humans? Why do they have to die? Are they also punished, and for what? There were probably two interpretations. The first one may have been that, being born material and on earth, they were mortal by definition. But there are also texts which clearly present them as culprits. 'Our tribute is death; awarded us in common *as merited*. And on earth there prevaileth the coming to pay

---

[24] Graulich, 'Myths of Paradise Lost'; *Myths of Ancient Mexico*, and *Quetzalcóatl y el espejismo de Tollan* (Antwerp, 1988).

[25] *Popol Vuh*; Fray Bartolomé de Las Casas, *Apologética Historia*, 2 vols (Mexico City, 1967) 2.650.

the tribute of death,' the priest of Tezcatlipoca prayed. The humans have to 'pay their debt' – a recurrent expression to designate sacrifice – to the gods.[26] The myth of the first sacred war and of the slaughter of 400 Mimixcoa ('Cloud Snakes') illustrates very well the guilt of the humans. But before we examine it some words are needed about the part played by animals in the sacrificial mythology.

According to the Quichés, the first living creatures were the animals, but because they were not able to talk, to pronounce the names of their creators and to praise them, they were condemned to be hunted and eaten.[27] In the Olmos version of the myth of Teotihuacan, the quails, grasshoppers, butterflies, and serpents were condemned to be sacrificed because they did not know on which side the sun would rise: in other words, not knowing where to look, they could not praise it.

The myth of the 400 Mimixcoas (plural of Mixcoatl) is told in the *Leyenda* immediately after the birth of the sun at Teotihuacan. In the year 1, Flint, the goddess of water gave birth to four hundred Mimixcoa and later to five younger children, Mixcoatl, Cuauhtli icohuauh, Tlotepetl, Apantecuhtli and the girl Cuetlachcihuatl. The latter five were suckled by the earth goddess Mecitli and are therefore Mecitins or Mexicas. The sun ('Tonatiuh') gave shields and precious darts to the 400 Mimixcoas, commanding them to feed and serve him and their mother Tlaltecuhtli ('Lady Earth'). However, the 400 did not obey; they only shot birds, and when they caught a jaguar, instead of offering it to the sun, they dressed up with feathers, slept with women, and got disgustingly drunk. Tonatiuh then summoned the five last-born, armed them with ordinary thorn-tipped darts and with shields, and ordered them to kill the 400 'who do not say "mother! father!".' The five poor younger brothers and sister hid themselves and when the 400 arrived they came out of their hiding and the four brothers attacked. Almost all of the 400 were destroyed.[28]

The importance of this myth appears very clearly from the fact that the prisoners of war to be sacrificed were dressed in the attire of

---

[26] Sahagún, *Florentine Codex*, bk. 1, ch. 1, p. 4. See also K.Th. Preuss, 'Die Sünde in der Mexikanischen Religion', *Globus* 83 (1903) 253-7, 268-73 at 256. Concerning the 'debt payment', *nextlahualli* (*Florentine Codex* bk.2, App., p. 199), the same word designates human sacrifices generally, as well as rituals without killing or even without bloodshed, like offerings of copal and paper.

[27] Graulich, 'Popol Vuh', 78f.

[28] *Leyenda de los Soles*, fol. 79, 2.150f.

the 400 Mimixcoas whom they represented. The very myth was reenacted every year in the 'gladiatorial sacrifice' during the 20-day month of Tlacaxipehualiztli, whose rituals celebrated the first rising of the sun, the beginning of sacred war, and the harvesting of food for sun and earth, gods and humans.[29] It clearly shows that at the beginning, the offerings expected by the sun and earth were animals, the first earthly creatures to have been condemned to (sacrificial) death because they did not recognize the superiority of their creators, or at least did not express it. But among the first humans, the 400 Mimixcoas also failed to do their duty: they did not offer their prey to the sun and earth, and therefore were condemned to become prey themselves. The myth proposes a passage from animal to human sacrifice. It tells about the beginning of the holy war, but a war that is actually a big hunting party.

It is remarkable that in this myth not all the humans are condemned, but only a category described as elders, rich, lazy, impious, and drunkards, while their opponents are poor but valiant younger ones, newcomers whose thorn-tipped darts evoke the weapons of Chichimec nomads. Here we meet again the basic overturning theme of the victorious newcomers stressed above, but with a clear political undertone: the guiltless victors are the innocent Mexicas, while the culpable vanquished are their enemies the Mexicas used to immolate.

As stated before, the *Leyenda* is with the *Historia de los Mexicanos por sus pinturas* one of the late Mexica compositions ordered by Motecuhzoma II, who wanted to rewrite the Aztec cosmogony. Both works share a common structure and present comparable versions of the 'legend of the Suns (or past eras)', but they nevertheless proceed from different schools of thought. Their versions of the creation of humans and the myth of Teotihuacan are rather different. The *Historia*'s mythical part includes a short theogony with the Mexica tutelar deity, Huitzilopochtli, mentioned among the first four children of the supreme creators. Any hint to the idea of transgression or culpability is carefully wiped out. Before autosacrifice or sacrifice began, there already existed war in order to nourish the sun. And,

---

[29] M. Graulich, 'Tlacaxipehualiztli ou la fête aztèque de la moisson et de la guerre', *Revista Española de Antropología Americana* 12 (1982) 215-54, 'Chasse et sacrifice humain chez les Aztèques', *Académie Royale des Sciences d'Outre-Mer, Bulletin des Séances* 43 (1997) 433-46 and 'Rituales aztecas: Las fiestas de las veintenas' (Mexico City, 1999).

the last peculiarity, the hearts and blood of victims are to feed only the sun, not the earth. In the *Leyenda* on the contrary, it is clearly father sun and mother earth that are to receive these offerings and there are transgressions from the very start of the present era, and notably that of the 400 Mimixcoas. And war is preceded first by autosacrifice, then by sacrifice of the gods, the same as in the other traditions.

Mixcoatepec and Coatepec

Two other well-known and important texts, the myths of Quetzalcoatl's victory at Mixcoatepec and of Huitzilopochtli's triumph at Coatepec, present prototypical victims of human sacrifice as transgressors.

It is again the *Leyenda* that tells the story of Quetzalcoatl's victory on the Mixcoatepetl, the Hill of Mixcoatl. According to this ancient myth with parallels in the *Popol Vuh*,[30] Quetzalcoatl was the son of Mixcoatl. His uncles, the 400 Mimixcoas, who hated Mixcoatl, killed and buried him. Quetzalcoatl looked for his father, found his bones and buried them in the Hill of Mixcoatl (Mixcoatepetl). Informed of this, the murderers, Apanecatl, Zolton and Cuilton told Quetzalcoatl that they would be angry if he inaugurated ('drilled with the fire sticks') his temple (on the hill) by sacrificing a rabbit or a serpent, because the required sacrifices were an eagle, a jaguar and a kind of wolf. Quetzalcoatl told the three animals that they would not die, but that, on the contrary, they would eat the three uncles to inaugurate the temple. He went to the temple through a subterranean gallery and lit the inaugural fire. His uncles were furious because they wanted to make this fire themselves. They stormed the hill, but Quetzalcoatl killed and sacrificed them.[31]

Not only are the Mimixcoas guilty for having assassinated their brother, but we also find again a passage from animal to human sacrifice. The uncles fancy that Quetzalcoatl will offer small animals while they would sacrifice bigger game, but after all it is

---

[30] Mixcoatl corresponds to Hun Hunahpu who was killed by the Lords of Xibalbá and his (in some versions posthumous) son Quetzalcoatl to the posthumous sons of Hun Hunahpú, the Twins, Xbalamqué and Hunahpú. Like Quetzalcoatl, the Twins sought for the bones of their father, descended to the underworld (the Mixcoatepec in the *Leyenda*), and avenged their father by killing the murderers in sacrifice.

[31] *Leyenda de los Soles*, fol. 81, 2.154f.

Quetzalcoatl who makes the most precious offering: his own uncles instead of animals.

The famous myth of Huitzilopochtli's birth at Coatepec, one of the few genuinely Mexica myths, is flatly copied from the Toltec Mixcoatepec story. Coatlicue (a name of the earth deity), the mother of the 400 Huitznahua and their older sister, Coyolxauhqui, lives on the Snake Hill, Coatepec, near Tollan, sweeping and doing penance. One day she sweeps a ball of feathers and puts it in her skirt, which leaves her pregnant. Her outraged children decide to kill her. The terrified Coatlicue is heartened by a voice coming from her womb that tells her not to fear. Coyolxauhqui and her brothers prepare for war and march in battle order to the Coatepec. When they reach the terrace at the top, Huitzilopochtli is born wholly armed. With his 'fire serpent' he pierces Coyolxauhqui and beheads her. Then the newcomer attacks the 400 and destroys them.[32]

The sources inform us that this myth was reactualized every year during the great festival of Panquetzaliztli. Revealing enough of the Toltec origin of the ritual, the prisoners who played the play of the Huitznahua were still dressed like Mimixcoas. The transgression of the would-be killers, who want to kill her mother and so impede the birth of their younger brother, but who are killed themselves, also recalls somewhat the sin in the heavenly city, where the gods ejected their unexpected and unusual flint brother, but found themselves expelled on earth and condemned to die.

The victims as culprits

Ritual practice also proves that sacrificial death was expiation.[33] According to Clavijero, Motecuhzoma would have said to Cortés that 'he didn't see any reason not to immolate to the gods men who for their personal misdemeanors or as prisoners of war were already

---

[32] Sahagún, *Florentine Codex*, bk. 3, pp.1-5; Sahagún, *Historia general de las cosas de Nueva España*, 4 vols, ed. A.M. Garibay (Mexico City, 1956) 1.271-3. It must be pointed out that Sahagún, in his book, tells the myth about the origin of the gods immediately after referring to the sun's birth in Teotihuacan. Aside from that, there is no context, but it is clear that it was an episode during the migrations.

[33] Seler, *Gesammelte Abhandlungen*, 3.286-7 questions some of Preuss' translations and the idea that sacrificial death is castigation. Duverger, *Fleur*, 147 thinks that human sacrifice is never a penalty and 'never must look like a repressive and barbarian act'. W. Krickeberg, *Las antiguas culturas mexicanas* (Mexico City, 1964) 158 also considers human sacrifice not a punishment but an honorable duty.

condemned to death'.[34] I do not know where Clavijero acquired this information, but we shall see that there is ample evidence to substantiate his claims.

Concerning the prisoners of war, sometimes called 'penitents', they impersonated Mimixcoas, who drank pulque and slept with women instead of doing their duty. Therefore they were given pulque, and sometimes women, before their immolation.[35] A ritual performed during the month of Etzalcualiztli illustrates very well the spirit of the immolation of warriors. Before the festival, the priests had to fast and do penance. Any neglect, like making a stain while eating, was severely castigated. They spied on one another and denounced the transgressors, who became the 'captives' of the denouncers or 'captors' – the terms used are those of warfare. If the culprits were unable to pay the fine to their 'captors', they were caught by the hair, like on the battlefield, and cast into the lagoon, beaten, submerged in the water until they suffocated and became 'like death'.[36] In other words, they were symbolically sacrificed like prisoners of war.

For a warrior, death on the battlefield or on the sacrificial stone was at the same time glorious and unfortunate, or even infamous. According to the divinatory almanach, dying in battle or in sacrifice was considered a 'bad end' and put on the same level as execution for adultery or robbery. To hear a wild animal crying or howling was a bad omen that announced death in war or some other 'misery' or 'disaster', like being sold as a slave or a prisoner of war or being condemned. Winning at the ballgame announced much adultery or death on the battlefield or by an outraged husband. Nahuatl proverbs also connote negatively the sacrificial death of a warrior. 'I have given you your banner, your strips of paper [part of the attire of the Mimixcoa victims]' is explained as follows: 'This is said when someone has reached the point of despair.' A metaphor collected by

[34] Francisco Javier Clavijero, *Historia antigua de México*, ed. M. Cuevas (Mexico City, 1964) 338. But this passage may be an eighteenth-century construction, like the phrase that follows, also attributed to Motecuhzoma: 'No contradigo la bondad del Dios que adoráis, pero si él es bueno para España, los nuestros lo son para México'.
[35] Cristóbal del Castillo, *Historia de la venida de los mexicanos y otros pueblos e Historia de la conquista*, transl. F. Navarrete Linares (Mexico City, 1991) 128-9; Durán, *Historia* 1.98, 2.160; Sahagún, *Florentine Codex*, bk. 2, ch. 21, p. 52. On penitents see Fernando Alvarado Tezozomoc, *Crónica mexicana precedida del Códice Ramírez*, ed. M. Orozco y Berra (Mexico City, 1878).
[36] Sahagún, *Florentine Codex*, bk. 6, ch. 25, pp. 83-86.

Olmos says 'I give you chalk and feather down, I give you your banner and *teteuitl* paper [also attire of the Mimixcoas], I place you before the mat, the seat, I drive you into the earth, I give you the spiny water, the water of pain', which means, 'now I cover your misdemeanor, but if you do not mend your ways, next time you will pay it all'.[37]

The other great category of victims were the slaves. The very condition of being a slave was regarded as one of the worst disasters one could suffer, a stain from which sacrificial victims had to be purified, and a punishment.[38] For them also, sacrifice was a disgrace and expiation. Only the unmanageable ones who had been sold two or three times, or those who had sold themselves to pay gambling debts and could not buy themselves back could be immolated.[39] The 300 beautiful Tlaxcaltec female slaves allegedly offered to Cortés and his men as a present to eat were women who had been condemned to be sacrificed for violations of the law.[40]

A third and much more limited category of victims comprises criminals and wrongdoers sentenced to death. Certain sentences were directly related to war, sacrifice. Noble warriors who had been caught on the battlefield but managed to escape were sacrificed in their home towns, and so were guards who let prisoners escape, commoners who refused to attend immolations, servants who let the domestic fire go out during the New Fire ceremony, warriors of

---

[37] Sahagún, *Florentine Codex*, bk. 4, ch. 27, pp. 93-94 and bk. 5, ch. 1, p. 151. Tezozomoc, *Crónica mexicana*, ch. 2, p. 228; T.D. Sullivan, 'Nahuatl proverbs, conundrums and metaphors collected by Sahagún', *Estudios de Cultura Náhuatl* 4 (1962) 93-178; K.Th. Preuss, 'Die Feuergötter als Ausgangspunkt zum Verständnis der mexikanischen Religion in ihrem Zusammenhange', *Mitt. Wiener Anthrop. Gesellschaft* 33 (1903) 129-233 at 190-1 and 'Die Sünde', 257.

[38] Durán, *Historia* 1, 64, 181-2, 185; Sahagún, *Florentine Codex*, bk. 4, 91; A.J.P. Anderson, 'The Institution of Slave-Bathing', *Indiana* 7 (1982) 81-91. In Fray Andrés de Olmos, *Grammaire de la langue nahuatl ou mexicaine*, ed. R. Siméon (Paris, 1875) 215: a slave was called '*teyo, quauhyo*', 'the one with the stone, the one with the stick', that is, the castigated one. See Preuss, 'Die Sünde', 256-7, and 'Feuergötter'; Sahagún, *Florentine Codex*, bk.5, 35, 93-5; bk.7, 23-4, quoted in Anderson.

[39] V.M. Castillo, *Estructura económica de la sociedad mexica* (Mexico City, 1972) 123; Motolinia (Fray Toribio de Benavente), *Memoriales e Historia de los Indios de la Nueva España* (Madrid, 1970) 174; Durán, *Historia* 1, 125, 183-4, 200, 210, who even mentions sacrifice as the fourth mode of execution for trespassers, especially slaves. Slaves paid as tribute – i.e., as a penalty – were also sacrificed: *Información de 1554. Sobre los tributos que los indios pagaban a Moctezuma*, ed. J.L. de Rojas (Mexico City, 1997); Durán, *Historia* 1, 82 and 2, 321.

[40] Muñoz Camargo, 'Descripción', 237.

the ritual 'flowery war' found in the land of their enemies, ambassa-
dors considered traitors, robbers of temple objects, and so forth.[41]
Other misbehaviors that had to do with religion, such as sorcery,
false predictions, rape of virgins and adulteries are also mentioned
in the sources.[42] Finally, ordinary criminals could also be immolated
according to information from different cities.[43]

Sacrifice was castigation, but also expiation, and it opened the
way to a better hereafter. This explains, first, why it was readily
accepted by many warriors – we have Spanish testimonies on victims they liberated in Mexico in 1520 and who rejoiced at being
immolated – and, second, why sometimes people volunteered to be
offered. The case of prostitutes who did so in honour of the goddess
of love Xochiquetzal, during her festival in Quecholli, and of musi-
cians to have the honour to play the drum during festivals, is also
documented. On the other hand, in the codices there are several representations of humans or gods killing themselves in sacrifice.[44]

[41] Mendieta, *Historia*, bk. 2, ch. 27, v.1 p. 144; Durán, *Historia* 1, 59; Tezozomoc,
Crónica, ch. 30, p. 321; Fernando de Alva Ixtlilxochitl, *Obras históricas*, 2 vols, ed. E.
O'Gorman (Mexico City, 1975-77) 2.111-3; Juan Bautista Pomar, *Relación de la ciudad
y provincia de Tezcoco = Relaciones geográficas del siglo XVI: México, tomo tercero*, ed. R.
Acuña (Mexico City, 1986) 89; Francisco López de Gómara, *Historia general de las
Indias*, 2 vols (Barcelona, 1965-66) 1.95; Hernán Cortés, *Cartas de Relación* (Mexico
City, 1963) 133; Motolinia, *Memoriales*, 41.

[42] 'Relación de la genealogía y linaje de los Señores…', in Icazbalceta, *Nueva colección de documentos para la historia de México*, 283; Torquemada, *Monarquía*, 2.386, 391;
Francisco Cervantes de Salazar, *Crónica de la Nueva España*, 2 vols (Madrid, 1971)
1.56; R. Castañeda Paganini, *La cultura tolteca-pipil de Guatemala* (Guatemala City,
1959) 33, quoting García Palacios' 1574 letter to Philip II; Codex Telleriano-Remensis,
in *Antigüedades de México*, 1.112, 201, 212-3, 216f.

[43] 'Relación de Metztitlan', in *Relaciones geográficas del siglo XVI: México, tomo
segundo*, ed. R. Acuña, (Mexico City, 1986) 66; 'Relación de Tecciztlan' and 'Relación
de Ocopetlayuca', both in *Papeles de la Nueva España*, ed. Francisco del Paso y Tron-
coso, 7 vols (Madrid, 1905-15) 6.257, 229 (also in *Relaciónes geográficas*, 242); Ixtlilxochitl, *Obras*, 39.

[44] *Documentos cortesianos*, 3 vols, ed. J.L. Martínez (Mexico City, 1990) 1.207: the
victims 'told him [Pedro de Alvarado] that they were kept to be sacrificed soon, and
that they rejoiced for that, because they would go to their gods'; 'Thomas Lopez
Medel, Relación, 1612', in Landa's *Relación de las cosas de Yucatán*, transl. and notes
A.M. Tozzer, *Papers of the Peabody Museum of American Archaeology and Ethnology,
Harvard Univ.*, vol. 18 (Cambridge, Mass. 1941) 222; Torquemada, *Monarquía*, 2.299;
'Costumbres, fiestas, enterramientos y diversas formas de proceder de los Indios de
Nueva España', ed. F. Gómez de Orozco, in *Tlalocan* 2,1 (1945) 37-63 at 59. For reasons unclear, in Sahagún, *Florentine Codex*, bk. 10, ch. 15, p. 55, the prostitute is compared to 'a sacrificial victim, a bathed slave [tlacamicqui, suchimicqui, tlaaltilli, teu-
micqui]…… She lives like a bathed slave, acts like a sacrificial victim; she goes about
with her head high – rude, drunk, shameless – eating mushrooms'. For suicide in
codices see the *Codex Borgia*, pp. 3-4, 7, 18, 23 and, possibly, 46.

Sacrifiers

The particular relationship established between the sacrifier and the victim he offers constitutes another argument that confirms that sacrifice is above all a means of gaining a worthy afterlife through expiation. The sacrifier identifies with the victim, in order to die symbolically through the victim. The end was obviously not only to feed the god, or simply to gain merit for this or the other world, since for that, the offered victim was sufficient. The only convincing explanation is that what the sacrifier wanted was to participate through the victim's death, to die through him, to offer himself, that is, to do as the gods in Teotihuacan who destroyed their material body to expiate and return to heaven. And, effectively, the prisoner of war killed on the sacrificial stone joined the House of Nanahuatl-Sun, and so did, or would do, the sacrifier assimilated with him.

Evidence for this identification is not abundant, but what exists is quite meaningful. When a warrior caught an enemy on the battlefield, he said 'he is like my beloved son' (*ca iuhquj nopiltzin*) and the captive replied: 'he is my beloved father' (*ca notatzin*). A son was regarded as the *ixiptla*, the image, the representation, of his father.[45] The same word is used to qualify the victims or impersonators of the gods. The identification of captor with captive is confirmed by the fact that the former could not eat the latter: 'would I eat my own self?' (*cuix çan no ninocuaz?*).[46] At certain moments, the captor dressed like his offering[47] or was called 'sun, chalk and feather down' (*tonatiuh tiçatl ihuitl*) because, like his substitute, he was a victim (covered with chalk and feather downs) and would join the sun.[48] More generally, when after a Mexica victory prisoners of war entered Mexico Tenochtitlan, they were told that they were at home, and they

---

[45] Sahagún, *Florentine Codex*, bk. 6, pp. 17, 189: The first prisoner made by a ruler was called 'his son' and revered as much as the very ruler, being saluted first, etc.: Motolinia, *Memoriales*, 161. People threatened to die from illness, war, perils of travel, etc., took a vow to sacrifice a slave or a son or daughter if they survived: their *ixiptla* died in their place, cf. Las Casas, *Apologética*, 2.226.

[46] Sahagún, *Florentine Codex*, bk. 2, ch. 21, p. 54.

[47] Sahagún, *Florentine Codex*, bk. 2, p. 45; bk. 9, pp. 63-64.

[48] Sahagún, *Florentine Codex*, bk. 2, p. 48. A much less convincing (but probably popular) interpretation of covering the captor with feather down accompanies the text: 'The captor's being pasted with feathers was done because he had not died there in war or else [because] he would yet go to die, would go to pay the debt. Hence his blood relatives greeted him with tears; they encouraged him' (transl. Dibble and Anderson).

were presented to the rulers and the gods. They were clothed, nourished, sometimes even received women and, in certain cases, could
even live freely in the city for years. The point was that they had to
be integrated as much as possible into the city, in order for them to
be assimilable to the Mexicas who would die through them.[49]

During the 'gladiatorial' sacrifice the sacrifier danced and watched
his captive, who had to fight before being put to death.[50] In another
context it is said that he wanted 'to see his god face to face', an
expression that in many religions expresses death, and we know of
cases in which the sacrifier effectively was allowed to ascend to the
top of the pyramid – the heaven, abode of the deity ['s image]–,
where the sacrifice took place and where he could effectively see 'his
god ['s image] face to face'.[51]

A myth and a pseudo-historical ritual recorded in the *Historia de
los Mexicanos por sus pinturas* both portray the victim as substitute for
the sacrifier. In the *Historia* version of the myth of Teotihuacan, the
sun is the son of Quetzalcoatl (usually identifiable with Nanahuatl)
and Moon the son of Tlaloc (remember that the moon is the Tlalocan, Tlaloc's paradise). The fathers both throw their sons into the
fire: they are the sacrificers and sacrifiers simultaneously, and we
have seen that their sons are their *ixiptlas*, their images or representations. To participate in the death of their sons Quetzalcoatl and
Tlaloc inflicted partial deaths on themselves by fasting and drawing
blood from the ears and the body before the immolation.

[49] Graulich, *Montezuma*, 85-9.
[50] Sahagún, *Florentine Codex*, bk. 2, p. 52.
[51] Face to face: see e.g. *Leviticus* 18.6. Sahagún, *Florentine Codex*, bk. 9, pp. 55, 67
and bk. 2, p. 49: the dead warrior goes in front of the face of the sun; Sahagún, *ibidem*, 48. According to a modern Totonac myth collected by A. Ichon, *La Religion des
Totonaques de la Sierra* (Paris, 1969) 45, 53, the gods contemplated to provide the
humans with a kind of visor that would prevent them seeing the heavens and therefore from dying, unless they wanted to die by lifting their heads and seeing the gods
face to face; but the gods changed their minds when the first creature committed a
transgression.
   While they climbed the stairs, the sacrifiers did something described as *moquai-
iauitiuh*, translated by Anderson and Dibble as 'they went putting breath to their
heads', drawing their inspiration from Sahagún's *Historia*, bk. 9, ch. 14, p. 55: 'y subi-
endo resollaban las manos y ponían el resuello en las cabezas con las manos', but it
is difficult to find *resollar*: *ihiyotia* (*nin*) in *iiauitiuh*. Another translation for this difficult verb is L. Schultze Jena, *Gliederung des Alt-Aztekischen Volks in Familie, Stand und
Beruf. Quellenwerke zur alten Geschichte Amerikas aufgezeichnet in den Sprachen der
Eingeborenen* V (Stuttgart, 1952) 340, based on *iyaua.nin*, 'ofrecerse alguno en sacrificio a dios; *nitla*: ofrecer algo desta manera, o incensar': 'he gave his head as an offering to Huitzilopochtli'. This is very interesting in our context but also debatable.

More telling still is the story of the Mexica-Tlatelolcas transgression during the wanderings of the Mexicas to their promised land. In the year 13 Reed, in Temazcaltitlan, the Tlatelolcas murmur at being led to disaster by Huitzilopochtli. To punish them, their god tells them in dreams that those who mumbled sinned like people with two faces and two tongues and that to be pardoned they had to make a seed image of a head with two faces and two tongues, shoot it with arrows, look for it blindfolded, and eat it. The image evidently represents the sinners who have to sacrifice themselves symbolically by killing their image to expiate.[52]

In Aztec ritual the sacrifier could be an individual (warrior, merchant, artisan), but also a group (corporation, ward, state) whose members contributed to buy the slave who would impersonate their tutelar deity. These members also 'died' through their victims but we may assume that they expiated less and earned less merit than the individual sacrifier.

The victim as substitute for the sacrifier is not uncommon in the history of religions.[53] The ancient substitution system still survives in Mexico, among the Huicholes, where the famous peyote hunt is assimilated with a deer hunt, the deer being the game *par excellence* and the animal equivalent of captured enemy. Peyote and deer are also assimilated with maize, as were captives in ancient Mexico, and with the Huicholes themselves: 'they form a unity, they are our life, they are ourselves'.[54] The peyote is shot with arrows and the hunters treat it as if it really were a deer. It is 'flayed' and eaten. The Indians, who die in or through the peyote cactus, then 'see their lives', and

---

[52] A comparable episode seems to be figured in the *Rollo Selden* (*Antigüedades de México* 2.111), a document depicting wanderings often closely related to the Mexica ones.

[53] On the frequent assimilation of sacrifier and victim (and addressee), see W.R. Smith, *Lectures on the Religion of the Semites* (London, 1894²); Comte Goblet d'Alviella, *Rites, croyances, institutions*, 3 vols (Paris, and Brussels, 1911) 1.303 even mentions Pre-Columbian America in this context; G. van der Leeuw, *Religion in Essence and Manifestation* (London, 1938 [1933¹]) 350-60; C. Lévi-Strauss, *La pensée sauvage* (Paris, 1962) 295-8; M. Biardeau and Ch. Malamoud, *Le sacrifice dans l'Inde ancienne* (Paris, 1976).

[54] On the Huichol peyote hunt, see C. Lumholtz, *El México desconocido*, 2 vols (Mexico City, 1904) 1.125-35; B.G. Myerhoff, *Peyote Hunt, The Sacred Journey of the Huichol Indians* (Ithaca and London, 1974); P.T. Furst, *La chair des dieux. L'usage rituel des psychédéliques* (Paris, 1974); S. Nahmad *et al.*, *El peyote y los huicholes* (Mexico City, 1979); P.T. Furst, *Los alucinógenos y la cultura* (Mexico City, 1980). The peyote quest practiced by the ancient Chichimecs is described by Sahagún, *Florentine Codex*, bk. 10, ch. 29. On hunting and sacrifice, see Graulich, 'Chasse'.

their shaman sees their gods face to face: they have ascended to heaven and recovered their lost paradise.

We have seen from the outset that the Aztec practice of human sacrifice was varied. In myth, not all the deaths of gods are expiatory, especially not the dema-type one of Tlalteotl, 'Earth Deity', a kind of saurian who haunted the primeval waters and whose body Quetzalcoatl and Tezcatlipoca tore into pieces to make from one part the earth, and from the other the sky. To console Tlalteotl, the angry gods (probably the supreme creators) made her body the source of all the fruits of the earth that humans need. Far from being expiation, her killing is a variant of the first transgression perpetrated by the gods.[55] When Tlalteotl's killing and the creation of the earth were reenacted in Ochpaniztli,[56] it certainly was no expiatory death for the goddess, but it was for the slave representing her and, of course, for the sacrifiers, in this case the midwives and healers who offered her. Ancient Mexican sacrifice consists of superimposed layers of meanings.

To conclude, expiation in view of a worthy afterlife is central to the theory and practice of Aztec human sacrifice. We have seen it at the core of the most important origin myth of sacrifice, misleadingly called the myth of the creation of sun and moon, where self-sacrifice was the only means for gods expelled on earth after a transgression to return to heaven. As for the terrestrial beings, first the animals were condemned for neglecting to venerate their creators, and, later, the humans were also condemned to sacrificial death for the same reason. An examination, first, of who the victims were and of how human sacrifice was regarded, and, second, of the sacrifiers and their particular relationship with the victims corroborates the central importance of expiation in Aztec sacrifice.[57]

---

[55] *Histoyre du Méchique*, 30-31. For an analysis of the myth in its context see Graulich, *Myths*, 49-62. The author of the *Histoyre du Méchique* goes on explaining that Earth only bears fruit if nourished with hearts and watered with human blood. Her death obviously is not expiation, but the payment of blood is: the humans have to pay for repeating constantly the prototypical transgression when they tear the earth open to cultivate it. This looks as a typically late Aztec and Mexica development aimed at explaining that both Earth and Sun need hearts to do their duty. The myth is also interesting because it presents life (plants) as proceeding from death. But it should be observed that the birth of the useful plants results from a decision of the gods who want to console the victim, who had returned to life.

[56] See note 4.

[57] This chapter was first published by the University of Chicago Press in *History of Religions* 39 (2000) 352-71; see now also my *Le sacrifice humain chez les Aztèques* (Paris, 2005).

II. HUMAN SACRIFICE
IN MEDIEVAL IRISH LITERATURE

Jacqueline Borsje

The earliest reference to Celtic religion mentions human sacrifice.[1] Sopater, a playwright from the late fourth century BC, writes about the Celts:

> Among them it is the custom, whenever they win any success in battle, to sacrifice their captives to the gods ...[2]

Sopater supplies us with the main elements for a definition of human sacrifice: people kill certain other human beings for a specific reason as an offering to supernatural beings.

There are three types of written sources available that give information about so-called Celtic human sacrifice. First, Greek and Latin writings mention several types of human sacrifice purported to have been performed by various Celtic populations.[3] Secondly, we have medieval texts from the inhabitants of countries, where a Celtic language is spoken: Ireland, Scotland, and Wales.[4] Thirdly,

---

[1] See P. Freeman, *War, women, and druids* (Austin, 2002) 33f.

[2] Sopater, fragment 6 Kassel-Austin, quoted by Athenaeus (*fl. c.* AD 200) iv.160, tr. C.B. Gulick, *Athenaeus* II (London and Cambridge MA, 1928) 230f.

[3] See, for instance, E. Anwyl, 'Communion with Deity (Celtic)', in J. Hastings (ed.), *Encyclopaedia of Religion and Ethics* III (Edinburgh, 1910) 747-51 at 749-50; E. Anwyl and J.A. MacCulloch, 'Sacrifice (Celtic)', *ibidem* XI (Edinburgh, 1920) 8-12; G. Dottin, *Manuel pour servir à l'étude de l'Antiquité Celtique* (Paris, 1906) 114-15, 255-58; idem, 'Divination (Celtic)', in Hastings, *Encyclopaedia* IV (Edinburgh, 1911) 787-8 at 787; L. Gougaud, *Les chrétientés celtiques* (Paris, 1911) 17-18; J. de Vries, *Keltische Religion* (Stuttgart, 1961) s.v. Opfer; F. Graf, 'Menschenopfer in der Burgerbibliothek. Anmerkungen zum Götterkatalog der "Commenta Bernensia" zu Lucan 1,445', *Archäologie der Schweiz* 14 (1991) 136-43. On the relationship between classical sources and recent archaeological finds, see F. Marco-Simón, 'Sacrificios humanos en la Céltica antigua: entre el estereotipo literario y la evidencia interna', *Arch. f, Religionsgeschichte* 1 (1999) 1-15.

[4] For medieval Irish examples, see F.N. Robinson, 'Human sacrifice among the Irish Celts', *Anniversary papers by colleagues and pupils of George Lyman Kittredge*

folklore customs from these same countries from the last centuries have been said to be survivals of the practice of human sacrifice.[5]

What strikes us immediately is that we have no direct witnesses from the Celts themselves: the information comes from Classical authors, Christian descendants of the Celts and modern scholarship.[6] A survey and analysis of all these texts could easily fill a book, which is why the present paper is limited to the literary motif of human sacrifice in medieval Irish literature.[7] The other sources will be referred to only when relevant.

In this survey, early Irish examples of human sacrifice are classified in four types.[8] The first type is human sacrifice in the strict sense: an offering to Gods for a certain purpose. The other types lack the mention of supernatural beings to whom the offering is made. They can be defined as foundation sacrifice (2), vicarious sacrifice

presented on the completion of his twenty-fifth year of teaching in Harvard University, June, MCMXIII (Boston and London, 1913) 185-97, and below. For Welsh examples, see H. Gaidoz, 'Review of "Zur Volkskunde", alte und neue Aufsätze von Felix Liebrecht (...)', *Revue Celtique* 4 (1879-80) 118-22 at 120-21; J.A. MacCulloch, *The Religion of the Ancient Celts* (Edinburgh, 1911) 190, and below; for Scottish examples, see G. Henderson, *Survivals in Belief among the Celts* (Glasgow, 1911) 276-89; A. Carmichael, *Carmina Gadelica. Hymns and Incantations* (Edinburgh & London, 1928) 338-41, and below. I did not come across any Breton examples.

[5] See, for instance, J. Brand, *Observations on popular antiquities chiefly illustrating the origin of our vulgar customs, ceremonies and superstitions*, ed. Sir Henry Ellis (London, 1900; 1777[1]) 125-26, 210-11, and the theories mentioned in MacCulloch, *Religion*, s.v. Sacrifice, human; R. MacilleDhuibh, 'Sating the river goddess', *West Highland Free Press*, 1–4–1994; 'The reason of the cow's hide', *West Highland Free Press*, 27–12–2002.

[6] It is beyond any doubt that there is a hidden agenda in most of our sources. To interpret and assess the information offered in the texts is not an easy task. See, for instance, N.K. Chadwick, *The druids*, ed. Anne Ross (Cardiff, 1997[2]) 6-30, on several classical texts ultimately deriving from the tradition of Posidonius (*c.* 135–*c.* 50 BC).

[7] At the turn of the 20th century, scholars debated the historical reality of human sacrifice among the Irish Celts: see, e.g., E. O'Curry in O'Curry and W.K. Sullivan, *On the Manners and Customs of the Ancient Irish* II (Dublin, 1873) 222; P.W. Joyce, *A social history of ancient Ireland* I (London, New York & Bombay, 1903) 239, 281-86; K. Meyer, 'Human sacrifice among the ancient Irish', *Ériu* 2 (1905) 86; Gougaud, *Chrétientés*, 17; MacCulloch, *Religion*, 236. This question is beyond the scope of this study. For references to archaeological finds in the Irish context, see Marco-Simón, 'Sacrificios', notes 43, 59; and R. Ó Floinn, 'Recent Research into Irish Bog Bodies', in R.C. Turner and R.G. Scaife (eds.), *Bog Bodies: New Discoveries and New Perspectives* (London, 1995) 137-145, quoted in Ailbhe MacShamráin, 'Iarsmaí 'Ceilteacha' na Danmhairge ón Iarannaois: Comharthaí ar Chaidreamh?', in R. Ó hUiginn & L. Mac-Cóil (eds.), *Bliainiris 2001* (Ráth Cairn, 2001) 181-202. With thanks to Ailbhe Mac-Shamráin for sending me an English version of his article.

[8] Initially, I distinguished even a fifth type – metaphorical sacrifice – but I dropped this category on second thought, because it stretches the definition too much.

(3), and burial sacrifice (4). The length of this paper dictates that I can analyse only the most important text in depth; the other examples will be dealt with more briefly.

In this paper, I use words, such as 'idol' and 'paganism'. These terms do not reflect my judgement of these religious concepts, but are translations of words from my sources. Finally, archaeology is not included in my discussion: this is a discipline in its own right and is beyond the scope of this paper.

1. Offerings to the Gods

The best-known Irish example of human sacrifice is from the tradition on place-names, the *Dindshenchas*, in which the place-name Mag Slécht is explained. The prose version goes as follows:

> *Ann roboi ri[g]idal Erenn.i. Crom Croich,⁹ 7 da idhal decc do clochaib ime, 7 eisium dí or, 7 is é ba déa do cach lucht rogab Erinn co toracht Patric. IS dó no ídpradis cétgeine cacha sotha 7 primgene cacha cloinde. IS cuca rosiacht Tigern[m]as mac Follaich ri Erenn dia samna co firu 7 co mna Erenn imalle dia adhradh, coro slecht uile fiadhu co ræm[d]etar tul a n-etan 7 maetha hi srona 7 faircledha a nglun 7 corra a n-uillend, co n-eplatar teora cethrama[i]n fer n-Erenn oc na slechtonaib sin. Unde Mag Slecht.*¹⁰

Tis there was the king-idol of Erin, namely the Crom Cróich, and around him twelve idols made of stones; but he was of gold. Until Patrick's advent, he was the god of every folk that colonized Ireland. To him they used to offer the firstlings of every issue (*suth*) and the chief scions of every clan (*clann*). 'Tis to him that Erin's king, Tigernmas son of Follach, repaired on the day of Samain¹¹ together with the men and women of Ireland, in order to adore him. And they all prostrated before him, so that the tops of their foreheads and the gristle of their noses and the caps of their knees and the ends of their elbows broke, and three fourths of the men of Erin perished at those prostrations. Whence *Mag Slecht* "Plain of Prostrations".¹²

---

⁹ Variant readings are: Crom Cruach (Book of Lecan 250va18), – Croich (Book of Ballymote 393a5); Crom Cruaich (Trinity College Dublin, MS 1322 (H.3.3) 51b24). I am grateful to Pádraig Ó Macháin for sending me a print-out from the manuscript's microfilm of this last page.

¹⁰ W. Stokes, 'The Prose Tales in the Rennes *Dindshenchas*', *Revue Celtique* 16 (1895) 31-83, 135-67, 269-312 at 35 (henceforth: Prose Tales 2).

¹¹ The translation of Stokes reads here 'on Hallontide', presumably meaning 'on All-Hallow's Tide'.

¹² Stokes, 'Prose Tales 2', 35-36.

The metrical version has extra information.[13] This chief idol (*ídal ard*)[14] or God of the Irish[15] is here called Crom Crúaich.[16] The poem confirms the detail that the idol is of gold and that there are twelve stone idols in the vicinity (lines 45-48). Whitley Stokes's translation of the prose version has led to theories concerning a sacrifice of first-fruit, firstborn animals and children to an earth or fertility god.[17] A literal translation of the relevant sentence is, however: 'It is to him that they used to sacrifice the firstborn of every offspring and the firstborn of every family.'[18] This could include animals, but it could also be limited to just human children. According to the metrical version, they kill their firstborn children (*clann*; line 14), amounting to one-third of their descendants (*suth*; line 19).[19] As *suth* and *clann* are here both referring to human offspring, it seems likely that the same is meant in the prose.[20] The method of the sacrifice is hinted at in the

[13] Three collections of the *dindshenchas* have been preserved: one collection of poems (Version A) and two collections in which prose and poems are found together (Versions B and C). The Mag Slécht *dindshenchas* is part of Collection C, in which 'the legend attached to each place-name is related first in prose and then in a poem', cf. T. Ó Concheanainn, 'The three forms of *dinnshenchas Érenn*', *Journal of Celtic Studies* 3 (1981-82) 88-131 at 88-89. This Collection C was, in Edward Gwynn's view, the work of a late twelfth-century reviser, but according to Tomás Ó Concheanainn, this 'reviser' was in fact the original redactor of the *dindshenchas*, Versions A and B being anthologies or extracts from C (*ibid*. 90-91, 131). For the edition and translation of the poem on Mag Slécht, see E. Gwynn, *The Metrical Dindshenchas* IV (Dublin, 1924) 18-23 (for an earlier edition and translation, see K. Meyer and A. Nutt, *The Voyage of Bran Son of Febal to the Land of the Living* II (London, 1897) 301-05).

[14] Gwynn (*Metrical Dindshenchas* IV, 19) translates 'a lofty idol', but it is likely that *ídal ard* is synonymous with *rígídal* (literally 'king-' or 'royal idol') in the prose, meaning 'chief idol'.

[15] *Ba hé a ndía*, 'He was their god' (Gwynn, *Metrical Dindshenchas* IV, 18-19). In line 31 he is called a demon (*demun*) and in line 56 an idol (*arracht*).

[16] Spelled 'Cruach' in the *Book of Lecan*.

[17] See, for instance, MacCulloch, who, obviously influenced by W. Mannhardt and J.G. Frazer (*Religion*, 269), speculates about the sacrifice, suggesting that the flesh of the victims (identified with the God) was either buried in the fields or mixed with the corn-seed (*ibid*. 237). There is no basis for this ritual in the Irish texts.

[18] *Cétgein* and *prímgein* are synonymous, both meaning 'firstborn'.

[19] *Suth* means 'fruit, produce; offspring, issue, progeny; milk'; *clann* is 'plant; springing locks, tress; children, family, offspring; a single child; descendants, race, clan'.

[20] The ambiguity of the Irish text is to be seen in the summary of this tradition by J. O'Donovan, *Annala Rioghachta Eireann. Annals of the Kingdom of Ireland, by the Four Masters from the Earliest Period to the Year 1616* I (Dublin, 1856) 43, n. *a*: he refers to the sacrifice of 'the firstlings of animals, and other offerings'. According to H. d'Arbois de Jubainville, *Les druides et les dieux celtiques á forme d'animaux* (Paris, 1906) 101, the firstborn of animals and women were sacrificed. It could be argued that the idea of the offering of the firstlings (fruit of the field, animals, children) was known from the Bible, but in this case the children were not seen as sacrifice to be slaughtered but

metrical version: they pour the blood of the children around the idol (lines 13-16). The reason for the sacrifice is furthermore given: they ask for milk and corn in return for their offer (lines 17-19). The adoration by Tigernmas king of Tara and the Irish is elaborated upon – besides kneeling, the beating of hand palms, bruising of their bodies, loud wailing and shedding of many tears are mentioned (lines 29-32). Only one fourth of the Irish population escaped death, and in this version the people die during Samain night (lines 33-40).[21] Samain is the night preceding and the day of 1 November, the beginning of winter in Ireland. Saint Patrick is then said to have ended the worship of this idol by using a sledgehammer (lines 49-56).

The Middle Irish *dindshenchas* collection was compiled in the eleventh or the first half of the twelfth century.[22] Thus it is a rather late witness of what is supposed to have happened in the fifth century. Moreover, the medieval etymology of the placename is based upon association with the verbal noun of the verb *sléchtaid*, an ecclesiastical term and a loan word from Latin (*flectāre*).[23] Yet it is the most

to be consecrated as servants of God. Sacrificing children was ascribed to 'pagans' or to sinning Israelites, and the receiving deity would be identified as Molech, Baal or another 'idol' (see further below); for human sacrifice in the Old Testament see Noort, this volume, Ch. V.

[21] The death of three-fourth of the population together with King Tigernmas is furthermore mentioned in *Lebor Gabála Érenn* (ed. and tr. R.A. Stewart Macalister, *Lebor Gabála Érenn. The Book of the Taking of Ireland* V (Dublin, 1956) 202-09, 432-37), in *Do fhlathiusaib hÉrend* (ed: R.I. Best, O. Bergin and M. A. O'Brien, *The Book of Leinster formerly Lebar na Núachongbála* I (Dublin, 1954) 56-93 at 63), in the *Annals of the Four Masters* (ed. and tr. O'Donovan, *Annala*, 42-43), and by Geoffrey Keating in the seventeenth century (ed. and tr. P. S. Dinneen, *The History of Ireland by Geoffrey Keating, D.D.* II (London, 1908) 122-23). Elsewhere in the *dindshenchas* 4000 people are said to have died on this occasion (Stokes, 'Prose Tales 2', 163). It should be noted, though, that some poems deviate from this tradition. Poem LXV from the *Lebor Gabála Érenn*-tradition, ascribed to Eochaid Ua Floind who died in 1003 according to the *Annals of Ulster*, calls Tigernmas *támda*, translated by Macalister as 'who suffered plague'; his death was in Slechta in Breifne (Macalister, *Lebor Gabála Érenn* IV (Dublin, 1940) 270-73). The eleventh-century poet Gilla Coemáin also mentions the death of Tigernmas with many Irish as caused by a plague (*tám*; ed. and tr. B. Mac Carthy, *The Codex Palatino-Vaticanus, no. 830* (Dublin, 1892) at 158-59). Gilla Coemáin does not mention a place name here, but in poem CXIV from the *Lebor Gabála Érenn*-tradition he identifies the place as Mag Slécht and he qualifies the death of Tigernmas as 'noble' (Macalister, *Lebor Gabála Érenn* V, 432-37, at 436-37, stanza 12).

[22] W. Stokes, 'The Prose Tales in the Rennes *Dindshenchas*', *Revue Celtique* 15 (1894) 272-336, 418-84 at 272 (Prose Tales 1). The Old Irish period is from about 600 to *circa* 900, the Middle Irish period from *c*. 900 to *c*. 1200, and the Early Modern Irish period from *c*. 1200 to *c*. 1650.

[23] J. Vendryes, *Lexique étymologique de l'Irlandais ancien* (Dublin and Paris, 1974) 129.

important early Irish text about human sacrifice, which is why it deserves further investigation concerning its literary development and its use of sources.

The beginning of the prose account is similar to a statement in the *Confessio*, written by Saint Patrick in the fifth century. He describes his advent to Ireland likewise as a crucial turning point in Irish history. The Irish used to worship *idola et inmunda*, 'idols and unclean things', he says, but since his arrival they have become the people of God.[24]

Idolum is the Latin equivalent of Irish *ídal*, used in our text. Saint Patrick uses biblical phrases in his writings. This is also the case when he describes the Irish pre-Christian religion.[25] We find, for instance, the same phrase – *idola colere* – in the Vulgate text of *Deuteronomy*, where the cults of Egypt and other nations are condemned:

> *Vidistis abominationes et sordes id est idola eorum lignum et lapidem argentum et aurum quae colebant* (29.17)

> You have seen abominations and filth, that is: their idols, wood and stone, silver and gold, which they worshipped.

The same phrase (*idola colere*) is also used in *Daniel* 14.4, in which chapter the Babylonians worship an image of clay covered with brass (*aereus*). A golden (*aureus*) statue is also venerated in this book: King Nebuchadnezzar demands that the people prostrate before this idol (*Daniel* 3.1-7). The worship of filth (*inmunditias colere*) is found in IV *Kings* 17.12, in which chapter not only the veneration of statues, molten calves and other idols is mentioned but also the sacrifice of children (twice: IV *Kings* 17.17, 31). Another parallel with Patrick's words is found in the same book: *figurae idolorum et*

---

[24] *Confessio* §41 (ed: L. Bieler, *Libri epistolarum Sancti Patricii episcopi. Introduction, text and commentary* (Dublin, 1993) 81). The parallel that Patrick here creates between Israel and the Irish is also found in e.g. §38, where he paraphrases the *Book of Jeremiah* (16.18-20) about the false idols that the (Israelite/Irish) fathers made for themselves as gods. Biblical references in this article are to the Vulgate, which was the version of the Bible used most in medieval Ireland.

[25] For instance, he tells how he declined a piece of wild honey, offered to him during his journey with 'pagan' sailors (*Confessio* §§18-19) and qualified as a sacrifice: *Immolaticium est* (Bieler, *Libri epistolarum*, 68). This is a quote from *I Cor* 10.28 (*hoc immolaticium est idolis*). It should be noted that Paul refers in this chapter to *Exodus* 32, in which the Israelites sacrificed to the idol of the golden calf and adored it as a god.

inmunditias (IV *Kings* 23.24) are mentioned in a chapter in which, again, child sacrifice is described (IV *Kings* 23.10).

Hagiographers of Saint Patrick appear to have filled in details concerning the *idola et inmunda* in Patrick's *Confessio*, using such biblical descriptions of idolatry as mentioned above. I suggest that these Patrician documents, biblical and other sources, have been used in the Mag Slécht tradition. I will delineate this literary development, starting with the *Lives* of Patrick that chronologically precede the Mag Slécht *dindshenchas*, and complementing them with the biblical sources that they refer to.[26]

At the end of the seventh century (circa 670 – 700), Bishop Tírechán wrote the *Collectanea* – a collection of local traditions about Saint Patrick. We read of Patrick sending a prophetic Irishman to the Moat of Slécht (*ad fossam Slecht*).[27] The idol there is not mentioned.[28]

Neither Mag Slécht nor its idol are mentioned in the *Life of Patrick* written by Muirchú in the seventh century. His narrative about the main conflict between Christianity and pre-Christian religion contains, however, a few relevant clues.[29] Muirchú explicitly draws a parallel between pre-Christian Ireland and Egypt when he writes that Patrick will celebrate the first Easter in 'the Egypt of this our island',[30] just as it once was celebrated for the first time in Goshen (I §13). He uses the word *caput*, 'head', four times in one sentence. Patrick celebrates the 'head' of all feasts – Easter – in Mag Breg, where the greatest Irish kingdom is and the head of all paganism and idolatry – the capitol Tara. It is there that the saint would smash the head of the dragon, just as the Psalmist wrote,[31] and he

---

[26] Previously, the importance of biblical and Patrician texts in this context has also been pointed out by M. Ó Duígeannáin, 'On the medieval sources for the legend of Cenn (Crom) Cróich of Mag Slécht', in J. Ryan (ed.), *Essays and studies presented to Professor Eoin MacNeill* (Dublin, 1940) 296-306. Because he was concerned with the historical evidence presented by the texts, he did not offer a detailed analysis of the sources.

[27] Ed. and tr. L. Bieler, *The Patrician Texts in the Book of Armagh* 10 (Dublin, 1979) 136, line 34.

[28] J.B. Bury ('The itinerary of Patrick in Connaught, according to Tírechán', *Proceedings of the Royal Irish Academy* C 24 (1902-04) 153-68 at 154-56) suggests that originally the story about the idol in Mag Slécht was here, but Bieler (*Patrician Texts*, 220) refutes this.

[29] Bieler, *Patrician Texts*, 62-123.

[30] Bieler, *Patrician Texts*, 83.

[31] PsG 73.14; the Psalmist refers to the heads (*capita*) of the dragon; the quotation has presumably been adapted to the symbolical and stylistic repetitive mention of *caput*. It should be noted, though, that the eighth-century *Psalm* text in Codex Palatinus

would drive a wedge into the head of all idolatry with the hammer of brave action and faith.[32] Muirchú tells furthermore (I §15) how King Loegaire summons nobility and druids to Tara, 'their Babylon', for a feast of idolatry, as once the biblical tyrant Nebuchadnezzar had done. Muirchú obviously refers here to *Daniel* 3, in which the obligatory veneration of the golden idol is described.[33]

There are five clues in this text that may have influenced the Mag Slécht tradition. Firstly, the confrontation takes place on a plain, in Muirchú's words: *in campo Breg maximo* – *campus* is the Latin equivalent of Irish *mag*. Significantly, according to Muirchú's source, King Nebuchadnezzar has set up the golden statue in the plain (*in campo Duram*) of Dura in the province of Babylon and demands that the people kneel down for it.[34] Just as the Babylonians, the pre-Christian Irish are described as kneeling down for a golden statue in a plain in the Mag Slécht *dindshenchas*.[35] Secondly, at first sight, the time of

---

Latinus, a manuscript from a Northumbrian or Irish monastery, reads here *caput* (ed. M. McNamara, *Glossa in Psalmos. The Hiberno-Latin Gloss on the Psalms of Codex Palatinus Latinus 68 (Psalms 39:11-151:7). Critical Edition of the text together with Introduction and Source Analysis* (Vatican City, 1986) 155.)

[32] ... *postremo inspirato divinitus sancto Patricio vissum est hanc magnam Domini sollempnitatem quasi caput omnium sollempnitatum in campo Breg maximo, ubi erat regnum maximum nationum harum, quod erat <caput> omnis gentilitatis et idolatriae, [ne possit ulterius] lib[er]ari, <ut iuxta vocem psalmistae> caput draconis confringeret <et> uti hic invictus cuneus in caput totius idolatriae (...) sub malleo fortis operis cum fide iuncti sancti Patricii et suorum manibus spiritalibus primus inlideretur,* '.... at last holy Patrick, divinely inspired, decided that this great feast of the Lord, being the principal feast of all, should be celebrated in the great plain of Brega, because it was there that there was the greatest kingdom among these tribes, the head of all paganism and idolatry; there, in the words of the Psalmist he would smash the head of the dragon, and for the first time an irresistible wedge would be driven into the head of all idolatry with the hammer of brave action joined to faith by the spiritual hands of holy Patrick and his companions' (Bieler, *Patrician Texts*, 82-85).

[33] His source is also obvious from the list of Loegaire's nobility (*congregatis etiam regibus, satrapis, ducibus, principibus et optimatibus populi, insuper et magis, incantatoribus, auruspicibus et omnis artis omnisque doni inventoribus doctoribusve vocatis ad Loigaireum velut quondam ad Nabucodonossor*: Bieler, *Patrician Texts*, 84), which is given in imitation of the nobility of Nebuchadnezzar (*itaque Nabuchodonosor rex misit ad congregandos satrapas magistratus et iudices duces et tyrannos et praefectos omnesque principes regionum; Daniel* 3.2; cp also *Daniel* 3.3: *tunc congregati sunt satrapae magistratus et iudices duces et tyranni et optimates* ...). See also T. O'Loughlin, 'Reading Muirchú's Tara-event within its background as a biblical "trial of divinities"', in J. Cartwright (ed.), *Celtic Hagiography and Saints' Cults* (Cardiff, 2003) 123-35.

[34] Another 'plain of the idol' (*campus Idoli*) is mentioned in *Amos* 1.5.

[35] Daniel's friends disobey this royal demand, just as Patrick and his followers break the royal rule when they light their paschal fire before King Loegaire lights the Tara fire, in Muirchú's narrative.

action looks different: Easter is closer to the feast of Beltaine (1 May). The start of summer in Ireland, however, could never have coincided with Easter,[36] whereas, significantly, the Feast of Tara is usually connected with Samain, just as the adoration in Mag Slécht.[37] Thirdly, Muirchú lets Patrick metaphorically smash the head of the dragon with a hammer – an instrument, which Patrick uses literally against the idol in the metrical *dindshenchas*. Fourthly, I already mentioned the repetitive use of *caput*: the head of the dragon equals the head of idolatry, which is represented by the feast and by Tara. The word *caput* or 'head' is also relevant in the context of the idol in Mag Slécht, because this is another 'head of idolatry' as chief idol – *rígídal* or *ardídal* – of Ireland.[38] Moreover, the earliest extant name of this idol begins with *Cenn*, 'head', instead of Crom. We read Cend Crúaich in the Irish *Life of Patrick* (*Vita Tripartita*), Cenn Cró[i]ch or Cenn Croth in the Latin *Vita Tertia* and no name at all in *Vita Quarta*.[39] Fifthly, in these Patrician *Lives* it is Muirchú's King Loegaire who is said to have worshipped the idol in Mag Slécht; no mention is made of the legendary King Tigernmas.

There is thus a description of the adoration of Cenn Crúaich in these Patrician *Lives*, but some details differ from what we find in the Mag Slécht *dindshenchas*. Cenn Crúaich is here described as covered with gold and silver (VT,[40] V3, V4). One version (V3) is very short: Saint Patrick's prayer pulverises the idol. The other two versions (VT, V4) tell how Patrick makes the earth swallow the twelve

---

[36] See J. O'Donovan, *Leabhar na g-Ceart, or The Book of Rights* (Dublin, 1847) xlviii-l; J.B. Bury, *The Life of St. Patrick and his place in history* (London, 1905) 107, 303.

[37] See, for instance, Gwynn, *Metrical Dindshenchas* IV, 296-99; cf. D.A. Binchy, 'The Fair of Tailtiu and the Feast of Tara', *Ériu* 18 (1958) 113-38 at 127-38.

[38] The length of this article does not allow the description and analysis of other Irish idols, such as Cermand Cestach, mentioned in the Middle Irish commentary of the *Martyrology of Oengus* (ed. & tr. W. Stokes, *Félire Óengusso Céli Dé. The Martyrology of Oengus the Culdee* (London, 1905) 186-87) and Crom Dubh, known from later folklore, see P.K. Ford, 'Aspects of the Patrician Legend', in Ford (ed.), *Celtic Folklore and Christianity. Studies in Memory of William W. Heist* (Los Angeles, 1983) 29-49.

[39] *Vita Tripartita* (VT), ed. and tr. W. Stokes, *The Tripartite Life of Patrick with Other Documents Relating to that Saint* (London, 1887) at 90-93 is dated to *c*. 900; it was revised in the eleventh century, cf. G. Mac Eoin, 'The Dating of Middle Irish Texts', *Proceedings of the British Academy* 68 (1982) 109-37 at 115; *Vita Tertia* (V3), ed. L. Bieler, *Four Latin Lives of St. Patrick. Colgan's Vita Secunda, Quarta, Tertia, and Quinta* (Dublin, 1971) at 150-51 is dated between *c*. 800 and *c*. 1130 (*ibid.* 26); *Vita Quarta* (V4), ed. *id.* at 99, is dated between the first half of the eighth and the eleventh century (*ibid.* 12).

[40] In *Vita Tripartita*, he is also called the chief idol (*ard ídal*) of Ireland.

idols covered with brass up to their heads.[41] The saint performs a miraculous action with the staff of Jesus without touching the idol, because of which the statue moves and is marked on its left side. These two versions describe how Saint Patrick expels the demon that lived in the statue (and who in *Vita Quarta* used to give answers to the people) to hell. This happens before the frightened eyes of King Loegaire and many Irish. *Vita Quarta* ends with their expression of gratitude towards God; *Vita Tripartita* tells how Patrick baptises many in 'Patrick's well', builds a church and leaves the prophetic Irishman there, who was probably also mentioned in Tírechán's *Collectanea* (see above). Place of action is in all these versions Mag or Campus Slécht (VT, V3, V4); in *Vita Tripartita* the statue's face is said to have been directed towards Tara.

Finally, this narrative is found in the *Life of Patrick* written by Jocelin of Furness in 1185/1186.[42] This late *Life* obviously depends upon the earlier ones, but a new element is the explanation of the name of the idol: *Ceancroithi id est caput omnium deorum*. *Cenn* is here explicitly connected with *caput* and used in the metaphorical sense as 'the head (or chief) of all gods'.

Comparing these other Mag Slécht traditions with the *dindshenchas*, it stands out that human sacrifice is mentioned only in the latter. The goal of the sacrifice – to get corn and milk – is said to have been achieved through other ways as well in early Irish literature: for instance, thanks to sacral kingship,[43] a contract with a supernatural person[44] or the holding of a fair at the first of August.[45] Samain

---

[41] Idols made of these materials are also found in the Bible: for instance, gold and silver (*Psalms* 113.12, 134.15; *Sap* 15.9; *Isaiah* 2.20, 30.22, 31.7; *Ezekiel* 7.19-20, 16.17; *Hosea* 8.4); clay and brass (*Daniel* 14.6); gold, silver, brass, stone and wood (*Revelation* 9.20).

[42] Ed. J. Colgan, *Trias Thaumaturga* (Dublin, 1997; facsimile reproduction of Louvain, 1647) 77, caput lvi.

[43] See, for instance, the Old Irish 'Testament of Morann', ed. and tr. F. Kelly, *Audacht Moraind* (Dublin, 1976) 6-7, in which milk and corn are successively mentioned (§§18-19) among other life-enhancing phenomena that are said to be produced by *fír flathemon*, 'the justice of the ruler'.

[44] The supernatural beings known as the Túatha Dé Danann destroyed corn and milk, until the Irish made a contract with the Dagda as related in an Old Irish tale, ed. and tr. V. Hull, 'De gabáil in t-shída (Concerning the seizure of the fairy mound)', *Zs. f. celtische Philol.* 19 (1931) 53-58. MacCulloch, *Religion*, 79, tentatively identifies him with Cenn/Crom Crúaich, pointing out that Crom-eocha was a name of the Dagda and that 'a motto at the sacrificial place at Tara read, "Let the altar ever blaze to Dagda"'. This remains, however, unverifiable: he says he bases these two things upon a lost text, referred to in *Collectanea de rebus Hibernicis* by Charles

is connected with many traditions,[46] but none mentions human sacrifice.[47] Where does this come from?

As we are dealing here with a Christian reconstruction of the pre-Christian past, a suitable source of inspiration was the Bible in which so-called 'pagan' practices were described.[48] As we have seen, Egypt,[49] Babylonia and Israel were used as symbols for Ireland. Loud cries, people cutting themselves and kneeling for a statue are also mentioned in the context of the cult of Baal.[50] Several biblical texts refer to the sacrifice of children to idols, such as Molech.[51] Statues[52] of idols are sometimes mentioned in the same context.[53] The

Vallancey (Dublin, 1786, IV.2, 495). It should be further noticed, that MacCulloch seems to have misread Vallancey's work: it is not on p. 495 but on p. 502 that the so-called motto at Tara is given, but no mention of a source is made, let alone a lost text. Moreover, concerning the name Crom-eocha (which I did not find in Vallancey's book), it should be noted that Vallancey excelled in highly speculative etymologies, translations and theories.

[45] See the *dindshenchas* on Carman (Stokes, 'Prose Tales 1', 311-15): the promise of corn and milk is followed by an enumeration of other good things. The *dindshenchas* on the Fair of Teltown has been mistakenly connected with human sacrifice, see Gwynn, *Metrical Dindshenchas* IV, 417.

[46] See M.-L. Sjoestedt, *Gods and Heroes of the Celts* (London, 1949) 52-56. It should be noted that Sjoestedt connects some deaths by burning and/or drowning in Samain tales with instances of human sacrifice mentioned in the *Scholia* on Lucan (see below). The crucial characteristic of a human being killed in offering to a supernatural being is, however, not present in these tales. More study is needed.

[47] Interesting in this context is the *Lebor Gabála* tradition, in which the supernatural people known as the Fomoire demanded from the Irish a yearly tribute, to be paid at Samain, of two thirds of the children, the corn and the milk in Mag Cetne (see Macalister, *Lebor Gabála Érenn* IV, 138-41, 172-75). I take this to refer to slavery, not to human sacrifice.

[48] Without further elaboration, already in 1899 Douglas Hyde, *A literary history of Ireland from earliest times to the present day* (London, 1980, reprint of 1899) 92-93 suggested that a 'Christian chronicler familiar with the accounts of Moloch and Ashtarôth' added this motif.

[49] Perhaps some association with the killing of children in Egypt may also have played a role. It is in Goshen in Egypt that at first the Jewish children are killed, and later the first-born of the Egyptians are killed as a result of the Tenth Plague. See also below, the text on Samson and the Gesteda. For human sacrifice in Egypt see the contributions of Van Dijk and Te Velde, this volume, Ch. VI and VII.

[50] III *Kings* 18.28, 19.18.

[51] See J. Day, *Molech: A god of human sacrifice in the Old Testament* (Cambridge, 1989). Molech is called 'idol' in e.g. Lv 18.21, 20.2; III *Kings* 11.5, 11.7; see also Noort, this volume, Ch. V.

[52] As indicated above, statues made from various materials also have a parallel in biblical descriptions.

[53] See IV *Kings* 16.3, 17.17, 17.31, 21.6, 23.10; 2 *Chronicles* 33.6; Sap 14.23; *Ezekiel* 20.31, 23.37-39.

[54] *Ezekiel* 16.36 (see furthermore verses 17, 20-21). Mention is also made of the devouring of children by idols (cf. *Ezekiel* 23.37).

most common form of this child sacrifice is 'passing them through fire', but we also encounter the offering of the blood of children to idols, just as in the Mag Slécht *dindshenchas*.[54] A description in *Psalm* 105.36-39 is quite similar to what is portrayed in the Irish text: Israel is accused of sacrificing their sons and daughters to demons; their innocent blood is shed and offered to the statues of the idols of Canaan. Sometimes blood-shedding is mentioned in the same context as child sacrifice,[55] which could also have influenced the description. Another possible source of inspiration for a bloody ritual may have been the name Cenn Crúaich itself, which might be translated as 'the Head of Slaughter'.[56]

Noteworthy are furthermore Classical sources, in which bloody human sacrifices by the Celts are mentioned. This should be seen as yet another example of 'pagan practices', and not as an example of the early medieval Irish identifying themselves with the Celts, because this identification was post-medieval.[57]

For example, Lucan (AD 39-65) writes in his *Civil War* concerning the Celts:

> *Et quibus inmitis placatur sanguine diro*
> *Teutates horrensque feris altaribus Esus*
> *Et Taranis Scythicae non mitior ara Dianae.*

> and the people who with grim blood-offerings placate
> Teutates the merciless and Esus dread with savage altars
> and the slab of Taranis, no kinder than Diana of the Scythians.[58]

---

[55] For instance, *Ezekiel* 22.3-4.

[56] *Crúach* as a feminine ā-stem means 'stack of corn, rick, mountain, hill'; as an adjective it means 'gory, bloody', and as a neuter o-stem 'slaughter, wounding'. In the Book of Lecan version of the Mag Slécht *dinshenchas* (see above, footnote 10), it seems to have taken the form of the adjective in Crom Cruach, 'the Bloody Bent One' (*cromm* means 'bent, stooped, crooked'). Alternatively, 'the Head/Bent One of the Hill' has been suggested, see J.P. Dalton, 'Cromm Cruaich of Magh Sleacht', *Proceedings of the Royal Irish Academy* C 36 (1922) 23-67 at 47, 62; he points out at 36 that his reconstructed location of the site has the form of a *crúach* or mound, but the form *Cenn/Crom Crúaiche* is not attested. For more about *crúach* and related forms, see R. Ó hUiginn, 'Crúachu, Connachta, and the Ulster Cycle', *Emania* 5 (1988) 19-23 at 21-23.

[57] See J. Leerssen, 'Celticism', in T. Brown (ed.), *Celticism* (Amsterdam and Atlanta, 1996) 1-20 at 5, who roughly dates the construction of 'the Celt' to the period from 1650 to 1850.

[58] Lucan I.444-46, tr. S.H Braund, *Lucan, Civil War* (Oxford, 1992) 14.

Diana or Artemis is the goddess who demanded from Agamemnon his daughter Iphigeneia as human sacrifice; Scythian Diana is Artemis of Tauris to whom strangers were sacrificed.[59]

This text leads us to our second example of 'human sacrifice to the Gods' in early Irish literature, for Lucan's *Civil War* was translated into Irish under the title *In Cath Catharda*, 'The Civil Battle'. This Irish version is dated circa 1100 or the early twelfth century.[60] The relevant section reads:

> *Tancadar ann popul na Teotonecdha. [is acu sen nó idpraitis fola daini i tempol Ioib 7 Mercuir 7 Mairt].*[61]

> There came the people of the Teutones. [It is by them that the blood of people used to be offered in the temple of Jupiter, Mercury and Mars.]

The Irish text summarizes here the Latin by offering the list of nations without the accompanying descriptions. The result is that the Celtic (i.e. Gaulish) names mentioned by Lucan have disappeared. Teutates seems to be mistaken for the people of the Teutones.[62] The second sentence, found in one manuscript only,[63] summarizes Lucan's description of the sacrifice of human blood, but the three Gaulish divine names have been replaced by their *interpretatio romana*. Could it be that its scribe knew the *Commenta Bernensia* or the *Adnotationes super Lucanum*?[64] These ancient commentaries on Lucan's work identify Mars, Mercury and Jupiter with the Gaulish deities.[65] The difference is that they do not start with Jupiter whereas

---

[59] On Iphigeneia, see J.N. Bremmer, 'Sacrificing a child in ancient Greece: the case of Iphigeneia', in E. Noort and E. Tigchelaar (eds), *The Sacrifice of Isaac. The Aqedah (Genesis 22) and Its Interpretations* (Leiden, 2002) 21-43.

[60] See A. Sommerfelt, 'Le Système Verbal dans *in Cath Catharda* (suite)', *Revue Celtique* 38 (1920-21) 25-47 at 39.

[61] W. Stokes, 'In Cath Catharda. The Civil War of the Romans. An Irish Version of Lucan's Pharsalia', in W. Stokes and E. Windisch (eds), *Irische Texte* IV.2 (Leipzig, 1909) 56.

[62] Stokes, 'In Cath Catharda', 57, n. 1.

[63] Royal Irish Academy, D.IV.2.

[64] The *Commenta Bernensia* are preserved in ninth-century Berne 370, ed. H. Usener, *M. Annaei Lucani Commenta Bernensia* (Leipzig, 1869, repr. Hildesheim, 1967). The *Adnotationes super Lucanum*, ed. I. Endt, *Adnotationes super Lucanum* (Leipzig, 1909) are extant in abbreviated form in Berne 370 and fuller in Bodmer lat. 182 from the eleventh century, see R.J. Tarrant, 'Lucan', in L.D. Reynolds (ed.), *Texts and Transmission. A Survey of the Latin Classics* (Oxford, 1983) 215-18 at 215 n. 4.

[65] The *Commenta Bernensia* offer two possibilities: (a) Teutates=Mercury, Esus=Mars, Taranis=Dis Pater, or (b) Teutates=Mars, Esus=Mercury, Taranis=Jupiter, see Usener,

the Irish text does. We cannot, therefore, be certain whether these commentaries were among the sources of the scribe.[66] What we do have is a Middle Irish tradition about 'Teutonic' sacrifice, in which human blood is offered to Jupiter, Mercury and Mars.

Our third example is a twelfth-century tale entitled 'How Samson slew the Gesteda'.[67] The editor Carl Marstrander suggested that the Gesteda should be located in the Land of Goshen in Egypt.[68] We are told how the angry Gods of the Gesteda have concealed all the waters from the people. The high king and chief priest of India arrives. He appears to be banished from his country and now advises the king of the Gesteda to sacrifice all their priests, druids, seers, physicians and learned people to the Gods. Twelve of them should be decapitated, offered and burned upon the altars daily for three months. Despite the protests of the victims, this happens. Then Hebrew people, descendants of Dan, suffer shipwreck in the vicinity and are taken captive. They were on their way to Troy in order to find out whether the Trojans were venerating the same God as they did. If so, Samson would go to Troy to help them fight against the Greek army. Now, however, they are under the threat of being sacrificed as well. They manage to arrange that one of them may go back to Samson for help. In the meantime each day twelve of them with a chief are sacrificed. In due time, Samson arrives together with his wife Lil(i)a and the priest Nehemias. Samson slays almost all of the Gesteda with the jawbone of a camel and sets fire to their dwellings. Then the waters rise up out of the earth and Samson kills

Commenta, 32. According to the *Adnotationes*, Teutates=Mercury, Esus=Mars, and Taranis=Jupiter (see Endt, *Adnotationes*, 28). See further Graf, 'Menschenopfer'.

[66] Three rituals are described in the *Commenta Bernensia* (32 Usener): a human being is suffocated head down into a kettle for Teutates, or hung in a tree for Esus or people are burned in a wooden vessel for Taranis. These descriptions of Gaulish rituals have been linked with the literary motif of the threefold death in a search for Celtic, cf. F. le Roux, 'Des chaudrons Celtiques à l'arbre d'Esus. Lucain et les Scholies Bernoises', *Ogam* 7 (1955) 33-58 or Indo-European, cf. D.J. Ward, 'The Threefold Death: An Indo-European Trifunctional Sacrifice?', in J. Puhvel (ed.), *Myth and Law Among the Indo-Europeans* (Berkeley, Los Angeles, London, 1970) 123-42, forms of sacrificial death. More critical research is needed, which, for instance, takes into account, firstly, that the Latin text presents three separate rituals and not a threefold ritual, and, secondly, that the Irish literary motif is always set in an explicitly Christian setting, see J.N. Radner, 'The Significance of the Threefold Death in Celtic Tradition', in Ford (ed.), *Celtic Folklore*, 180-99 at 183.

[67] Ed. and tr. C. Marstrander, 'How Samson slew the Gesteda', *Ériu* 5 (1911) 145-59 from one manuscript: Royal Irish Academy, D.IV.2. Marstrander presumably gave the tale its title; for the date, see p. 145.

[68] Marstrander, 'Samson', 145.

the last survivors: the Indian priest, the king and the queen. Samson thanks the heavenly Gods and God; Nehemias writes this all down in the annals of the Hebrews. Just as the previous example, this text ascribes human sacrifice to 'pagan' foreigners. The killing of these people by Samson is seen as a divine punishment.

In the fourth example of this group, human sacrifice is part of a divine punishment. In the Old Irish *Letter of Jesus*,[69] people are told to keep Sunday holy. Many sanctions are enumerated; one of them is that people, who do not observe the rules pertaining to Sunday, will be taken in bondage abroad by 'pagans', who will sacrifice these transgressors to their Gods.[70] This text is the oldest in this group and it is our final example of human sacrifice in the strict sense. Only the first example ascribes human sacrifice to the pre-Christian Irish; in the other three texts, 'pagan' foreigners perform this act. The Gods to whom this sacrifice is offered are named in the first two instances only: Cenn Crúaich and the Roman interpretations of Gaulish Gods. Cenn Crúaich is believed to give corn and milk in return; in the tale about Samson the Gods do not return the waters in exchange for human sacrifice, but the waters flow forth when Samson takes his divine revenge on the sacrificing people.

The other examples that will be described below do not refer to Gods as recipients of human sacrifice, although, as we will see, the God of the Christians sometimes plays a role.

2. Foundation sacrifice

The earliest possible reference to foundation sacrifice is one of the etymological explanations of the name Emain Macha, the royal fortress of Ulster. We read in the early Irish *Glossary of Cormac*, ascribed to King Bishop Cormac mac Cuilennáin (831–908):

> *Nó Em- ab ema [αῖμα] i.e. sanguine, quia ema sanguis est; -uin i.e. unus, quia sanguis unius hominis [effusus est] in tempore conditionis eius.*[71]

---

[69] Ed. and tr. J.G. O'Keeffe, 'Cáin Domnaig. I. The Epistle concerning Sunday', *Ériu* 2 (1905) 189-214; the text dates possibly from the ninth century: see J. Borsje, *From Chaos to Enemy: Encounters with Monsters in Early Irish Texts. An investigation related to the process of Christianization and the concept of evil* (Turnhout, 1996) 335-41.

[70] O'Keeffe, 'Cáin', 196-97, §10. The motif of being taken into exile by foreign peoples as a divine punisment can of course be traced back to the Old Testament.

[71] Ed. K. Meyer, 'Sanas Cormaic. An Old-Irish Glossary', *Anecdota from Irish Manuscripts* 4 (1912) 42. The glossary is translated by J. O'Donovan and W. Stokes, *Sanas Chormaic. Cormac's Glossary* (Calcutta, 1868).

Or *Em-* is from *ema* ['blood' in Greek] that is: from blood, because *ema* is blood. *Uin* that is: one, because the blood of one man [was shed] at the time of its founding.

It is a well-known tradition that one needs human blood or human sacrifice for the construction of a stable building.[72] This etymology, however, only supplies us with the barest details – there is neither reference to stability nor any further detail that could confirm that a sacrifice was performed at Emain Macha's construction.

A variation on this theme without human sacrifice is found in the late Old Irish tale 'Fíngen's night watch'.[73] What the builders of a palisade lift one day falls down the next morning.[74] Miraculously, one Samain night the palisade suddenly is stable. I mention this example, because it appears that human sacrifice is often absent in the oldest sources, but comes up in later variant versions. We saw this in the Mag Slécht tale and we shall see this presently again.

When Vortigern, king of the Britons, wants to build a fortress on a hill overlooking the sea, three nights in a row the building material (stone and wood) disappears. His druids, who had pointed out this place, now tell him to kill a son whose father is not known and to sprinkle his blood on the hill. The boy's blood should consecrate the fortress. This boy is found, but he appears to outwit the druids. He shows that a red and a white worm are living under the ground. When dug up, they fight and the red one wins. The boy explains that they symbolise the Saxons and Britons. In the end, nobody is sacrificed: the king and the druids go north to build a fortress and the boy, Ambrose son of a Roman consul, builds his fortress on the hill.

---

[72] See J.H. Todd, *Leabhar Breathnach. The Irish Version of the Historia Britonum of Nennius* (Dublin, 1848) xxiv-xxv; W. Stokes, *Three Irish Glossaries* (London and Edinburgh, 1862) xli-xlii; idem, 'Mythological Notes. X. Human sacrifice', *Revue Celtique* 2 (1873-75) 200-01; Joyce, *Social history*, 284-86; H. d'Arbois de Jubainville, 'Des victimes immolées par les constructeurs pour assurer la solidité des édifices', *Revue Celtique* 26 (1905) 289; E.S. Hartland, 'Foundation, foundation-rites', in Hastings, *Encyclopaedia* VI (Edinburgh 1913) 109-15; Anwyl and MacCulloch, 'Sacrifice', 12; A.H. Krappe, 'The Foundation Sacrifice and the Child's Last Words', in his *Balor With the Evil Eye. Studies in Celtic and French Literature* (New York, 1927) 165-80; S. Ó Súilleabháin, 'Foundation Sacrifices', *J. Roy. Soc. Antiq. Ireland.* 75 (1945) 45-52.

[73] Ed. J. Vendryes, *Airne Fíngein* (Dublin, 1953) at 16-17, §10, tr. T.P. Cross and A.C.L. Brown, 'Fingen's Night-watch', *The Romanic Review* 9 (1918) 29-47 at 43; Vendryes, *Airne*, xxii dates the text to the ninth or tenth century.

[74] Cross and Brown, 'Fingen's Night-watch', 29-30 suggest that the failure is due to the fact that one attempts to build on a *síd* or elfmound, and that the success may be the result of a compact with the dwellers in the *síd*.

This tale is from *Lebor Bretnach*,[75] the early Middle Irish translation of the Latin *Historia Brittonum*.[76]

It is likely that this narrative influenced an Early Modern Irish tale, called 'The adventurous journey of Art son of Conn'.[77] In this tale, druids advise to slay the son of sinless couple before Tara and to mix his blood with the earth of Tara (§8) or with the blighted earth and the withered trees (§12). This is, however, not a foundation sacrifice. The boy's killing is supposed to bring back Ireland's fertility: ever since the king married the wrong woman,[78] there is neither corn nor milk in Ireland (§8). Just as in the tale about Mag Slécht, child sacrifice is suggested as a kind of exchange for corn and milk. I note in passing that the king's druid is called Cromdes (§8), which name bears reminiscence to Crom Crúaich. As in our previous example, the human sacrifice does not take place. The boy is found on a wondrous island and brought to Ireland. He is willing to undergo the sacrifice, but his mother appears on the scene, bringing

---

[75] Ed. and tr. Todd, *Leabhar Breathnach*, 90-99; for a more recent edition without translation, see A.G. van Hamel, *Lebor Bretnach. The Irish version of the Historia Britonum ascribed to Nennius* (Dublin, 1932) at 53-61, who has added the Latin text (based on Mommsen's edition) at the bottom of the pages. The Irish translation is ascribed to Gilla Coemáin and dated to the middle of the eleventh century, cf. D.N. Dumville, '"Nennius" and the *Historia Brittonum*', *Studia Celtica* 10-11 (1975-76) 78-95 at 87-88.

[76] The Latin original was written in Wales in 829-30, cf. D.N. Dumville, 'Some aspects of the chronology of the *Historia Brittonum*', *Bulletin of the Board of Celtic Studies* 25 (1972-74) 439-45; on the Latin original of the Irish text, see *idem*, '"Nennius"'. For a wide-ranging theory based on this episode, see Krappe, 'Note sur un épisode de l'*Historia Britonum* de Nennius', *Revue Celtique* 41 (1924) 181-88.

[77] Ed. and tr. R.I. Best, 'The Adventures of Art son of Conn, and the Courtship of Delbchaem', *Ériu* 3 (1907) 149-73.

[78] This is a supernatural woman, banished from the lands of the supernaturals (the so-called Túatha Dé Danann) because of a transgression with another man (§3). When she arrives in Ireland, she declares she wants to marry the king's son Art, but she marries his father instead and demands that Art be banished from the court for a year (§§5-7). As a result, milk and corn are lacking in Ireland. The druids declare that this is caused by the *corbbad*, 'pollution, corruption, incest', and unbelief of the wife of the king (§8). See further B. O Hehir, 'The Christian revision of *Eachtra Airt meic Cuind ocus Tochmarc Delbchaime ingine Morgain*', in Ford (ed.), *Celtic Folklore*, 159-79. Interesting is the presence of the motif of a sexual (more or less incestuous) transgression with a younger female, which is also found in two other human sacrifice tales. Vortigern marries his own daughter and has a son with her. This is told just before the 'human sacrifice' episode. The Indian priest in 'How Samson slew the Gesteda' was banished from his land because he had raped his stepdaughter. Note also that the appointed victim in two tales is supposed to have been conceived either without sex (*Lebor Bretnach*) or by a single sexual act ('The adventurous journey of Art').

a cow that is slaughtered instead. The cow's blood is mingled with the earth of Tara and put on the doors of Tara. This cow was carrying two bags, filled with two birds, one with one leg and the other with twelve legs. The birds fight and the one-legged bird prevails. The woman explains that the birds symbolise the druids and the boy. She advises to hang the druids and to banish the queen, who causes the milk and corn blight (§§12-14).[79] Obviously, not only the *Historia Brittonum* but also biblical tales have been used as sources, such as the intended sacrifice of Isaac by Abraham with the replacement by a ram and the blood of lambs put on the doorposts of the Israelites in Goshen in Egypt, because of which the firstborn children in those houses are not killed.[80]

Our next example of foundation sacrifice belongs to hagiography. Again, this motif is not found in the oldest source – the Latin *Life of Columba* by Adomnán (†704)[81] – but in the later Irish *Life of Colum Cille*, dated to 1169.[82] This text relates how Colum Cille meets two bishops on his arrival on the eve of Whitsuntide in Iona, where he will establish his monastery. These bishops want to expel him. Colum Cille knows, however, that they are false and he reveals their true identity. Thereupon they abandon the island to him. The text then reads:

> At-bert Colum Cille ind sin rá muntir: 'Is maith dún ar fréma do dul fó thalmain súnd', 7 at-bert friu: 'Is cet díb nech écin uaib do dul fo úir na hinnsi-se dia coisecrad.' Atracht suas Ódran erlattad 7 is ed at-bert, 'Dianam-gabtha,' olse, 'is erlom lem sin.' 'A Odrain,' ol Colum Cille, 'rotbia a lóg sin.i. ni tiberthar a itghe do neoch icom ligesi mina fortsa shirfes ar thús.' Luid iarum Odran docum nime. Fothaigissium eclais Híía iarum.[83]

Then Colum Cille said to his company: 'It would benefit us if our roots were put down into the ground here', and he said to them:

---

[79] This does not happen, however, and the woman and boy return home. The narrative continues, but does not concern us here any further.

[80] See *Genesis* 22.13 and *Exodus* 12.7; cf. also Bremmer, 'Sacrificing a child'.

[81] Ed. and tr. A.O. and M.O. Anderson, *Adomnán's Life of Columba* (Oxford, 1991; revised edition of Edinburgh and London, 1961); see also W. Reeves, *The Life of St. Columba, Founder of Hy; written by Adamnan, ninth abbot of that Monastery* (Dublin, 1857) 203-04, note c.

[82] Ed. and tr. M. Herbert, *Iona, Kells and Derry. The History and Hagiography of the Monastic Familia of Columba* (Oxford, 1988) 218-69, for the date, see 193. Latin *Columba*, 'dove', is essentially the same as Irish *Colum Cille*, 'dove of the church'.

[83] Herbert, *Iona*, 237, lines 414-20.

'Someone among you should go down into the soil of the island to consecrate it.' The obedient Odrán rose up and said: 'If I be taken, I am prepared for it', said he. 'Odrán,' said Colum Cille, 'you will be rewarded for it. No one will be granted his request at my own grave, unless he first seek it of you.' Then Odrán went to heaven. Colum Cille afterwards founded the church of Iona.[84]

This tale about the sacrifice of Odrán appears to have been a popular tradition,[85] because various later versions are extant. There is a sequence of motifs: first, inimical presences in the land that is new to Colum Cille and his company must be banished or appeased. Second, the death of one companion is needed, either to consecrate the earth in preparation of the building or to stabilise the building of the church.[86] The false bishops that try to send Colum Cille away are druids in the guise of bishops in the sixteenth-century version.[87] Later versions refer to evil spirits or demons that make the construction of the sacred building impossible until Odrán is buried alive.[88]

---

[84] Herbert, Iona, 261.

[85] Odrán is also the name of Patrick's charioteer; he is mentioned in an interesting anecdote in VT (Stokes, Tripartite Life, 216-19) and in the Life of Patrick in the Book of Lismore, ed. and tr. W. Stokes, Lives of Saints from the Book of Lismore (Oxford, 1890) 1-19, 149-67, at 13 and 161. The latter text is one of the later, abridged versions of the Vita Tripartita, which also contain new material, cf. J.F. Kenney, The Sources for the Early History of Ireland: Ecclesiastical. An Introduction and Guide (New York, 1929, repr. Dublin, 1979) 345. A man called Foilge (or Failge) Berraide wants to kill Patrick in revenge for the idol Cenn Crúaich, because he was Foilge's God. On the day that they happen to be in the district of Húi Failge, Patrick's charioteer (who knows of Foilge's plan) wants to sit in Patrick's seat with Patrick being the charioteer. Because of this change of positions, Foilge kills Odrán by mistake. Shortly afterwards, Foilge dies and his soul goes to Hell. The later Life of Patrick adds that his body lives on being possessed by the Devil until Patrick visits him. This anecdote is also found in V3 and V4 (Bieler, Four Latin Lives, 106, 157-58) but without the mention of the name Cenn Crúaich. For more about the sacrificial aspect of the death of Patrick's charioteer, see J.F. Nagy, Conversing with angels and ancients. Literary myths of medieval Ireland (Dublin, 1997) 208-10, who also discusses Colum Cille's Odrán at 281-84.

[86] One could compare this with some of the traditions discussed above: the expulsion of a demon, followed by the building of a church (Vita Tripartita) and the suggestion to sacrifice a boy in order to consecrate the king's fortress, which could not be built because of the building material being removed by inimical presences (Lebor Bretnach).

[87] See A. O'Kelleher and G. Schoepperle, Betha Colaim Chille. Life of Columcille. Compiled by Manus O'Donnell in 1532 (Urbana, 1918) 200-03. Colum Cille calls them 'druids of Hell'.

[88] See Joyce, Social history, 285-86, and W.G. Wood-Martin, Traces of the Elder Faiths of Ireland I (London, 1902) 304-05, who do not specify their sources; Thomas Pennant (1726-1798), Second Tour in Scotland, quoted in Todd, Leabhar Breathnach, xxv; Henderson, Survivals, 282-83.

It appears that Odrán does not die immediately, according to these later tales, and gives an unorthodox report about the afterlife. For instance, in a version from 1771 Colum Cille receives a revelation that he should bury someone alive so that the building of his monastery will be successful. The lot falls on Oran.[89] After three days Colum Cille wants to see his friend again and opens the grave. Oran says then 'There is no wonder in death, and hell is not as it is reported', to which Colum Cille reacts with flinging the earth back on him.[90]

In this section on foundation sacrifice I also discussed, for reasons mentioned above, the tale 'The adventures of Art'. Human sacrifice is suggested in this narrative as a way to restore the fertility of Ireland, in which the boy would function as a 'scapegoat' for the transgressions of the new queen. This type of sacrifice is known as vicarious sacrifice, which will now be dealt with.

3. Vicarious sacrifice

Vicarious human sacrifice plays a role in yet another variant version of the Colum Cille and Odrán tale.[91] According to an oral tradition recorded in 1698,[92] Colum Cille dreams that he has to bury a man alive in order to stop a famine. Oran volunteers provided that the saint will build a chapel in his name. The 'scapegoat' is thus given a reward for his voluntary death. This motif is also found in the other

---

[89] 'Oran' is a later, variant spelling of 'Odrán'.

[90] See R. Sharpe, *Adomnán of Iona. Life of St Columba* (Harmondsworth, 1995) 362. A. Carmichael (*Carmina Gadelica*, 338-41) refers to version in which Odrán is buried alive for three days and nights as part of a bet between him and Colum Cille about the afterlife.

[91] This belief in vicarious sacrifice is also ascribed to the Gauls: according to Caesar (*Bellum Gallicum* VI.16), they sacrificed humans in case of illnesses and war, believing 'that, unless for a man's life a man's life be paid, the majesty of the immortal gods may not be appeased', tr. H.J. Edwards, *Caesar. The Gallic War* (London and Cambridge MA, 1917) 340f. The Gauls of Massilia (Marseilles) are said to have applied the following 'scapegoat' ritual when there was a pestilence. A poor man was fed for a year, then led through the city while symbolically taking on him the transgressions of the population and finally thrown from a height, cf. G. Thilo and H. Hagen, *Servii grammatici qui feruntur in Vergilii carmina commentarii* I (Leipzig, 1923) 346 (ad *Aeneid* III.57). For the scapegoat ritual in Massilia see Petronius fr. 1; scholion on Statius, *Thebais* 10.793, cf. J.N. Bremmer, 'Scapegoat Rituals in Ancient Greece', in R. Buxton (ed.), *Oxford Readings in Greek Religion* (Oxford, 2000) 271-93 at 277, 285-88; E. Courtney, *A Companion to Petronius* (Oxford, 2001) 43-45.

[92] See Sharpe, *Adomnán*, 361.

examples of vicarious sacrifice: the people who die for the sake of others receive some privileges.

The first early Irish example of vicarious sacrifice is found in 'The regulation of Éimíne Bán' from the late Old Irish or early Middle Irish period.[93] When a pestilence threatens Leinster, the king and his nobles consider becoming monks in order to avert this disease. The abbot Éimíne Bán realises the monastery's predicament: they cannot refuse the aristocracy, but if they stay and die it will be a shame for the monastery. The solution he comes up with is that he and an equal number of monks will die on their behalf. Lots are cast which monks will die, and then indeed, each day of a whole week seven monks die.[94] In the end, the abbot dies for the king, after having secured privileges for the monastery.

Another hagiographical example is found in the Middle Irish[95] *Life of Finnian of Clonard*.[96] In a passage that compares Saint Paul with Saint Finnian it is said that Paul died in Rome so that the Christians would not go to Hell and Finnian died in Clonard to save the Irish from the Yellow Plague. This is followed by an angelic promise, which takes the form of a privilege for Finnian's congregation: their prayer will banish every pestilence and illness from Clonard and their fasting will banish disease from Ireland.

The last example is from the narrative 'The expulsion of the Déssi'. Two groups of people are at war. It has been prophesied that the party that delivers the first killing or wound will lose the battle. One party is tricked into killing an animal, which turns out to be a transformed human being. This human being is thus sacrificed in order to win the battle. In the Old Irish version of this tale, druids transform an old slave into a red cow. He rushes in this form at the enemies, who kill him and then see his real form.[97] In

---

[93] Ed. and tr. E. Poppe, 'A new edition of *Cáin Éimíne Báin*', *Celtica* 18 (1986) 35-52; for the date, see 38. The tale is situated in the seventh century. For more about the historical context, see idem, 'The list of sureties in *Cáin Éimíne*', *Celtica* 21 (1990) 588-92.

[94] This means 49 monks and the abbot. Strangely enough, the text speaks of fifty noblemen and their king, which would not be compatible with the previous number.

[95] Robinson, 'Human sacrifice', 193.

[96] Ed. and tr. Stokes, *Lives*, 75-83, 222-30 at 82 and 229-30. Ingrid Sperber kindly pointed out to me that this anecdote is absent from the Latin *Lives*. For more about the *Lives* of Finnian, see Kenney, *Sources*, 375f.

[97] Ed. and tr. K. Meyer, 'The Expulsion of the Dessi', *Y Cymmrodor* 14 (1901) 101-35 at 118-21. Meyer dates the text to the second half of the eighth century (at 102). The slave receives a privilege for his descendants, who will be free forever. Incidentally, a woman who was reared on the flesh of little boys suggests this trick.

the later version, it is a druid who transforms and then sacrifices himself in this manner.[98]

4. Burial sacrifice

The fourth type of human sacrifice is burial sacrifice. The following funeral rites are mentioned in the context of the burial of Fiachra, king of Connacht:

> *Ro claidead a leacht 7 ro laigeadh a feart 7 ro hadhnadh a cluichi caintech, 7 ro scribad a ainm oghaim, 7 ro hadnaiced na geill tuctha andeas 7 siad beoa im fhert Fhiachra, co mba hail for Mumain dogrés 7 co mbeth i comruma forro.*[99]

> His grave was dug, and his tomb was laid, and his funeral game was started, and his ogham name was written, and the hostages who had been brought from the south were buried alive around Fiachra's tomb, that it might always be a shame for Munster and be as a triumph over them.[100]

There are several texts that refer to funeral rituals but only this Middle Irish tale entitled 'The Death of Crimthann son of Fidach and of the three sons of Eochaid Muigmedón, Brian, Ailill and Fiachra' mentions the ritual killing of people.[101]

5. Conclusions

Of the twelve medieval Irish examples of human sacrifice described in this survey, only four refer to a proper human sacrifice: a human being killed as an offer to the Gods. Of these, only the *Letter of Jesus* dates from the Old Irish period. The tales about Mag Slécht, Samson

---

[98] Ed. and tr. V. Hull, 'The Later Version Of The Expulsion Of The Déssi', *Zeitschrift für Celtische Philologie* 27 (1958-59) 14-63 at 39-44 and 60-63. This version was compiled before 1106 (*ibid.* 15). The druid receives immunity from the Déssi for his children forever.

[99] W. Stokes, 'The death of Crimthann son of Fidach, and the adventures of the sons of Eochaid Muigmedón', *Revue Celtique* 24 (1903) 172-207 at 184, §17.

[100] Stokes, 'The death', 185, §17.

[101] Stokes, 'The death'; M. Dillon, *The Cycles of the Kings* (Oxford, 1946; reprint Blackrock, 1994) 30 tentatively dates the text to the eleventh century. Funeral rites mentioned in the Second Tale of *The wooing of Étaín*, ed. and tr. O. Bergin and R.I. Best, 'Tochmarc Étaíne', *Ériu* 12 (1938) 137-96 at 166-67, dated to the ninth century, at 139, include the digging of one's grave, the making of one's lamentation and the slaying of one's cattle.

and the Irish translation of Lucan's *Civil War* date from the late Middle Irish period. The earliest and only mention of Irish people sacrificing human beings to a God is the Middle Irish Mag Slécht tradition. As pointed out above, sometimes a related motif is found in Old Irish sources, which develops into the motif of human sacrifice in later sources. This is surprising. The ascription of this horrible ritual to the pre-Christian Irish would have fitted Christian anti-propaganda against the competing religion. There are traces of this competition in the earliest texts in the form of condemnation of druids with their arts, divination and 'idol' worship.

I suggest that we should connect the virtual absence of the motif of human sacrifice in the oldest sources with two other literary phenomena: the suppression of reference to pre-Christian Gods and the identification of the Irish with the Israelites. The authors of early Irish literature used the Christian reading of the Old Testament as a model. In their view, the Irish were a chosen people receiving divine revelations about Christianity before Patrick's advent. Thus, although the pre-Patrician Irish were considered to be still in 'the dark' as so-called 'pagans', the authors of the texts did not consider their own ancestors to be so 'pagan' as other nations. Like Israel, they were supposed to be more enlightened.[102] Therefore, reference to the old Gods seems often to have been suppressed or euhemerised.

On the other hand, in the Middle Irish period the reconstruction of the pre-Christian past seems to have entered a new phase: more details were filled in, and sometimes this past is even somewhat romanticised.[103] Although we would not qualify the description of child sacrifice in the *dindshenchas* romantic, I do think that we should see the literary development of the Cenn/Crom Crúaich tradition in this light. Chronologically, we see in Patrick's *Confessio* of the fifth century an abstract condemnation of idol worship. In the Irish and Latin *Lives of Patrick* details about this worship have been filled in, in which influence from biblical 'idol worship' is undeniable. These texts point out the veneration led by the king. Divination is another characteristic, supplied by the Fourth Live. The God or demon is said to have answered questions of the people from within the statue. It is in the eleventh- or twelfth-century *dindshenchas* that the

---

[102] See also J. Borsje, 'Fate in early Irish texts', *Peritia* 16 (2002) 214-31.
[103] See J. Carey, 'The three things required of a poet', *Ériu* 48 (1997) 41-58.

motif of child sacrifice and the enigmatic death of King Tigernmas together with many Irish people are found.[104] My conclusion is, finally, that the further in time we get away from the supposed veneration of Cenn or Crom Crúaich, the more detailed the information becomes. This information seems to be more a key towards understanding in what way the pre-Christian past was viewed in the Middle Irish period than a key to disclose knowledge about the historical veneration of Cenn Crúaich.[105]

[104] This latter motif also occurs in other sources (see n. 22). It should be noted that Tigernmas not only has an alternative death tradition but he is also described as a 'culture hero', introducing novelties to the Irish, such as the use of drinking horns, the smelting of gold, the use of gold and silver for adornment, and the use of certain colours in clothing. As the statue of Cenn Crúaich was made of gold and silver according to the Patrician *Lives*, I wonder whether this explains why Tigernmas was taken up in the tradition concerning this 'idol'. Or should we see this king as a euhemerised pre-Christian God of the Irish, see K. Murray, 'A Reading from *Scéla Moshauluim*', *Zeitschrift für celtische Philologie* 53 (2003) 198-201? More research on Tigernmas is needed.

[105] I am indebted to Ronald Black, Philip Freeman, Michael Herren, Bart Jaski, Kevin Murray and Józsi Nagy for bibliographical information, and I am grateful to John Carey and Ingrid Sperber for comments on an earlier draft of this paper. Translations are mine, unless stated otherwise.

III. MYTH AND RITUAL
IN GREEK HUMAN SACRIFICE:
LYKAON, POLYXENA AND
THE CASE OF THE RHODIAN CRIMINAL

Jan N. Bremmer

Greek human sacrifice has long been of interest to scholars. The two dissertations of the nineteenth and the first monograph of the twentieth century concentrated on collecting the material and investigating its reliability. These efforts resulted in the conclusion that ancient Greece once indeed practised human sacrifice, but in the course of time had replaced the ritual by animal sacrifice or the expulsion of the human victim.[1] After a long period of neglect, the end of the twentieth century suddenly became interested again in the theme.[2] These recent studies could profit from a century of archaeological activity and from the attention to the patterns of myth and ritual as exemplified by the work of Walter Burkert and Jean-Pierre Vernant.[3]

---

[1] R. Suchier, *De victimis humanis apud Graecos* (Diss. Marburg, 1848); J. Becker, *De hostiis humanis apud Graecos* (Diss. Münster, 1867); F. Schwenn, *Die Menschenopfer bei den Griechen und Römer* (Giessen, 1915).

[2] A. Henrichs, 'Human Sacrifice in Greek Religion: Three Case Studies', in J. Rudhardt and O. Reverdin (eds), *Le sacrifice dans l'antiquité* = *Entretiens Hardt* 27 (Vandoeuvres-Geneva, 1981) 195-242 (discussion included); D. Hughes, *Human Sacrifice in Greek Religion: Three Case Studies* (London and New York, 1991); P. Bonnechere, *Le sacrifice humain en Grèce ancienne* (Athens and Liège, 1994); idem, 'La notion d'"acte collectif" dans le sacrifice humain grec', *Phoenix* 52 (1998) 191-215; S. Georgoudi, 'À propos du sacrifice humain en Grèce ancienne: remarques critiques', *Arch. f. Religionsgeschichte* 1 (1999) 61-82; J. Scheid, 'Menschenopfer. III', in *Der neue Pauly* VII (Stuttgart, 1999) 1255-58; T. Fontaine, 'Blutrituale und Apollinische Schönheit. Grausame vorgeschichtliche Opferpraktiken in der Mythenwelt der Griechen und Etrusker', in H.-P. Kuhnen (ed.), *Morituri. Menschenopfer, Todgeweihte, Strafgerichte* (Trier, 2000) 49-70 (well illustrated, poorly argued).

[3] For the relation between myth and ritual in ancient Greece see most recently W. Burkert, 'Mythos und Ritual: im Wechselwind der Moderne', in H. Horstmannshoff *et al.* (eds), *Kykeon. Studies in honor of H.S. Versnel* (Leiden, 2002) 1-22; Bremmer, 'Myth and Ritual in Ancient Greece: Observations on a Difficult Relationship', in

Yet they did not all systematically pursue questions such as: which gods were the recipients of these sacrifices, who were the victims, why were they sacrificed and, not to be neglected, what was the rhetoric of human sacrifice?[4] It is along these lines that I would like to discuss three cases of human sacrifice: a ritual example, a mythical case, and one that nicely illustrates the complicated relationship between myth and ritual in ancient Greece.

1. Kronos and the case of the Rhodian criminal

The philosopher Porphyry (ca. 234-305) mentions that on the sixth of the month Metageitnion the Rhodians used to sacrifice a man to Kronos. Later the custom was changed, and somebody who was condemned to death was kept in prison until the Kronia festival. When the day of the festival had arrived, he was guided out of the gates of the city, opposite the temple (hedos) of Artemis Aristoboule, given wine to drink and slaughtered. The custom is related in the past and was apparently no longer practised in Porphyry's time.[5] The source of Porphyry's information is not known, but must have been, directly or indirectly, a Hellenistic author who wanted to explain this strange case of ritual killing.[6]

Unfortunately, the text is not crystal clear about the exact place of the criminal's execution. Earlier scholars interpreted the notice as if he was slaughtered in front of a statue of Artemis Aristoboule.[7] The thought is not wholly absurd, as Artemis is regularly associated with human sacrifice. This is well illustrated by Euripides' *Iphigenia in Tauris*,[8] and, moreover, in Athens the bodies of executed criminals

R. von Haeling (ed.), *Griechische Mythologie und frühes Christentum* (Darmstadt, 2005) 21-43.

[4] This question is well discussed by A. Henrichs, 'Drama and *Dromena*: bloodshed, violence, and sacrificial metaphor in Euripides', *Harvard Stud. Class. Philol.* 100 (2000) 173-88.

[5] Porphyry, *On Abstinence* 2.54, quoted by Eusebius, *Praep. Ev.* 4.16.1 and *De Laude Constant.* 13.7.6; Theodoretus, *Graec. aff. cur.* 7.41; D. Morelli, *I culti in Rodi* (Pisa, 1959) 59, 157f. The most recent edition of Porphyry's treatise is: J. Bouffartigue and M. Patillon, *Porphyre, De l'abstinence* II (Paris, 1979).

[6] For aetiological myths of Hellenistic Rhodian cults see H.-U. Wiemer, *Rhodische Traditionen in der hellenistischen Historiographie* (Frankfurt, 2001) 207-18.

[7] M.P. Nilsson, *Griechische Feste* (Leipzig, 1906) 38; H.S. Versnel, *Transition and Reversal in Myth and Ritual* (Leiden, 1993) 100f.

[8] For the various examples see F. Graf, *Nordionische Kulte* (Rome, 1985) 411; Georgoudi, 'À propos du sacrifice humain', 68, 70, 74-79; Th. Grünewald, 'Menschenopfer im klassischen Athen? Zeitkritik in der Tragödie Iphigenie in Aulis', *Archiv f. Kulturgeschichte* 83 (2001) 1-23.

were exposed in an area where once the temple of Artemis Aristoboule had been.[9] Yet it is unlikely that Artemis would be so prominent during a festival for Kronos, since there is no other parallel for a close association of the two divinities. Moreover, Rhodes knew an association of Aristobouliastai, and the name Aristoboulos was extremely popular on Rhodes.[10] It is surely improbable that the Rhodians would give their children the name of a cruel goddess, as the Greeks also did not name their children after the child eating Kronos.[11] *Hedos* therefore more likely means 'temple' here, and indicates the location of the execution: outside the gates and opposite the temple of Artemis Aristoboule, Artemis being a protectress of gates also elsewhere in Greece.[12]

Both the procession out of the city and the drinks for the criminal resemble the Greek scapegoat rituals, as sometimes the scapegoat was also feasted before being led out of the city in a procession.[13] This resemblance is perhaps not purely chance. We now know that the Kronia festival originated in exactly the same small area on the western coast of Turkey where the scapegoat festival is first attested – both rituals eventually deriving from Northern Syria.[14] The Kronia were always celebrated after the completion of the harvest.[15] It fits this time of year that the month Metageitnion (Rhodian: Pedageitnyos) found its place in the Rhodian calendar just before the summer until the second half of the second century BC, although afterwards it was shifted to a place in the winter.[16]

A human sacrifice to Kronos is not improbable. He was connected with human sacrifice in Crete,[17] and in Carthage he was identified

[9] Plutarch, *Life of Themistocles* 22.
[10] Aristobouliastai: *Inscriptiones Graecae* (= *IG*) XII 1.163; G. Pugliese Carratelli, *Annuario della Scuola Archeologica di Atene* n.s. 1-2 (1939-40) 151 no. 6. Name: there are more than 60 examples.
[11] Bremmer, 'Remember the Titans!', in C. Auffarth and L. Stuckenbruck (eds), *Fall of the Angels* (Leiden, 2004) 35-61 at 45.
[12] Graf, *Nordionische Kulte*, 173f.
[13] Thus Nilsson, *Griechische Feste*, 38, wrongly rejected by Hughes, *Human Sacrifice*, 125. For the scapegoats see most recently U. Kron, 'Patriotic heroes', in R. Hägg (ed.), *Ancient Greek hero Cult* (Stockholm, 1999) 61-83; Bremmer, 'Scapegoat Rituals in Ancient Greece', in R. Buxton (ed.), *Oxford Readings in Greek Religion* (Oxford, 2000) 271-93 and 'The Scapegoat between Hittites, Greeks, Israelites and Christians', in R. Albertz (ed), *Kult, Konflikt und Versöhnung* (Münster, 2001) 175-86.
[14] See my 'The Scapegoat', 175-7 and 'Remember the Titans!', 46-8.
[15] Bremmer, 'Remember the Titans!', 44.
[16] For the date see C. Börker, 'Der Rhodische Kalender', *Zs. f. Papyrologie und Epigraphik* 31 (1978) 192-218; C. Trümpy, *Untersuchungen zu den altgriechischen Monatsnamen* (Heidelberg, 1997) 187.
[17] Istros *FGrH* 334 F 48; Eusebius, *Praep. Ev.* 4.16.7, cf. Graf, *Nordionische Kulte*, 417.

with the originally Phoenician god to whom children were sacrificed.[18] This identification took place at an early stage, since Sophocles already connects Kronos with human sacrifice by barbarians.[19] In all these cases we may assume the influence of Kronos' mythical devouring of his children; in fact, an imperial inscription still calls him 'Kronos the child-eater'.[20] Now the Greeks were sensitive to the happy or sombre connotations of particular dates. For example, we know that the death of Sophocles was located on the most sombre day of the Anthesteria festival and the death of Demosthenes on the most gloomy day of the Thesmophoria festival, even if these dates were probably historically incorrect.[21] Similarly, the sixth of Metageitnion must have had sombre connotations too: Epicurus forecast that he would die on that day, as he actually did.[22] Admittedly, Epicurus did not come from Rhodes, but his birth-place Samos was not that far away and actually one of the few places where Kronos and the Kronia had surfaced in the Greek world.[23]

So where does this all leave us? Apparently, every year the Rhodians executed a criminal for reasons that no longer are clear to us. Evidently, at a certain point in time the ritual had become associated with Kronos, as he was perhaps the most prominent one of the many Greek gods and heroes that were associated with human sacrifice.[24] However, as this connection was firmly dated to the hoary past, it seems reasonable to assume that the myth was used to legit-

---

[18] Clitarchus *FGrH* 137 F 9; Diodorus Siculus 5.66.5, 13.86.3; 20.14.6; Curtius Rufus 4.3.23; Plutarch, *Moralia* 171C, 552A, 942C; Tertullian, *Apol.* 9.2; Porphyry, *On Abstinence* 2.27. For these much debated sacrifices see most recently E. Lipinski, 'Sacrifices d'enfants à Carthage et dans le monde sémitique oriental', in *idem* (ed.), *Studia Phoenicia VI: Carthago* (Leuven, 1988) 151-85; S. Moscati and S. Ribichini, *Il sacrificio dei bambini: un aggiornamento* (Rome, 1991); S. Brown, *Late Carthaginian Child Sacrifice and Sacrificial Monuments in Their Mediterranean Context* (Sheffield, 1992); Versnel, *Transition and Reversal*, 101 (with older bibliography); J.B. Rives, 'Tertullian on Child Sacrifice', *Museum Helveticum* 51 (1994) 54-63; K. Koch, 'Molek astral', in A. Lange *et al.* (eds), *Mythos im Alten Testament und seiner Umwelt* (Berlin and New York, 1999) 29-50; C. Grottanelli, 'Ideologie del sacrificio umano: Roma e Cartagine', *Arch. f. Religionsgesch.* 1 (1999) 41-59 F. Ruggiero, 'La testimonianza di Tertulliano, *Apologeticum* 9, 2-4 sul sacrificio del bambini nell'ambito del culto di Saturno', *Annali di Storia dell' Esegesi* 18 (2001) 307-33; J. Lightfoot, *Lucian, On the Syrian Goddess* (Oxford, 2003) 523-8.

[19] Sophocles F 126 Radt; note also *TrGF* Adesp. 233 Snell-Kannicht.

[20] *Supplementum Epigraphicum Graecum* (= *SEG*) 31.1285: *teknophagos*.

[21] Bremmer, *Greek Religion* (Oxford, 2003³) 77.

[22] A. Vogliano, *Epicuri et Epicureorum scripta in Herculanensibus papyris servata* (Berlin, 1928) 53.

[23] Bremmer, 'Remember the Titans!', 43.

[24] See the enumeration by Georgoudi, 'À propos du sacrifice humain', 65f.

imate a ritual in the present, which happened more often in ancient Greece.[25] Yet, in the end, the precise historical circumstances of the Rhodian sacrifice remain totally obscure.

2. Polyxena and the representation of human sacrifice

How did the Greeks represent a human sacrifice? The question is generally easier posed than answered, but we have an interesting case in this respect in the myth of Polyxena, the daughter of the Trojan king Priam.[26] The oldest testimonium does not yet speak of a human sacrifice in her case, since according to the *Cypria* (F 43 Bernabé = F 27 Davies) Odysseus and Diomedes fatally wounded Polyxena during the capture of Troy.[27] Virtually at the same time, though, a more gruesome variant arose. According to Proclus' summary of the *Ilioupersis* (p. 89 Bernabé), Stesichorus (S 135 Davies), Ibycus (F 307 Davies),[28] and Simonides (F 557 Page), Polyxena was sacrificed to the ghost of Achilles and slaughtered by his son Neoptolemos. The idea was probably inspired by the myth of Iphigeneia: just as the Greeks had to sacrifice a maiden because of bad weather in order to be able to sail to Troy, so they also had to sacrifice a maiden to be able to return home.[29] These treatments soon inspired sculptors and vase painters, and the myth remained popular well into Roman times.[30]

[25] For many examples of this process see Graf, *Nordionische Kulte*, 74-80.

[26] For the literary and iconographical evidence see O. Touchefeu-Meynier, 'Polyxene', in *Lexicon Iconographicae Mythologiae Graecae* (= *LIMC*) VII.1 (Zurich and Munich, 1994) 431-35; add *Supplementum Epigraphicum Graecum* 45.2150; Y. Tuna-Norling, 'Polyxena bei Hektors Lösung. Zu einem attisch-rotfigurigen Krater aus Tekirdag (Bisanthe/Rhaidestos)', *Arch. Anz.* 2001, 27-44.

[27] For a slightly different interpretation of the passage see G. Hedreen, *Capturing Troy* (Ann Arbor, 2001) 136f. For the varying versions of the *Cypria* see J.S. Burgess, 'The Non-Homeric Cypria', *Trans. Am. Philol. Ass.* 126 (1996) 77-99; M. Finkelberg, 'The *Cypria*, the *Iliad*, and the Problem of Multiformity in Oral and Written Tradition', *Class. Philol.* 95 (2000) 1-11. It is increasingly realised that Homer drew on this poem for his *Iliad* and *Odyssey*, cf. J.S. Burgess, *The Tradition of the Trojan War in Homer and the Epic Cycle* (Baltimore and London, 2001); M. Finkelberg, 'The Sources of *Iliad* 7', *Colby Quarterly* 28 (2002) 151-61.

[28] M. Robertson, 'Ibycus. Polycrates, Troilus, Polyxena', *Bull. Inst. Class. Stud.* 17 (1970) 11-15.

[29] For the myth of Iphigeneia now see Bremmer, 'Sacrificing a Child in Ancient Greece: the case of Iphigeneia', in E. Noort and E.J.C. Tigchelaar (eds), *The Sacrifice of Isaac* (Leiden, 2001) 21-43; G. Ekroth, 'Inventing Iphigeneia? On Euripides and the Cultic Construction of Brauron', *Kernos* 16 (2003) 59-118.

[30] For Polyxena in Roman times see G. Schwarz, 'Achill und Polyxena in der römischen Kaiserzeit', *Römische Mitteilungen* 99 (1992) 265-99; J. Mossman, *Wild Justice. A Study of Euripides'* Hecuba (Oxford, 1995) 247-51.

In the fifth century, the sacrifice of Polyxena also became the subject of tragedies by Sophocles and Euripides.[31] From Sophocles'
Polyxena (F 522-28 Radt) we have only a few fragments left and
none about the sacrifice proper,[32] but in his *Hecuba* (*ca.* 424 BC)
Euripides described Polyxena's death in detail.[33] In this play, the
reason for the sacrifice was the sudden appearance of Achilles in
golden armour (110) above his tomb at the Hellespont, when the
Greek fleet had already put out to sail home (37-41), asking to have
Polyxena as 'his victim and special prize' (41). The idea of such an
appearance had occurred first to Simonides and was visualised on
stage by Sophocles.[34] Euripides apparently felt that he could not
improve on his fellow tragedian and let the appearance relate by
Polyxena's dead brother. After a debate in the Greek assembly it
was decided to grant Achilles his request and the Greeks dis-
patched Odysseus to fetch the *prosphagma* (41), 'victim'.[35] As a
recently published sacred law from Sicilian Selinous has shown,
'*thyein* is the unmarked term that epitomizes the sacrificial process
as a whole, whereas *sphazein* refers more specifically to the act of
slaughtering the animal. As the marked term, *sphazein* carries associations of violence and bloodshed that the tragedians exploit'.[36] An
attentive reader of the *Hecuba* immediately notices that in his sacrificial vocabulary Euripides uses virtually only words connected
with *sphazein*, 'cutting the throat' instead of words connected with
thyô, 'to sacrifice'. And indeed, the observation is nicely confirmed
by Porphyry's choice of words about the case of the human sacrifice

[31] For Polyxena in Euripides' *Trojan Women* see G. Petersmann, 'Die Rolle der
Polyxena in den Troerinnen des Euripides', *Rheinisches Museum* 120 (1977) 146-58.
Nothing is known about the *Polyxena* of Euripides Junior (*TrGF* 17 T 1) and Nico-
machus (*TrGF* 127 T 1).

[32] For a discussion see Mossman, *Wild Justice*, 42-47.

[33] The earlier reports are too scanty to give any indication about the reason for
her death, but later passages stress the romance between Achilles and Polyxena.
Note also the interesting information, perhaps deriving from an early treatment, that
Polyxena's sacrifice was meant as a primal offering: *Suda* α 1007: Ἀκρόλιον· ἀπαρχή:
ὥσπερ ἀκρόλιον. Πολυξένην καταθῦσαι τοὺς Ἕλληνας ἀκρόλιον.

[34] Longinus, *On the Sublime*, 15.7; Mossman, *Wild Justice*, 31-34; P. Michelakis,
Achilles in Greek Tragedy (Cambridge, 2002) 76-80.

[35] For the exact meaning of *prosphagma*, which here seems to have the same meaning as *sphagma*, see J. Casabona, *Recherches sur le vocabulaire des sacrifices en Grec*
(Paris, 1966) 170-74.

[36] Henrichs, 'Drama and *Dromena*', 180, referring to M. Jameson *et al.*, *A Lex Sacra
from Selinous = Greek, Roman, and Byzantine Stud.* Suppl. 11 (1993) 17: B 12f. For *sphazô*
and related words see Casabona, *Recherches*, 155-96.

on Rhodos (§1): at first a man was sacrificed to Kronos (*ethyeto*), but later they slaughtered a criminal (*esphatton*).

The difference is also clear in the term *prosphagma* for Achilles' request (41, 265), in the use of *sphagion* as the terminology for the victim of the sacrifice (109, 119, 135, 305), in the use of *sphagê* for the sacrifice itself (522, 571) and, finally, in the use of the verb *sphazô* for the act of sacrificing (188, 221, 433, 505).[37] In striking contrast, it is only once that we hear of a word connected with *thyô*. When Odysseus announces the verdict to Polyxena's mother, he tells her that the son of Achilles will preside as the priest over the *thyma*, the whole of the sacrificial ritual (223).[38] Naturally, Odysseus could not use a term for the sacrifice that would attract attention to its brutal character. Given the contrast, we can well understand that Hecuba asks Odysseus: 'Or did necessity compel them "to perform a human sacrifice" (*anthrôposphagein*) on (Achilles') tomb, where "the sacrifice of an ox" (*bouthytein*) is more fitting?' (260-61). The audience of the *Hecuba* was clearly left in no doubt at all about the brutality of the act.

It is rather exceptional that we can illustrate the procedure of the sacrifice as described by Euripides with a series of images that were all produced in the late sixth and early fifth century, when images of comparable real sacrifice scenes with animals were extremely rare.[39] However, Polyxena's request to Odysseus to wrap her garment about her head and take her away to her death (432) is not yet represented. The gesture itself, though, was not uncommon for people who were going to die. Just before his death Socrates covered up his face; Diogenes the Cynic was found dead wrapped up in his cloak, although he never used to sleep this way, and Caesar wrapped himself up when Brutus and the other senators butchered him. The covering up is an act of separation, and dying in this way immediately separates them from the living.[40]

---

[37] Similarly in Euripides' *Heraclids* where we find *sphazô* for the sacrifice of Makaria (408, 490, 493, 502, 562), but *thyô* for normal animal sacrifices (877).

[38] For this meaning of the term see Casabona, *Recherches*, 146f.

[39] See the insightful discussions by P. Blome, 'Das Schreckliche im Bild', in F. Graf (ed.), *Ansichten griechischer Rituale* (Stuttgart and Leipzig, 1998) 72-95 at 82-84; J.-L. Durand and F. Lissarrague, 'Mourir à l'autel', *Arch. f. Religionsgesch.* 1 (1999) 83-106 at 91-102.

[40] Plato, *Phaedo* 118 (Socrates); Aristotle, *Rhet.* 2.6.1385a9; Valerius Maximus 4.5 (Caesar); Pausanias 4.18.6; Diogenes Laertius 6.77 (Diogenes); Procopius, *Pers.* 2.9. Polyxena's gesture is wrongly interpreted by R. Rehm, *Marriage to Death* (Princeton, 1994) 175 note 37.

At the tomb itself, Neoptolemos took Polyxena by the wrist (523). The gesture was a sign of taking possession of someone and thus part of the Greek wedding ceremony,[41] and its mention here adds to the poignancy of the situation of a young girl who should have been led as a bride to a new house, but instead would become a 'bride of Hades'. As Polyxena herself noted, she would be 'without the bridegroom and wedding' that she should have had.[42] Now we see this wedding gesture already on a cup attributed to Macron, *ca.* 500 BC, where Neoptolemos, sword in hand, leads Polyxena to the grave mound of Achilles.[43] The association with a wedding must naturally have occurred to others as well, and we may perhaps wonder whether Euripides does not depend on his predecessors for this detail.

Near Polyxena, there were 'picked youths of the Achaean army' to check 'any leap your calf' should make, as the herald Talthybios tells her mother (525-6).[44] The expression is telling. Young girls were often compared to calves or foals because of their playfulness,[45] but here the expression also suggests a possibly unruly animal victim. It was indeed normal that ephebes guided the animal to the altar to check possible attempts at escape.[46] Moreover, voluntariness of the victim was an important part of Greek sacrificial ideology, which stressed that the victim was pleased to go up to the altar, sometimes could even hardly wait to be sacrificed![47] Obviously, ideology and practice did not always concur, and vases show

[41] Pindar, *P.* 9.122; Euripides, *Alcestis* 916-7 (cf. H. Foley, *Ritual Irony* [Ithaca, 1985] 87-8) and *Medea* 21-2 (cf. S. Flory, 'Medea's Right Hand', *Trans. Am. Philol. Ass.* 108 [1978] 69-74); Iamblichus, *VP.* 84; G. Neuman, *Gesten und Gebärden in den griechischen Kunst* (Berlin, 1965) 59-66; R. Sutton, *The Interaction between Man and Woman portrayed on Attic Red-Figure Pottery* (Diss. Univ. of North Carolina, 1981) 181-4; Rehm, *Marriage to Death*, 35; Tuna-Norling, 'Polyxena', 38 note 56, 42-3; Hedreen, *Capturing Troy*, 46 (with more bibliography in note 79).

[42] Euripides, *Hecuba* 416, cf. Rehm, *Marriage to Death*, 167 note 34.

[43] Touchefeu-Meynier, 'Polyxene', no. 23, cf. Durand and Lissarrague, 'Mourir', 97f.

[44] D. Kovacs, *Euripides* II (Cambridge Mass. and London, 1995) 447 translates 'any leap your daughter might make', which neglects the reference to animal sacrifice in the expression.

[45] Mossman, *Wild Justice*, 147-51; C. Calame, *Choruses of Young Women in Ancient Greece* (Lanham and London, 1997) 238-44.

[46] J.-L. Durand, 'Le boeuf à la ficelle', in C. Bérard *et al.* (eds), *Images et société en Grèce ancienne* (Lausanne, 1987) 227-41.

[47] K. Meuli, *Gesammelte Schriften*, 2 vols (Basel, 1975) II.950, 982, 995-6; F.T. van Straten, *Hierà kalá* (Leiden, 1995) 100-02; N. Himmelmann, *Tieropfer in der griechischen Kunst* (Opladen, 1997) 38-40.

us ephebes struggling with the victim or the ropes tied to its head or legs in order to restrain it.[48]

At the tomb Neoptolemos poured out a libation for his father during a prayer. The text does not mention the substance of the libation, which could be water or pure wine, but his words 'Come and drink the dark, undiluted blood of a maiden' (536-7) shows that the cup contained the latter substance. The Greek word used, *choas* (529), indeed denotes those libations used especially in purificatory and funerary circumstances, often to appease the dead or to call them up for necromantic purposes.[49] It was also common to pronounce a prayer just before the actual kill.[50] This is already the case in the *Odyssey*, where the participants in Nestor's sacrifice 'threw the barley-groats forward' only after a prayer was pronounced (3.447).

After the prayer Neoptolemos gave a sign to the youths that they should hold Polyxena (545). At this point Euripides is actually less dramatic than the vase painters. Normally, in order to demonstrate their physical prowess, ephebes, 'in the way of the Greeks' (Eur. *Helen* 1562), lifted the animal up to have its throat cut.[51] Although representations of Polyxena's sacrifice are rather rare,[52] at the beginning of the sixth century at least one archaic Attic vase painter and in its last decades an Ionian sculptor pictured Polyxena being lifted up like an animal, with Neoptolemos actually cutting her throat with his sword:[53] Aeschylus describes the sacrificing of Iphigeneia in his

[48] P. Stengel, *Opferbräuche der Griechen* (Leipzig and Berlin, 1910) 109-10; Van Straten, *Hierà kalá*, 101-02, 111; S. Peirce, 'Death, Revelry, and *Thysia*', *Classical Antiquity* 12 (1993) 219-66 at 255-6; note for an unwilling victim also Menander, *Dyskolos* 393-9.

[49] J. Rudhardt, *Notions fondamentales de la pensée religieuse et actes constitutifs du culte dans la Grèce classique* (Geneva, 1992²) 246-48; Casabona, *Recherches*, 231-97; W. Burkert, *Greek Religion* (Oxford, 1985) 70-3 (with earlier bibliography); P. Veyne, 'Images de divinités tenant une phiale ou patère. La libation comme "rite de passage" et non pas offrande', *Métis* 5 (1990 [1993]) 17-31.

[50] Euripides, *El.* 803; Isaeus 8.16; Agatharchides *FGrH* 86 F5; Apollonius of Rhodes 1.425.

[51] See the bibliography in Henrichs, 'Drama and *Dromena*', 187 note 61; add F. Graf, *Museum Helveticum* 36 (1979) 14-5.

[52] For Etruscan representations see D. Steuernagel, *Menschenopfer und Mord am Alter. Griechische Mythen in etruskischen Gräbern* (Wiesbaden, 1998) 42-44, reviewed by P. Bonnechere, 'Mythes grecs de sacrifice humain en Étrurie: problèmes iconographiques et socio-historiques', *Kernos* 13 (2000) 253-65.

[53] N. Sevinç, 'A new sarcophagus of Polyxena', *Studia Troica* 6 (1996) 251-64; Durand and Lissarrague, 'Mourir', 97-98; G. Schwarz, 'Der Tod und das Mädchen: frühe Polyxena-Bilder', *Athen. Mitt.* 116 (2001) 35-50.

Agamemnon in the same manner.[54] However, Euripides prefers more pathos and lets his heroine exclaim (548-49): 'Let no one touch my skin, for I shall offer you my neck bravely!' We are here reminded again of the motif of voluntariness. However, Euripides could not use his favorite theme of girls dying voluntarily for their community,[55] as Polyxena was dying for the enemy. Instead, he let Polyxena, somewhat unpersuasively, exclaim: 'In the gods' name, leave me free when you kill me, so that I may die a free woman! For since I am a princess, I shrink from being called a slave among the dead' (515-52, tr. Kovacs).

Just before being killed Polyxena made a last, theatrical gesture: she bared her bosom down to her navel. There is an element of tradition in this baring, since Iphigeneia dropped her saffron garment before being slaughtered in Aeschylus and Makaria asked to be covered up after her death in Euripides' *Heraclids* (561).[56] Then Neoptolemos cut her throat as he would have done with an animal victim, 'and blood gushed forth' (567), just as animals are sacrificed by having their throats cut in order that their blood will gush directly on the altar.[57] That is how Polyxena died, 'of captives the choicest and most beautiful maiden' (267-68), as her mother Hecuba called her or, as she said herself, 'amidst the maidens conspicuous, like the gods in all but my mortality' (355-56). The repeated mention of Polyxena's beauty heightens of course the poignancy of the occasion, but it also fits the descriptions of scapegoat sacrifices where the beauty of the victim is always stressed.[58]

---

[54] Aeschylus, *Agamemnon* 231ff., to be read with the observations by P. Maas, *Kleine Schriften* (Munich, 1973) 42 and S. Radt in A. Harder *et al.* (eds.), *Noch einmal zu...Kleine Schriften von Stefan Radt zu seinen 75. Geburtstag* (Leiden, 2002) 111.

[55] J. Schmitt, *Freiwilliger Opfertod bei Euripides* (Giessen, 1921); P. Roussel, 'Le thème du sacrifice volontaire dans la tragédie d'Euripide', *Revue Belge Philol. Hist.* (1922) 225-40; H.S. Versnel, 'Self-Sacrifice, Compensation and the Anonymous Gods', *Entretiens Hardt* 27 (Geneva, 1981) 135-94 at 179-85, with an interesting discussion; C. Nancy, 'Φάρμακον σωτηρίας: Le mécanisme du sacrifice humain chez Euripide', in *Théâtre et spectacles dans l'antiquité* (Leiden, 1983) 17-30; E.A.M.E. O'Connor-Visser, *Aspects of Human Sacrifice in the Tragedies of Euripides* (Amsterdam, 1987); J. Wilkins, 'The State and the Individual: Plays of Voluntary Self-sacrifice', in A. Powell (ed.), *Euripides, Women, and Sexuality* (London, 1990) 177-94; S. O'Bryhim, 'The Ritual of Human Sacrifice in Euripides', *Class. Bull.* 76 (2000) 29-37; P. Oikonomopoulou, 'To kill or not to kill? Human sacrifices in Greece according to Euripidean thought', in D.-C. Naoum *et al.* (eds), *Cult and Death* (Oxford, 2004) 63-7.

[56] Iphigeneia: Aeschylus, *Agamemnon* 239, to be read with the observations by Radt in Harder, *Noch einmal zu...Kleine Schriften von Stefan Radt*, 111f.

[57] Van Straten, *Hierà kalá*, 104-05.

[58] Bremmer, 'Scapegoat Rituals', 276f.

It is clear that the ritual of this human sacrifice closely follows that of normal animal sacrifice, and the familiarity of the latter may have helped to lessen the gruesome character of the representation.[59] It is also possible that the 'perverted echo of real-life ritual practices would have connected the world of the play to that of the audience through contrast, which distanced the human sacrifice and the world in which it took place from the audience's realities'.[60] However this may be, we cannot but remain puzzled by the fact that Greek civilisation was so keen to put especially maidens on the stage. This problem is not solved by declaring it an exercise in the unthinkable or stating that it was 'due far more to the greater vulnerability of women to the violence of men, and the consequent poetic opportunities for pathetic contrast between victim and sacrificers, than to any sexual impulse'.[61] Moreover, our discomfort is not lessened by the picture of the half-naked Polyxena. When all is said and done, maiden sacrifices in these plays cannot be separated from the male dominated nature of Athenian theatre.

3. Mount Lykaion, Lykaon and the Arcadian werewolves

In antiquity Arcadia was not seen in the utopian colours of modern European tradition. On the contrary, this region in the centre of the Peloponnese was known for its backward customs. That is why the other Greeks mocked the Arcadians as *proselênoi*, 'people from before the moon',[62] and *balanêphagoi*, 'acorn-eaters',[63] that is, eaters of the food of the pre-cereal agriculture era, cereal agriculture in the eyes of the Greeks being associated with the arrival of civilisation. Here, not that far from Olympia, on one of the wooded crests of Arcadia's highest mountain range Mt Lykaion (the present Ai Lias), there was a sanctuary of Zeus Lykaios.[64]

[59] Blome, 'Das Schreckliche', 94.

[60] C. Sourvinou-Inwood, *Tragedy and Athenian Religion* (Lanham, 2003) 339.

[61] N. Loraux, *Tragic ways of Killing a Woman* (Cambridge Mass, 1987) 32; Mossman, *Wild Justice*, 143-7, respectively.

[62] P. Borgeaud, *Recherches sur le dieu Pan* (Rome, 1979) 19-23; M. Jost, 'Image de l'Arcadie au IIIe siècle avant J.-C. (Lycophron, *Alexandra*, v. 479-483)', in M.-M. Mactoux and E. Geny (eds), *Mélanges Pierre Lévêque*, vol. 2 (Paris, 1989) 285-93 at 289-90; T.H. Nielsen, *Arkadia and its Poleis in the Archaic and Classical Periods* (Göttingen, 2002) 71.

[63] Herodotus 1.66; Pausanias 8.1.6; Galen VI.621; scholion on Lycophron 482; Jost, 'Image de l'Arcadie', 290; Nielsen, *Arkadia*, 72.

[64] Wooded character: Callimachus, *Hymn to Zeus*, 10-1; Virgil, *G.* 1.16, 3.314; Ovid, *Met.* 1.217; Pausanias 8.38.3-4; Nonnus, *D.* 13.288. Sanctuary: see the excellent, chronological survey of the sources by F. Hiller von Gaertringen in *IG* V 2, 140.

Zeus clearly derived his epithet Lykaios from the name of the mountain, just like Zeus Olympios was named after the Olympus; in fact, Zeus was often connected with tall mountains, as befitted the supreme god.[65]. The name Lykaios, to which we come back below, must have been typical of the neighbourhood, since nearby there were two small communities called Lykaia.[66] Zeus Lykaios' cult was limited mainly to Arcadia, but it also existed in Tegea on the road to Laconia, and the seventh-century poet Alcman composed hymns to Zeus Lykaios in neighbouring Sparta.[67] Yet, by all accounts, it was a typically local cult.

At the top of the mountain crest, there was a circular earth-and-ash altar that was excavated at the beginning of the twentieth century. The sanctuary possessed the archives of the region,[68] and its festival the Lykaia was considered to be one of the oldest in Greece, being founded by the first Arcadian, Lykaon;[69] its antiquity is confirmed by Pindar, who already mentions it several times.[70] Inscriptions tell us that both men and boys had their separate, if largely overlapping, programme, which consisted of athletic contests such as running, wrestling, boxing and the *pankration*. The prize was a bronze tripod and an oak wreath,[71] the latter undoubtedly referring to the fact that the Arcadians believed they were descended from an oak.[72] The festival was probably celebrated in the spring and, given the resemblance of its athletic program to the Olympic games,[73] it will have taken place every four years.[74]

---

[65] See A.B. Cook, *Zeus*, 3 vols (Cambridge, 1914-40) 2.868-987; add M.K. Langdon, *A sanctuary of Zeus on Mount Hymettos* = *Hesperia* Suppl. 16 (1976) 76-95, 100-12; R. Parker, *Athenian Religion* (Oxford, 1996) 29-33.

[66] For the places and the problems connected with the names see E. Meyer, *RE* 13 (1927) 2229-31.

[67] Tegea: Pausanias 8.53.11. Sparta: Alcman F 24 Davies = T 29 Calame; note also the Spartan king Pleistoanax's refuge in Zeus Lykaios' sanctuary (Thucydides 5.16.3) and the mention of the sanctuary in Euripides, *Electra* 1274.

[68] *SEG* 20.716, re-edited and commented upon by A. Laronde, *Cyrène et la Libye hellénistique* (Paris, 1987) 149-60.

[69] *Marmor Parium FGrH* 239 A 17; Pliny, *NH* 7.205 and Pausanias 8.2.1 mention that only the Eleusinia was older; Aristotle F 637 Rose puts it in fourth place after the Eleusinia.

[70] Pindar, *O.* 7.83-4, 9.96, 13.107-8 and *Nem.* 10.48; see also W. Immerwahr, *Die Kulte und Mythen Arkadiens* (Leipzig, 1891) 5; add *IG* II² 993; *IDelos* 4.1957; *IG* IV.I² 629; *IG* IV 428; *IG* V 2.142, 436; *SEG* 49.1999.

[71] Tripod: Scholia on Pindar, *O.* 7.153d and 9.143a, *Nem.* 10.48. Oak wreath: P. Charneux, 'Inscriptions d'Argos', *Bull. Corresp. Hell.* 109 (1985) 357-83 at 364-68.

[72] Lycophron 480; Plutarch, *Mor.* 286A.; Jost, 'Image de l'Arcadie', 287f.

[73] K. Kourouniotis, 'Anaskaphai Lykaiou', *Arch. Ephem.* 1904, 153-214 at 173, 175.

[74] E. Meyer, *RE* 13 (1927) 2229-31.

An Arcadian winner in the games advertised himself not, as was customary, with the name of his city but only as 'Arcadian';[75] in other words, the festival was clearly seen as a 'national' event. This is confirmed by Xenophon who tells us in his *Anabasis* (1.2.10) that Xenias the Arcadian 'performed the sacrifice for the Lykaia and organised games'. The games must have been such a splendid spectacle that even the younger Cyrus, the pretender to the Persian throne, attended them. Apparently, the festival aroused the same emotional feeling that the Anthesteria evoked among Athenians, and Christmas once in the hearts of many colonists and immigrants.[76] The presence of a sanctuary of Zeus Lykaios on the agora of Megalopolis, the fourth-century newly founded capital of Arcadia,[77] is one of the indications that Zeus' sanctuary on Mt Lykaion must have been the centre of a kind of Arcadian confederacy or tribal state before the fourth century.[78]

It was at this sanctuary that the sacrifice reported by Skopas (*FGrH* 413 F 1) in his *Olympic Victors* must have taken place: 'Demainetos the Parrhasian, at the sacrifice to Zeus Lykaios that the Arcadians were still making at that time with a human victim, tasted the entrails of a sacrificed boy and was turned into a wolf. And when he had been restored to his own form he competed as an athlete in boxing and returned from Olympia a victor'.[79] Pausanias, the late second-century 'Baedeker', relates the same story in more detail: 'But concerning the boxer named Damarchos, an Arcadian of Parrhasian (the area around Mt Lykaion) origin, except for his victory at

---

[75] *IG* V 2.549f.

[76] J. Roy, 'Arcadian Nationality as Seen in Xenophon's *Anabasis*', *Mnemosyne* IV 25 (1972) 134-5. Anthesteria and Christmas: Bremmer, *Greek Religion*, 50.

[77] Pausanias 8.30.2. For the cult of Zeus Lykaios in Megalopolis see M. Jost, 'The Distribution of Sanctuaries in Civic Space in Arkadia', in S.E. Alcock and R. Osborne (eds), *Placing the Gods* (Oxford, 1994) 225-28.

[78] The exact nature of this political institution remains uncertain, see Th. Nielsen, 'Was there an Arkadian Confederacy in the Fifth Century B.C.?' in M.H. Hansen and K. Raaflaub (eds), *More Studies in the Ancient Greek Polis* (Stuttgart, 1996) 39-61 and his *Arkadia*, 61, 113-57 (with illuminating discussions of the Arcadian coinage depicting Zeus Lykaios); J. Roy, '*Polis* and Tribe in Classical Arkadia', in Hansen and Raaflaub, 107-12; R. Parker, *Cleomenes on the Acropolis* (Oxford, 1998) 32-3; C. Morgan, *Early Greek States Beyond the Polis* (London and Sydney, 2003) 82-5.

[79] For the sacrifice see most recently W. Burkert, *Homo necans* (Berkeley, Los Angeles, London, 1983) 84-93; M. Jost, *Sanctuaires et cultes d'Arcadie* (Paris, 1985) 180-5, 249-69; Hughes, *Human Sacrifice*, 96-117; M. Halm-Tisserant, *Cannibalisme et immortalité* (Paris, 1993) 127-58; Bonnechere, *Sacrifice humain*, 85-96; M. Jost, 'À propos des sacrifices humains dans le sanctuaire de Zeus du mont Lycée', in R. Hägg (ed.), *Peloponnesian Sanctuaries and Cults* (Stockholm, 2002) 183-6.

Olympia I do not believe the other things said by pretentious men, namely that he was changed from a man to a wolf at the sacrifice of Zeus Lykaios and that in the tenth year after these events he again became a man. Nor did it seem to me at all that this was said about *him* by the Arcadians, for in this case it would also be said in the inscription at Olympia, which runs as follows:

> Damarchos son of Dinyttas dedicated this statue,
> a Parrhasian by birth from Arcadia.'[80]

Pausanias makes it thus very clear that he does not believe the story. Yet elsewhere in his work he supports the Arcadian werewolf tradition: 'For they say that ever since Lykaon (below) a man would become a wolf at the sacrifice of Zeus Lykaios, but that he would not become one for all his life. They say that if he refrained from human flesh while he was a wolf, later, in the tenth year, he would turn again from a wolf into a man, but that if he tasted it he would remain a beast for ever' (8.2.6).

Pausanias' information is supplemented by the Latin author Varro (116-27 BC), whose information illustrates the Roman interest in Arcadia since the second century BC, which had been prompted by Rome's dealings with the Achaean league.[81] A short summary of Varro is provided by Augustine in his discussion of metamorphosis in the *City of God* (18.17),[82] but in his *Natural History*, from which we have already quoted the information given by Skopas, Pliny the Elder (8.81) supplies a much fuller account: 'Euanthes, not despised among the writers of Greece, relates that the Arcadians write that someone from the clan of a certain Anthos, chosen by drawing lots

---

[80] Pausanias 6.8.2 = D.L. Page, *Further Greek Epigrams* (Cambridge, 1981) no. 137 (the epigram); L. Moretti, *Olympionikai* (Rome, 1957) 117, no. 359 dates Damarchos to the end of the fifth or the beginning of the fourth century. However, one cannot escape the impression that Pausanias confused two Arcadians, since it is hard to see how the name Damarchos became corrupted into Demainetos (= Damainetos), and the epigram provides only the name but no other information about Damarchos: *contra* Jost, *Sanctuaires*, 259; Burkert, *Homo necans*, 85 note 11; Hughes, *Human Sacrifice*, 98.

[81] See Bremmer and N. Horsfall, *Roman Myth and Mythography* (London, 1987) 13 (by Horsfall).

[82] For Augustine's interest see now J.R. Veenstra, 'The Ever-Changing Nature of the Beast. Cultural Change, Lycanthropy and the Question of Substantial Transformation (from Petronius to Del Rio)', in J.Í. Bremmer and J.R. Veenstra (eds), *The Metamorphosis of Magic from Late Antiquity to the Early Modern Period* (Leuven, 2002) 133-66 at 144-6; add to his bibliography D. Kraatz, 'Fictus Lupus: the Werewolf in Christian Thought', *Classical Folia* 30 (1976) 57-79.

among the family, is led to a certain pool in the area, and that after hanging his clothes on an oak, he swims across and goes off into the wild; and that he is turned into a wolf and consorts for nine years with others of the same species. If during this period he has abstained from eating humans, he returns to the same pool, and having swum across it he resumed human shape, but with nine years added to his former appearance. And he adds a still more fabulous detail (the text is unfortunately uncertain here) that he receives again the same clothing'.

It is somewhat strange that Pliny calls Euanthes 'a not negligible author', since he is completely unknown otherwise. As the names Euanthes, Euantha and Euanthidas are well attested for Arcadia,[83] the author may have been a descendant of the Anthos family too. Pliny does not tell us Euanthes' place of origin, but it seems clear that his information is not connected to the sanctuary of Zeus Lykaios. That leaves the possibility open that Euanthes was the product of a scribal mistake for the name of the much better known fourth-century historian Neanthes.[84] However this may be, although we have no certain information about the protagonist of the ritual, the future 'wolf' will hardly have been an established Arcadian with a career to lose. That strongly suggests a youth, just as the Olympic victor can hardly have been an older man, and this conclusion is supported by myths that we will discuss presently.

What was the ritual that the youth had to perform? Apparently, it started with a sacrifice to Zeus Lykaios at his altar; in front of it were two pillars, with gilded eagles on top of them, towards the rising sun. On this altar, so Pausanias tells us (8.38.7), 'they sacrifice (*thyousin*) in secret to Zeus Lykaios. I could see no pleasure in trying to find out the contents of this sacrifice (*thysia*): let is be as it is and as it was from the beginning'. Skopas is less squeamish and mentions that the Arcadians sacrificed a young boy, whose entrails – the best part of the flesh – had to be tasted by the youth. Plato supports this information about 'the sanctuary of Zeus Lykaios in Arcadia': 'the story goes that he who has tasted of human innards – one of these

---

[83] P.M. Fraser and E. Matthews, *A Lexicon of Greek Personal Names* IIIA (Oxford, 1997) 159.

[84] For writing Euanthes in stead of Neanthes see the manuscripts of Diogenes Laertius 3.4; scholia on Apollonius of Rhodes 1.1063 and 1065. For Neanthes' date see now W. Burkert, 'Philodems Arbeitstext zur Geschichte der Akademie', *Zs. f. Papyrologie und Epigraphik* 97 (1993) 87-94 at 92.

having been minced up with the innards of the other victims – is inevitably turned into a wolf'.[85] Since Plato calls it a story (*mythos*!), he is clearly sceptical in this passage about the reality of the sacrifice. Yet in his later *Laws* (6.782c) he speaks about the Greeks still performing human sacrifices, and the pseudo-Platonic, if still fourth-century, dialogue *Minos* (315C) also connects the Lykaia with human sacrifice. In his *Piety*, Theophrastus (*ca.* 372-287 BC) informs us that they periodically sprinkle kindred blood on the altar in remembrance of the custom.[86] Both the secrecy mentioned by Pausanias and the fact that Lykaon's son was called Nyktimos, 'Mr. Night', suggest that the sacrifice actually took place in the dark, as would indeed befit a gruesome sacrifice.[87]

After the sacrifice the youth seems to have been led out of the community in a procession before hanging his clothes on an oak. Given the importance of the oak for the Arcadian community, leaving his clothes behind on this particular tree will have signified his leaving Arcadian civilisation. Stripping and water are both associated with metamorphosis in antiquity and later: in Apuleius' *Golden Ass* (3.21, 24), Pamphile and Lucius strip before their metamorphoses take place, just as in Petronius' *Satyricon* (61-2) the werewolf removes his clothes before changing shape.[88] Similarly, clothes function as a boundary marker in medieval werewolf episodes, such as in Maria di Francia's *Bisclavret*. Water, too, is a familiar means of effecting a transition in Greek culture, as washing corpses, bathing newly born babies and baptising abundantly illustrate.[89]

---

[85] Plato, *Republic* 8.565de, quoted, perhaps not surprisingly, by the Arcadian Polybius 7.13.7. The innards were reserved for the more important persons: *Odyssey* 3.9, 40, 461; Herodotus 6.67-8; Euripides, *Electra* 838-9; Eupolis, fr. 99.43 Kassel-Austin; Aristophanes, *Peace* 1040, 1092-1115, *Birds* 519, 975.

[86] Theophrastus fr. 584A Fortenbaugh (= Porphyry, *On Abstinence* 2.27.2).

[87] Nyktimos: Lycophron 480-1; Apollodorus 3.99; Clement of Alexandria, *Protr.* 2.36.5; Nonnus, *D.* 18.21; scholion on Euripides, *Or.* 1646.

[88] For Petronius' werewolf see M. Schuster, 'Der Werwolf und die Hexen', *Wiener Studien* 48 (1930) 149-78; W. Kroll, 'Etwas vom Werwolf', *ibidem* 55 (1937) 168; R.O. James, 'Two Examples of Latin Legends from the Satyricon', *Arv* 35 (1979) 122-5; A. Borghini, 'Lupo mannaro: il tempo della metamorfosi: (Petr. Satyr. LXII 3)', *Aufidus* 14 (1991) 29-32; T. Pàroli, 'Lupi e lupi mannari, tra mondo classico e germanico, a partire da Petronio 61-62', in *Semiotica della novella Latina* (Rome, 1986) 281-317; B. Baldwin, 'The Werewolf Story as Bulletinstil', *Petronian Society Newsletter* 22 (1992) 6-7.

[89] For stripping and water see the excellent analysis by R. Buxton, 'Wolves and Werewolves in Greek Thought', in Bremmer (ed.), *Interpretations of Greek Mythology* (London and New York, 1988²) 60-79 at 69-74; add now to his bibliography on *Bisclavret*, D.B. Leshock, 'The Knight of the Werewolf: *Bisclavret* and the Shape-Shifting Metaphor', *Romance Quarterly* 46 (1999) 155.

Once being outside the community, the 'wolf' had to stay in the wild for nine years and was forbidden to eat human flesh. At the end of his 'jungle period' the 'wolf' could return, would find his clothes and could thus re-enter Arcadian civilisation. Admittedly, the fact that the 'wolf's' clothes were said to be still awaiting him after nine years hardly looks credible. The idea behind this detail seems to be that it is normal clothes that would make him again a proper civilised Arcadian. It is this clearly transitional character of the ritual, combined with the youthful age of the protagonist, which points into the direction of initiation, as several students of the ritual have argued.[90]

Do all three elements of this story – the 'wolf', cannibalism and the stay of nine years – indeed point into that direction? As regards the 'wolf', there clearly was a close connection between Arcadians and wolves, since the historian Myron mentions that the Arcadians used to carry the skins of wolves and bears instead of shields.[91] For the Greeks, the wolves were characteristic of co-operation in their packs but also of wildness, trickery and solitariness.[92] We see this association already in Homer's *Iliad* (X.334) where Dolon, 'Mr. Trickery', dons a wolf cap for a raid,[93] and in the association of Apollo Lykeios, 'Wolfish Apollo', with initiation and the world of the ephebes, the young Greeks on the brink of adulthood.[94] The image of wolves, then, would certainly fit groups of wandering novices who had to live, presumably, from plundering or joining the retinue of aristocrats (below).

On the other hand, the mention of 'wolves' also suggests the one-time occurrence of werewolves. It might seem strange that these ever occurred in ancient Greece, but notices on lycanthropy in

[90] H. Jeanmaire, *Couroi et Courètes* (Paris, 1939) 558-65; similarly Burkert, *Homo necans*, 90; Hughes, *Human Sacrifice*, 103-4; Bonnechere, *Le sacrifice*, 90-2, 173; Buxton, 'Wolves', 70-2.

[91] Pausanias 4.11.3; Statius, *Theb.* 4.303f.

[92] C. Mainoldi, *L'Image du loup et du chien dans la Grèce ancienne d'Homère à Platon* (Paris, 1984); Buxton, 'Wolves', 60-67 (splendid); G. Baudy, 'Die Herrschaft des Wolfes. Das Thema der 'verkehrten Welt' in Euripides' 'Herakles', *Hermes* 121 (1993) 159-80; A. Marcinkowski, 'Le loup et les Grecs', *Ancient Society* 31 (2001) 1-26.

[93] F. Lissarrague, 'L'iconographie de Dolon le Loup', *Rev. Arch.* 1980, 3-30; D. Williams, 'Dolon', *LIMC* III.1 (1986) 660-4; A. Burlando, 'Bâlla coi lupi (ovvero il travestimento di Dolone)', *Orpheus* 14 (1993) 255-74.

[94] M. Jameson, 'Apollo Lykeios in Athens', *Archaiognosia* 1 (1980) 213-36; Graf, *Nordionische Kulte*, 219-26; C.-F. de Roguin, 'Apollon Lykeios dans la tragédie: dieu, protecteur, dieu tueur, "dieu de l'initiation",' *Kernos* 12 (1999) 99-123.

Byzantine medical authors mention patients imitating wolves and gathering in cemeteries until dawn in the month of February;[95] interestingly, their notices were taken up and translated by Arab authors.[96] All these notices probably eventually go back to the second-century medical author Marcellus of Sidon, who mentioned the werewolf in his great work *Iatrika*.[97] Now February was the month of the Roman Lupercalia festival, the name of which suggests wolves (Latin: *lupus*), and the festival itself remained popular well into Late Antiquity.[98] The behaviour of the 'wolves', then, is clearly culturally determined and suggests narrative models of werewolves, such as that in Petronius (above).[99] In fact, werewolves are also attested for other Indo-European traditions where they are equally associated with initiation, outlaws and tribal names.[100]

[95] Burkert, *Homo necans*, 89 compares Marcellus of Sidon *apud* Aëtius of Amida 6.11; Oribasius 8.9; Paulus Aeginatas 3.16, all collected by R. Foerster, *Scriptores Physiognomonici Graeci et latini*, 2 vols (Leipzig, 1893) II.282-3; add *Sicamii Aetii libellus De Melancholia*, in C.G. Kühn, *Claudii Galeni opera omnia*, vol. 19 (Leipzig, 1830) 719-20; Psellus, *Poemata* 9.838-42 Westerink; Johannes Actuarius, *De diagnosi* 1.35 in J. Ideler, *Physici et medici Graeci minores*, 2 vols (Berlin, 1842) II.387 and Anonymus, *ibidem*, 282; E. Rohde, *Kleine Schriften*, 2 vols (Tübingen and Leipzig, 1901) II.216-23; P. Balin, 'Diagnostic: lycanthrope', in O. Bianchi and O. Thévenaz (eds.), *Mirabilia – Conceptions et représentations de l'extraordinaire dans le monde antique* (Bern, 2004) 295-305.

[96] M. Ullmann, 'Der Werwolf. Ein griechisches Sagenmotiv in arabischer Verkleidung', *Wiener Zs. z. Kunde des Morgenlandes* 68 (1976) 171-84.

[97] Suda, μ 205.

[98] Y.-M. Duval, 'Des Lupercales de Constantinople aux Lupercales de Rome', *Rev. Ét. Lat.* 55 (1977) 222-70; R.A. Markus, *The End of Ancient Christianity* (Cambridge, 1990) 131-5; C. Schäublin, 'Lupercalia und Lichtmess', *Hermes* 123 (1995) 117-25.

[99] For its contemporary occurrence, even if not identical with ancient lycanthropy, see most recently H.F. Moselhy and A. Nasr, 'Lycanthropy: A Dangerous Reverse Intermetamorphosis. Review of 23 Cases with the Syndrome of Lycanthropy', *European J. Psychiat.* 13.3 (1999) 145-50.

[100] See more recently M. Eliade, *Zalmoxis, the vanishing God* (Chicago and London, 1972) 1-20; M.R. Gerstein, 'Germanic Warg: The Outlaw as Werwolf', in G.J. Larson (ed.), *Myth in Indo-European Antiquity* (Berkeley, Los Angeles, London, 1974) 131-56; M. Jacoby *Wargus, vagr "Verbrecher" 'Wolf'* (Uppsala, 1974) and 'Nordische Ortsnamen mit varg-'Wolf',' *Beiträge z. Namenf.* 11 (1976) 425-36; K. McCone, 'Hund, Wolf und Krieger bei den Indogermanen', in W. Meid (ed.), *Studien zum indogermanischen Wortschatz* (Innsbruck, 1987) 102-54; C. Ginzburg, *Ecstasies* (Harmondsworth, 1991) 153-81; S. Cataldi, 'Popoli e città del lupo et del cane in Italia meridionale e in Sicilia tra realtà e immagine', in M. Sordi (ed.), *Autocoscienza e rappresentazione dei popoli nell'antichità* (Milan, 1992) 55-82 (conceptually weak); A. Ivancik, 'Les guerriers-chiens. Loups-garous et invasions scythes en Asie Mineure', *Rev. d'Hist. Rel.* 210 (1993) 305-29; F. Bader, 'Le renard, le loup, le lion razzieurs', *Bull. Soc. Ling. Paris* 90 (1995) 85-147; G. Ortalli, *Lupi, genti, culture. Uomo e ambiente nel medioevo* (Turin, 1997) 90-95.

As regards cannibalism, our sources tell that the boy would become human only if he had not eaten human flesh. Is this not rather odd? As if eating human flesh was the normal thing to do! No, it must have been that in an older, less 'civilised', version the novice could only become human again if he had really tasted human flesh: it is cannibalism that belongs to initiation, not its absence.[101] The feature of cannibalism during initiation and among secret societies is well known, although its presence in Greece may still be surprising. Yet, cannibalism and necrophagy, its alternative, are also ascribed to Indo-European werewolves. The Iranian members of the men's societies, the 'two pawed-wolves' (!), were accused of living on corpses.[102] Mircea Eliade has suggested that this accusation was a kind of stereotype used by Zarathustran polemicists,[103] but similar accusations were levelled against the worshippers of Shiva, the *agorapanthis*, and in Western-Europe the *wargus*, 'werewolf', was regularly associated with cannibalism and necrophagy.[104] In fact, the evidence mentioned above that Greek 'werewolves' spend the night mostly in cemeteries does suggest the notion of necrophagy; Petronius' werewolf also metamorphoses on a road beside some tombstones. Necrophagy was still in full force among novices of Kwakiutl secret societies at the end of the nineteenth century and was reputed to be somewhat easier than cannibalism.[105]

Several authors have objected to an initiation interpretation of this ritual by pointing to the nine-year period of absence, and Richard Buxton reasonably states that we must make sense of the nine years 'in relation to the life of a historical Arcadian community'.[106] There are two answers that can be given here. First, we may perhaps compare the famous Trojan War. Long ago I pointed out that the myths of this war, which lasted for ten years, bristle with initiatory themes;

[101] As is suggested by G. Widengren, *Religionsphänomenologie* (Berlin, 1969) 166.

[102] Two-pawed wolves: S. Wikander, *Der arische Männerbund* (Diss. Lund, 1938) 64ff.; G. Widengren, *Hochgottglaube im alten Iran* (Uppsala, 1938) 328ff, 344. Cannibalism: Widengren, *ibidem*, 331ff.

[103] Eliade, *Zalmoxis*, 8.

[104] Shiva: Widengren, *Hochgottglaube*, 331ff. Europe: W. Hertz, *Der Werwolf* (Stuttgart, 1862) 104ff.; Gerstein, 'Germanic Warg'; Jacoby, *Wargus*, 22-27.

[105] F. Boas, *The Social Organization and the Secret Societies of the Kwakiutl Indians* (Washington, 1897) 440f.

[106] Buxton, 'Wolves', 72; Bonnechere, *Sacrifice humain*, 90; Jost, 'À propos des sacrifices humains', 183-6.

moreover, in the Homeric epic it is normal to find 'for nine days ... but on the tenth'.[107] In other words, a period of nine years would fit early Greek culture. Second, we find long periods of initiation also among the ancient Celts, Germans and Ossetes. In fact, the Irish initiatory legends about the wandering Finn and his *fian* belong to the oldest part of Irish literature. In this case, we can also see how initiation could be integrated into other institutions of society, since the *fian* sometimes served in the retinue of a king during their period away from home.[108] Now it was a distinctively Arcadian custom to leave the region and enlist as a mercenary abroad.[109] The most famous Arcadian mercenaries probably were those that had joined Cyrus the Younger (above), but well before them they had joined the service of Sicilian tyrants, and this will explain why Zeus Lykaios has recently turned up in Sicilian Himera too.[110] It seems not implausible that this Arcadian speciality has to be connected to the long stay away from home during initiation.

It might be held against this interpretation that we hear of only one 'wolf'. It is indeed unclear if the Arcadian youth, who undoubtedly was of aristocratic stock, disappeared all alone or took some other youths of lower social standing with him. A famous description of initiatory pederasty in Crete shows that only aristocratic youths had to submit to a pederastic relationship, but also that, during their stay in the mountains, they were accompanied by other youths who, presumably, were not aristocrats.[111] On the other hand, in the course of the archaic period all over Greece, the original tribal initiation became limited to a few symbolic representations, except for Sparta and Crete where initiation was re-organised to serve the

---

[107] See my 'Heroes, Rituals and the Trojan War', *Studi Storico-Religiosi* 2 (1978) 5-38. Nine: *Lexicon des frühgriechischen Epos*, s.v. *ennea, ennêmar*; N.J. Richardson, *The Homeric Hymn to Demeter* (Oxford, 1974) 165f.

[108] Giraldus Cambrensis, *Topographica Hibernica* 2.19 (seven years as wolf); J. Nagy, *The Wisdom of the Outlaw* (Berkeley, Los Angeles, London, 1985) 140ff. (retinue of kings); Felix, *Life of Saint Guthlac*, ed. B. Colgrave (Cambridge, 1956) Ch. 18 (initiation lasts nine years); Ivancik, 'Les guerriers-chiens', 319 (Ossetes: seven years).

[109] Nielsen, *Arkadia*, 79-83; Morgan, *Early Greek States*, 204.

[110] See *SEG* 40.1675; L.B. Bergese, *Tra ethne e poleis. Pagine di storia Arcade* (Pisa, 1995) 111-12 for the dedication of a silver bar by a woman to Zeus Lykaios; for other Arcadian immigrants see L. Dubois, *Inscriptions grecques dialectales de Sicile* (Rome, 1989) 73 (a perhaps sixth-century Arcadian in Selinus); S. Hornblower, *Thucydides and Pindar* (Oxford, 2004) 185f.

[111] Bremmer, 'An Enigmatic Indo-European Rite: Paederasty', *Arethusa* 13 (1980) 279-98.

military needs of the state.[112] Unfortunately, then, we simply do not have the information to know what happened during (the development of) Arcadian initiation in this respect.

Having looked at the ritual, let us now see if the myth of Lykaon perhaps supports the presence of human sacrifice on Mt Lykaion.[113] During his visit to the site Pausanias (8.2.3) recorded the following myth: '... but Lykaon brought a human baby to the altar, sacrificed the baby and poured its blood on the altar. They say that at the sacrifice he was immediately turned into a wolf'. It is understandable that the locals told Pausanias the most 'innocent' version of human sacrifice: the cutting up of a baby. Authors outside Arcadia could present a more gruesome version and imagined that it was Lykaon's own son Nyktimos.[114] The myth evidently reflects the stories about the sacrifice and confirms Theophrastus' notice about the pouring of the blood on the altar. It also nicely illustrates two characteristics of Greek myth in its relation to ritual. Greek myth often concentrates on the more unusual or gruesome aspects of the ritual and it often turns the temporality of ritual into permanence.[115] Our myth does not mention circumstantial details about the initiatory ritual but clearly focuses on its most horrible aspect and, unlike human novices, Lykaon is turned into a wolf forever. Lykaon was considered the founder of the Arcadians and in the course of time mythology ascribed to him several inventions and made him a paradigm of righteousness.[116] What better way to support the youth in his difficult future ahead than this association with the founder of his community?

Yet Lykaon's myth is so closely connected to the ritual of Mt Lykaion that we are not surprised that there is a more interesting variant. According to 'Hesiod', Lykaon cut up a baby and put him as a dish on the table when hosting Zeus. Zeus turned the table in disgust, which gave the city Trapezous ('Table': near Mt Lykaion) its name, and hurled a bolt of lightning at the house of Lykaon, whom

---

[112] F. Graf, 'The Locrian Maidens', in Buxton, *Oxford Readings*, 250-70 at 261f.

[113] For all testimonia see G. Piccaluga, *Lykaon* (Rome, 1968). The myth was apparently the subject of several tragedies: Achaeus, *Azanes* (*TrGF* 20 F 2: *ca*. 450 BC?); Xenocles, *Lykaon* (*TrGF* 33 F 1: 415 BC: of which nothing has remained); Astydamas, *Lykaon* (*TrGF* 60 T 6: 340 BC).

[114] Lycophron 480-81; Clement of Alexandria, *Protr*. 2.36.5; Nonnus, *D*. 18.20-24.

[115] Bremmer, 'Myth and Ritual'.

[116] P. Forbes Irving, *Metamorphosis in Greek Myths* (Oxford, 1990) 216-18.

he turned into a wolf. Later traditions combined the Lykaon myth with that of Kallisto and her son Arcas, the ancestor of the Arcadians. However, the myth of Arcas originally belonged to the eastern side of Arcadia,[117] where the richest agricultural land lies and the most Early Iron Age evidence is found,[118] whereas Lykaon is closely tied to the western Mt Lykaion.[119] Moreover, Lykaon is consistently associated with wolves, whereas Arcas, via his mother Kallisto, is consistently associated with bears;[120] in fact, the names Arcas and Arcadia cannot be separated from Greek *arkos*, 'bear', a variant of the more frequent *arktos*.[121] Consequently, these combinations need not concern us here.[122]

There is a noteworthy parallel to the myth of Lykaon. Tantalus offered his son Pelops to the gods during a banquet in order to test their divinity. As Demeter was thinking of Persephone's kidnap by Hades, she did not notice the cannibalistic feast and ate Pelops' shoulder. However, Zeus revived Pelops, although he had to live with an ivory shoulder blade.[123] Originally, Tantalus comes from Sipylos (*Iliad* XXIV.615), an area above Smyrna, and Homer already knew the story of his son Pelops' wooing of Hippodameia. This supports the suggestion that a version of the myth of Tantalus and Pelops was already known to the Asiatic Aeolians.[124] From Asia

---

[117] M.L. West, *The Hesiodic Catalogue of Women* (Oxford, 1985) 154f.

[118] Morgan, *Early Greek States*, 38f.

[119] For Arcadia in the Late Archaic period see Nielsen, *Arkadia*, 92-97.

[120] For the myth of Kallisto and its many variants see most recently K. Dowden, *Death and the Maiden* (London and New York, 1989) 182-91; Forbes Irving, *Metamorphosis in Greek Myths*, 72-4, 202-5; *LIMC* V.1 (1990) s.v. Kallisto (I. McPhee); M. Jost, 'Versions locales et versions "panhelléniques" des mythes arcadiens chez Pausanias', *Kernos*, Suppl. 8 (1998) 227-40 at 231-4; K. Waldner, 'Kallisto', in *Der neue Pauly* VI (Stuttgart and Weimar, 1999) 205.

[121] Compare nouns like *arkulos*, 'bear cub', and names like Arkoleon, 'Bear-Lion': L. Robert, *Hellenica* 5 (1948) 88-89; O. Masson, *Onomastica Graeca selecta*, 2 vols (Paris, 1990) II.617-20; C. Dobias-Lalou, *Le Dialecte des inscriptions grecques de Cyrène = Karthago* 25 (2000) 61; add to her linguistic and onomastic analysis *IG* XIV.1302, 1308; W.J. Slater on Aristophanes Byz. F 174b; S. Amigues, *Revue Philologique* 75 (2001) 135f.

[122] As Henrichs, 'Three Approaches', 261-2 has seen, the connection with Kallisto and Arcas in Hesiod, fr. 163 Merkelbach-West, quoting Eratosthenes as printed by Merkelbach and West, is a later combination. This is confirmed by the fact that poems or prose works in which both traditions are combined are all fairly late: Ovid, *Met.* 1.198-239; Hyginus, *Fab.* 176; Apollodorus 3.98-99; Nonnus, *D.* 18.20-24.

[123] Pindar, *Ol.* 1.26-7, 47-53; Bacchylides F 42 Maehler; Euripides, *IT* 386-88; Lycophron 152-55; Apollodorus, *Epit.* 2.2-3; E. Krummen, *Pyrsos hymnon. Festliche Gegenwart und mythisch-rituelle Tradition bei Pindar* (Berlin and New York, 1990) 168-84.

[124] West, *Hesiodic Catalogue*, 158-59 (Asiatic Aeolians); R. Janko, *The Iliad: A Commentary* IV (Cambridge, 1992) 101 (Homer).

Minor, both father and son were 'exported' to the west of the Peloponnese, to Olympia, at some time in the eighth or seventh century.[125] Here, Pelops' shoulder blade remained long on display, but had disappeared in the time of Pausanias.[126] Given the prominence of Olympia and the copying of the Olympian games by the organisers of the Lykaia, it seems more likely that the Arcadians had copied the Olympian myth than the other way round.

Now the altar of Zeus Lykaios is not older than *ca.* 600 BC, perhaps constructed shortly after the Arcadians decided to perform their (tribal?) rites of initiation in a new sanctuary for Zeus Lykaios on Mt Lykaion, and it remained in use into the fourth century BC.[127] Given the prominence of the wolf in their ritual, the Arcadians will have chosen the spot because of the popular etymological connection of Lykaios with Greek *lykos*, 'wolf', as the 'real' etymology of Lykaion is unclear.[128] Zeus himself is associated with both human sacrifice and initiation in ancient Greece, which may well explain the choice of this particular god.[129] Popular etymology must also have played a role in the choice of the name Lykaon, who is only a minor figure in Homer's *Iliad*. The recent publication of a Hittite fragment has definitively demonstrated that Lykaon (from *Lykawon) derives from *Lukkawanni*, 'inhabitant of Lukka (= Lycia)'.[130] It is one of a slowly growing number of names in the *Iliad*, such as Priam and Paris, which have been shown to derive from Anatolian languages.[131] Such a choice can indeed hardly have been made before the seventh century, as influence of the *Iliad* on the Peloponnese is not attested before that century.[132]

What can we now conclude from our discussion so far? In the earlier fourth century the Arcadians apparently brought a secret

---

[125] They are already mentioned together in a Peloponnesian context by *Cypria* F 15.4 Bernabé.

[126] Burkert, *Homo necans*, 99.

[127] Kourouniotis, 'Anaskaphai Lykaiou', 167-8, 178-84.

[128] See the survey of the etymological explanations by Jost, *Sanctuaires*, 250f.

[129] Bonnechere, *Sacrifice humain*, 96-107 (human sacrifice), 144-6 (initiation).

[130] R. Lebrun, 'Syro Anatolica Scripta Minora I', *Le Muséon* 114 (2001) 245-51 at 252; the connection with Lycia had already been suspected by C.J. Ruijgh, *Scripta minora*, 2 vols (Amsterdam, 1991-96) 1.252. Note that the name is more frequent in the area south of Lycia, especially Rhodes, than in Arcadia itself, cf. Fraser and Matthews, *Lexicon of Greek Personal Names* I, 290.

[131] Janko, *Iliad: A Commentary*, 358-9; C. Watkins, *Selected Writings*, 2 vols (Innsbruck, 1994) 2.711-12.

[132] Burkert, *Kleine Schriften* I (Göttingen, 2001) 175.

sacrifice to Zeus Lykaios during the Lykaia festival in which, reportedly, human and animal innards were mixed up. After this sacrifice, a youth had to leave the community, was turned into a 'wolf' and returned after nine years in order to become again a respected member of the Arcadian community. Plato himself is already sceptical about the human sacrifice, but the *Minos* and Theophrastus accept its reality. The Arcadians apparently continued to talk about this sacrifice until the second century AD when Pausanias visited the sanctuary. It is not impossible that the need for tourists kept the story alive, since it is unlikely that the Romans would have permitted the custom to continue. They were rather keen on abolishing human sacrifice among the Carthaginians and Celts, and certainly would not have liked to be associated with such an abominable practice.[133] Yet all our information should not prevent a certain amount of scepticism about our knowledge of the ritual. Damarchos' winning of the 'gold medal' in boxing in the Olympic Games straight after being a 'wolf' rather suspiciously resembles the structure of fairy-tales, where the 'outlaw' on his return often marries the princess and becomes king.[134] Evidently, these descriptions are idealised representations of an ancient ritual rather than accurate reports by trained anthropologists.

Where does this all leave us? I am afraid that we cannot pierce through the darkness of the Arcadian night in which the ritual took place. Our reports are pretty clear that the Arcadians did practise human sacrifice, but the excavation of the altar of Zeus Lykaios did not reveal a single human bone,[135] although we must allow for the fact that excavations of a century ago were not as systematic as those of the present. Modern sensibility would make us prefer to suppose that it was all pretence, and that was evidently already the opinion of Plato. Yet the persistent rumour about the ritual until Pausanias' time, its mythological reflection and the ethnological parallels of cannibalism and necrophagy in male initiation rituals indicate that we must keep open the possibility of a real human sacrifice. Whether the Arcadian 'wolves' were real 'cannibals' we will probably never know.

---

[133] For the Roman opposition to human sacrifice see J. Rives, 'Human Sacrifice among Pagans and Christians', *J. Roman Stud.* 85 (1995) 65-85.

[134] See the classic studies by V. Propp: *Morphology of the folktale* (Austin, 1968²) and *Les racines historiques du conte merveilleux* (Paris, 1983).

[35] Kouroniotis, '*Anaskaphai Lukaiou*', 162-70.

4. Conclusion

We have seen that a discussion of human sacrifice in Greece teaches us that we must be prepared to accept a variety of possibilities. A report of a past human sacrifice may have served to legitimate an execution via a religious ritual. The telling of a myth can test the arguments as to whether the community can exact the death of an individual for the common good, but a dramatist can also use the same myth to entertain his male audience with a mixture of *eros* and *thanatos* that would not have been amiss in a modern pornographic film. Finally, a human sacrifice, real or fictitious, can signify a total break with civilisation. Herodotus mentions only one Greek human sacrifice, that of two Egyptian boys to secure favourable winds, and calls the deed 'an unholy act' (2.119.2-3); elsewhere in his work he ascribes human sacrifice only to foreigners.[136] And indeed, human sacrifice, like cannibalism,[137] has always been the crime *par excellence* to impute to foreigners or outsiders. As such, it was already used to slander Jews and Christians in antiquity, and especially against Jews the accusation had a long and evil life.[138]

Given the nature of our sources, in the end we are left wondering whether our evidence really enables us to establish with certainty the historicity of reports of human sacrifice in an initiatory context. It is perhaps not the worst side of us that maintains some faith in human decency amidst all these cruelties.[139]

---

[136] J. Mikalson, *Herodotus and Religion in the Persian Wars* (Chapel Hill and London, 2003) 78f.

[137] W. Arens, *The man-eating myth: anthropology and anthropophagy* (New York, 1979); G. Obeyesekere, *Cannibal Talk. The Man-Eating Myth and Human Sacrifice in the South Seas* (Berkeley, Los Angeles, London, 2005).

[138] Antiquity: H. Jacobson, 'Apion, the Jews, and Human Sacrifice', *Class. Quart.* 51 (2001) 318-19; A. Nagy, 'La forme originale de l'accusation d'anthropophagie contre les chrétiens, son development et les changements de sa représentation au IIᵉ siècle', *Rev. Ét. Augustiniennes* 47 (2001) 223-49; Roig Lanzillotta, this volume, Ch. IV. Modern times: R. Po-chia Hsia, *The myth of ritual murder: Jews and magic in Reformation Germany* (New Haven, 1988).

[139] For comments and corrections I would like to thank Jitse Dijkstra, Ralf von den Hoff, Hans-Ulrich Wiemer and, especially, Ken Dowden.

IV. THE EARLY CHRISTIANS
AND HUMAN SACRIFICE

Lautaro Roig Lanzillotta

Among the many accusations levelled by pagans against the early Christians, those that accuse them of cannibalism or child sacrifice deserve special attention. The interest of such charges is certainly not their novelty. Thanks to the role played by the motif of human sacrifice in the age-old discussion about civilisation and barbarism, it has appeared in numerous contexts.[1] It served not only as a way of opposing the civilisation of the Greco-Roman world to the barbarism outside it,[2] but also as a means to draw a line between culture and humanity and barbarity and inhumanity within the same cultural world.[3] In a religious context, the motif also frequently established

---

[1] J.B Rives, 'Human Sacrifice among Pagan and Christians', *J. Roman Stud.* 85 (1995) 65-85.

[2] The examples that underline this opposition are numerous. Scythians (Ephorus, *FGrH* 70 F 4a), androphagoi (Herodotus 4.106), Taurians (Herodotus 4.103; Euripides, *Iphigeneia in Tauris*; see other references in Cicero, *Rep.* 3.15; Ovid, *Trist.* 4.4.61-82, *Pont.* 3.2.45-96; Hyginus, *Fab.* 120; Lucan 1.446; Juvenal 15.116-19), people of the Pontus in general (Aristotle, *Ethica Nicomachea* [= *EN*] 1148b 19-23; *Pol.* 1338b 19-22), Carthaginians (Sophocles, *Andromeda* fr. 126 Radt, on which Rives, 'Human Sacrifice', note 21; Tertullian, *Apolog.* 9. 2-3; see in general S. Brown, *Late Carthaginian Child Sacrifice Monuments in their Mediterranean Context* (Sheffield, 1991) and J.B. Rives, 'Tertullian on Child Sacrifice', *Museum Helveticum* 51 (1994) 54-63) and Gauls (Caesar, *Bellum Gall.* 4.16; Strabo 4.4.5; Diodorus Siculus 5.31.3-4) alike were accused of performing such rituals.

[3] Political enemies were the favourite targets of such accusations (see already Plato, *Rep.* 571c-574e; 619 b-c, about the tyrant; Aristotle, *EN* 1448b 24 about Phalaris, tyrant of Acragas in the sixth century; so, also, Tatian, *Or. ad Graec.* 34.1-35), such as the supporters of the Tarquinii (Plutarch, *Publ.* 4.1), Apollodorus of Cassandreia (Diodorus Siculus 22.5.1; Polyaenus 6.7.2; Plutarch, *Sera Num. Vind.* 556d; cf. Aelian, *VH* 14.41) and Catilina (Sallust, *Cat.* 22.1-2; Plutarch, *Cic.* 10.4; Florus 2.12.4; Cassius Dio 37.30.3; Tertullian, *Apol.* 9.9; Minucius Felix, *Oct.* 30.5). See in general G. Marasco, 'Sacrifici umani e cospirazioni politiche', *Sileno* 7 (1981) 167-78. Secret associations were equally accused of human sacrifice. So, for example, the boukoloi (Cassius Dio 71.4.1; Achilles Tatius, *Leucippe and Cleitophon* 3.15.4; Lollianos, *Phoinikika*, on which A. Henrichs, 'Pagan Ritual and the Alleged Crimes

the difference between good and bad religion (and still does),[4] but could also be used as a means to condemn religion altogether.[5]

What is interesting about the alleged accusation of child sacrifice against Christians is the fact that in spite of its great echo in Christian sources, there is not a single pagan source explicitly documenting it. If Christians were in fact accused of such crimes, how can it be that not a single document records such charges? In the other known instances concerning barbarous peoples, political enemies and religious groups, not only the charges but even simple suspicions of human sacrifice found an enormous echo.[6] In the case of the many vices attributed to Jews by their enemies, of which Josephus attempts to exonerate them, several are also attested by other sources.[7] When approaching the alleged charges of child sacrifice against early Christians, however, we surprisingly have to rely exclusively on Christian sources.

On the other hand, it is also striking that orthodox Christians did not hesitate to use the same charges, first against numerous splinter

of the Early Christians. A Reconsideration', in *Kyriakon. Festschrift J. Quasten* I (Münster, 1970) 18-35 and *Die Phoinikika des Lollianos. Fragmente eines neuen griechischen Romans* (Bonn, 1972) 28-37); Parthenios, *Amat.* 35, with the commentary of J. Lightfoot *ad loc.*

[4] See the treatment of Celtic Religion by Caesar (*Bellum Gall.* 6.16.1), Pomponius Mela (3.18) and Pliny (*Nat. Hist.* 30.13). Human sacrifice in these cases served both to distinguish good from bad religion, namely *religio* from *superstitio*, since the latter appeared to arise from an excessive and irrational attitude towards the gods. Other foreign religions, however, were also suspect. Dio (42.26.2) reports that in a shrine to Bellona in Rome, jars full of human flesh were found, see R.M. Grant, 'Charges of "Immorality" Against Various Religious Groups in Antiquity', in R. van den Broek and M.J. Vermaseren (eds), *Studies in Gnosticism and Hellenistic Religions Presented to G. Quispel on the Ocassion of his 65th Birthday* (Leiden, 1981) 161-70. As for the participants in the Bacchanalia of 186 BC, these were also suspected of obscure crimes (Livy 39.8-18) and Apion accused the Jews of sacrificing a Greek every year (Josephus, *C. Apion.* 11.52-113). Magic was also widely suspected of involving human sacrifice (Juvenal 6.550-52) and different individuals were believed to sacrifice children in order to achieve various goals (Cassius Dio 73.16: Didius Julianus; Cassius Dio 79.1 and *Historia Augusta* 8.1-2: Elagabalus). See in general F.J. Dölger, '"Sacramentum infanticidii". Die Schlachtung eines Kindes und der Genuß seines Fleisches und Blutes als vermeintlicher Einweihungsakt im ältesten Christentum', *Antike und Christentum* IV (Münster, 1934) 188-228 at 211-17 and Rives, 'Human Sacrifice', 79 note 67.

[5] Lucretius, *De rerum natura* 1.82-101, with his denouncement of the 'crimes of religion', was not the first to focus on human sacrifice to criticise religion. According to Porphyry's *De abstinentia* (2.27.1-3), Theophrastus in *On Piety* already attacked the traditional Greek blood sacrifice on the grounds that its origin was human sacrifice.

[6] Above notes 2-4.

[7] Josephus, *C. Apion.* 2.145-50. Compare Diodorus Siculus 34.1-3; Tacitus, *Hist.* 5.5, *Annals* 15.44; Philostratus, *Life of Apollonius* 5.33, etc.

groups in their crusade against heresy, and later on against the Jews. If they were really being accused of performing ritual murders, and if they were conscious of the fallacy of these defamatory attacks, how could they now seriously press them against others?

The purpose of this contribution is, first, to critically review the pagan testimonies that allegedly contain accusations against Christians in order to examine whether the existence of such charges can be established only on the basis of the Christian testimonies. Secondly, it surveys the far more numerous orthodox Christian allegations of child sacrifice against different heterodox groups. Thirdly, it raises the question of whether there is a connection between the reputed pagan charges and the orthodox accusations against heterodox groups or whether they are independent developments. Within this scope attention is paid both to various hypotheses that explain the origin of these accusations and to the sources upon which these explanations rely.

1

Even though our pagan sources on the issue are scanty and not always explicit, the vague testimonies of the apologists and Church Fathers are customarily provided as proof that the accusation of human sacrifice, at least in the *vox populi*, might have been rather extensive. Let us first examine the alleged pagan sources documenting this indictment.

The claim that the Christians had 'unlawful meals' seems to be a typically second-century issue, although the accusation may already have been known earlier: Tacitus reports that in Nero's time Christians were hated for their 'crimes'.[8] It was the German scholar Hans Achelis who first interpreted this allusion as referring to the charge of cannibalism and thus concluded that the accusation already existed in the first century.[9] Although following Achelis' interpretation of *flagitia*, Jean Pierre Waltzing suggested that Tacitus was actually referring to the rumours of his time.[10] This view has recently

---

[8] Tacitus, *Annals* 15.40.

[9] H. Achelis, *Das Christentum in den ersten drei Jahrhunderten* I (Leipzig, 1912) 294.

[10] J.P. Waltzing, 'Le crime rituel reproché aux chrétiens du IIᵉ siècle, *Académie royale de Belgique. Bulletins de la classe des lettres et des sciences morales et politiques* 5e série tome 11 (Brussel, 1925) 205-39 at 210. Even if Dölger, 'Sacramentum infanticidii', 196 has rightly remarked that Waltzing's reservation seems to be contradicted

been restated by Albert Henrichs,[11] who not only thinks that Tacitus' pregnant use of *flagitia* may reflect the opinion of his contemporaries, but even suggests his dependence upon Pliny's *Letter to Trajan* in this instance (below). Despite the weight given by these scholars to Tacitus' passage, this text is, as Dölger has rightly and more cautiously pointed out, too short and ambiguous to allow such an assumption.[12] Besides, Tacitus' use of *exitiabilis superstitio* ('destructive superstition') to refer to Christianity and his reference to the *odium humani generis* normally attributed to the Jews[13] seem to suggest that he considered Christians to be a Jewish sect and consequently endowed them with the same troublesome, conflictive and violent characters.[14] This appears to be a preferable explanation for the 'crimes' or *flagitia* he is referring to, since it is difficult to understand why he would not mention the accusations of anthropophagy if he had had them in mind while writing this section of the *Annals.*

The second reference customarily adduced as testimony for the accusation is Pliny's *Letter to Trajan.* Whereas Tacitus' passage vaguely referred to *flagitia*, the testimony of Pliny the Younger appears to furnish some more evidence for the accusation that Christians had 'unlawful meals'. Indeed, this letter written in the second decade of the second century might even seem to imply it, for Pliny reports to the emperor that according to his inquiries the Christians 'come together to take food but of an ordinary and harmless kind'.[15] The view that Pliny is referring here to allegations of cannibalism is widely held. Waltzing and Dölger clearly defend such an interpretation;[16] Henrichs not only believes that the accusation was known to Pliny (and Tacitus), but also that it was the result of an anti-Christian campaign by Roman Jews,[17] Benko also apparently gives credence to this interpretation,[18] although he rightly points out the interesting similarities between Pliny's report and Livy's account of

by Tacitus' use of the imperfect, the latter's opinion has recently received the support of Henrichs (see next note) and Benko (see note 14).

[11] Henrichs, 'Pagan Ritual', 20-21.

[12] Dölger,'Sacramentum infanticidii', 196.

[13] Above note 7.

[14] S. Benko, 'Pagan Criticism of Christianity', *Aufstieg und Niedergang der Römischen Welt* II.23.2 (1980) 1055-1118 at 1064-65.

[15] Pliny, *Ep.* 10.96.8, *cf.* A.N. Sherwin-White, *The Letters of Pliny: A Historical and Social Commentary* (Oxford, 1966) 707.

[16] Waltzing, 'Le crime', 210; Dölger, 'Sacramentum infanticidii', 195-96 and note 20.

[17] Henrichs, 'Pagan Ritual', 24. See also below note 68.

[18] Benko, 'Pagan Criticism', 1074, 1089.

the suppression of the Bacchanalia in 186.[19] Both descriptions focus on the same elements: nightly meetings, a common meal by the participants and accusations of promiscuity and murder[20]. These obvious similarities seem to suggest that Pliny's report was not so much based on the alleged charges of cannibalism as on the pattern provided by Livy, which offered him a precedent for his inquires into a secret association. As for the apparent reference to 'unlawful meals', it should be noted that Pliny's expression *cibum innoxium* can be interpreted not only as 'impure food' but also as 'innocent', that is, as 'not harmful for a third party'.[21] Given the parallelism with Livy and the possibility of understanding the passage otherwise, Pliny's affirmation that Christians 'come together to take food but of an ordinary and harmless kind' should perhaps rather be explained in the light of the Bacchanalia precedent, during whose feasts poisonings were not unknown.

The astrologer Vettius Valens, whose floruit was between *ca.* AD 140 and 170, is sometimes adduced as testimony for the existence of the same accusation as well. He may be referring to it when he says that 'some of them deny the divine and have a different worship or eat unlawful meals', although he does not explicitly mention Christians.[22]

However, the most important of the alleged pagan sources documenting the charge of cannibalism against Christians is the supposed testimony of Marcus Cornelius Fronto. On the basis of the *Octavius* by Minucius Felix, some scholars believe that the famous Roman orator who lived between 100 and 166 (or 176)[23] may have

---

[19] Livy 39.8-19. According to Livy, there were nightly meetings and secret rites, which included wine and feastings, promiscuity and, occasionally, murder.

[20] See Benko, 'Pagan Criticism', 1072. The similarity between both passages was also noted by Grant, 'Charges of Immorality', 161 who thinks that 'something like Livy's account seems to have been in his mind when he investigated the activities of Bithynian Christians', even though we cannot be sure that Pliny read about the Bacchanalia; see also Rives, 'Human Sacrifice', 74 note 44.

[21] Compare Minucius Felix, *Oct.* 9.5, *innoxius ictus*; see Dölger, 'Sacramentum infanticidii', 195-96, note 20.

[22] Vettius Valens, *Anth.* 4.15.4; see Rives, 'Human Sacrifice', 65, note 3. For Vettius Valens' date see now Vettius Valens, *Anthologiae*, ed. D. Pingree (Leipzig, 1986) v-vi.

[23] The existence and the character of Fronto's alleged attack on Christians still are a matter of controversy. See J.H. van Haeringen, 'Circensis Noster (Minucius Fel. 9.6)', *Mnemosyne* 3 (1935) 29-32; P. Frasinetti, 'L'orazione di Frontone contro i cristiani', *Giornale italiano di filologia clasica* 3 (1949) 238-54, who even dates it to between AD 162-166; W.H.C. Frend, *Martyrdom and Persecution* (New York, 1967) 187-8; G.W. Clarke, *The Octavius of Minucius Felix* (New York, 1974) 221-24; Henrichs, 'Pagan Ritual', 26ff. For the dating of Fronto's life, below note 31.

played an important role in the formation of the story about human sacrifice among Christians.[24] Others go even further and suggest that he may have included these charges in a specific speech *contra Christianos*,[25] although nothing of the kind has been preserved among Fronto's writings. As a matter of fact, the *Octavius* never says that Fronto referred to the charges of cannibalism. Q. Caecilius Natalis, one of the interlocutors in *Octavius*, neither cites Fronto as his source when he affirms that Christians 'establish a herd of a profane conspiracy, which is leagued together by nightly meetings, and solemn fasts, and inhuman meats',[26] nor when he describes child sacrifice as performed by Christians.[27] Rather, Caecilius' reference to Fronto opens his description of the banqueting and the promiscuity after it[28] and this, consequently, is the only detail we may consider as being referred to by the Roman orator.[29] Despite the fact that the conversation recreated by Minucius Felix is a clear literary fiction,[30] and that consequently we should be careful when evaluating the facts referred to in it, scholars tend to magnify the importance of the role played by Fronto.[31] They not only believe in the existence of the supposed speech against the Christians, but also speculate that Fronto's accusations may have had their origin in peculiar practices of various splinter groups.[32]

---

[24] Dölger, 'Sacramentum infanticidii', 200; S. Benko, *Pagan Rome and the Early Christians* (London, 1985) 60-68.

[25] E. Champlin, *Fronto and Antonine Rome* (Cambridge, MA, 1980) 64-66.

[26] Minucius Felix, *Oct.* 8.4.

[27] Minucius Felix, *Oct.* 9.5. See *infra* note 62.

[28] Minucius Felix, *Oct.* 9.6, cf. Rives, 'Human Sacrifice', note 4.

[29] Despite this, after speculating on the occasion and the general character of Fronto's speech, Henrichs, 'Pagan Ritual', 27 states the following: 'That he (*scil.* Minucius) should have limited his attack to the *convivium* and omitted the far more spectacular charge of homicide, is hard to believe, if this is really what Minucius wanted to imply'. Nevertheless, he rightly criticises the attempt to reconstruct Fronto's alleged speech on the basis of the *Octavius*.

[30] See already G. Boissier, *La fin du paganisme* I (Paris, 1891) 321 and J.P. Waltzing, *Octavius* (Louvain, 1902) 75; see also W. Speyer, 'Zu den Vorwürfen der Heiden gegen die Christen', *Jahrbuch für Antike und Christentum* 6 (1963) 129-135 at 129 note 1.

[31] R.M. Grant, 'The Chronology of the Greek Apologists', *Vigiliae Christianae* 9 (1955) 25-33 at 25, 30 already speculated that the apologies by Aristides and Justin may be a response to a speech pronounced by Fronto in 143. See also R. Freudenberger, 'Der Vorwurf ritueller Verbrechen gegen die Christen im 2. und 3. Jahrhundert', *Theol. Zs.* 23 (1967) 97-107 at 103-05; differently, Henrichs, 'Pagan Ritual', 26-28, thinks that the occasion of the speech may have been either the trial of Justin and his companions (between 165 and 167) or the persecution of Lyons (177). For a later date for his death see ibid. p. 27 note 46.

[32] Speyer, 'Zu den Vorwürfen', passim; Henrichs, 'Pagan Ritual', 25, 26 note 40, 29, and, notably, Benko, 'Pagan Criticism', 1081-89, who produces a battery of

This is all the information we can obtain from pagan sources concerning the alleged crimes committed by the early Christians, which, regrettably, is not very substantial. The references by Pliny and Tacitus refer vaguely to 'crimes', Vettius Valens does not mention what or who he is referring to, and Fronto, if at all, was probably referring to the presumed incestuous banquets of Christian reunions. But what about Christian sources? Do they provide us with a clearer picture of the nature of these charges? Let us now take a look at the Christian testimonies.

It is in the works of the apologists of the second half of the second century that the accusations acquire a clear and distinct enunciation. Justin already alludes to 'impious accusations' levelled against 'all the Christians' in passing, but without specifying what these accusations actually were.[33] It is only after referring to various heretics that he becomes more explicit and specifies the accusations, namely 'the upsetting of the lamp, and promiscuous intercourse, and eating human flesh'.[34] Tatian remains as vague as Justin. He denies that cannibalism was practised among Christians.[35] As far as Theophilus of Antioch is concerned, in the third book of his *Ad Autolycum*, dedicated to refuting all pagan accusations against Christianity, he again includes the indictment of anthropophagy together with those of incest and promiscuity.[36]

However, it is Athenagoras, in a work written in 177, who first gives this threefold charge its familiar form, namely 'atheism, Thyestean meals and Oedipodal intercourse',[37] which also appears in *The Letter of the Churches of Vienna and Lyons* dated to the second century. This testimony as preserved by Eusebius records the persecution of the Christians in Lyons in 177/8.[38] As has been pointed out, *The Letter* furnishes perhaps the clearest proof that the accusation of cannibalism and child sacrifice had an eminently popular

(mostly later) references to associate the testimony of the *Octavius* with the alleged rituals by heretics; see also his 'The Libertine Gnostic Sects of the Phibionites according to Epiphanius', *Vigiliae Christianae* 21 (1967) 103-19. See the criticism on the issue by M.J. Edwards, 'Some Early Christian Immoralities', *Ancient Society* 23 (1992) 71-82 at 72 note 4.

[33] See Justin, *Apol.* 1.4.7; see also *Apol.* 1.10.6; 1.23.3; *Dial. c. Tryph.* 10.1.
[34] Justin, *Apol.* 1.26.6-7 at 7, also 2.12.1-2.
[35] Tatian, *Or. ad Graec.* 25.3.
[36] Theophilus of Antioch, *Ad Autolycum* 3.4.9.
[37] Athenagoras, *Legatio* 3.1, see also 34.3, 35.1-2.
[38] Eusebius, *Historia Ecclesiastica* (= HE) 5.1.1-2, 8.

character. In this persecution, Christians appear to have been charged primarily with impiety and atheism, and the accusations of cannibalism present a clearly secondary character.[39] It is only after a series of tortures that some heathen household slaves accuse their masters of 'Thyestean banquets and Oedipodal intercourse'.[40] Despite the euphemism, the accusation was probably more precise, since the testimony of a Christian woman called Biblis clearly implies the charge of child murder and cannibalism.[41] Be that as it may, it is noteworthy that *The Letter* uses exactly the same expressions that we first find in Athenagoras. We cannot doubt that these expressions were coined by Athenagoras, since they perfectly fit the character of his text and his intention to turn the accusations against the pagans by his use of mythological examples. Given the *terminus a quo* of *The Letter*, we must conclude either that its anonymous author depended upon Athenagoras or, perhaps more likely, that Eusebius interpolated these expressions into the source he was working on.

We now turn to the testimonies of Tertullian and Minucius Felix. These authors deserve more detailed attention, since according to most investigators they illustrate an important turning point in the development of the charge against the Christians. Whereas thus far the accusation has vaguely been described as cannibalism or, with a more mythological allure, as 'Thyestean banquets', Tertullian and Minucius clearly refer to child sacrifice as an initiatory rite performed by Christian neophytes. The interpretation of these testimonies, however, is beset with difficulties that have not yet been surmounted. To begin with, they do not seem to present independent reports of the same incident. Due to their important similarities, it is generally assumed that both expositions are related to each other.[42] The question whether Minucius depends upon Tertullian or

---

[39] A.A. Nancy, 'La forme originale de l'accusation d'anthropophagie contre les chrétiens, son développement et les changements de sa représentation au IIe siècle', *Revue des Études Augustiniennes* 47 (2001) 223-49 at 229-30; see Eusebius, *HE* 5.1.9.

[40] Eusebius, *HE* 5.1.14.1-9.

[41] Eusebius, *HE* 5.1.26: 'How could those to whom eating the blood of irrational beasts is not allowed eat children?'

[42] Another possibility is that both depended upon a common source. This theory, which was first defended by F. Wilhelm, 'De Minucii Felicis Octavio et Tertulliani Apologetico', *Breslauer philol. Abhandl.* 2 (1887), has received support from M. Sordi, 'L'apologia del martire romano Apollonio, come fonte dell' *Apologeticum* di Tertulliano e i rapporti fra Tertulliano e Minucio', *Rivista di Storia della Chiesa in Italia* 18 (1964) 169-88.

vice versa is still a matter of controversy today,[43] although in our opinion a comparison between both testimonies clearly speaks in favour of Tertullian's priority (below).

Beyond their mutual relationship, however, the accounts also present difficulties. With regard to Tertullian, the interpretation of his testimony is no simple matter since he deals with the issue in two different works and his accounts are always intertwined with a high degree of irony and sarcasm. With Minucius we do not even know the exact dates of his life, and his *Octavius* is roughly dated between 160 and 260.[44] An additional problem with his exposition is that he allegedly based (partially or totally?) his account on the Roman orator Fronto (above). Finally, his report, even though very similar to that of Tertullian, nevertheless presents important divergences. In the following, we shall analyse their testimonies separately.

In defending Christians from the numerous vices attributed to them by the pagans, Tertullian includes the following passage in the *Apology*:[45]

> Come, plunge your knife into the babe, enemy of none, accused of none, child of all; or if that is another's work, simply take your place beside a human being dying before he has really lived, await the departure of the lately given soul, receive the fresh young blood, saturate your bread with it, freely partake. Then while as you recline at table, take note of the places which your mother and your sister occupy; mark them well, so that when the dog-made

---

[43] See on the issue H. v. Geisau, 'Minucius Felix', *RE* Suppl. XI (1968) 988ff; Henrichs, 'Pagan Ritual', 25-26; M.E. Hardwick, *Josephus as a Historical Source in Patristic Literature through Eusebius* (Georgia, 1989) 19-23 and C. Tibiletti, 'Il problema della priorità Tertulliano-Minucio Felice', in J. Granarolo (ed.), *Hommage à R. Braun* II (Paris, 1990) 23-34.

[44] For this *terminus a quo*, based on Minucius' reference to Fronto, see A. Harnack, *Die Chronologie der altchristlichen Literatur bis Eusebius*, vol. 2 (Leipzig, 1904) 324. The *terminus ante quem* is based on Novatian's alleged use of the *Octavius* in his *De Trinitate*, see Harnack, ibid. and J. Beaujeu, *Minucius Felix: Octavius* (Paris, 1964) lxvii-lxviv, who suggested that Cyprian and the pseudo-Cyprianic *Ad Novatianum* depend upon the *Octavius*. Moreover, in his opinion, internal evidence suggests that the *Octavius* was composed after the persecution of the Church by Gallus and Volusion (251-253).

[45] Tertullian also deals with the issue in *Ad nat.* 1.7.20ff, although his exposition in this work is somewhat bewildering. The version of the *Apologeticum* includes exactly the same basic elements, but in a much clearer fashion. Owing to a lesser degree of irony, Tertullian's intention in the *Apology* is easier to follow. It seems as though Tertullian, aware of the confusing character of his earlier work, intended to provide a better organised and therefore more effective enunciation.

darkness has fallen on you, you may make no mistake, for you will be guilty of a crime, unless you perpetrate a deed of incest.[46]

According to most commentators, this text proves that the charges against Christians may have experienced a clear transformation at the beginning of the third century.[47] What used to be simply anthropophagy has now become ritual child sacrifice performed by neophytes in their initiation into Christian mysteries. But does this text allow such an interpretation? Isolated from its immediate context, this interpretation is certainly possible. A closer examination, however, shows that the passage in question is but the culmination of a longer section which must, consequently, be analysed as a whole. From this perspective, Tertullian appears to simply amplify and develop in a sarcastic manner the threefold accusation that we already know from the apologists of the second century.

The passage occupies the central segment of a longer section of the *Apology* (Chapters 7-9), in which Tertullian deals with the accusation. Whereas in chapter 7 he presents the charges against Christians and approaches them from different angles, in Chapter 9 he intends to turn them against the accusers. In this context, Chapter 8 – the chapter that includes our passage – has a clear transitional function, since it allows him to focus on his main goal: providing a number of examples of human sacrifice that will present it as a token of paganism.[48]

The beginning of Chapter 7 of the *Apology* is clear as to Tertullian's intention to refute the known threefold charge of anthropophagy, promiscuous banqueting and incest:

> Monsters of wickedness, we are accused of observing a holy rite in which we kill a little child and then eat it; in which, after the feast,

---

[46] Tertullian, *Apolog.* 8.2-3, cf. *Ad nat.* 1.7.31-32.

[47] Nancy, 'Forme originale', 231ff.

[48] As already pointed out (above note 45), Tertullian deals with the matter in two different places. A comparison between *Ad nationes* and the *Apology* is instructive in understanding the intention of Tertullian's recast. Whereas in the former work all the arguments are presented chaotically and are equally affected by a strong sarcasm, in the *Apology* they are conveniently organised into two sections and irony, when necessary, excluded. For example, the first of these sections, chapter 7, serves now as an introduction and the role of irony has been reduced to a minimum. In turn, the second section, in chapter 8, not only preserves the same degree of irony but also allows a more effective *reductio ad absurdum* in its last part, due to a better organisation of the material.

we practise incest, the dogs – our pimps, forsooth, overturning the lights and getting us the shamelessness of darkness for our impious lusts.[49]

After this opening, Tertullian immediately points out the fact that there has never been a true investigation; that no proof was ever furnished to substantiate the alleged crimes[50] and that no witnesses have ever provided testimony to support the charges.[51] The author then ironically describes Christianity as a mystery, comparable to known pagan mysteries, in order to rhetorically question how it is possible that those of the 'Christian mystery' are known to everyone, whereas the contents of other mystery rituals are unknown.[52] If the accusation nevertheless persists, the conclusion is obvious: it is simply rumour.[53]

Chapter 8 is completely dedicated to a parody of the threefold charge. This is facilitated by Tertullian's surreptitious presentation of Christianity as a 'mystery' in the previous Chapter. After referring to the promise of eternal life provided by the Christian mysteries,[54] Tertullian urges his addressee to join in their secret rites. It is in this context that the text quoted above is included. But just in case his sarcasm was not enough for his reader, Tertullian, loyal to his tiresome style, repeats it once again:

it is the custom for persons wishing initiation into sacred rites, I think, to go first of all to the master of them, that he may explain what preparations are to be made. Then, in this case, no doubt he would say, 'You must have a child still of tender age, that knows not what it is to die, and can smile under thy knife; bread, too, to collect the gushing blood; in addition to these, candlesticks, and lamps, and dogs – with tid-bits to draw them on to the extinguishing of the lights: above all things, you will require to bring your mother and your sister with you'.[55]

---

[49] Tertullian, *Apol.* 7.1, cf. *Ad nat.* 7.20. Even though an excess of sarcasm may obscure his intentions, the threefold charge can nevertheless be recognised in the enunciation.

[50] Tertullian, *Apol.* 7.2, cf. *Ad nat.* 7.21-22.

[51] Tertullian, *Apol.* 7.5-6.

[52] Tertullian, *Apolog.* 7.6-7, cf. *Ad nat.* 7.25-28.

[53] Tertullian, *Apol.* 7.8-14.

[54] On the issue Dölger, 'Sacramento infanticidii', 189-92.

[55] Tertullian, *Apol.* 8.7.

Besides, Tertullian's purpose is obvious in the opening to Chapter 9:
'To refute these charges more effectively, I will show that these
crimes are perpetrated by you both in public and in secret, which is
perhaps the reason that you have come to believe them about us
also'. He begins precisely by referring to the alleged child sacrifices
performed in Africa till Tiberius' time[56] and continues with some
mythical examples of infanticide. Even though he briefly speaks
about other known cases of cannibalism among barbarous peoples,
he finally returns to his time and place and focuses mainly on the
abortions practised by Romans. Had Tertullian presented the charge
against Christians as simple cannibalism, many of the examples
included in his counterattack would not have been effective. By
transforming it into child sacrifice and by presenting it as a part of a
Christian initiation ritual, he paves the way for his use of the numerous known instances (real or unreal) of ritual child sacrifice, notably
the alleged sacrifices in the temple of Saturn in North Africa.

Consequently, Tertullian's detailed description of the alleged initiation ritual should not be understood literally, i.e. as an echo of an
actual rumour, but rather as a parody or an intentional deformation
that had to serve his argument. Given the context and character of
this section of the *Apology*, his adaptation of the known threefold
charge perfectly suits the tenor and the intention of his own work,
which is an attack on paganism rather than a defence of Christianity
against pagan charges. This reading gains some support when one
notes that, as Dölger has already pointed out, Tertullian's description accurately follows the pattern of ancient initiation rituals[57] and
his vocabulary deliberately includes the terminology current in the
context of blood sacrifices.[58]

Incidentally, it is also interesting that Tertullian emphasises the
lack of witnesses and documents in order to sustain the charges, and
that no serious investigation had ever been instituted to substantiate
them.[59] In his opinion, the accusation has always been pure rumour.
This later affirmation indeed seems to support the suggestion,

---

[56] For Tertullian's deformation of facts in this particular, see Rives, 'Tertullian on
Child Sacrifice' (see above, note 2).

[57] See Dölger, 'Sacramentum infanticidii', 188 note 1, who refers to Apuleius, *Met.*
11.22; 23; see also Henrichs, 'Pagan Ritual', 25 and *Die Phoinikika*, 35, notes 34-38.

[58] See Dölger, 'Sacramentum infanticidii', 189 note 2 and, especially, 189-195;
Henrichs, *Die Phoinikika*, 35. See also *infra* note 63.

[59] Tertullian, *Apol.* 7.2.

pointed out above, that the accusation had an eminently popular nature and that it never actually acquired an official character.

The version by Minucius Felix presents many points of contact with that of Tertullian, although it also includes some divergences.[60] At first sight, these differences might seem to speak in favour of either the independence of Minucius' account or, at least, of his priority. However, as we will immediately see, this false impression is due to Minucius' reworking and adaptation of his source to the plan of his own work. After referring to 'secret and nocturnal rites' performed by Christians, Caecilius includes the following statement:

> Now the story about the initiation of young novices is as much to be detested as it is well known. An infant covered with meal, that it may deceive the unwary, is placed before him who is to be stained with their rites: this infant is slain by the young pupil, who has been urged on as if to harmless blows on the surface of the meal, with dark and secret wounds. Thirstily – O horror! they lick up its blood, eagerly they divide the limbs. By this victim they are pledged together; with this consciousness of wickedness they are covenanted to mutual silence.[61]

Minucius not only transforms the ritual pattern by adding new issues and eliminating others,[62] he also reinterprets the function and meaning of both the sacrifice and the partaking in the blood of the victim. In Minucius' version, child sacrifice is no longer the first step in an initiation into a mystery, but rather the means by which the participants in a conspiracy pledge faith to each other.[63] This reading is confirmed not only by the disappearance of every reference to a 'Christian mystery',[64] but also by Caecilius' introductory remark

---

[60] Beaujeu, *Minucius Felix*, liv-lv provides a complete list of the parallels between Minucius Felix and Tertullian; see also, more recently, Nancy, 'Forme originale', 232-36.

[61] Minucius Felix, *Oct.* 9.5.

[62] Regarding the additions, we may note the complete transformation of the ritual, the preparation of the victim and its sacrifice. See on the issue Henrichs, 'Pagan Ritual', 25-26 and *Die Phoinikika*, 35-36. Among the omissions, the most obvious are the promiscuous banquet and the incest, which are no longer conceived of as successive steps in the ritual and are, consequently, referred to somewhere else. For Minucius' transformation of his sources, see M.M. Sage, *Cyprian* (Philadelphia, 1975) 53.

[63] See Henrichs, 'Pagan Ritual', 35 note 33, who compares the last words of Minucius' passage in *Oct.* 9.5; see also ibid. 26 and note 37 for Henrichs' comparison of the function of the killing of the victim in Minucius with the Greek oath sacrifice.

[64] Tertullian opens the passage *Apolog.* 7.1 with the term *sacramentum* or 'holy rite', but the references are numerous in the whole section: see 7.6, *mysteriis silentii*,

regarding the 'secret and nocturnal rites', and certainly by his previous statement that Christians 'establish a herd of a profane conspiracy, which is tied together by nightly meetings, and solemn fasts,
and inhuman food.[65] In this sense, Minucius deconstructs Tertullian's *mise en scène* and connects the accusation with the Bacchanalia
scandal of 186 BC.

This reinterpretation obviously influences the form and the character of Octavius' reply in Chapter 30, which nevertheless presents
many echoes of Tertullian's text.[66] In fact, Octavius does not begin
his reply with the numerous instances of pagan child sacrifice as
Tertullian did. Rather, he focuses firstly on different cases of infanticide, notably those of abortions practised by Roman women, and
only then proceeds to refer to Saturn's devouring of his children. In
this manner it provides an aetiological explanation for his next reference, viz. the child sacrifices performed 'in different parts of Africa'
at Saturn's temples. It is in this context that he includes the numerous exempla of human sacrifices, also partially quoted by Tertullian,
which form the core of his reply. The mention of Catilina, finally,
allows him to change direction and to introduce cases of the consumption of human blood for medical purposes. The organisation of
this response appears to be more logical and effective than Tertullian's. The examples follow an ascending line that reaches the core of
Octavius' reply, namely human sacrifice by Romans, and then
descends again in order to finish with a couple of certainly disgusting but not very horrible examples. This conscious reorganisation of
the material is, in our opinion, the clearest proof of Minucius'
dependence upon Tertullian. If this interpretation is correct, the testimonies of both, Tertullian and Minucius Felix, do not seem to
imply any relevant change in the popular rumour about the Christians, which might still be as vague as those recorded by second century sources.

Origen documents the persistence of the accusations in the middle
of the third century. In his book against Celsus, he argues that the
charges of child sacrifice and incestuous unions were invented by

---

and the references to the mysteries of Samothrace and Eleusis; see also the beginning
of Chapter 8.1, *vitam eternam*; 8.4, *talia initiatus et consignatus vivis in aevum*; and,
finally, 8.7, *atque volentibus initiari* and *patrem illum sacrorum*. See also *Ad nat.* 1.15.2,
nos infanticidio litamus sive initiamus.

[65] Cf. Minucius Felix, *Oct.* 8.4.

[66] Compare Tertullian, *Apol.* 8.2 to Minucius Felix, *Oct.* 30.1.

the Jews and found good ground in the pagan mob ignorant of the word of God.[67] In his opinion, the accusation had its origin in popular rumours.

2

But if popular rumour is a possible explanation for the accusations against Christians, the same cannot be said about the charges of ritual infanticide and incest levelled by orthodox Christians against many different heretical groups. In contrast to the absolute absence of explicit pagan references to these indictments, polemic writings against heretics not only widely attest such charges but also provide meticulous and atrocious descriptions of the alleged rituals.

As early as the middle of the second century, Justin's *Apology* already documents the accusation against the Marcionites. After affirming that they wrongly called themselves 'Christians', he comments, 'Whether they do these shameful things described in rumours, the upsetting of the lamp and the licentious couplings and the meals of human flesh, we do not know'.[68] Justin does not pretend to have certain information,[69] but nevertheless, this is the first attempt to deflect the charges towards the heretics.

In line with Justin, Irenaeus also intends to turn the charges against the heretical Carpocratians, although he does not refer to specific vices and generally affirms that as Carpocratians 'practice every kind of impious act and godless deed', all Christians alike receive the blame for their conduct.[70] Clement of Alexandria refers to the Carpocratians as well, but even though his testimony is more explicit, he only refers to the promiscuity and incest.[71] However, it is Eusebius who not only reinforces these vague accusations but

---

[67] Origen, *C. Cels* 6.27.24-29 and 6.40. Origen's theory that Jews, who in their turn had also been accused of ritual murder by Apion (Josephus, *C. Apion.* II.92-6, cf. H. Jacobson, *Class. Quart.* 51, 2001, 318-9), were responsible for the origin of the slander was already pointed out by Justin (*Dial. c. Tryph.* 10.1; 17.1; 108.2) and would also be echoed in the third century by Commodianus (*Carmen Apologeticum* 847ff). Testimonies such as Clement's first letter (1Clem 5.2), Eusebius (*HE* 4.26.9) and Tertullian (*Apol.* 7.3) have further been adduced as support for the Jewish origin of the accusation, so Henrichs, 'Pagan Ritual', 22-24 and notes 21-29.

[68] Justin, *Apol.* 1.26.7.

[69] Edwards, 'Christian Immoralities', 72 note 4.

[70] Irenaeus, *Adv. haer.* 1.25.3-4.

[71] Clement of Alexandria, *Strom.* 3.2.10.1.

also gives them a specific form. Indeed, he asserts both that the Carpocratians committed all these crimes and that this is the reason why Christians were accused of having 'unlawful intercourse with mothers and sisters and eating unlawful meals'.[72]

From the fourth century onwards, the Montanists become the favourite goal of orthodox accusations. The first to record the allegation is Cyril of Jerusalem, although it has been suggested that the charge might have its origin in one of the apologetic works by Apollinaris of Hierapolis.[73] In a work written around 350, Cyril says that the Montanists 'slaughter the wretched little children of women and cut them up into unlawful meat for the sake of what among them are called mysteries'.[74] The story became widely diffused and appears, with slight differences, in the heresiological works of the fourth and fifth centuries. Epiphanius of Salamis records the charge, adds some macabre details and specifies that the real objective of the ritual was the blood of the victim. According to his testimony, the Montanists 'take a child, a mere infant, and pierce him throughout his body with bronze needles and so procure his blood for themselves, for the performance of a sacrifice'.[75] Philaster also records the story[76] and so does Augustine, who provides some additional details in his account as well.[77] The same charges appear in the letters of Isidore of Pelusium,[78] and we have to wait until Jerome's testimony to find the first scepticism regarding the accusation.[79]

However, the weirdest and most detailed exposition of the charges of ritual infanticide and incest against heretic groups appears in the *Panarion* by Epiphanius of Salamis. In his treatment of the customs of a Gnostic sect generally known as the Phibionites, Epiphanius reports that, after having sex with one another, if a woman becomes pregnant:

---

[72] Eusebius, *HE* 4.7.10-11; cf. 2.13.7 about the Simonians and 4.7.9 about the Nicolaits.

[73] J.B. Rives, 'The Blood Libel Against the Montanists', *Vigiliae Christianae* 50 (1996) 117-24 at 120-22; see, in general, P. de Labriolle, *Les sources de l'histoire du Montanisme* (Paris, 1913) and R.E. Heine, *The Montanist Oracles and Other Testimonia* (Macon, 1989).

[74] Cyril of Jersualem, *Catech.* 18.8.

[75] Epiphanius of Salamis, *Pan.* 48.14.5-6.

[76] Philaster, *Haer.* 49.

[77] Augustine, *Haer.* 26.7.

[78] Isidore of Pelusium, *Ep.* 1.242.

[79] Jerome, *Ep.* 41.4.1; Theodoretus of Cyrrhus, *Haer. fab. comp.* 3.2.

They extract the foetus at the stage appropriate for their enterprise, take this aborted infant, and cut it up into a trough shaped like a pestle. And they mix honey, pepper, and certain other perfumes and spices with it to keep from getting sick, and then all the revellers in this <herd> of swine and dogs assemble, and each eats a piece of the child with his fingers. And now, after this cannibalism, they pray to God and say, 'We were not mocked by the archon of lust, but have gathered the brother's blunder up!' And this, if you please, is their idea of the 'perfect Passover'.[80]

Even though some scholars consider that Epiphanius's report may reflect an actual ritual,[81] the horrific and exaggerated character of the story make this supposition rather unlikely.[82] It should be noted, furthermore, that the very same story, with a couple of disgusting additions, has turned up in the eighth century in the Great Book of Mandeans, but now told about Christians.[83]

Child sacrifice would also be attributed by Psellos to the Euchites and Gnostics, since he affirms that they kill children and threw them into the fire and then mixed their blood with their ashes and ate them. Before him, in the fifth century, Maruta of Maipherkat[84] accused the Borborians and, at the end of the eighth century, Theodor bar Konai did the same against the Manichaeans.[85] These testimonies are the last examples of the accusation in the context of inner conflicts within Christianity. From now on the accusation of child sacrifice would be directed towards the Jews. A clear sign of the new development appears in a recast of the *Acts of Andrew and Matthias in the City of Cannibals*, the so-called *Laudatio Andreae*, an anonymous composition probably written in the ninth or tenth century.[86] Whereas the original text speaks of the city of cannibals in general and simply calls

[80] Epiphanius of Salamis, *Pan.* 25.5.5-6.

[81] Notably Speyer, 'Zu den Vorwürfen', 129-31; Henrichs, 'Pagan Ritual, 28-29, although he points out that the alleged Gnostic rituals alone cannot account for the accusations; however, in his *Die Phoinikika*, 36 his opinion is less nuanced; Benko, 'Pagan Criticism', 1085-87.

[82] K. Rudolph, *Gnosis. The Nature and History of Gnosticism*, tr. R. MacLachlan Wilson (San Francisco, 1987) 249ff. See also Edwards, 'Christian Immoralities', 72.

[83] Great Book, 228, 14-27.

[84] O. Braun, *De sancta Nicaena synodo: Syrische Texte des Maruta von Maipherkat übersetzt* (Münster, 1898) 48.

[85] A. Adam, *Texte zum Maichäismus* (Berlin, 1954) 77.

[86] See M. Bonnet, 'Acta Andreae apostoli cum laudatione contexta', *Analecta Bollandiana* 13 (1894) 309-52.

its inhabitants anthropophagoi, 'man-eaters',[87] the *Laudatio* describes them not only as cannibals but also as Jews.[88] Thus, the accusations against the Jews experience exactly the same evolution as those issued against Christians and heretics. What in the beginning was anthropophagy gradually became the well-known myth of the ritual murder of children. This myth would be responsible for the persecutions of Jews in the Middle Ages and the numerous processes against them from the twelfth to the sixteenth centuries on the charge of child murder.

3

Studies of the charges of child sacrifice against the early Christians tend to give credit to these reports by orthodox writers and suggest that actual ritual Gnostic practices might have provided grounds for the appearance of the accusation. In the 1930s, and after an exhaustive analysis of the evidence, Dölger proposed five possible origins for the accusations, among which the 'Gnostic theory' made its first appearance:[89]

1. The alleged ritual murder performed by the Jews was later on extended to Christians.
2. The Greek and old-Italic oath sacrifice with a human victim as the ritual foundation of a *coniuratio*.
3. Ritual infanticide for magical purposes.
4. Actual initiation rituals performed by Gnostics.
5. Misunderstanding of the Eucharist.

Until the end of the twentieth century, studies on the issue curiously remained within the framework established by Dölger and either presented a combination of these factors or else chose one of them to state their point. Thus, for example, Wolfgang Speyer in 1963, even though admitting that it was not the only reason, argued that the use of Syrian and Egyptian Gnostics was a determinant in the genesis of the accusation.[90]

---

[87] Bonnet, *Acta Apostolorum Apocrypha* II/1 (Leipzig, 1898) 65-127.
[88] Bonnet, 'Acta Andreae cum laudatione contexta', 317.13-319.2 at 318.14ff.
[89] Dölger, 'Sacramentum infanticidii', 227f.
[90] Speyer, 'Zu den Vorwürfen', 130.

In 1967, Rudolph Freudenberger, in turn, argued that the first and the second possibilities proposed by Dölger were already combined before the charge was pressed against Christians. He traced the motif back to 2, namely to the *coniuratio*, as he considered that the third and fifth explanations may simply be attributed to Fronto and that the fourth alternative is impossible because the accusation existed long before the appearance of Gnostics.[91]

In his studies from 1970 and 1972, Albert Henrichs presents a synthesis of both previous approaches.[92] After combining 1 and 2 in the same way as Freudenberger, he suggests that although the Jews were responsible for the extension of the charge to Christians, its contents proceed from similar ritualistic practices of pagan origin. Ritual practices actually committed by Gnostics, however, might have provided grounds for the accusation against the whole Church.

In 1980 Stephen Benko adopted approximately the same approach. He combined 1 and 5 and thus concluded that Jews were responsible for the first accusation against Christians. Fronto's misinterpretation of the Eucharist further supported the defamation. In his view, however, the suspicion that Christians in general were guilty of *flagitia* could only arise from the actual committing of the crime by Gnostics.[93]

Excluding Freudenberger, consequently, all these scholars take actual Gnostic practices as the origin of the slanders. This explanation is certainly striking since it seems to obviate the fact that later on the same or very similar accusations would be extended against the Jews. In the case of the medieval blood libel against the Jews, which practices, and performed by whom, were the origin of the slanders? But the most remarkable thing about this explanation is that while no single scholar gives credit to the charges when they are pressed against mainstream Christians, most investigators do tend to believe them when told about heretics.[94] However, this is perhaps not as strange as it may seem, since in a last analysis these splinter

---

[91] Freudenberger, 'Der Vorwurf', 106-07.

[92] Henrichs, 'Pagan Ritual' and *Die Phoinikika*, respectively.

[93] Benko, 'Pagan Criticism', 1084-85 and 1087.

[94] Already C. Schmidt, *Gnostische Schriften in koptischer Sprache aus dem Codex Brucianus* (Leipzig, 1892) 573ff. gave credit to Epiphanius' account on the grounds of his direct knowledge of the Egyptian sects. Despite the reservations of Dölger, 'Sacramentum infanticidii', 220-21, Speyer, *passim*, and Benko, 'Pagan Criticism', 1085-87 accept Epiphanius' report as trustworthy.

groups are still today frequently seen as representatives of a deviant way of thought concerning the orthodox standard values.[95] Even though the reliability of the accounts of the fathers of the Church has recently been seriously questioned,[96] their black and white testimony concerning Gnostics is still seen by many as normative.

Consequently a new approach is necessary, and in 1992 M.J. Edwards, following a suggestion by Marcel Detienne,[97] compared early Christian ethics with the rejection of social and religious standard values by the Cynics.[98] After refuting one by one the five possibilities suggested by Dölger, Edwards surmised that the accusations were maliciously inferred from the Christian disdain of social customs, which was expressed in two very public shows of abstinence – from the altar and from the bed.

J.B. Rives developed this line of investigation in a comprehensive and excellent paper about human sacrifice among pagans and Christians.[99] He claimed an understanding of 'the stories told about Christians not as distorted accounts of an actual practice, but as accurate if metaphorical accounts of the Christians' place in Greco-Roman society'. According to Rives, then, instead of relating the charges against Christians with this or that practice, they should be placed in the wider context of Greco-Roman discourse about civilisation and religion.

These two scholars, however, mainly explained how or why the accusation was levelled against the early Christians and left aside the origin of the charges by orthodox Christians both against heretics and Jews. Edwards comments in passing that the extension of the charges of cannibalism against the heretics may have arisen from an orthodox attempt to deflect the charges originally levelled against them onto different splinter groups.[100] Similarly, Rives considers that this might be the origin of the charges against the Montanists.[101] Our

---

[95] The so-called inner Gnostic polemics in *Pistis Sophia* 147 and the *Second Book of Jeu* 43 (Schmidt, *Gnostische Schriften*, 196), sometimes adduced as a proof for the existence of these rites, only attest, if at all, sexual practices of libertine sects, but certainly not the charge of child sacrifice.

[96] M.A. Williams, *Rethinking Gnosticism: an argument for dismantling a dubious category* (Princeton, 1996); K.L. King, *What is Gnosticism?* (Cambridge Mass., 2003).

[97] M. Detienne, *Dionysos mis à mort* (Paris, 1977) 108ff.

[98] Edwards, 'Christian Immoralities'.

[99] Rives, 'Human Sacrifice', 65-67 and 83ff.

[100] Edwards, 'Christian Immoralities'.

[101] Rives, 'The Blood Libel', 120.

evidence, however, seems to indicate the contrary. On the one hand, we have seen that explicit references to the charges from the pagan side are rather scarce, if not wholly nonexistent, and that these are mainly attested by Christian sources. On the other, we have also seen that orthodox accusations against heretics and the alleged pagan charges against Christians appear exactly at the same time, namely in the second century. Is it not possible to think, then, that it was the other way around? If mainstream Christians fallaciously accused other Christian groups whom they considered heretical of committing all kind of crimes, these accusations may easily have reached pagan ears. Given that pagans would not necessarily distinguish between Christian sects, if there were in fact rumours about secret child sacrifices performed by Christians it is very plausible that they were simply repeating what Christians were saying about other Christians.[102] Consequently, on the basis of our evidence the question arises whether we are not just dealing with an exclusively Christian motif.

In the first pages of his *Homo necans*, W. Burkert asserted that 'blood and violence lurk fascinatingly at the very heart of religion'.[103] Two thousand years earlier, Lucretius, the great Roman poet, seems to have held the same opinion. Indeed, after praising his master Epicurus for freeing humanity from the fear of the gods, Lucretius begins an indictment against the crimes of religion (*scelerosa atque impia facta*), the core of which is the narration of Agamemnon's sacrifice of his daughter Iphianassa, a lesser known variant of Iphigenia.[104]

But Burkert also suggestively asserted that the death of God's innocent son for the redemption of humanity shows that murder is also at the core of Christianity. Two recent studies on human sacrifice in two remote contexts come to similar conclusions. We are referring to P. Tierney's *The Highest Altar* and to R.P. Hsia, *The Myth of Ritual Murder. Jews and Magic in Reformation Germany*. In commenting on

---

[102] So already Dölger, 'Sacramentum infanticidii', 217 and 223, although with reservations.

[103] W. Burkert, *Homo Necans. Interpretationen altgriechischer Opferriten und Mythen* (Berlin/New York, 1972) 8.

[104] See now J.N. Bremmer, 'Sacrificing a Child in Ancient Greece: the case of Iphigeneia', in E. Noort and E.J.C. Tigchelaar (eds), *The Sacrifice of Isaac* (Leiden, 2001) 21-43; G. Ekroth, 'Inventing Iphigeneia? On Euripides and the Cultic Construction of Brauron', *Kernos* 16 (2003) 59-118.

a recent case of ritual murder committed by individuals belonging to the 'Evangelical Army of Chile', the first author states that 'The core of human-sacrifice ideology is that a surrogate victim in one way or another saves others by his or her death. Christians believe they are saved by the blood of the sacrificed Jesus. If God the Father sacrificed His own Son (...), to save humanity from the power of Satan', he argues, 'a simple person (...) might not see any difference in driving a stake through her own son to save her father and vanquish the demonic powers threatening the community...'.[105] According to Hsia, the medieval blood libel against the Jews had a similar background. 'The essential underlying ritual-murder-discourse was the Christian belief in sacrifice, the dominant form of its representation being the story of Christ's Passion. In accusing the Jews of child murders, and in extracting confessions from the suspects, the magistrates and the people thus created repetitions and variations on the theme of Christian sacrifice. The tortured Christian children, the bleeding little martyrs, and the abused Eucharist became symbols by which a society created its own moments and loci of sanctity'.[106] It should be noted that most accusations against the Gnostics worked on the same elements and seem to present exactly the same background.

In our view, the persistence and recurrence of the accusations of child sacrifice against or by the Christians not only shows that the motif may very well be a typically Christian one, but also offers indirect evidence for the relevance of an obscure myth that – whether well founded or unfounded – has accompanied Christianity throughout its 2000 years of history.

---

[105] P. Tierney, *The Highest Altar. The History of Human Sacrifice* (New York, 1989) 368-69.

[106] R.P. Hsia, *The Myth of Ritual Murder. Jews and Magic in Reformation Germany* (New Haven and London, 1988) 226f.

V. CHILD SACRIFICE IN ANCIENT ISRAEL: THE STATUS QUAESTIONIS

Ed Noort

The last five years have heralded a change in the way we regard violence and the willingness of men and women to sacrifice themselves.
The attack on the Twin Towers of the World Trade Centre in New
York 2001 succeeded because nobody expected hijackers to fly into
the towers themselves without the chance to escape. The same
applies to the suicide attacks in Israel since the start of the second
intifada in 2000. Of course, there are also many examples in the past,
from the Jewish defenders of Massada in 73 AD to the Japanese
kamikaze pilots of the Second World War.[1] However, never on this
scale and with such enormous effect. We have to deal with the fact
that young men and women are prepared to sacrifice themselves in
the strong belief that they are fighting a just war even if they are
killing non-combatants.

The methodologically interesting question is: does this radical
change in how human life is valued change our own view of the
past too? In relation to our subject: is sacrificing one's own life or
that of loved ones part of the reality of the belief system in Ancient
Israel? I am not wholly sure, but I guess that the willingness to
accept a praxis of child sacrifice in the past because of experiences
today, is growing.

There seem to be two barriers to this acceptance, however. First,
there is the psychological barrier – the texts involved are still relevant to many communities of faith today. Human sacrifice is something difficult for them to deal with. Secondly, where the Hebrew
Bible speaks about child sacrifice it is always referring to 'others',
other people, other gods. The main stream of religions emerging
from the Hebrew Bible has nothing to do with it at all.

---

[1] See Harimoto, this volume, Ch. XII.4.

So what has changed? It is not only the fact that we are now experiencing the devastating power of self-sacrifice and viewing what could have happened in the past with different eyes. Maybe the most important reason is that our view of Israel's religious past has changed. The picture of the black-and-white oppositions between Baalism and Yahwism has disappeared. Israel and Judah's religious experience must have been more colourful than the Deuteronomistic pictures tell us.

Dealing with child sacrifice

A study of the historical and ideological backgrounds of human sacrifice in Ancient Israel can resort only to literary sources,[2] of which the Hebrew Bible with all its problems of interpretation and dating is the most prominent. Palestine itself does not provide any desperately needed conclusive archaeological evidence. Therefore we have to involve the world outside Palestine. Here, with the help of indirect links, cemeteries in Carthage can play an important role in the discussion thanks to Punic inscriptions.

The first real problem is the canonical character of the texts referring to child sacrifice. They all have a history of their own and their own ideological context; none of them are eye-witness reports which can be trusted historically; they were consolidated at a given time and, finally, they have been passed down as a canon. In this final text, it is transparently clear that every human sacrifice was considered ultimately detestable. Texts deploring child or human sacrifice are the climax of a movement framed by prophetical complaints

---

[2] O. Eissfeldt, *Molk als Opferbegriff im Punischen und Hebräischen und das Ende des Gottes Moloch* (Halle, 1935); P.G. Mosca, *Child Sacrifice in Canaanite and Israelite Religion: A Study in Molk and mlk* (Diss. Harvard, 1975); H.P. Müller, 'mlk', in *Theol. Wört. z. Alt. Test.* IV (1984) 957-68; G.C. Heider, *The Cult of Molek: A Reassessment* (Sheffield, 1985); J. Day, *Molech. A God of Human Sacrifice in the Old Testament* (Cambridge, 1989); H.P. Müller, 'Genesis 22 und das *mlk*-Opfer', *Bibl. Zs.* 41 (1997) 237-46; G.C. Heider, 'Molech', in K. van der Toorn *et al.* (eds), *Dictionary of Deities and Demons in the Bible* (Leiden, 1999²) 581-5; H.P. Müller, 'Malik', *ibidem*, 538-42; K. Koch, 'Molek astral', in A. Lange *et al.* (eds), *Mythos im Alten Testament und seiner Umwelt. Festschrift für Hans-Peter Müller zum 65. Geburtstag* (Berlin and New York, 1999) 29-50. For a non-sacrificial interpretation see M. Weinfeld, 'The Worship of Moloch and the Queen of Heaven and Its Background', *Ugaritische Forschungen* 4 (1972) 133-54; M. Weinfeld, 'Burning Babies in Ancient Israel. A Rejoinder to Morton Smith's Article in *JAOS* 95 (1975), 477-79', *ibidem* 10 (1978) 411-13; D. Platorati, 'Zum Gebrauch des Wortes *mlk* im Alten Testament, *Vetus Testamentum* 28 (1978) 286-300.

about ethical behaviour in which the ritual of sacrifice as a whole is criticized:

> Even though you offer me (YHWH) your burnt offerings[3] (*'olot*) and grain offerings (*minḥotekèm*), I will not accept them, and the offering of the well-being[4] (*šèlèm*) of your fatted animals I will not look upon! (*Amos* 5.22)

What started here with a criticism of the usual offerings in the eighth century BC by Amos ends in the sixth century with what is experienced at that time as the most abominable offering: child sacrifice. The existence of texts about child sacrifice in the own tradition and handing over those texts with a supposed religious validity to the next generation leaves only two solutions:

1. To describe the 'otherness' of the sacrificer and the deity to whom the child is sacrificed. They must be foreign to the own (religious) community.
2. To characterise the bogeyman in the own community as a child sacrificer.

Child sacrificers are by definition religiously and culturally 'other', or acknowledged villains from the own history.

Concerning the first solution, the Hebrew Bible uses four ways to restrict child sacrifice to the religious world outside a faithful Israel. The first scheme is a chronological one, where child sacrifice belongs to the gods of pre-Israelite Canaan. Israel is warned about taking over this religious custom or accused of having mixed with the pre-Israelite inhabitants, e.g. *Deuteronomy* 12.31: 'You must not do the same for YHWH your god, because every abhorrent thing that YHWH hates they (the Canaanites) have done for their gods. They would even burn their sons and daughters in the fire to their gods.' In the eyes of the Deuteronomists, child sacrifice was only a danger for Israel if it adopted the religious customs of the Canaanites. Their gods could demand human sacrifices. For YHWH, however, it was an abomination, he hated it. The technical term for the sacrifice is the remarkable 'to burn in fire' (*śāraf bā-'eš*).

---

[3] The textual difficulty of v.22a calls for a missing second part of the verse. The whole tone of the passage is negative. The addition (cf. BHK, BHS app.) of a possible exception for the *'olot* by a glossator is implausible.

[4] Only singular here, usually it is *zèvaḥ šĕlāmim* (pl.).

The second category of foreign deities referred to as receivers of child sacrifices are contemporaries, described generally as 'idols'. These idols, probably represented by phallic symbols, are used in the simile of the unfaithful wife from *Ezekiel* 16.[5] The accusation runs: 'And you (Jerusalem) took your sons and your daughters, whom you had borne to me,[6] and you sacrificed them to be consumed. Were your harlotries so small a matter, that you (also) slaughtered my sons and delivered them up as an offering (by fire) to them?' (v. 20-1). In the preceding verses Jerusalem has misused the gifts of YHWH, making illegal sacred places (v. 16), sacred images (v. 17) and phallic symbols (v. 18-9). The climax of the complaint is child sacrifice. The terminology used is 'to slaughter' (*šāḥaṭ*) and 'to make [sons/daughters] pass (through fire)', ([the usual *bā-'eš* is lacking here] *hè'ĕvīr*).

The third scheme ascribes child sacrifice to the most prominent rival of YHWH, Ba'al. *Jeremiah* 19.5 states explicitly: 'They (Judah/ Jerusalem) have built shrines to Ba'al, to burn their sons in fire as burnt offerings (*'olot*) to Ba'al, which I (YHWH) did not command or require, and which I never contemplated.' The same formulation without Ba'al, but with the topographical specification of the Topheth in the valley of Ben Hinnom, to which we will return later, is used in *Jeremiah* 7.31.

The fourth way of labelling child sacrifice as a foreign tradition is the characterization as a *mlk*-offering. Due to the translations of the *Septuaginta* and *Vulgata*, *mlk* became Moloch and was understood as a separate deity to whom children were sacrificed. Most modern translations handle the expression in this way. Opposition to this sacrifice can be seen in the Holiness Code, e.g. 'You shall not have (any of) your offspring pass as a *mlk*-sacrifice and so profane the name of your god: I am YHWH' (*Leviticus* 18.21, cf. 20.2-5).[7] The antithesis between (Deuteronomistic) Israel and the supposed child-eating deity is stressed by the reform actions of the ideal king of

---

[5] *Ezekiel* 16 uses the verb *zānā*, 'to prostitute, to play the harlot' 12 times, the most dense concentration of the verb in the prophetic book.

[6] *lī* 'me' in the Massoretic text is lacking in the *Septuaginta*, probably for dogmatic reasons.

[7] NRSV: 'You shall not give any of your offspring to sacrifice them to Molech'; Luther-Translation 1984: 'Du sollst auch nicht eins deiner Kinder geben, dass es dem Moloch geweiht werde....; Nederlands Bijbelgenootschap: 'en gij zult geen van uw kinderen overgeven, om het aan den Moloch te wijden...'

Judah, Josiah, in 2 Kings 23.10: 'He (Josiah) defiled Topheth, which is in the valley of Ben-Hinnom, so that none would make a son or a daughter pass through fire as a *mlk*-offering.' We will return to the *mlk*-offering later. For the moment it is enough to note that large parts of the traditions have connected child sacrifice with a foreign, pagan deity Moloch/Molech.

The second solution, to ascribe child sacrifice to persons judged negatively by the Deuteronomists, can easily be demonstrated. The following is said about King Ahaz: 'He (Ahaz) even made his son pass through fire, according to the abominable practices of the nations whom YHWH drove out before the people of Israel' (2 *Kings* 16.3). Here the king of Judah is portrayed as a man who does not listen to Isaiah (*Isaiah* 7.1ff.) and the divine word of the prophet during a politically life-threatening crisis. Such a king is painted black and accused of having his own son sacrificed. By doing so, he has acted like the pre-Israelite Canaanites with their 'abominable practices'[8] (see above, chronological solution).

The message is clear. YHWH has driven away the people who performed abominations, such as making their sons pass through fire. But now a king of Judah was accused of doing the same. The conclusion of this accusation is obvious. Just as YHWH drove away the foreign nations, so will he with his own people. Exile is in the air.

The second king accused of child sacrifice is Manasseh, the predecessor of the ideal king Josiah. In the catalogue of the sins of Manasseh, 2 *Kings* 21.6 relates: 'He made his son pass through fire; he practiced soothsaying and augury, and dealt with mediums and with wizards....Manasseh misled them (Judah) to do more evil than the nations had done that YHWH destroyed before the people of Israel' (v. 9). Here, the chronological argument is used in a more negative way, as is the case with Ahaz. Manasseh did even more evil than the pre-Israelites. The catalogue of sins is a stereotypical one – the Deuteronomistic authors desperately needed Manasseh to be a great sinner. Otherwise the king after him could not reform the Yahwistic cult in the radical way he is supposed to have done and earn the praise of the Deuteronomists: 'There was no king like him (Josiah), who turned to YHWH with all his heart, with all his soul,

---

[8] The 'chronological' argument is used only for Ahaz, Manasseh and Rehobeam (1 *Kings* 14.24). Rehobeam is accused of promoting male temple prostitution, not of child sacrifice.

and with all his might, according to all the law of Moses; nor did any like him arise after him' (2 *Kings* 23.25). The relationship between Manasseh and Josiah in both ideological portrayals is rightly described by Spieckermann: 'Weil Manasse mit dem Massstab Josias gemessen wird…ist es nicht widersinnig Manasse, den Vorgänger des Reformators Josia, einen Gegenreformator zu nennen. Was historisch barer Unsinn wäre, ist literarisch möglich, denn die Deuteronomistische Charakterisierung Manasses ist von Josias Reform her und folglich auch auf sie hin gestaltet.'[9]

To sum up, the tendency to declare child sacrifice a foreign institution belonging to Canaanites, idols, Baʿal and 'Molech' keeps this phenomenon outside the domain of the YHWH religion. Within the own tradition, the already negative portraits of Ahaz and Manasseh are intensified by the accusation of child sacrifice. The polemical and ideological character of the texts complicates every historical analysis.

Not only the texts themselves make it difficult to analyse the possible historical background to the practice of child sacrifice in Judah. Hidden behind the mask of objective scholarship, personal preferences and ethical and religious views play an enormous role in judging text and reality. At the beginning of the twentieth century, a dissertation focusing on the history of religion was written, defending the impossibility of a relationship between the YHWH religion and human sacrifice: 'Wer möchte da die Stirne haben, zu behaupten, die Geistesheroen des Alten Testaments, die Propheten, seien aus einer Menschenmörderbande hervorgegangen? Sowenig eine schöne Blume aus dem Kot wächst, obgleich sie Erde und Dünger zu ihrer äusseren Existenz bedarf, so gewiss sie aus sich selbst und aus ihrem Keime sich entwickelt, so gewiss ist auch, dass der reine Jahvedienst der Propheten nicht ein reformierter Molochdienst gewesen ist, sondern schon bei seinem ersten Erwachen in einer ganz anderen Ideeenwelt stand.'[10] For this scholar, human or child sacrifice belonged to a world totally different from the world of the prophets. The foreign allocation of the phenomenon pushed forward by the Deuteronomistic and priestly authors is taken for granted.

---

[9] H. Spieckermann, *Juda unter Assur in der Sargonidenzeit* (Göttingen, 1982) 161.
[10] E. Mader, *Die Menschenopfer der alten Hebräer und der benachbarten Völker. Ein Beitrag zur alttestamentlichen Religionsgeschichte* (Diss. Freiburg/Breisgau, 1909).

This is the view of the majority of modern scholars too. It is not by accident that the standard works of reference have no or only a short passage about child sacrifice within the entry 'sacrifice'. *Pars pro toto*, we may refer to the *Anchor Bible Dictionary*. G.A. Anderson gives a good overview of the sacrificial theories, especially from the priestly source (P). Although he writes about 'prophetic critique', he only discusses that critique in general.[11] There is no reference to child or human sacrifice. Only the entry 'Molech' produces the information longed for and is linked to the entries 'Tophet' and 'Cult of the dead'.[12] The idea behind it is crystal clear. Cultic sacrifice in Ancient Israel had nothing to do with child sacrifice. The theme of child sacrifice does not appear in the authoritative German *Religion in Geschichte und Gegenwart* either.[13]

The biblical material
The books of Kings

Starting with the literary sources, the debate itself concentrates on three themes: 1) child sacrifice, sometimes connected to 2) sacrifice of the firstborn, and 3) human sacrifice as a general background. In fact, there is only one text that we can locate historically without doubt. In this text the polemic tendencies against child sacrifice are missing because Israel itself is involved only indirectly. Therefore, this text may partly reflect a historical event, not necessarily linked, however, to the two kings mentioned here: Jehoram and Jehoshaphat.[14] Framed by the Elisha miracle stories, 2 *Kings* 3.25ff. tells about the campaign of Israel, Judah and Edom against King Mesha of Moab and the siege of the capital Kir Haresheth (el-Kerak) in the ninth century BC. The text continues:

[11] G.A. Anderson, 'Sacrifice and Sacrificial Offerings', in *Anchor Bible Dictionary* V (New York, 1992) 870-86.

[12] G.C. Heider, 'Molech', in *Anchor Bible Dictionary* IV (New York, 1992) 895-8.

[13] A. Marx, 'Opfer (Vorderer Orient und Altes Testament)', in *Religion in Geschichte und Gegenwart*[4] VI (Tübingen, 2003) 572-6. An exception is H. Seebass, 'Opfer II', in *Theologische Realenzyklopädie* XXV (Berlin, 1995) 258-67 at 260.

[14] The striking parallels between 1 *Kings* 22 and 2 *Kings* 3 and the schematic elements of 2 *Kings* 3 (three kings; seven days, every city conquered, every tree felled, all the water wells stopped) do not favour the historical interpretation of 2 *Kings* 3.4-25a, cf. J.R. Bartlett, 'The "united" campaign against Moab in 2 Kgs 3:4-27', in J.F.A. Sawyer and D.J.A. Clines (eds), *Midian, Moab and Edom. The History and the Archaeology of late Bronze and Iron Age Jordan and North-West Arabia* (Sheffield, 1983) 135-46.

26. And the king of Moab saw that the fighting was too hard[15] for him, and he took with him[16] seven hundred swordsmen to break through, opposite the king of Edom[17], but they could not. 27. Then he took his firstborn son who was to succeed him and offered him as a burnt offering (*wayya'alehu 'olā*) on the wall. And great wrath came upon Israel, so they withdrew from him and returned to their own land.

The fact that this text is focused upon an 'other', the Moabite king, is probably the reason for the natural place in the narrative. No Israelite or Judean king needs to be defended or attacked. After the failure of his attempted escape, the Moabite king seizes a desperate last resort and sacrifices his eldest son, the heir-apparent, on the wall. Chemosh, the national god of Moab, receives the sacrifice and transfers his anger to the enemies outside the walls. Chemosh, who had punished Moab through the victory of Israel, now turns his great wrath against Israel, which is left with no other choice than to flee. In order to transfer the divine anger from Moab to Israel, the crown prince is sacrificed on the wall, where not only the deity but also the enemies may watch the spectacle. It is interesting to see that the Hebrew narrator has no doubt at all about the effectiveness of the sacrifice of the firstborn. He mentions it without any hesitation or comment.

This is different in the case of another 'historical' text which is regularly mentioned in the debate about child sacrifice: the cursing of Jericho in *Josh* 6:26 and its fulfilment in *1 Kings* 16.34. The texts read:[18]

---

[15] Read *ḥzqh*.

[16] Read *'tw*.

[17] The conjectural emendation of Edom > Aram by J. Gray, *I & II Kings* (London, 1997³) 484 is unnecessary.

[18] For details see E. Noort, 'Joshua, The History of Reception and Hermeneutics', in J.C. de Moor and H.F. van Rooy (eds), *Past, Present, Future: The Deuteronomistic History and the Prophets* (Leiden, 2000) 199-215 at 207ff.

Joshua 6.26	1 Kings 16.34
26Aa Joshua let them swear the following oath 26Ab in those days: 26Ba "Cursed [before YHWH] be the man, 26Bb who undertakes to build up this city [Jericho] (again). 26Bc at the cost of his firstborn he shall lay its foundations, 26Bd and at the cost of his youngest, he shall set up its gates."	34A In his days Hiel the Bethelite rebuilt Jericho. 34Ba At the cost of Abiram, his first born, he laid its foundation, 34Bb and at the cost of Segub, his youngest, he set up its gates. 34Bc According to the word of YHWH, 34Bd which he had spoken 34Be by the service of Joshua, the son of Nun.

In the *Septuaginta* version of *Joshua* 6.26 'before YHWH' is missing (26Ba) as is the explanation of the object Jericho (26Bb). The reading is supported by the Dead Sea Scrolls (4Q175, 4Q379 22ii). If this is the original reading, it seems probable that the curse and the note of its fulfilment originate from *1 Kings* 16.34.[19] Arguments in favour of this are the unknown Bethelite Hiel and his sons Abiram and Segub, and the explicit mention of Jericho, which is necessarily mentioned in *1 Kings* 16.34, but is superfluous in Joshua 6.26 because it is very clear which city is cursed. This also applies to 'before YHWH'. According to *1 Kings* 16.34, the curse is explicitly the word of YHWH (34Bc), so there the phrase is not needed. If *Joshua* 6.26 derived from *1 Kings* 16.34 the addition 'before YHWH' seeks to demonstrate that the curse is the word of YHWH indeed. So the *Septuaginta* version also supports the primacy of *1 Kings* 16.34 based on content.[20]

---

[19] W. Dietrich, *Prophetie und Geschichte: Eine redaktionsgeschichtliche Untersuchung zum Deuteronomistischen Geschichtswerk* (Göttingen, 1972) 110-2; K. Bieberstein, *Josua-Jordan-Jericho: Archäologie, Geschichte und Theologie der Landnahmeerzählungen Josua 1-6* (Fribourg and Göttingen, 1995) 394-7 *contra* R. Then, *'Gibt es denn keinen mehr unter den Propheten?' Zum Fortgang der alttestamentlichen Prophetie in frühjüdischer Zeit* (Frankfurt, 1990) 98-103.

[20] This raises new questions, for the *Septuaginta* in *Joshua* 6.26 has an extensive addition, with a note of fulfilment that, however, differs from *1 Kings* 16.34, while certain manuscripts of the *Septuaginta* (boc₂e₂) do not have a note of fulfilment in *1*

What is the background of this report and the curse? Is the wide-spread opinion that a building sacrifice is presupposed here correct? Should we add *1 Kings* 16.34 to the texts demonstrating child or human sacrifice? The answer is probably not. In contrast to the bib-lical view and to the curse, Jericho was inhabited during the Iron Age. It was most likely an accident that happened during the expan-sion from village to city that formed the historical basis for the curse.[21] The main reason for thinking of an accident is the obscurity of the names of the rebuilder and his sons. They are totally unknown. If a building sacrifice had played any role here, the names of the sons of Ahab, i.e. the evil king par excellence, would have appeared. On the other hand, if the event was pure fiction, the nar-rator would have seized the opportunity to fill in the names of the sons of any king, not the names of a moderate man from Bethel. The accident, however, is explained as a curse. This curse is connected with great skill and precision to the Ahab stories.[22] What is told here is a fatal accident, not a sacrifice. The accident has to demonstrate the power of the curse of Joshua.

The later prophets

The really exciting texts, however, can be found in the prophetic cor-pora of the exilic priest-prophet Ezekiel, living in Babylon from 597 on, and his somewhat older contemporary Jeremiah, who was not deported to Babylon but stayed in Judah. Later he was forced by a group of oppositionists to go to Egypt, where he probably died. In the corpus of the priest-prophet Ezekiel, torah, statutes and laws play an important role. Then, suddenly, in *Ezekiel* 20.25-6, the most peculiar sentence on the role of torah in the Hebrew Bible appears:

> 25. I (YHWH) also gave to them (Israel) bad statutes and laws, through which they could NOT live! 26. and I (YHWH) made them unclean through their offerings, when they offered (*bĕ-ha'avīr*) all the firstborn (by fire) – that I might fill them with horror.

Kings 16.34. Parts of the tradition of *Septuaginta* render the fulfilment of the curse immediately with *Joshua* 6.26. This does not make the matter any easier, however, because this fulfilment is not a duplicate of *1 Kings* 16.34.

[21] Archaeological evidence: H. and M. Weippert, 'Jericho in der Eisenzeit', *Zs. Deutschen Palestina Ver.* 92 (1976) 105-48. Textual evidence: *Joshua* 16.1,7; 18.12, 21; *2 Samuel* 10.5; *2 Kings* 2.4, 5, 18-22.

[22] C. Conroy, 'Hiel between Ahab and Elijah-Elisha: 1 Kgs 16:34 in its immediate literary context', *Biblica* 77 (1996) 210-8.

It is YHWH himself who provides the laws leading to death instead of life.[23] He allows Israel to taint itself by the sacrifice of the first-born. The verb *hè'ĕvīr* is used, its basic meaning being '(to have) ... pass through'. This verb is used for the law concerning the firstborn who, as YHWH's property, has to be released by the sacrifice of an animal. At the same time it forms the *terminus technicus* for 'to pass through the fire', the expression for child sacrifice. This double use of the verb *hè'ĕvīr* leads to a conscious mingling of both interpretations of the verb. The bad statutes of v. 25 lead to the way of death. In v. 26 this is interpreted as a real child sacrifice of the firstborn. The combination of both verses leads to the unique conclusion that it was YHWH himself who ordered the death of the firstborn, giving 'bad statutes' and deadly laws.

The relationship between the firstborn offering and child sacrifice returns in *Ezekiel* 16.20-1, the text already mentioned above. It should be clear that Ezekiel and the traditions surrounding him (Holiness code *Leviticus* 18.21, 20.2-5) consider child sacrifice as *to'evā* 'abomination'. So in general child sacrifice was transferred to the 'other gods' for ethnic-religious reasons. Whoever sacrificed children did so to please 'other gods'. But the enigmatic *Ezekiel* 20.5-6 leaves the possibility wide open that it was YHWH himself who issued laws and ordinances connected to child sacrifice. This means that child sacrifice during a certain period – whether or not connected to the sacrifice of the firstborn – was ascribed to the will of YHWH by a certain religious segment. At least, there was a religious praxis that thought this to be the case.

The aspect of the view from inside to outside, from the own religion to the 'foreign' cult of Ba'al, plays a role in *Deuteronomy* too and in the texts of *Jeremiah* related to it (*JerDtr*). Here again it is expressly stated that the 'abominations' YHWH hates are part of the cultic praxis of the Canaanites and their gods. 'They (the Canaanites) even burn their sons and daughters with fire for their gods' (*Deuteronomy* 12.31).[24]

---

[23] The harshness of the statement of the divine speech is demonstrated by the mirror of later exegesis. The targum of v. 25 reads: 'But I rejected them because they were rebellious against my word and would not receive my prophets. I expelled them to a place far away and handed them over to the ones who hated them. And they followed their own foolish impulses and *they made for themselves bad statutes and laws, through which they could not have life.*'

[24] Child sacrifice appears as the culmination point of the cultic practice of the Canaanites after *Deuteronomy* 12.29-31. Its formulation and structure indicate that later Deuteronomistic hands were responsible for the addition to the main corpus.

The allocation of responsibility is perfectly clear here; it is not Israel, but the Canaanites who burn their children in fire, and that is an abomination to YHWH. The next step is the accusation that Israel/Judah took over these cultic practices from outside. This is reflected in the same way in *JerDtr*. Three texts play an important role here:

> And they (Judah) go on building the high place(s) of Topheth, which is in the valley of Ben-Hinnom, to burn their sons and their daughters in the fire – which I (YHWH) did not command, nor did it come into my mind (*Jeremiah* 7.31).

> 4. Because the people (Judah/Jerusalem) have forsaken me (YHWH), and have profaned this place by making offerings in it to other gods whom neither they nor their ancestors nor the kings of Judah have known, and because they have filled this place with blood of the innocent (5) and gone on building the high places of Baal to burn their children in the fire as burnt offerings to Baal, which I did not command, nor did it enter my mind (*Jeremiah* 19.4, 5).

> They built the high places of Baal in the valley of Ben-Hinnom, to bring their sons and daughters as a mlk-offering, though I did not command them, nor did it enter my mind that they should do this abomination, causing Judah to sin (*Jeremiah* 32.35).

These three texts from Jeremiah provide some interesting information. Here it is no longer an indefinite idolatry practised somewhere by the outside religion, but the child sacrifice is connected with two well-known names within Judah: a) The toponym 'valley of Ben Hinnom' and b) the Tofeth. The valley of Ben-Hinnom can be located. It is the deep valley on the south side of Jerusalem, which, coming from the west, encloses the current hill of Sino and the south-eastern hill where Jerusalem once originated, before it encounters the eastern valley of Kidron, the deep crevice between Jerusalem and the Mount of Olives. Topheth is more difficult. It is not an actual toponym – though connected with the valley of Ben-Hinnom – but rather a description of the function of the place. From the author's point of view it is seen as a place to 'burn children', therefore it will not be called Tophet, or valley of Ben-Hinnom any longer, but 'valley of the Slaughter' (*Jeremiah* 7.32). The best explanation for Topheth seems to assume an original *tèfèt*,[25] meaning 'altar of fire',

---

[25] For the philological discussion see W.McKane, *Jeremiah* I (Edinburgh, 1986) 179f.

later on adjusted with a so-called *bošèt*-vocalisation. *Bošet* means 'shame' and was applied to words of which the final redactors of the texts wanted to express their abhorrence. Due to the change of the o-e vocalisation, *tefet* became *tofet*.[26]

With this topographical remark, child sacrifice is located in Judah; it has come home from the outside religion to the very heart of the Southern Kingdom. As stated above, the Deuteronomistic judgement on the kings of Judah accuses two kings of child sacrifice: Ahaz (741-725) and Manasseh (696-642), the successor to Hezekiah. The latter is portrayed as the villain par excellence, but at the same time had the longest reign of all kings (55 years).[27]

Though Ba'al plays a role in these texts too, he is not the main figure. The Jeremiah texts stress the innocence of YHWH in a particular way. The denial: '(child sacrifice) which I (YHWH) did not command, nor did it come into my mind' (Jer 7:31; 19:5; 32:35 [var.]) is a very rare formulation. The fact that YHWH 'does not command something, that something did not come into his mind' assumes an opposition to something which was thought possible or necessary or even commanded by him. The formulation denies in a powerful way that YHWH could ask for these sacrifices; it opens up the possibility, however, that there were groups or opinions stating that something like child sacrifice was indeed commanded by YHWH: that child sacrifice indeed 'had come into his mind'. This brings us back again to Ezek 20:25f. '(25) I (YHWH) also gave to them (Israel) bad statutes and laws, through which they could NOT live! (26) and I (YHWH) made them unclean through their offerings, when they offered all the firstborn (by fire) – that I might fill them with horror.' Are the bad statutes and laws ordered by YHWH himself, laws which kill and make unclean, laws about the offering of the firstborn, understood as real child sacrifice, a possibility which is denied so passionately by Jeremiah?

---

[26] Some prudence is called for here. Anyone who 'googles' Tofeth is quickly led to sites on the excavations at Carthage, and presented with beautiful colour prints of these excavations, especially of the cemeteries, where hundreds of gravestones bear witness to numerous child burials. There is currently a heated discussion on the interpretation of these graves and the inscriptions, but as soon as the interpretation of child sacrifice in Carthage had taken hold, the name Tofeth from the Hebrew Bible was applied to the cemetery in Carthage.

[27] Since a long reign is seen as a blessing, 2 *Chronicles* 33.11-13 had to develop a fictitious 'conversion' to be able to explain his long reign.

From the deity Moloch to molk-*offering*

The fourth piece of information from the Jeremiah texts complicates
the matter at hand. It considers the formulation which is usually
translated as 'to sacrifice to Molech (*lmlk*) '. As observed before, this
'Molech' is understood as a Phoenician and/or Assyrian deity and
linked to child sacrifice and/or to the cult of the dead.[28] Besides *Jeremiah* 32.35, important texts about Molech can be found in *Leviticus*
18.21, 20.2-5; *2 Kings* 23.10.[29] The discussion concerns the question of
whether there was a separate deity Molech 'specializing' in child sacrifice, as later developments seem to suggest, connected to many stelae with Punic, Neo-Punic and Latin inscriptions in the burial
grounds of Carthage. And in addition to other narratives by classical
authors there is the famous story by Diodorus Siculus (20.6-7: first
century BC), writing about Carthage during a crisis in 310 BC: 'There
was in their city a bronze image of Kronos, extending its hands,
palms up and sloping toward the ground, so that each of the children
when placed thereon rolled down and fell into a sort of gaping pit
filled with fire'. In the history of reception it became the most famous
story about child sacrifice. Koch describes the result of this interpretation as follows: 'Das ergab das Bild eines scheußlichen kanaanäischen
Götzen, von dem nichts anderes bekannt war, als dass er Kinder zum
Fraß begehrte. Auch rabbinische Legenden haben diese Verbindin-
dungslinie gezogen. Christlichen (wie jüdischen) Auslegern hat das
zwei Jahrtausende lang Anlass gegeben, sich über den unmen-
schlichen heidnischen Götzendienst zu ereifern'.[30]

It was the great Old Testament scholar O. Eissfeldt (1887-1973),
who turned the discussion in another direction.[31] He understood
mōlek in relation to the Punic *molk/mulk*, a cognate common name as
part of child sacrifice terminology. The *lmlk* phrases should be rendered in the following way: 'to cause one's son/daughter to pass
through the fire as a *molk*-sacrifice'. After Eissfeldt's widely accepted

---

[28] Through a Masoretic distortion by a *bošèt*-vocalisation *Molek*, Hebrew *lmlk*
became rendered in the *Septuaginta* as *Molech* in *2 Kings* 23.10 and *Jeremiah* 39.35
(= Masoretic Text 32.35) and the *Vulgata* as *Moloch*. From there it led a separate existence as a Canaanite god, Moloch.

[29] Some scholars suggest including *Isaiah* 30.33. *1 Kings* 11.7 confuses Molech with
Milcom.

[30] Koch, 'Molek astral', 30.

[31] O. Eissfeldt, *Molk als Opferbegriff im Punischen und Hebräischen und das Ende des
Gottes Moloch* (Halle, 1935).

proposal,[32] *mōlek* was no longer a divine name but a sacrificial terminus. But Molek/Moloch had still not died because scholars started to look for a divine candidate elsewhere and earlier than the Hebrew and Punic texts. Thus an Ancient Near Eastern predecessor Malik entered the stage.[33] A wide range of names and places has been taken into account: Ebla (*[(d)]Ma-lik* +PN); Ur III (*[(d)]Ma-al-ku-um ŠÈ*, 'for the god Malkum'), Mari (*Malik* +PN; plural *Mālikū*), Ugarit (*mlk* [in Athtarot]), Phoenicia (*mlk.'štrt*).[34] Sometimes *mlk* is mentioned in connection with the *kispum* ceremony in the cult of the dead (kings), and sometimes *mlk* is identified with the death god Nergal. The geographical name Athtarot from the Ugaritic texts plays a role in the cult of the dead. Malik's character as an underworld deity can be confirmed, but death is not the same as child sacrifice. More importantly, no text can be found which links Malik with child sacrifice. Moreover, as Koch has shown, the Ugaritic *mlk* does not appear in the offering lists and did not receive any offerings at all. He disappeared completely in the history of religion of the Ancient Near East at the beginning of the first millennium. In Koch's words, this would mean: 'dass ein schon in Ugarit in den Hintergrund tretender und dann völlig abgetauchter Gott nach rund einem halben Jahrtausend in Jerusalem – und nur hier – wieder emporgekommen und unheimlich bedeutsam geworden ist'.[35] If Malik/Molek was a Canaanite god who suddenly appears round about the seventh or sixth century BC in the surroundings of Jerusalem, he appeared out of nowhere, which is very doubtful considering the amount of information we have nowadays. For this reason a connection between Malik and Molech is unlikely; this also applies to a supposed relationship with the Ammonite chief god Milcom.[36]

This means that we have to look again at the character of the *mlk*-sacrifice, without the burden of a presupposed Ancient Near Eastern deity Malik. According to Müller, the Masoretic *lmlk* is a causative nominal formation from the root *jlk > wlk* 'to go', or in the causative

---

[32] For critical points see Heider, 'Molech', 581f.

[33] Molech as a deity and related to Malik is defended by G.C. Heider, *The Cult of Molek: A Reassessment* (Sheffield, 1985); J. Day, *Molech. A God of Human Sacrifice in the Old Testament* (Cambridge, 1989); Heider, 'Molech'.

[34] F. Israel, 'Materiali per 'Moloch',' *Rivista di Studi Fenici* 18 (1990) 151-5; Müller, 'Malik', 540-1 and 'Genesis 22 und das *mlk*-Opfer'.

[35] Koch, 'Molek astral', 32.

[36] S. Pardee, 'G.C. Heider, The cult of Molek. A Reassesment', *JNES* 49 (1990) 320-72.

'to present, to offer'. The noun with the prepositional l[e]-essentiae[37] means 'as a presentation, as an offering';[38] in fact, it means a special way of offering. The 'end of the god Moloch' announced by Eissfeldt in 1935 has indeed come with the additional material worked in by Müller. The change from divine name to sacrificial phrase, as suggested by Eissfeldt and Müller, can indeed be related to Phoenician and Punic inscriptions.[39] The link between the Hebrew and the Phoenician can be found in the inscription of Nebi Yunis where a *molk*-offering is commemorated.[40] But is the *mlk*-offering really related to child sacrifice?

Denying Child Sacrifice

Weinfeld has argued 'that is it is just as hard to prove the existence of child sacrifice in the ancient world as it is to disprove it'.[41] His thesis that the *mlk*-sacrifice had to do with initiation and dedication rather than with slaying and 'burning babies' is deduced from idiom. The terminology of the *mlk*-offering in the Hebrew Bible is connected with 'to give' (*nātan*) and 'to cause ...to pass' (*hè'èrīv*) not to normal offering terminology such as 'to slaughter' (*zāvaḥ*, *šāḥaṭ*), 'to offer' (*hiqrīv*) or 'to burn (*śāraf*).[42] The most incriminating expression from the Hebrew Bible, 'to cause his sons and daughters pass through the fire', finds an innocent explanation in Weinfeld's eyes as a possible initiation rite proved by means of passing between torches, as known in the pagan world. Weinfeld has an important point with the idiom, but his interpretation of it as dedication, not sacrifice is based on the *Book of Jubilees*, the *Septuaginta* and later Rabbinic sources. He does not have any direct proof from the Hebrew Bible itself. For that reason, Weinfeld has to admit that *Ezekiel*, *Deutero-Isaiah*, and *Dtr-Jeremiah* may have had 'sporadic child sacrifice' in mind.

---

[37] The same use in *Genesis* 22.2; *Leviticus* 15.18. *l[e]* does not mean here 'for *mlk*', but 'as'.

[38] Müller 1984, 965-967; Müller 1995, 1006.

[39] For a short survey of the terminology, see H.P. Roschinski, 'Punische Inschriften zum MLK-Opfer und seinem Ersatz', *TUAT* II/4, 606-20.

[40] RES 376 I,1; B. Delavault, A. Lemaire, 'Une stèle »molk« de Palestine, dédiée à Eshmoun? RES 367 reconsidéré', *Revue Bibl.* 83-84 (1976) 569-83; *TUAT* II/4, 597f.

[41] Weinfeld, 'The Worship of Moloch' and 'Burning Babies'; Platorati, 'Zum Gebrauch des Wortes *mlk* im Alten Testament.

[42] Weinfeld, 'Burning Babies', 411f.

The last alternative is to understand the child sacrifices of the Punic inscriptions and stelae not as real sacrifices but as the burning of the dead bodies of prematurely deceased children,[43] buried together with foetuses and sacrificed sheep and goats. Following this opinion the *mlk*-sacrifice is 'die Bitte des Opfernden an die zuständige Gottheit, das verstorbene Kind in die göttliche Sphäre aufzunehmen'.[44] There are two objections – there is no proof that children who had died young played an exceptional role in the 'normal' cult or in the rites around death and life and their numbers cannot be explained by this solution. The number of cemeteries in the Punic settlements with burials of children aged 1-4 surpasses by far the normal number expected in cases of natural death. This is true even if the high infant mortality rate is taken into account. The most plausible explanation is that the Punic cemeteries are indeed evidence of child sacrifice. The combination of the stelae with vows to Tinnit and Ba'al Hammon and urns containing the remains of young children speaks in favour of a real history of child sacrifice. As is the case in the Hebrew laws concerning the firstborn, however, a praxis of substitution can be noted here too.[45] But not every child was lucky enough to have a substitute.

The dilemma of contradictory evidence

To sum up, the following conclusions may be drawn:

1. There is a general tendency in the Hebrew Bible to ascribe child sacrifice to the barbarian Other: either to Canaanites before the settlement of Israel or to worshippers of foreign gods.
2. Another Other is built up in the judgement about the two Judean kings Ahaz and Manasseh. They situate themselves outside Yahwism by causing their sons and daughter to pass through the fire.

---

[43] Osteological evidence demonstrates that there were no anomalous conditions.

[44] So recently again, D. Volgger, 'Es geht um das Ganze – Gott prüft Abraham (Gen 22,1-19)', *Biblische Zs.* 45 (2001) 1-19 at 13.

[45] Most clearly in a Neo-Punic inscription from N'gaus: where a lamb is mentioned as a substitute: *vita pro vita, sanguis pro sanguine, agnum pro vika(rio)*. In addition to the inscriptions concerning *mlk 'dm* (human) *bšrm* ([his] flesh), *mlk 'mr* (lamb) appears in many inscriptions, cf. L.E. Stager, 'Carthage. A View from Tophet', in H.G. Niemeyer (ed.), *Phönizier im Westen* (Mainz, 1982) 158f. For the inscriptions see A. Berthier and R. Charlier, *Le sanctuaire punique d'El Hofra* (Paris, 1955), cf. *TUAT* II/4 (Gütersloh, 1988) 606ff.

3. The tendency to blame the otherness of gods and worshippers practising child sacrifice can already be observed in the Hebrew Bible and its reception itself. The *molk*-offering as a cultic expression became a foreign god: Moloch!
4. The denial of human sacrifice in the Jeremiah texts is a particular one. In an I-speech, YHWH declares that 'he did not command, nor did it come into his mind' to accept child sacrifice.
5. Nowhere in the Hebrew texts is there a clear 'yes' to child sacrifice. Where the item is referred to, it is strictly forbidden.
6. On the other hand, *Ezekiel* 20.25 states that YHWH has given 'bad statutes and laws'. The enigmatic statement appears in a context of child sacrifice. *Micah* 6.7 'Shall I give my firstborn for my transgression, the fruit of my body for the sin of my soul' could be understood as a reflection of a possible praxis of child sacrifice. *2 Kings* 3.27 states that it was the Moabite king who sacrificed his son, but the Israelites have to flee after the sacrifice. It is told that the crisis management of Mesha works. The intensive and particular denial of YHWH's involvement in child sacrifice feeds the suspicion that there might have been other times and forms of worship.
7. The accusations of Jeremiah and Ezekiel and the Deuteronomistic blackening of Ahaz and Manasseh are too strong to suppose that we are dealing with a totally invented tradition.
8. In the 'Umwelt' we have proof of child sacrifice. It will be difficult, however, to extrapolate this proof automatically to a *praxis pietatis* in Israel.

How to find a background

We have seen that two kings are blackened by Deuteronomistic hands for practices of child sacrifice. Is this one hundred percent invented tradition? Probably not. It is difficult, however, to find a historical situation where Ahaz could have passed his sons through the fire. It is possible to imagine that the march of Northern Israel and Aram/Syria during the spring of 733 led to a situation comparable to *2 Kings* 3.25, where the Moabite King sacrificed his son during the siege of his endangered capital. How desperate the situation of Jerusalem was is poetically described in *Isaiah* 7.2 'When the house of David heard that Aram had allied itself with Ephraim, his (i.e. Ahaz') heart and the heart of the people shook as the trees of the forest shake before the wind'; technically shown because Ahaz meets Isaiah 'at the end of the conduit of the upper pool' – the text suggests that Ahaz is inspecting the water supply of the city in case of a siege; theologically proven because Isaiah offers Ahaz a sign to be asked from YHWH, your God (7.11),[46] but isolates the king religiously after his refusal to do so with 'that you weary my God also?' (7.13); and last but not least politically demonstrated because the second text about Ahaz and the Syrian-Ephraimite war, 2 Kings 16.7, tells that Ahaz calls on Tiglath-Pileser and the Assyrians to protect him from Aram and Israel. It will take more than a century to get rid of them. The overall tendency of the Isaiah text is anti-Ahaz. If Ahaz had sacrificed one of his sons during the march of the enemy troops on his capital, the text would have used it against him. At the same time the accusation of 2 Kings 16.3 is a general one, a concrete situation is not being related. With the material now available it is not possible to connect Ahaz' supposed child sacrifice with the political disaster and the military threat of his northern neighbours. It must have another background.

The same seems to be the case for Manasseh, the other king accused of child sacrifice, as stated above. Heavily laden with Deuteronomistic ideology, the account of his time on the throne of Judah is described as the climax of cultic sins during the monarchy. Manasseh, the apostate, does almost every single thing Deuteronomy forbids. Even the report about Manasseh in 2 Chronicles 33.1-20, which pretends to know much more about Manasseh and his deeds, only reflects his cultic sins, not his political ones. The only passage that can be understood as a description of his military and political government is 2 Kings 21.16: 'Moreover Manasseh shed very much innocent blood, until he had filled Jerusalem from one end to another….' This is a reference either to child sacrifice or to the persecution of YHWH prophets or oppositional groups. Both possibilities presuppose a king in full power, able to control his own country as long as he was a loyal Assyrian vassal. This loyalty to Assyria is again demonstrated by two inscriptions of the Assyrian kings Esarhaddon and Assurbanipal.[47] Here Manasseh co-operates with Esarhaddon in public works in Nineveh and is an ally of Assurbanipal on his campaign to Egypt.[48]

---

[46] The subject of Isaiah 7.10 must be Isaiah, not YHWH (Masoretic Text).

[47] J.B. Pritchard, Ancient Near Eastern Texts Relating to the Old Testament (Princeton, 1969³) 291.

[48] Pritchard, ibidem, 294.

Neither account reflects any occasion where child sacrifice would be necessary and/or useful. For Manasseh, too, we need another background for the supposed child sacrifice.

Is there a possibility to find another background? One popular thesis thinks that the firstborn offering is the real background to child sacrifice. But only *Exodus* 22.28b, taken up by *Micah* 6.7, speaks of offering the firstborn without substitution. All the other texts refer to substitutes or presuppose them. Still more important is the difference in the use of the cultic terms. 'To cause one's son/daughter to pass through the fire (as a *molk*-sacrifice)' never appears in the context of offering the firstborn. And the 'sons and daughters' of the specific texts are never related to that firstborn offering. Indeed, it was the impact of a combination of the sacrifice of Isaac narrative (*Genesis* 22), the laws on the firstborn and the story about the Moabite king (2 *Kings* 3.27) that related child sacrifice with the firstborn. Klaus Koch observed that the Punic *mlk*-texts suggest that not the oldest but the youngest child was sacrificed.[49] This means we have to look for another background to the *molk*-sacrifice. Koch starts with the context of the reforms of King Josiah (2 *Kings* 23.4ff.) and argues that all the measures taken have one common ground, the astral cult in Jerusalem.[50] In v. 4 all the vessels made for Ba'al, Asjerah and the host of heaven are burned. The heavenly Ba'al and Asjerah the 'Queen of Heaven' speak for themselves as they surely represented an astral cult in Jerusalem. V. 11 tells of the removal of the horses dedicated to the sun; the chariots of the sun are burned. V. 12 mentions altars on the roof. All these characteristics point in one direction: a cult in which the astral powers, with the sun at the centre, guaranteed good fortune.

Returning to the Carthage material, it seems clear that the deity Tinnit/Tanit had astral connections, too. As the 'face of Ba'al Šamem', she was 'un intermediaire entre le monde terrestre et le monde céleste'.[51] The reason why not the eldest son but younger ones were sacrificed could be that the concept of pureness played an important role.

---

[49] Koch, 'Molek astral', 35.
[50] Koch, 'Molek', 39-41.
[51] E. Lipiński, quoted by Koch, 'Molek', 47.

Should the Jerusalem *mlk*-cult be understood in this context? *Jeremiah* 7.31 accuses the kings of Judah of burning children. In the addition to 8.1-3, their judgement is announced:

> 1. At that time, says YHWH, the bones of the kings of Judah, the bones of its officials, the bones of the priests, the bones of the prophets, and the bones of the inhabitants of Jerusalem shall be brought out of their tombs (2) and they shall be spread before the Sun and the Moon and all the Host of Heaven, which they have loved, and served, which they have followed, and which they have inquired of and worshipped...' (*Jeremiah* 8.1-2).

Here a connection is made between the *mlk*-offering, the child that was 'caused... to pass through the fire' and the heavenly powers, represented by the Syrian Ba'al Šamem (YHWH), Asjerah and the Host of Heaven. Koch suggests that the Hebrew concept of *ruach* which can mean 'spirit', 'breath' and 'wind' at the same time, is one of the cornerstones of the motivation behind child sacrifice.[52] The negative statement of *Qohelet* (3.19-21) about the individual human spirit going to heaven after death presupposes a tradition in which this was thought to be a possibility, maybe by the smoke of a burnt offering. As Koch himself admits, this is only a hypothesis.[53] For me, the relationship with the *ruach* is one bridge too far. Too many steps between the concept of the moving spirit and child sacrifice must be taken without any evidence. On the other hand, the connection between the *mlk*-offering and the divine sphere of heavenly powers playing a role in an astral cult seems a promising approach. In the world of these specific Jeremiah texts, YHWH, among others, wears the face of an astral deity. The situation in Judah at this time must have been a period with a great variety of religious possibilities, as *Jeremiah* 44 demonstrates. Here the women of Jerusalem answer Jeremiah:

> 17. Instead, we will do everything that we have vowed, make offer sacrifices to the queen of heaven and pour out libations to her, just as we and our fathers before us, our kings and our officials, used to do in the towns of Judah and in the streets of Jerusalem. Then we had more than enough food and we enjoyed prosperous times; we did not experience disasters. 18. But from the time we stopped making offerings to the queen of heaven and pouring out libations

---

[52] Hebrew texts were aware of this tripartite meaning. *Ezekiel* 37.9-10 plays with the combination 'breath', 'wind' and 'spirit'.

[53] Koch, 'Molek astral', 44.

to her, we have lacked everything and have perished by the sword and by famine. 19. And the women said, 'Indeed we will go on making offerings to the queen of heaven and pouring out libations to her; do you think that we made cakes for her [in her image], and poured out libations to her without our husbands' being involved?

The text reflects a situation where Jeremiah represents the voice of a radical YHWH-alone movement in the eyes of the women of Jerusalem.[54] Without doubt these women are referring to the prosperous times of the pre-Josiah era, i.e. the time of Manasseh. Disaster came to Judah after an exclusive Yahwism was centralized in Jerusalem: the death of Josiah himself (609), the twofold surrender/ conquest of Jerusalem (597/587), the humiliation and mutilation of King Zedekiah, the murder of Gedaliah and all the horrors of deportation and occupation by a foreign power. Of course the overall tone of the chapter is clear: it was idolatry that caused the fall of Jerusalem and will cause the extermination of the Jews in Egypt. Here the fall of Pharaoh Hophra (570) is taken as a sign.[55] This setting makes it clear that arguments and parties are coloured by Deuteronomistic interests. The historical credibility of 'a general assembly' of Jewish men and/or women in Egypt as presupposed in *Jeremiah* 44 is not very high. The argument, however, that disaster followed the suppression of the cult of the Queen of Heaven (Asjerah/Ishtar) is impressive and mirrors with high probability the religious spectre at the end of the seventh century BC. There is no reference here to the *mlk*-offering. But the description fits the increasingly astral character of religion at that time. If child sacrifice was located in the surroundings of astral religion it seems probable that the accusations to the account of Manasseh were not made without reason. Confronted with the different faces of YHWH in the last century of Judah's existence as a vassal state, it is possible that child sacrifice belonged to the belief system of those days. If child sacrifice did exist in ancient Israel, they were made to YHWH as well. Maybe there are also traces of a more or less accepted religious praxis referring to child sacrifice in an earlier time.[56]

---

[54] It is tempting to connect Jeremiah's speech with the reforms of Josiah. The view of Jeremiah himself about Josiah's reforms, however, is uncertain. There is no 'positive' text of Jeremiah which can be related to the actions of the king.

[55] *Jeremiah* 44.30 does not suggest that Hophra was overthrown by Nebuchadrezzar himself.

[56] *Micah* 6.7. Even if exaggeration is part of the construct in which the 'right' answer is given in v. 8 ('but to do justice, and to love kindness') and the rhetorical

The harsh critics of the later prophets suggest that at a certain stage and under certain circumstances child sacrifice did indeed belong to the religious belief system and praxis of Ancient Israel. The statement by Ezekiel that YHWH did give Israel 'statutes that were not good and ordinances by which they could not live' (20.25) and the astral character of Yahwism at the end of the monarchic period could refer to the background of that praxis.

Such a *praxis pietatis* may seem strange to students of religion in the twenty-first century. But in the long run of history it is not that long ago that we were burning witches.[57]

questions of v. 7 should be answered with 'no', the fact remains that in the imagery of Micah it was esteemed to be a real possibility to sacrifice the firstborn.

[57] This paper is a reworked and extended version of E. Noort, 'Genesis 22: Human Sacrifice and Theology in the Hebrew Bible', in E. Noort and E.J.C. Tigchelaar (eds), *The Sacrifice of Isaac: The Aqedah (Genesis 22) and Its Interpretations* (Leiden, 2002) 1-20 at 6-14.

VI. HUMAN SACRIFICE IN ANCIENT EGYPT

Herman te Velde

At first sight, human sacrifice does not seem to be anything special – people can sacrifice money, but also flowers, animals, and thus also other people. In his book on sacrifice, the Dutch historian of religion Theo van Baaren (1912-1989) writes: 'If, for example, we wanted to organise offerings by the material offered, then this list would be rather disappointing and we would be forced by this system to group completely different phenomena under the same heading. (…) there is no such thing as a systematic unit of "human sacrifice".'[1] But in the chapter about 'The Sacrificed God', he writes: 'This does not mean that the occurrence of human sacrifice was not an important phenomenon in religion which has naturally attracted a lot of attention. It is also true that a large number of the human sacrifices we know can be derived from the same basic concept. The crucial point with these offerings lies in the killing. Burkert even goes so far as to say: 'Sacrificial killing is the basic experience of the "sacred". *Homo religiosus* acts and attains self-awareness as *homo necans*'.[2] When objects are used, the killing can be replaced by the breaking or destruction of the objects.'[3]

An offering is of course not always or automatically a presentation offering. In Predynastic and Early Egypt, the servants and wives of the deceased pharaoh were buried with him. This seems also to have been the case later in the Sudan, in the kingdom of Kerma (± 2300-1650 BC) and in the kingdom of Ballana and Qustul. Although this simultaneous burial can indeed be interpreted as a presentation offering, the actual killing is also an essential element here.[4]

[1] T.P. van Baaren, *Het Offer. Inleiding tot een complex religieus verschijnsel* (Utrecht, 1975) 19f.
[2] W. Burkert, *Homo necans* (Berkeley, Los Angeles, London, 1983) 3.
[3] Van Baaren, *Het Offer*, 88.
[4] See also J. van Dijk, this volume, Ch. VII.

However, what scholars of Egyptian religion tend to call an offering is usually not so much something presented by people to the gods but rather a ritual act by which men can contribute to the restoration or maintenance of cosmic harmony in the world.[5] An offering in Egypt, therefore, is not so much an offering *to* a god as an offering *of* the god. However, in Egypt, this offering of the gods can hardly, if at all, be compared with the offerings of the gods we are familiar with from the hunter-gatherer and early farming cultures. In Egypt the killing and offering of the bull is not directly a celebration of the death of the god. It is well known that life and death or death and resurrection are important themes in Egyptian religion, for example the death and resurrection of Osiris, and even the rising and setting of the sun god. The death of Osiris, and particularly the killing of Osiris, is never directly but only indirectly celebrated – it is as if it was too awful and too cosmic-order shattering to be celebrated and repeated in ritual. What does happen is that the killer or murderer is killed during the ritual. As early as in the pyramids from the third millennium BC it can be read that when sacrificing a bull, the following words are recited to Osiris or to the deceased pharaoh who has become the deceased and resurrected Osiris: 'I have killed for you the one who killed you' (*Pyr.* 1544b). That mythical murderer or killer is the god Seth, who by his murderous deed has introduced death into the world and disrupted the cosmic order, and who must be killed in his turn in the ritual so that the disturbed cosmic order can be re-established and balance achieved again.

The sacrificial animal is killed, cut into pieces, butchered or burnt, that is, eaten or destroyed. The well-known and famous cannibal spell from the Pyramid Texts, which relates in dramatic terms that the deceased and resurrected pharaoh has eaten the smaller gods as breakfast and the greater ones as his evening meal, should be understood in this framework.[6] Rather than killing an animal, it was also possible to bake cakes in the shape of an animal, for example a hippopotamus, and to break that into pieces and eat it during the ritual. It was also possible to make statuettes of the sacrificial animal or of the god Seth, for example from wax, and then to burn them. The

---

[5] Th.P. van Baaren, *Mensen tussen Nijl en Zon. De godsdienst van het oude Egypte* (Zeist and Antwerpen, 1963) 68; H. te Velde, *Seth, God of Confusion* (Leiden, 1967) 50.
[6] Cf. C. Eyre, *The Cannibal Hymn: A Cultural and Literary Study* (Liverpool, 2002).

creature being sacrificed in the representations that have survived is sometimes a goose, or a hippopotamus or a bull, and sometimes even a human figure. This led a prominent Egyptologist like Hermann Junker (1877-1962) to conclude that in Ancient Egypt, and in particular on the island of Philae at the southern Egyptian border, human beings were sacrificed, and he referred to Procopius, who lived in the time of Justinian, that is, the sixth century AD.[7] Procopius wrote that local tribes, the Blemmyes, were in the habit of sacrificing people to the sun before Justinian ended the temple cults on Philae.[8]

There are quite a number of reports by Greek and Roman authors about human sacrifice in Egypt. Even Herodotus (II 45) dismissed these reports as fairy tales, calling them stupid (euêthês) stories: 'By telling this story, the Greeks in my opinion show that they have absolutely no understanding of the nature and customs of the Egyptians. People who regard the sacrifice of animals as improper, with the exception of pigs, bulls and bull calves, at least if they are pure, and geese – how on earth would they be able to sacrifice humans?'

In 1948 J.G. Griffiths presented an overview of this Classical evidence. He discusses the story of the Egyptian king Busiris who sacrificed foreigners, the tradition that Sethian or Typhonic people in particular were sacrificed, and gives a list of the places in classical literature where human sacrifice in Egypt is mentioned. His final conclusion is as follows: 'The evidence suggests that human sacrifices were not frequent in Egypt in the period of the Egyptian dynasties, but that in a later era they became common in certain areas and cults. ... It must be concluded that human sacrifice was practised in Egypt during the Roman period'.[9]

The idea that human sacrifice was not the rule in Ancient Egypt but only occurred very exceptionally and that it was something marginal appeals to many contemporary Egyptologists, as does the idea that human sacrifice was imported by African Nubians to Philae and by Asiatic Semites to Tanis in the north-east of the Delta. Sometimes people refer to traces of ancient Egyptian humanism. The stories

[7] H. Junker, 'Die Schlacht- und Brandopfer und ihre Symbolik im Tempelkult der Spätzeit', Zs. Ägypt. Sprache 48 (1911) 69-77.

[8] Procopius, Pers. 1.19.36, cf. J. Dijkstra, Religious Encounters on the Southern Egyptian Frontier in Late Antiquity (Diss. Groningen, 2005) 34.

[9] J.G. Griffiths, 'Human Sacrifices in Egypt: the Classical Evidence', Annales du Service des Antiquités de l'Egypte 48 (1948) 409-23.

from the Westcar Papyrus, which are set in the time of Khufu but date from the Hyksos Period, relate that a great magician was summoned to the court of Khufu to show off his skills. One of his tricks was that he was apparently even able to reattach a severed head. Pharaoh then wants to summon a convict from prison and cut off his head, but the magician Djedi states that such an experiment should not be performed on a human being and instead cuts off the head of a goose. Naturally, Djedi's magic spell is able to make the goose and its head waddle towards each other and a short time later the goose is again honking happily to itself. It appears from this, then, that the life of a human was considered to be more valuable than that of an animal. Incidentally, the distinctions between human and animal and god are never considered to be as hard and fast as in the modern western world – instead there was more of a gradual difference in life between gods, spirits, men and animals. Not only humans but also animals were mummified. We also know of animals – young cats – who were killed by having their necks wrung in order to be able to produce a beautiful cat mummy, but not of people who were murdered in order to turn them into mummies!

There is one story about a pharaoh who according to his physician had become mortally ill, and who according to his court magicians would only be able to escape death by sending a named courtier to the underworld instead of dying himself.[10] However, the courtier/ magician in question, who is offered a state funeral with all the trimmings as well as mummification and all the rest of it – his son would be treated preferentially and he himself would be granted a mortuary cult in the temple – is not really attracted by the idea. Because he is not able to escape the request of the pharaoh to act as his deputy in death, he gives in, more or less because he has to.

The belief that the life of someone dying could be saved, and even that someone who had died could be resurrected by another human being acting as a replacement and offering himself in his stead is not unparalleled elsewhere in the ancient world. In classical mythology and Euripides, for example, what springs to mind is the story of Alcestis who sacrificed herself to save her husband Admetus who had been condemned to an early death by the Fates. However, I do not know of any specific ritual that turns such a replacement human sacrifice into reality. As mentioned above, this is all just a story.

[10] G. Posener, *Le Papyrus Vandier* (Cairo, 1985).

Near the Egyptian fortress of Mirgissa in the Sudan, 'the first indisputable evidence for the practise of human sacrifice in classical ancient Egypt' has been found.[11] It is a human skull in or on a pot with traces of beeswax painted with red ochre, that is, the remains of melted wax figurines. Not far away were thousands of sherds of deliberately broken pots inscribed with the names of foreign peoples and princes, etc., as well as the skeleton of a decapitated person and limestone statuettes of handcuffed enemies. The skull and the skeleton may have been of a Nubian. It is assumed that this was a cursing ritual or *rituel d'envoûtement* from *c.* 1800 BC. The ritual of the breaking of the red pots is also known from elsewhere, as well as the accompanying texts.[12] Because only the circumstances of the find at Mirgissa are known, we do not know whether the killing or sacrificing of a human during such a ritual was the exception or the rule.

As early as 1900, Lefébure published a 35-page article on human sacrifice in the Swedish journal *Sphinx*.[13] He gave a rather roundabout summary of what classical authors had written about human sacrifice and also a description and explanation of the so-called *tekenu*. This was believed to be a human sacrifice that was performed during the funerals of notables. In the fifth volume of the *Wörterbuch der Ägyptischen Sprache* (335), which appeared in 1931, the *tknw* is still called 'Das (symbolische) Menschenopfer beim Totenkult', but nowadays no-one subscribes to this explanation. In his 1994 dissertation, Harco Willems[14] refers to J.G. Griffiths, who interpreted the *tekenu* as a 'living human being covered by an animal hide',[15] apparently the sem-priest who as the beloved son of the deceased, searches for and finds his deceased father while asleep or in a dream, and who is thus not killed or sacrificed.

An important contribution to the study of human sacrifice in Ancient Egypt is formed by a substantial article by Jean Yoyotte.[16]

[11] R.K. Ritner, *The Mechanics of Ancient Egyptian Magical Practice* (Chicago, 1993) 162-3.

[12] J. van Dijk, 'Zerbrechen der roten Töpfe', *Lexikon der Ägyptologie* VI (1986) 1389-96; *The New Kingdom Necropolis of Memphis* (Groningen, 1993) 173-88.

[13] E. Lefébure, 'Le sacrifice humain d'après les rites de Busiris et d'Abydos', *Sphinx* 3 (1900) 129-64.

[14] H.O. Willems, *The Coffin of Heqata (Cairo JdE 36418). A Case Study of Egyptian Funerary Culture of the Early Middle Kingdom* (Leuven, 1996) 110ff.

[15] J.G. Griffiths, 'The Tekenu, the Nubians and the Butic Burial', *Kush* 6 (1958) 111-19.

[16] J. Yoyotte, 'Héra d'Héliopolis et le sacrifice humain', *Annuaire de l'Ecole Pratique des Hautes Etudes* 89 (1980-81) 31-102.

Yoyotte begins with Manetho, who reports that a certain pharaoh Ahmose (probably not the Ahmose of the 18th Dynasty (*c.* 1500 BC) but Amasis of the 26th Dynasty (*c.* 600 BC) had apparently abolished the practise of sacrificing humans to the goddess Hera of Heliopolis and replaced it by the burning of wax statuettes. He also investigates the sacrifices and burnt offerings of the Egyptians and how the victims were selected, for example because they had red hair or other characteristics. This is the cleanliness or suitability mentioned above. It appears that the offerings were identified with the followers of the demonic primeval snake Apophis or with the god Seth, the murderer of Osiris. The burnt offerings, which were called 'human cattle' (*rmt-'wt*), were thrown into the fiery oven or cauldron ('*h*) of the goddesses Mut or Hera of Heliopolis and burnt. Yoyotte concludes that the sacrificing of humans was practised in the Third Intermediate Period (*c.* 1070-712 BC), and that the burnt offerings were selected on political and biological grounds. Plutarch, too, mentions that Typhonic or Sethian people with red or blond hair were sacrificed.

It looks very much as if criminals, rebels, people who did not follow the cosmic order, *ma'at*, in word or deed, or even in biological characteristics such as hair colour, were eliminated, destroyed or sacrificed. It was a ceremonial execution packaged in religion. Nowadays, the death penalty is still exercised by, among others, the American, Chinese and Iranian cultures, and the death penalty has been imposed in many times and cultures, including the culture of Ancient Egypt. Incidentally, Ancient Egyptians were in general careful of human life, as has already been mentioned in connection with the Westcar Papyrus. The Instructions of Merikare say in so many words: 'Do not kill, it is not useful. Punish by beating with sticks and with a prison sentence so that the land remains well organised – except for the rebel whose plan has been discovered.' With regard to a rebel: 'Throw him out, kill him, destroy his name and destroy those who belong to him.' Rebels were the opponents of the goddess Ma'at and, being followers of Apophis and Seth, they were the enemies of Re and Osiris. Human rebels against the pharaoh and the gods were burned in the fiery ovens or on the altar of the god whom they had insulted. This is the background to the passage in the Maxims of Ankhsheshonq where it is stated that conspirators against the life of the pharaoh would be burned in a cauldron or on a brazier ('*h*) placed on a clay altar built near the door of the palace. Conspiracy against the pharaoh, but also theft of temple property, was punished by death by fire or impalement.[17]

Harco Willems has demonstrated that at a festival with a procession of the god Hemen in Moalla during the Middle Kingdom, representatives of Apophis, i.e. a bull, a hippopotamus and fish, were sacrificed and that criminals and tomb desecrators could be added and that humans could replace the usual animal representatives.[18] Willems emphasises that living humans were indeed sacrificed, as seems to be convincingly demonstrated by his textual analysis. Capital punishment existed in Egypt, and this could be performed as a sacrifice. This immediately gives rise to the question of how far Egypt regarded the performance of capital punishment on a human being as a human sacrifice. Religion and law are not separate matters in Egypt but rather overlap each other. The execution of the death sentence is a *Tötungsritual*. The fundamental disruption of the world and legal order by a human must be set right by the killing or sacrificing of a human.[19]

Finally, I would like to mention a representation which appears numerous times from the Predynastic Period down to Roman times, namely the pharaoh grasping an often kneeling and handcuffed enemy or enemies by the hair in one hand, while in the other he raises a club to administer the decisive death blow. It is an image of the invincible pharaoh triumphing over chaos and the representatives of rebellious peoples, thus maintaining cosmic order. It has been suggested that this image is based on what were originally actual executions or human sacrifices.[20] This representation can also be found on some private stelae, probably mainly coming from Memphis during the New Kingdom. Alan Schulman has argued that these representations of the victory over his enemies by the pharaoh, for example representations of the presentation of the gold of honour, were reminders of memorable moments in the lives of the owners of

---

[17] A. Leahy, 'Death by Fire in Ancient Egypt', *J. Econ. Soc. Hist. Orient* 27 (1984) 199-206.

[18] H. Willems, 'Crime, Cult and Capital Punishment (Mo'alla Inscription 8)', *J. Egypt. Arch.* 76 (1990) 27-54.

[19] See also J. Assmann, 'When Justice Fails: Jurisdiction and Imprecation in Ancient Egypt and the Near East', *J. Egypt. Arch.* 78 (1992) 149-63.

[20] Thus for example F. Jesi, 'Rapport sur les recherches relatives à quelques figurations de sacrifice humain dans l'Egypte pharaonique', *J. Near-Eastern Stud.* 17 (1958) 194-203.

the stelae.[21] The owners may have attended ceremonial executions or human sacrifices being performed by the pharaoh. However, he cannot produce a single text to support his hypothesis, which rests only on this analogous reasoning. I remain unconvinced. Schulman's hypothesis is based on the idea that Egyptian culture enjoyed bloody human sacrifices, that the Egyptians thanked the gods by smashing the skulls of human beings. Schulman believes that conquered enemies who were the prisoners of war of the victorious army on its return were ceremonially sacrificed as thank offerings. The Egyptians certainly condemned rebels to death and undoubtedly practiced war with sometimes barbaric methods. However, the regular killing of people during temple rituals is rather different to killing in the heat of battle or execution after a legal trial. For the time being, I believe that the rebels or enemies of the pharaoh were generally symbolically killed, for example in representations. The Egyptian culture was careful of human life. However, I do not want to imply that in the thousands of years of Egyptian history there were no instances when attitudes hardened, when men turned symbolism into reality and literally rather than symbolically sacrificed other men. To sum up, the human sacrifices they occasionally practised were more often the exception than the rule in Ancient Egypt.

---

[21] A.R. Schulman, *Ceremonial Execution and Public Rewards. Some Historical Scenes on New Kingdom Private Stelae* (Freiburg and Göttingen, 1988).

VII. RETAINER SACRIFICE
IN EGYPT AND IN NUBIA

Jacobus Van Dijk

'The truth of the doctrine of cultural (or histori-
cal-it is the same thing) relativism is that we can
never apprehend another people's or another
period's imagination neatly, as though it were
our own. The falsity of it is that we can therefore
never genuinely apprehend it at all. We can
apprehend it well enough, at least as well as we
apprehend anything else not properly ours; but
we do so not by looking *behind* the interfering
glosses that connect us to it but *through* them.'[1]

Human sacrifice has long been, and perhaps still is, a somewhat controversial subject among Egyptologists. The ancient Egyptians have
often been considered too civilized for such a barbaric custom. As
the Canadian anthropologist and archaeologist Bruce Trigger put it,
'the cruel forms of human sacrifice practised by the Aztecs have
caused many Egyptologists to wonder if such people can really be
considered to have been civilized'.[2] Invariably, a famous episode
from an early New Kingdom literary text, the Westcar Papyrus, is
cited in this context.[3] It is a collection of fairy tales set in a distant
past, the time of the Old Kingdom pharaohs. One of the stories tells
of the magical skills of a man called Djedi, who is able to reconnect

---

[1] C. Geertz, 'Found in Translation: On the Social History of Moral Imagination',
in *Local Knowledge: Further Essays in Interpretive Anthropology* (New York, 1983) 44.

[2] B.G. Trigger, *Early Civilizations: Ancient Egypt in Context* (Cairo, 1993) 84.

[3] A.M. Blackman, *The Story of King Kheops and the Magicians. Transcribed from
Papyrus Westcar (Berlin Papyrus 3033)*, ed. W.V. Davies (Reading, 1988). The text has
often been translated; recent English translations are available in M. Lichtheim,
Ancient Egyptian Literature I (Berkeley, Los Angeles and London, 1973) 215-22 and
R.B. Parkinson, *The Tale of Sinuhe and Other Ancient Egyptian Poems 1940-1640 BC*
(Oxford, 1997) 102-27.

a severed head and restore the victim to life. King Cheops, the builder of the Great Pyramid at Giza, is keen to have a demonstration of this and gives orders to fetch a prisoner and use him as a guinea pig, but Djedi tells the King that 'it is forbidden to do such a thing to the noble cattle', i.e. human beings. A duck, a goose, and a bull are then used instead. King Cheops is clearly depicted here as a barbarian who does not acknowledge the value of human life.

In modern popular imagination the idea of the pharaoh as a cruel despot is still very much alive. In many a film or novel the pharaoh has the people who have built his pyramid buried alive with him in order to ensure that nobody will disclose the secret of its construction and rob his tomb, and these people then often return as vengeful mummies risen from the dead. Of course this is all nonsense, but on the other hand it cannot be denied that the custom of having the King's servants killed and buried with him in order to serve him in the afterlife did actually exist in Ancient Egypt, albeit only for a brief period at the very beginning of pharaonic civilization.

Two main forms of human sacrifice can be distinguished. On the one hand there is the ritual killing of a human being, either as a regular or as an exceptional form of the offering cult. In this case human beings – usually, though not always, convicted criminals or prisoners of war – are sacrificed to the gods in order to maintain or re-establish cosmic order and to emphasize the role of the King as its main guarantor. In some cases this type of human sacrifice may be no more than a ritualized form of the legal death penalty.[4] On the other hand there is the practice of retainer sacrifice, where the death of the king is followed by the killing of people who are supposed to accompany him to the hereafter.[5] It is on this latter custom that we shall focus here, although it is possible that the two forms of human sacrifice may sometimes overlap, for example if, as sometimes has been suggested, prisoners of war were selected to be killed on the occasion of the royal funeral.[6]

---

[4] See for the various forms of cultic human sacrifice H. te Velde, this volume, Ch. VI.

[5] Sometimes rather inappropriately called *sati*-burial, after the Indian rite of widow-burning, see e.g. H. Yule and A.C. Burnell, *Hobson-Jobson: The Anglo-Indian Dictionary* (1886, repr. Ware, Hertfordshire, 1996) 878-83, s.v. *suttee*. As B.G. Trigger, 'The Social Significance of the Diadems in the Royal Tombs at Ballana', *J. Near Eastern Stud.* 28 (1969) 255-61 at 257 has pointed out, 'in India, where *sati* was widespread, retainer sacrifice is unreported'.

[6] On the various problems of interpretation of archaeological and anthropological data in this context see the special volume of the journal *Archéo-Nil* (10, 2002) devoted to *Le sacrifice humain en contexte funéraire*.

The earliest instances of retainer sacrifice from Egypt appear to date from the last phases of Egyptian prehistory, particularly the Naqada II (Gerzean) period (*c.* 3500-3200 BC). In some cemeteries there is evidence for dismemberment of the body, a burial custom not attested in earlier times. Parts of the body were buried or reburied separately; in a number of cases the skull has been detached from the body and in a tomb at Naqada several skulls and long bones have been carefully laid out along the walls of the tomb. Evidence of post mortem decapitation has recently come to light not only at Hierakonpolis[7] but also at near-by Adaïma, where at least two cases are known where the victim had been decapitated after his throat had been slit.[8] These examples have been interpreted as cases of 'self-sacrifice' and the beginning of the practice of retainer sacrifice,[9] but caution is needed since the status in life of the victims remains unknown.

Firmer and more substantial evidence of retainer sacrifice comes from the royal burial grounds of the Early Dynastic Period at Abydos. The kings of Dynasties 0 and I, when the centralized Egyptian state was formed, as well as those of the second part of Dynasty II were buried here. The unification of the country under one central government is traditionally ascribed to Menes, the legendary first king of the First Dynasty, but although military operations may ultimately have played a decisive role, this unification is now usually seen as the result of a gradual process which took several decades. The identity of 'Menes', whose name does not appear in contemporary records, is still uncertain; he is most often identified either with Narmer, who is depicted as king of both Upper and Lower Egypt on a famous slate palette from Hierakonpolis now in the Cairo Museum, or with his successor Aha.[10] Be this as it may, retainer sacrifice in the necropolis of Abydos is first attested in the

---

[7] R. Friedman *et al.*, 'Preliminary Report on Field Work at Hierakonpolis 1996-1998', *Journal of the American Research Center in Egypt* 36 (1999) 1-35.

[8] B. Midant-Reynes, E. Crubézy and T. Janin, 'The Predynastic site of Adaïma', *Egyptian Archaeology* 9 (1996) 13-5; E. Crubézy and B. Midant-Reynes, 'Les sacrifices humains à l'époque prédynastique: L'apport de la nécropole d'Adaïma', *Archéo-Nil* 10 (2000) 21-40; B. Ludes and E. Crubézy, 'Le sacrifice humain en contexte funéraire: problèmes posés à l'anthropobiologie et à la médecine légale. L'exemple prédynastique', ibid., 43-53.

[9] Midant-Reynes, in I. Shaw (ed.), *The Oxford History of Ancient Egypt* (Oxford, 2000) 53-4.

[10] On this debate see T.A.H. Wilkinson, *Early Dynastic Egypt* (London and New York, 1999) 67-8.

burial complex of King Aha and continues to be a feature of all royal tombs of the First Dynasty. The burial complexes of these kings consist not only of the tomb proper, an impressive mud-brick structure built on the high desert which was once covered by a rectangular tumulus,[11] but also of a separate funerary enclosure situated nearer the edge of the cultivation.[12] The necropolis has suffered extensively both from looting and from less than careful digging by early excavators, but the work carried out by Petrie in 1899-1903 and 1922 and the excavations of the German and American missions presently working there have nevertheless yielded important results.

Both the tomb and the funerary enclosure are surrounded by rows of small, square or rectangular subsidiary graves each containing one burial, usually in a wooden coffin.[13] The tomb of Aha had three parallel rows of 36 subsidiary graves containing the skeletal remains of young males, none of whom was older than 20-25 years. This uniform age is a strong indication that they were all killed simultaneously, apparently by strangulation.[14] It is interesting to note that the remains of at least seven young lions were found near one of these burials.[15] Further confirmation of the practice of retainer sacrifice

---

[11] G. Dreyer, 'Zur Rekonstruktion der Oberbauten der Königsgräber der 1. Dynastie in Abydos', *Mitt. d. Deutschen Arch. Inst. Kairo* 47 (1991) 93-104.

[12] See Wilkinson's chapter 7 for a survey of the royal mortuary architecture of this period.

[13] The following information on individual tombs and enclosures has chiefly been gained from Petrie's excavation reports; cf. also W.B. Emery, *Archaic Egypt* (Harmondsworth, 1961) 62, 67-8, 73, 81, 85, 90, 135-8. For a detailed analysis of the subsidiary graves at Abydos see G.A. Reisner, *The Development of the Egyptian Tomb down to the Accession of Cheops* (Cambridge, Mass., Oxford and London, 1936) 75-121, who also assessed the problem of the retainer sacrifices, 117-21; cf. M.A. Hoffman, *Egypt Before the Pharaohs: The Prehistoric Foundations of Egyptian Civilization* (London and Henley-on-Thames, 1980) 275-9.

[14] As suggested by a recent re-examination of the victims' teeth by Nancy Lovell, see K.A. Bard, in I. Shaw (ed.), *The Oxford History of Ancient Egypt*, 71. Strangulation, besides cutting of the throat and interment alive, has also been observed in the much later retainer sacrifices at Ballana and Qustul, where the remains of a rope were found around the necks of some individuals, see A.M. el Batrawi, *Mission archéologique de Nubie 1929-1934. Report on the Human Remains* (Cairo, 1935) 79. In a scene in the New Kingdom Theban tomb of Mentuherkhepshef, which I hope to discuss elsewhere, two Nubians are put to death by strangulation as part of the funerary rites of the tomb-owner.

[15] Three young lions, two of whom wore amulets, were found in individual sand burials in the Napatan non-royal cemetery at Sanam in Lower Nubia, see F.Ll. Griffith, *Liverpool Annals of Archaeology and Anthropology* 10 (1923) 81-2.

comes from the very recent excavation of Aha's funerary enclosure by the American mission.[16] Here the expedition uncovered six subsidiary burials containing the skeletons of what appear to be court officials, servants and artisans. Although the graves had been looted they still contained funerary goods such as jars with the royal seal of Aha and precious items of ivory and lapis lazuli jewellery, indicating that these people were no mere servants but persons of some standing. That they were all buried at the same time is made probable by the fact that the wooden roofs over the individual graves were covered by a continuous layer of mud plaster laid down over all the graves very soon after the enclosure was constructed.

Aha was succeeded by Djer, whose tomb was surrounded by the graves of no fewer than 317[17] individuals, while a further 242 were found buried around his funerary enclosure, a total of 559 individuals, among whom were a considerable number of women. Many of these subsidiary graves were originally marked by simple tombstones inscribed with the names of their occupants, a further indication that these people were not just nameless slaves. Not all of the subsidiary burials are necessarily retainer sacrifices, however. In the case of the burials at Djer's tomb, Reisner, after careful consideration of the archeological and constructional evidence, considered 63 cases probable and a further 99 possible. After Djer the numbers gradually decrease. The tomb of his successor Djet (Wadji) had 174 subsidiary burials (assessed by Reisner as 14 probable and 99 possible cases of retainer sacrifice); his funerary enclosure counted a further 161. The tomb of Queen Merytneith, who appears to have acted as regent during the minority of her son Den, contained 41 (33 probably sacrificial) subsidiary graves, and Den's own tomb had 133 (40 probable, 83 possible), while his ritual enclosure, perhaps originally associated with Merytneith, counted 77. The tomb of the next king, Andjib, was surrounded by 64 poorly constructed graves; his enclosure, if he had one, is as yet unidentified.

The last two kings to be buried in the First Dynasty necropolis at Abydos were Semerkhet and Qaa. Semerkhet's tomb is particularly interesting in that the 68 subsidiary graves have been constructed directly around the king's own burial chamber and were almost

---

[16] The find was officially announced on 14 March 2004 and is as yet unpublished. The details given here are based on the press release issued by New York University on 16 March 2004 and the report in *The New York Times* of that day.

[17] The number given by Emery is 338.

certainly covered by the same roofing timbers and superstructure, a further strong indication that these burials were simultaneous with the royal funeral (Reisner considers all 68 burials as probable cases of retainer sacrifice). Some of the retainers buried were dwarfs, as evidenced by skeletal remains as well as depictions on some of the seven stelae found in the tomb. Semerkhet's funerary enclosure is unknown, although it has been identified with the so-called 'Western Mastaba', a building neighbouring (and similar to) the enclosure of Den; if so, there do not seem to have been any subsidiary burials. Qaa's tomb contained only 26 subsidiary graves which were again constructed around the core of the royal tomb itself, and are therefore very probably all cases of retainer sacrifice; his enclosure has not yet been identified.

Elsewhere in Egypt monumental funerary structures are also sometimes accompanied by subsidiary graves of sacrificed retainers. In the Early Dynastic cemeteries of the capital Memphis, at Giza and Saqqara, several cases have been found. At Nezlet Batran, near Giza, 56 subsidiary graves were found around a large rectangular mud-brick structure with a palace façade surrounded by an enclosure wall, the so-called mastaba Giza V, dated by Petrie to the reign of Djet (Wadji). The interpretation of this massive building is uncertain; it may be the tomb of Djet's mother or one of his wives, or possibly a cenotaph of Djet himself,[18] a symbolic tomb representing the king's continued presence in the north. The same problem arises with the huge palace façade mastabas of the First Dynasty found by Emery at Saqqara. Emery believed these to be the true royal tombs of the early rulers of Egypt, whereas he saw Petrie's Abydos tombs as royal cenotaphs erected in the sacred domain of the god Osiris, a view still held by some scholars today.[19] The size of the Saqqara mastabas in particular is an important argument: they are much larger and much more imposing than the tombs at Abydos, that is, if the funeral enclosures belonging to the latter are left out of the equation. This makes it rather unlikely that the Saqqara mastabas belong to high officials even if these were of royal blood themselves, for as Michael Hoffman has pointed out, it is hardly conceivable that they would have been allowed to outshine the king by the grandeur of their funerary monuments, and there is much to be said for Hoffman's

---

[18] Hoffman, *Egypt Before the Pharaohs*, 280.

[19] See W.B. Emery, *Great Tombs of the First Dynasty* II (London, 1954) 1-4; Hoffman, 280-88; Wilkinson, *Early Dynastic Egypt*, 259-60.

solution that at least some of the Saqqara mastabas are in fact the northern cenotaphs of the kings buried at Abydos.

The question is not without interest for the subject of this article, for if the Saqqara monuments did not belong to kings, it would mean that even private individuals, albeit of the highest rank, could have retainer sacrifices with their burials. Mastaba 3504 at Saqqara, associated with King Djet, which is nearly twice as large as the king's tomb at Abydos, contained 62 retainer burials. Mastaba 3503, associated with Queen Merytneith, also had 20 subsidiary burials which were largely undisturbed and contained not only the remains of the sacrificed servants, but also 'the objects denoting their particular service to their royal mistress, such as model boats with her shipmaster, paint pots with her artist, stone vessels and copper tools with her vase maker, pots of every type with her potter, etc.'[20] Four subsidiary graves were found adjoining mastaba 3500, dated to the reign of Qaa, which according to Emery, 'all showed evidence of having been buried at the same time'.[21]

At Abu Rawash, a little to the north of Giza, at least two of the First Dynasty mastabas excavated by Montet in 1913-14 (nos. I and VII) were flanked by rows of subsidiary graves similar to the ones found at Giza and Saqqara.[22] At tomb I, dated to the reign of Den, there were seven, each of them covered with a miniature tumulus and marked with a small stela. The contents had been disturbed in antiquity, but some of the graves still contained skeletal material and remains of wooden coffins; the surviving grave goods consisted mainly of pottery and stone vessels. In one of the graves the relatively well-preserved coffin contained not only a human skeleton but also (unspecified) animal bones. A similar arrangement, this time of eight burials, was found at Tomb VII, also from the time of Den, although the superstructure was no longer extant here. The tombs at Abu Rawash are smaller than those at Saqqara and must have belonged to members of the elite, perhaps of the royal family. The grave goods are of the same type and quality as those at Saqqara and presumably came from the same royal workshops.[23] There is no

---

[20] Emery, *Archaic Egypt*, 66-8 and 137-9.

[21] *Archaic Egypt*, 90.

[22] P. Montet, 'Tombeaux de la Ière et de la IVe dynasties à Abou-Roach', *Kêmi* 7 (1938) 11-69.

[23] Cf. A. Klasens, *Oudheidkundige Mededelingen uit het Rijksmuseum van Oudheden te Leiden* 42 (1961) 108.

certain archaeological evidence that we are dealing with retainer
sacrifice here, but the similarity with the arrangements at Saqqara
and Abydos suggests that this is indeed the case. This means that at
this time retainer sacrifice was not an exclusively royal prerogative.

The kings of the Second Dynasty initially broke with the tradition
of having themselves buried in the ancestral cemetery at Abydos;
instead, they moved to Saqqara. Many kings of this dynasty are
ephemeral rulers of whom little beyond their names is known. The
tombs of only two of these kings, Hetepsekhemwy and Ninetjer,
have been identified with reasonable certainty. They are of a new
type, with a very long underground gallery cut into the bedrock and
containing a large number of rectangular niches. The superstruc-
tures of these tombs have disappeared completely and the underground parts were emptied out long ago.[24] Later in the history of the
dynasty the kings returned to Abydos. The first to do so was Perib-
sen, who built a tomb similar to those of his First Dynasty predecessors. No subsidiary burials have been found with it, and although
Reisner thought that such burials 'in the main tomb continued to be
made', he admitted that neither their number nor their placing could
be determined.[25] The last king of the dynasty, Khasekhemwy, built a
tomb unlike any of the others at Abydos; it looks like a mud-brick
adaptation of the Saqqara gallery tombs. It is an oblong structure of
about 70 m with the royal tomb proper in the centre; a sloping
entrance corridor leads to a series of 40 niches on either side of the
compound, with a further 9 in the middle, behind the royal tomb.
According to Reisner, 'the central burial-complex ... certainly contained two or more *sati*-burials, and it is to be presumed that other
chambers ... contained other *sati*-burials. The numbers of these burials would probably not have exceeded ten or fifteen'.[26] If there were

---

[24] The same applies to a possible further Second Dynasty royal tomb recently dis-
covered at Saqqara, which was reused and extended first at the end of the Eighteenth
Dynasty and then again in the Late Period; see M.J. Raven *et al.*, *Jaarbericht Ex Oriente
Lux* 37 (2001-2002) 95-100.

[25] Reisner, *Tomb Development*, 125.

[26] Reisner, *Tomb Development*, 128. It should be pointed out that Reisner uses the
term *sati*-burial not only for sacrificed retainers in subsidiary graves, but also for
wives of the king who were killed to accompany him to the other world and who
were buried within the royal tomb itself. As far as I can see, however, there is no
hard evidence for this practice in the Early Dynastic cemeteries at either Abydos or
Saqqara. It is true that the tomb of Djer introduced the multiple-room substructure
(Reisner, 350ff.) and that a human arm bedecked with precious jewellery, thought to
have belonged to the body of a queen, was found in a robbers' hole in the wall of the
tomb, but the arm may equally well have belonged to Djer himself and a queen of

retainer sacrifices at these Late Second Dynasty tombs, it is likely that they also existed in the earlier gallery tombs at Saqqara, but it should be stressed that there is no evidence for any such burials in either location; indeed, it is usually supposed that the custom died out after the First Dynasty. On the other hand, the function of the niches in the walls of the galleries, usually assumed to be magazines, has yet to be determined and it has to be admitted that their arrangement resembles the rows of subsidiary graves along the exterior walls of First Dynasty royal tombs.

Two further possible cases of retainer sacrifice in Egypt must be mentioned here, both from the Nile Delta. In the Late Middle Kingdom stratum at Tell ed-Dab'a (c. 1680-1660 BC), a Canaanite settlement was found which was characterized, among other things, by donkey burials, usually a pair of them, near the entrance of the tomb. In three cases human bodies were also found outside the tomb, in front of and facing the entrance; in one instance two completely disarticulated bodies were found together with five donkeys and an ox. To Van den Brink these circumstances 'strongly suggest that the dead were intentionally killed and buried together with the owner of the tomb in front of which they were buried. Probably they were servants who followed their master to the Next World'.[27] This interpretation has been called into question, however. The skeletons actually appear to predate the tomb in front of which they were found. They probably belong to a multiple burial such as have been found in earlier strata at Tell ed-Dab'a, which was disturbed when the tomb above them was dug out.[28]

In 1978, a team from the University of Mansura carried out excavations at Tell el-Balamun, in the far north of the Nile Delta. Unfortunately only a very brief preliminary report has been published so far,[29] and many intriguing questions must remain unresolved for the

Djer called Herneith appears to have been the owner of the large mastaba 3507 at Saqqara.

[27] E.C.M. van den Brink, *Tombs and Burial Customs at Tell el-Dab'a* (Vienna, 1982) 48-50.

[28] M. Bietak, *Tell el-Dab'a V: Ein Friedhofsbezirk der Mittleren Bronzezeitkultur mit Totentempel und Siedlungsschichten*, Teil I (Vienna, 1991) 58, with figs. 24-25 on pp. 52-3. P. Montet, the excavator of Tanis, which he believed was the Hyksos capital Avaris, claimed that he had found 'Canaanite' human sacrifices (as part of foundation rituals) there as well, but his interpretations have since been convincingly refuted, see P. Brissaud, 'Les prétendus sacrifices humains de Tanis', *Cahiers de Tanis* 1 (1987) 129-44.

[29] F. Abd el-Malek Ghattas, 'Tell el-Balamoun 1978 (Fouilles de l'Université de Mansoura)', *Annales du Service des Antiquités de l'Egypte* 68 (1982) 45-9.

time being. Most of the finds appear to date from the Late Period, but there is also a mastaba-like structure of a 'much earlier' date. It contains a large T-shaped room; at one end of the transverse room were found the skeletons of two individuals, whose faces had been covered by crude masks made of gold foil. At the opposite end of the same room were 'further skeletons', but without any trappings. More skeletons were found in the long room taking off from the centre and these had a circular hole in the front of the skull, just above the forehead, leading the excavator to suspect that they had been 'systematically, or even ritually' killed by a blow with a blunt instrument in order to let them follow the individuals wearing the gold masks into the hereafter. More skeletons were found in another room in the tomb; the only objects found were pottery, which unfortunately has not been included in the report, depriving us of a ready means to date this curious ensemble. It is difficult to assess this find; it is not even certain how many skeletons there were and how many of them had pierced skulls. The method by which these people were killed has not been observed before in clear cases of retainer sacrifice, and other interpretations are also possible. Moreover, the date of the tomb is uncertain; although the excavator thought it was much earlier than the Late Period, it is quite possible that it is in fact later, perhaps as late as Roman.[30]

In Nubia, retainer sacrifice is a recurring phenomenon from at least the Classic Kerma Period (*c.* 1750-1500 BC) to the time of the kingdoms of Ballana and Qustul (5th/6th century AD).[31] The kings of Kerma, just south of the Third Cataract, were buried in very large tumulus tombs which were accompanied by massive mud-brick mortuary chapels. The tombs, excavated by G.A. Reisner shortly before World War I,[32] contained not only large quantities of all sorts of luxury objects such as furniture, model ships, pottery, jewellery, and weapons, but also various sacrificial animals as well as the

---

[30] Cf. the use of gold leaf on (parts of) the faces of Roman mummies, W.A. Daszewski, in M.L. Bierbrier (ed.), *Portraits and Masks. Burial Customs in Roman Egypt* (London, 1997) 63.

[31] Cf. the brief surveys in e.g. B.G. Trigger, *Nubia under the Pharaohs* (London, 1976) 89-96; W.Y. Adams, *Nubia, Corridor to Africa* (London, 1977) 198-9, 203-5; D.A. Welsby, *The Kingdom of Kush: The Napatan and Meroitic Empires* (London, 1996) 88-91. For the period preceding Kerma see J. Reinold, 'Le problème des sacrifices humains: cas du néolithique soudanais', *Archéo-Nil* 10 (2000) 89-96.

[32] G.A. Reisner, *Excavations at Kerma* I-V, Harvard African Studies V-VI (Cambridge, Mass, 1923).

skeletons of sacrificed human beings who had apparently been buried alive. One of the largest tumuli contained the bodies of at least 322 people, a great many of them female, perhaps members of the royal harem. Retainer sacrifice was not just a royal prerogative here, however, for smaller numbers of victims have also been found in subsidiary graves belonging to court officials, dug into the royal tumulus itself. These massive royal burial sites evidently represent the Kingdom of Kerma at its most powerful. In the northern parts of the cemetery human sacrifices are less in evidence. Reisner ascribed this difference to a period of decline, but Adams has suggested that it may instead reflect the period of development leading up to the cultural heyday of Kerma.[33] Neither the A-Group culture which preceded it nor the C-Group culture of Lower Nubia which was partly contemporaneous with Kerma appear to have known retainer sacrifice, although Kerma-type burials with smaller numbers of victims have been found in the region where the two overlap, near the Second Cataract, at Mirgissa,[34] where evidence for cultic human sacrifice, briefly discussed elsewhere in this volume, has also been found, and at Ukma.[35]

During the Egyptian New Kingdom, Nubia was an Egyptian colony governed by 'The King's Son of Kush', the Egyptian viceroy. It was dominated politically, economically and culturally by Egypt, which also meant that 'slaves were protected from grim Nubian customs such as retainer sacrifice'.[36] By the end of the New Kingdom Egypt had lost control over Nubia, and not much is known about the period which follows; it is not until c. 850 BC that the archaeological evidence becomes more abundant again. Egyptian religious traditions, and especially the cult of the god Amun at Gebel Barkal, appear to have been preserved among the elite. This may explain why retainer sacrifice does not seem to have been practiced in the royal cemeteries at Kurru and Nuri, near the capital city Napata at Gebel Barkal, although sacrificial burials of animals, especially horses and guardian dogs, are common there. The earlier tombs at Kurru were covered by tumuli, but from the reign of Piye (Piankhy) onwards the kings both here and at Nuri erected pyramids with adjacent mortuary chapels over their tombs. Piye is the king who

---

[33] Adams, *Nubia*, 212-3.
[34] A. Vila, in J. Vercoutter, *Mirgissa I* (Paris, 1970) 223-305.
[35] A. Vila, *Le cimetière kermaïque d'Ukma Ouest* (Paris 1987).
[36] Trigger, *Nubia under the Pharaohs*, 130.

invaded Egypt and whose successors ruled over it for close to a century as the Twenty-fifth Dynasty. Both in their inscriptions and in their monuments they portray themselves as 'more Egyptian than the Egyptians'.

The period of Nubian rule over Egypt came to an end in 657 BC, when King Tanutamani fled to his native country before the plundering troops of the Assyrian King Assurbanipal. The kings continued to be buried in the cemeteries of Napata (chiefly Nuri), however, and it was not until after Arkamaniqo (*c.* 270-260 BC) decided to move the royal cemetery much further to the south to Meroe, between the Fifth and Sixth Cataracts, that we see a revival of the ancient practice of retainer sacrifice.[37] The first kings and queens were buried in the existing elite cemetery at Meroe South, but the later North Cemetery is the true royal necropolis with no fewer than thirty-eight royal pyramid tombs. Queens and members of the court elite were buried in the adjacent West Cemetery. The last royal tomb, the owner of which is unidentified, dates from *c.* AD 320. Reisner, who excavated these cemeteries, stated that evidence of '*sati*-burial' was found in almost all of these tombs, but on the basis of his published reports it is now thought that he 'exaggerated the frequency of the phenomenon'.[38] Nevertheless, it is certain that at least sixteen tombs (five kings, a queen, a prince, and a further eight of unknown status) dating from the first century BC onwards contained additional sacrificial burials, with a maximum of seven in any one tomb. Here too, however, human interments are outnumbered by those of horses, dogs, and later, camels.

In the post-Meroitic period (4th-6th century AD) 'royal' cemeteries are found at el-Hobagi, some 75 km upstream from Meroe, north of the Sixth Cataract. The exact status of the tumulus graves found there is not certain; Patrice Lenoble, the excavator of the site, sees them as the direct successors of the royal tombs of Meroe and as proof that Meroitic culture continued after the political decline of Meroe itself, but others prefer to view them as the tombs of local chiefs.[39] Whatever the truth may be, it seems certain that these peo-

---

[37] Adams, *Nubia*, 308-9.

[38] Welsby, *The Kingdom of Kush*, 89.

[39] P. Lenoble and N.M. Sharif, 'Barbarians at the gates? The royal mounds of El Hobagi and the end of Meroe', *Antiquity* 66 (1992) 626-35, and the comment on this paper by P.L. Shinnie and J.H. Robertson in *Antiquity* 67 (1993) 895-9. See also Lenoble, 'Le rang des inhumés sous tertre à enceinte à El Hobagi', *Meroitic Newsletter* 25 (1994) 89-124.

ple saw themselves as kings, as Lenoble's analysis of the grave goods shows. But, although vast quantities of weaponry were found in these tombs, only one of them contained a horse burial and no human sacrifices were found at all.[40]

Large tumuli of the post-Meroitic period are also present in many other sites, both in the north (Qasr Ibrim, Ballana, Qustul, Gemai, Firka, Kosha, Wawa) and further south, from Tanqasi and Zuma, near Gebel Barkal, to Gebel Qisi, south of the Sixth Cataract. Most of the latter sites are unexcavated; limited work by Shinnie at Tanqasi has not revealed human sacrifices.[41] By contrast, clear evidence of the custom has emerged from the huge burial mounds at Ballana and Qustul in Lower Nubia, discovered in the early 1930s by Emery and Kirwan.[42] These two places, situated on opposite sides of the Nile just north of the Egyptian-Sudanese border, constitute the most important sites of the so-called X-Group Culture, nowadays usually referred to as the Ballana Culture. The average height of the tumuli is about 4.5 m, with a diameter of between 4 and 12 m, but the royal burial mounds are much larger, the largest measuring some 77 m in diameter and 12 m high. Concealed underneath them is a long sloping corridor, usually from the east, which leads to a number of barrel-vaulted, mud-brick rooms constructed in pits cut out of the bedrock. Their massive size as well as the opulence of their contents make these tombs stand out as 'the only symbolic representations of state authority which we are able to recognize in the post-Meroitic era'.[43]

Several of the royal tombs were undisturbed and full of archaeological treasures such as wooden, bronze, and iron furniture, bronze and silver vessels, lamps, jewellery, tools, and weapons. Sacrificial victims, both animals and humans, were found in the burial compartments themselves as well as in the sloping corridors. In some of the larger tombs the queen, 'who was undoubtedly sacrificed' was in a separate room 'with her attendant slaves', in smaller tombs 'the sacrificed queen was placed beside her consort'. After the entrance to the tomb proper had been blocked, 'the owner's horses, camels,

---

[40] D.A. Welsby, *The Medieval Kingdoms of Nubia. Pagans, Christians and Muslims along the Middle Nile* (London, 2002) 41, 44.

[41] P.L Shinnie, 'Excavations at Tanqasi, 1953', *Kush* 2 (1954) 66-85.

[42] W.B. Emery, with L.P. Kirwan, *The Royal Tombs of Ballana and Qustul*, 2 vols (Cairo, 1938).

[43] Adams, *Nubia*, 405.

donkeys, and dogs, together with their grooms and possibly soldiers, were ... sacrificed in the courtyard and the ramp'.[44] Among
the human victims were men, women and children. The horses were
pole-axed and then buried on the spot wearing their saddles and
harnesses, some of which were richly wrought with silver, and some
of the dogs had collars and leashes. Finally, the whole burial site was
covered by a massive tumulus, the surface of which was, at least at
Ballana, covered with white pebbles.

The number of sacrificed victims appears to have been relatively
small; the highest count in any one tomb was seventeen.[45] In recent
years the interpretation of these human sacrifices has been the subject of debate. The excavators described them as retainer sacrifices,
and so have subsequent authors like Trigger and Adams. Lenoble,
however, who strongly advocates the continuity of Kushite funerary
beliefs and practices from Napata to Ballana, has interpreted the Ballana and Qustul finds as well as the earlier ones in the royal tombs
in the North Cemetery at Meroe as victims of the ritual slaughter of
enemies on the occasion of a king's funeral.[46] He refers to reliefs in
Meroitic temples and royal mortuary chapels showing rows of
bound prisoners and kings and queens grasping groups of captive
enemies by the hair and raising a club or a sword in order to kill
them. However, these scenes are a direct borrowing from ancient
Egypt, where they are commonplace on temple pylons and elsewhere. They represent the pharaoh, whose main task it is to maintain *ma'at*, the order of creation, subduing the powers of chaos represented by Egypt's enemies, and although a literal ('historical')
interpretation has been suggested recently for these Egyptian scenes
as well,[47] they are almost certainly purely symbolic.

[44] Emery, *Ballana and Qustul* I, 25-6.
[45] Trigger, 'The Royal Tombs at Qustul and Ballâna and their Meroïtic
Antecedents', *J. Egypt. Arch.* 55 (1969) 117-28 at 123; but cf. Welsby, *Medieval Kingdoms of Nubia*, 43, who specifies 'a maximum of nineteen at Qustul, nine at Ballana
and four in one of the elite burials at Firka'.
[46] P. Lenoble, 'Les "sacrifices humains" de Meroe, Qustul et Ballana. I: Le massacre de nombreux prisonniers', *Beiträge zur Sudanforschung* 6 (1995) 59-87. In his *The
Kingdom of Kush*, 90, Welsby is still reluctant to accept Lenoble's interpretation, but in
The Medieval Kingdoms of Nubia, 43, he appears to have accepted it. Cf. now also
Lenoble's contribution 'Le "sacrifice humain" des funérailles impériales de Méroé:
un massacre de prisonniers triomphal?", *Archéo-Nil* 10 (2000) 99-110.
[47] A.R. Schulman, *Ceremonial Execution and Public Rewards. Some Historical Scenes
on New Kingdom Private Stelae* (Freiburg and Göttingen, 1988). See the final paragraphs of H. te Velde's contribution to the present volume.

Lenoble's interpretation is part of a long-standing debate about continuity and change in the various stages of Nubian culture, from the early Kerma civilization to the Ballana culture of Byzantine times, and particularly on the position of the latter vis-à-vis its predecessors.[48] It would take us beyond the scope of this paper to discuss this problem here in detail. Nevertheless, the differences between the Ballana tumuli and the Meroitic royal tombs seem greater to me than the similarities. For starters, the latter all take the shape of pyramids; even at the very end of the Meroitic period, when retainer sacrifice is revived and Nubian customs begin to regain the upper hand over the Egyptianizing trends of the previous centuries, the tombs are still covered by (badly constructed) pyramids. By contrast, as Adams pointed out, 'the domed earth tumulus, which is the standard superstructure for all burials of the Ballana period, is much more nearly comparable to the tumulus of Kerma times than to anything which was built in the intervening 2,000 years' and even the custom of covering the earth mound with white pebbles was widespread in Kerma times.[49]

Another important point is the custom of bed burials. This is an 'un-Egyptian form of burial' which had been practised from Kerma to the early kings of the Twenty-fifth Dynasty until it was abandoned first for royal burials at the time of Taharqa, and then by lesser members of the elite.[50] It then reappeared in post-Meroitic graves at Meroe and also at Ballana and Qustul. Furthermore, the royal North Cemetery of Meroe was, as we have seen, exclusively royal, whereas the elite and even the queens were buried in the West Cemetery. At Ballana and Qustul, the royal tumuli and smaller graves are in the same cemetery, as had been the case at Kerma.[51]

In fact, the only indisputable evidence for an ideological link between the kings of Ballana and their Meroitic predecessors are the silver crowns in Meroitic, that is Egyptianizing, style found in

[48] See in particular Trigger, 'The Royal Tombs at Qustul and Ballâna and their Meroïtic Antecedents', *JEA* 55 (1969) 117-28; Adams, *Nubia*, 407ff.; L. Török, *Late Antique Nubia* (Budapest, 1988) 216ff.; Welsby, *Medieval Kingdoms of Nubia*, 23ff.

[49] Adams, *Nubia*, 408-9. Cf. the recently introduced term 'post-pyramidal Meroitic' for the 4th-6th centuries.

[50] D.M. Dixon, 'The Origin of the Kingdom of Kush (Napata-Meroë)', *J. Egypt. Arch.* 50 (1964) 121-32, esp. 129-30.

[51] Adams, *Nubia*, 204-6, 411.

several of the Ballana royal tombs.[52] While these are obviously potent symbols of kingship, they have in fact little to do with funerary customs *per se*, and in this respect their significance has probably been overrated. It seems more likely to me, therefore, that Adams is right when he says that 'many aspects of the post-Meroitic burial complex seem to represent a deliberate break with tradition, and a revival of much older, pre-pharaonic practices'.[53]

Apart from these general considerations there is also the actual location of the bodies of the sacrificed victims in the Ballana tombs to take into account. Some of them were found in the underground complex, some even within the royal burial chamber itself. Thus in one case, the king's body 'was placed on a canopied wooden bier below which were placed bronze and silver vessels for his immediate use. He was dressed in his royal regalia, and weapons for his protection were left leaning against the foot of the bier, and at its head lay the sacrificed bodies of a male slave and an ox.'[54] Clearly, this sacrificed man was there to serve the king in the afterlife; that this should be the body of an enemy prisoner slaughtered in the course of a triumphal celebration seems wholly unbelievable to me. Lenoble has interpreted the presence of the ox along the same lines, viz. as part of 'un rite de confirmation du charisme de la famille royale', whose main function was 'de célébrer et d'adapter l'idéologie royale lors des successions'.[55] Even if one accepts this, however,[56] this does not necessarily exclude the possibility that an ox placed in the king's burial chamber was supposed to be of use to him in the afterlife, as were the human victims buried with the king. The same holds true for the men buried with the king's saddled horses, which were clearly not just there for triumphal ostentation,[57] but ready to be used and therefore needing the continued attention of grooms. Batrawi, in his report on the skeletal material found at Ballana and Qustul, observed that 'it is a most significant fact that the animals

[52] Emery, *Ballana and Qustul* I, 22-3; cf. Trigger, 'Social Significance'; L. Török, *The Royal Crowns of Kush* (Oxford, 1987).

[53] Adams, *Nubia*, 409-11.

[54] Emery, *Ballana and Qustul* I, 25-6; Adams, *Nubia*, 407.

[55] P. Lenoble, 'Le sacrifice funéraire de bovinés de Méroé à Qustul et Ballana', in *Hommages à Jean Leclant* II (Cairo, 1994) 269-83.

[56] Lenoble's iconographic evidence comes from Meroitic pyramid chapels, but the scenes in question have again been borrowed from common Egyptian examples.

[57] P. Lenoble, 'Une Monture pour mon Royaume: Sacrifices triomphaux de chevaux et de méhara d'el Kurru à Ballana', *Archéologie du Nil Moyen* 6 (1994) 107-30.

buried inside the tombs were invariably edible, while all the animals found in the ramp and pit are usually used for carrying, riding or hunting'.[58]

Retainer sacrifice is a custom which can be found in many societies, in a variety of times and places, and in many forms.[59] There are, however, also some common features. The custom occurs only in developed root-crop cultures,[60] not in more primitive societies, and only in societies with centralized power in the person of a king or chief who has control over the lives of his retainers, and who is seen as having a special relationship with the supernatural, not in more equalitarian societies.[61] It is also more frequent in territorial states than in city-states. Finally, there appears to be a correlation between retainer sacrifice and other forms of human sacrifice: it occurs only in societies where human beings were regularly sacrificed to the gods, and when cultic human sacrifice is no longer practised, retainer sacrifice also dies out.[62] All of these factors are at work in Early Dynastic Egypt, a developed agricultural society governed by a powerful divine king who had recently established a centralized territorial state after the 'incipient city-states'[63] of Late Predynastic times. After the First Dynasty, the practice of retainer sacrifice appears to have died out quickly, and it is probably no coincidence that the only pictorial evidence we have of cultic human sacrifice dates from the same period. A scene found on a few Early Dynastic wooden labels[64] shows a kneeling figure, apparently with his hands tied behind his back, being stabbed in the chest by an officiant holding a bowl to catch the blood. On the best preserved label the context is clearly a royal religious ceremony, but the status of the person killed (a willing victim? a prisoner of war?) is unknown. That this is a real event and not just a symbolic representation of the kind that is

---

[58] A.M. el Batrawi, *Mission archéologique de Nubie 1929-1934. Report on the Human Remains* (Cairo, 1935) 139.

[59] Cf. the brief survey given by Trigger, 'Social Significance', 256f.

[60] A.E. Jensen, *Mythos und Kult bei Naturvölkern* (Wiesbaden, 1960) 185-217; cf. A. de Waal Malefijt, *Religion and Culture* (New York and London, 1968) 212.

[61] Trigger, 'Social Significance', 257.

[62] B.G. Trigger, *Early Civilizations* (Cairo, 1993) 97-8.

[63] B.J. Kemp, *Ancient Egypt: Anatomy of a Civilization* (London and New York, 1989) 52.

[64] Wilkinson, *Early Dynastic Egypt*, 266-7 with fig. 8.2; M. Baud and M. Etienne, 'Le vanneau et le couteau. Un rituel monarchique sacrificiel dans l'Égypte de la Ire dynastie', *Archéo-Nil* 10 (2000) 55-77; B. Menu, 'Mise à mort cérémonielle et prélèvements royaux sous la Ire dynastie (Narmer-Den)', *Archéo-Nil* 11 (2001) 165-77.

so often depicted in later temple reliefs is made likely by the fact that it is not the king who is shown killing the victim, but a nonroyal officiant. This scene is never depicted again after the First Dynasty and cultic human sacrifice appears to have become a highly exceptional event in later times.

There is, then, no indisputable evidence of retainer sacrifice in Ancient Egypt after the First Dynasty. But, as Trigger rightly remarks, 'the ethical and socio-economic factors that have resulted in the abandonment of this custom in the course of social evolution are no less worthy of investigation than is the custom itself'[65] – so why was the practice of retainer sacrifice discontinued after the First Dynasty? This is an intriguing problem for which there is no easy solution. It is usually assumed that in Nubia the practice of retainer sacrifice was initially abandoned after the Kerma period because of the political and cultural colonization of the area by the Egyptians, who had not practised retainer sacrifice for well over a millennium. The revival of the custom after the end of the Egyptian domination and its aftermath under the Egyptianizing Kushite rulers tends to confirm this. The final abandonment of the practice appears to have been the result of the introduction of Christianity in Nubia,[66] although as late as the 11th century AD the Arabic writer 'Abd-el-'Aziz El-Bekri still describes a royal burial in a tumulus grave with sacrificed retainers which is strikingly similar to those found at Ballana and Qustul.[67] For Early Dynastic Egypt, however, no such external influence can be found, unless one wants to assume, as some scholars have suggested, that the custom was rooted in a distinct Upper Egyptian culture and that it was abandoned under the civilizing influence of the north.[68]

[65] Trigger, 'Social Significance', 257.

[66] On Christian burial practices in Nubia see Welsby, *The Medieval Kingdoms of Nubia*, 48ff.

[67] The passage, as translated by W. Vycichl, 'The Burial of the Sudanese Kings in the Middle Ages. A survival of the Kerma Civilization', *Kush* 7 (1959) 221-2, is worth quoting in full: 'When a king of the Sudan dies, they make him a big cupola from the wood of the plane-tree and put it on his burial place. Then they bring a bed with a few covers and cloths and introduce it (or him) into the cupola. They put beside him his jewellery, his arms, his eating and drinking vessels and they bring food and beverages with him as well as some of the men who served him with his food and drink. Then they shut the door of the cupola and put over the cupola mats and objects. Then the people gather and heap earth on it until it becomes like a huge hill. Then they make a moat around it so that one can arrive at this hill only from one side. And they slaughter animals to their dead'.

[68] Emery, *Archaic Egypt*, 90.

One of the main obstacles to our understanding of the process which led to the discontinuation of the practice in Early Dynastic Egypt is that we know very little about the status in life of the sacrificed victims. That they were supposed to serve the king in the hereafter seems reasonably certain, but had they also been his servants when he was still alive, in other words, were the king's own servants sacrificed? This is usually assumed, and is perhaps the most likely option, but it is also possible that the victims were selected from among the chief families of the elite[69] or contributed by them from among their servants. This would make it a collective form of sacrifice, a symbol of group unity emphasizing the social bonds of the participants, their shared belief that by sacrificing some of their servants they contributed to the king's continued existence in the hereafter and thereby to the prosperity of the state, and their loyalty to the king's successor.

Apart from these ideological components, however, such a practice, like all forms of conspicuous consumption or indeed like any sacrifice, also involves an important economic factor.[70] For although, as John Baines put it somewhat apodictically, 'life was cheap in most pre-modern societies and this was a striking example of that cheapness',[71] such a statement does not take into account the economic value servants may have represented for their owners. 'Even at the heart of primitive religious ideology in such a basically important phenomenon as sacrifice, notions of rationality and prudent calculation enter',[72] and the sacrifice of a servant does not only despatch an easily replaceable human body to the other world but also deprives the surviving community of his professional skills and experience. The retainer burials excavated by Emery at Saqqara demonstrate that these people were not mere menial labourers but specialized servants, such as craftsmen, painters, potters, sailors etc., who were buried with the particular tools of their trade. The precious items of lapis lazuli and ivory recently found in the subsidiary graves at

---

[69] This appears to have been the case in fourteenth-century Sudan, according to the report of Ibn Batûtah quoted by E.A. Wallis Budge, *Osiris and the Egyptian Resurrection* (London, 1911) 225.

[70] R. Firth, 'Offering and Sacrifice: Problems of Organization', *J. Roy. Anthrop. Inst.* 93 (1963) 12-24.

[71] J. Baines, in D. O'Connor and D.P. Silverman (ed.), *Ancient Egyptian Kingship* (Leiden, 1995) 137.

[72] Firth, 'Offering and Sacrifice', 22.

Aha's funerary enclosure at Abydos[73] point in the same direction. With the establishment of a centralized state and the growing demand for luxury goods and services the elite may well have started to think about more economical ways to meet their ritual obligations to the deceased king and to 'serve God without losing touch with Mammon'.[74] These considerations are equally pertinent if, as seems likely, the sacrificed retainers were the deceased king's own servants, for their deaths would then deprive his successor's royal workshops of their expertise. Such economic considerations may have been strengthened by a development during the later First Dynasty, when retainer sacrifice no longer appears to have been an exclusively royal prerogative.

John Baines has drawn attention to a potential conflict between the idea that 'the prosperity of the land depended on the deceased king's destiny' (which was presumably enhanced by the sacrifice of his retainers) and the position of his successor as guarantor of the country's well-being.[75] This may be so, but such a conflict would not have been resolved by abandoning the custom of retainer sacrifice – a similar conflict may conceivably have existed in later times, when an incredible amount of luxury goods for the king's life in the hereafter was amassed in his tomb, but no human beings were included. Moreover, this would only work if one assumes that the absence of buried retainers in his tomb made the deceased king 'powerless', and this can hardly have been the intention in view of the later substitution of sacrificed retainers by depictions of servants and their activities in tomb and mortuary temple reliefs. A conflict there was, but it was between the perceived interests of the deceased king and the earthly economic interests of his survivors. In the end the latter outweighed the former. I would suggest, then, that socio-economical rather than ideological factors were responsible for the gradual decline of the number of sacrificed retainers after the reign of Djer, and the eventual discontinuation of the custom after the First Dynasty. Ideological justification of this abandonment in terms of the inviolability of human life probably followed later. In the age of the great pyramid builders the conspicuous consumption of human life was replaced by other potent symbols of royal

---

[73] See p. [6] above.
[74] Firth, *ibidem*, 23.
[75] Baines, in *Ancient Egyptian Kingship*, 136.

status and authority, although according to the folktale in the Westcar Papyrus quoted at the beginning of this article, King Cheops still had to be reminded by one of his subjects that the life of the 'noble cattle'[76] was not cheap.[77]

[76] It is important to note that this term does not refer to human beings in general, but to the Egyptians, the king's subjects. Cf. J.M.A. Janssen, 'De farao als goede herder', in *Mens en dier* [Fs. F.L.R. Sassen] (Antwerpen and Amsterdam, 1954) 71-79; D. Müller, 'Der gute Hirte. Ein Beitrag zur Geschichte ägyptischer Bildrede', *Zs. f. Ägyptische Sprache und Altertumskunde* 86 (1961) 126-44. The implications of this observation for the interpretation of human sacrifice in Ancient Egypt cannot be discussed here.

[77] For help I would like to thank my colleagues Jitse Dijkstra (Ottawa), Wolfram Grajetzki (London), and Louis Zonhoven (Leiden).

VIII. HUMAN SACRIFICE IN INDIA IN VEDIC TIMES AND BEFORE

Asko Parpola

Human sacrifice in the Veda has been the object of scholarly study for two hundred years now.[1] It was first discussed in the pioneering article of 1805 by Henry Thomas Colebrooke,[2] who knew horse sacrifice *(aśvamedha)* and human sacrifice *(puruṣamedha)* at first hand from the *Vājasaneyi-Samhitā* and the *Śatapatha-Brāhmaṇa*.[3]

---

[1] For an overall account of Vedic religion see H. Oldenberg, *Die Religion des Veda* (Berlin, 1917²); A.B. Keith, *The Religion and Philosophy of the Veda and Upanishads*, 2 vols (Cambridge, Mass., 1925); J. Gonda, *Die Religionen Indiens, I: Veda und älterer Hinduismus* (Stuttgart, 1960, 1978²); J.C. Heesterman, 'Vedism and Brahmanism', in M. Eliade (ed.), *The Encyclopedia of Religion*, 15 vols (New York, 1987) 15.217-42. Sacrificial rites occupied a prominent position in Vedic religion. The earliest text collection, the *Ṛgveda(-Saṃhitā)*, attests to the worship of gods with recited and chanted hymns and offerings of an invigorating drink called *soma*; see T. Oberlies, *Die Religion des Ṛgveda*, 2 vols (Vienna, 1998-99). The next oldest text collection, the *Atharvaveda(-Saṃhitā)*, attests to a rather different ritual background, with emphasis on royal rites (with bloody sacrifices), rites of 'white' and 'black magic' as well as domestic ceremonies; see M. Bloomfield, *The Atharva-Veda and the Gopatha-Brāhmaṇa* (Strassburg, 1899). In subsequent literature (the later *Saṃhitās*, the *Brāhmaṇas* and the *Śrautasūtras*) we meet a very complex *śrauta* ritual, with hundreds of rites divided into different categories according to the sacrificial substance (vegetable, animal or *soma* offerings or combinations of these) and their duration (from one day up to a thousand years), and with a varying number of specialized priests (as many as seventeen); see A. Weber, 'Zur Kenntniss des vedischen Opferrituals [I-II]', *Indische Studien* 10 (1868) 321-96 and 13 (1873) 217-92; A. Hillebrandt, *Ritual-Litteratur, vedische Opfer und Zauber* (Strassburg, 1897); F. Staal (ed.), *Agni: The Vedic ritual of the Fire Altar*, 2 vols (Berkeley, 1983). The relatively simple domestic *(gṛhya)* rites are discussed at greater length only in the youngest category of Vedic texts, the *Gṛhyasūtras;* see J. Gonda, *Vedic ritual (non-solemn rites)* (Leiden, 1980).

[2] H.T. Colebrooke, 'On the *Védas* or Sacred Writings of the Hindus', *Asiatick Researches*, vol. 8 (Calcutta, 1805) 369-476, reprinted in Colebrooke's *Miscellaneous Essays*, I (London, 1837) 9-113.

[3] The oldest preserved Indian texts are *Saṃhitās*, collections of hymns or verses composed in Sanskrit and addressed to deities, and used as formulae *(mantra)* accompanying ritual acts in Vedic rites. The later *Saṃhitās*, representing the several branches of the Black Yajurveda, also contain prose formulae *(yajus)* used as *mantras,*

According to him, the Veda teaches their performance 'as emblem-
atic [that is, symbolic] ceremonies, not as real sacrifices' (p. 61), and
hence 'human sacrifices were not authorized by the Véda itself'
(p. 61). This is evident from the fact that in the *puruṣamedha*, 'a hundred and eighty-five men of various specified tribes, characters,
and professions are bound to eleven posts; and after the hymn concerning the allegorical immolation of Náráyaṅa has been recited,
these human victims are liberated unhurt; and oblations of butter
are made on the sacrificial fire.'[4]

as well as prose passages *(brāhmaṇa)* commenting on the ritual and anticipating the
chronologically next literary category of *Brāhmaṇa* texts written in prose. The
Brāhmaṇas comment on the origin, meaning and purpose of sacrificial rites; they
contain mythical, legendary, cosmogonic and cosmological passages with rudiments
of philosophy (especially in their esoteric portions called *Upaniṣad*). In the younger
White Yajurveda, the *Vājasaneyi-Saṃhitā* contains only *mantras*, and all *brāhmana* passages appear in the very extensive *Śatapatha-Brāhmaṇa*. See J. Gonda, *Vedic Literature
(Saṃhitās and Brāhmaṇas)* (Wiesbaden, 1975). The next literary category of *Sūtra* texts
(in prose) aims at a systematic description of all the numerous rites. See J. Gonda,
Ritual Sūtras (Wiesbaden, 1977). It is difficult to date the Vedic texts, but the following very rough approximations may be given for the completion of the texts mentioned in this paper: the *Rgveda(-Saṃhitā)* (the oldest preserved Indian text collection), c. 1200 BC; the *Atharvaveda(-Saṃhitā)*, c. 1000 BC; the *Maitrāyaṇī Saṃhitā*,
the *Kaṭha-Saṃhitā* and the *Taittirīya-Saṃhitā*, c. 900 BC; the *Aitareya-Brāhmaṇa* and the
Tāṇḍya-Brāhmaṇa, c. 800 BC; the *Vājasaneyi-Saṃhitā* and the *Śatapatha-Brāhmaṇa*,
c. 700 BC; the *Baudhāyana-Śrautasūtra* and the *Vādhūla-Sūtra*, c. 600 BC; the
Śāṅkhāyana-Śrautasūtra, c. 500 BC; the *Kātyāyana-Śrautasūtra*, c. 300 BC. Cf. three
studies by M. Witzel: 'Tracing the Vedic Dialects' in C. Caillat (ed.), *Dialectes dans les
littératures indo-aryennes* (Paris, 1989) 97-265; 'Early Indian history: Linguistic and
Textual Parameters', in G. Erdosy (ed.), *The Indo-Aryans of Ancient South Asia: Language, Material Culture and Ethnicity* (Berlin, 1995) 85-125, and 'The Development of
the Vedic Canon and Its Schools: The Social and Political Milieu', in his *Inside the
Texts, Beyond the Texts: New Approaches to the Study of the Vedas* (Cambridge, Mass.,
1997) 257-345. The great Sanskrit epics have a complex history, but the first book of
the *Rāmāyaṇa* figuring in this paper dates from about c. AD 200; see J. Brockington,
The Sanskrit Epics (Leiden, 1998).

    [4] E. Pirart, 'Le sacrifice humain: Réflexions sur la philosophie religieuse indo-
iranienne ancienne', *Journal Asiatique* 284 (1996) 1-35, concludes: 'Human sacrifices, it
seems, were only fictitious amongst Indo-Iranian tribes in the Antiquity. Probably
their raison d'être was theoretical: there were no real human immolations except as
a punishment' (English summary on p. 2). Just like Colebrooke, Pirart (p. 8-9) bases
his view mainly on *Śatapatha-Brāhmaṇa* 13,6,2,12-13, which expressly enjoins the
release of the (166) human victims of the *puruṣamedha* after they have been consecrated for immolation. The *Śatapatha-Brāhmaṇa* recognizes only 166 (released) victims, but the 13th book of the *Vājasaneyi-Saṃhitā* contains a list of 184 victims, the difference being due to a later addition in the last-mentioned source; cf. A. Weber,
'Ueber Menschenopfer bei den Indern der vedischen Zeit', *Zs. Deutschen Morgen-
ländischen Gesellschaft* 18 (1864) 262-87 at 270-3, revised and enlarged reprint in
Weber's *Indische Streifen* I (Berlin, 1868) 54-89 at 67-70.

The issue has since been debated on a much broader textual basis than was available to Colebrooke. In 1864 Albrecht Weber published an impressive study on human sacrifice in India in Vedic times, republished in an enlarged version in 1868.[5] Weber offers an exhaustive and accurate description of all places in Vedic literature known to him at that time that contain material related to human sacrifice. In 1876, Rājendralāla Mitra published a well-reasoned paper on the subject, in which he defended the view that human sacrifice has been a reality in India, in both early and later times.[6] New textual material of high interest was added in 1926-28 when Willem Caland published extracts from the previously unknown Vedic text *Vādhūla-Sūtra*.[7] It is obvious that the whole discussion and its results are hardly known to many contemporary scholars writing on this subject. In a widely used textbook on Hinduism published for the first time in 1996, for example, we find altogether three statements on this topic that do not show much progress beyond Colebrooke:

'There was also a human sacrifice *(puruṣamedha)* modelled on the horse sacrifice, though the human victims were set free after their consecration.
'Indeed the human sacrifice, the sacrifice of the 'great beast' *(mahā paśu)*, is regarded in the Veda as the highest sacrifice, even though human sacrifices may never have actually taken place.'
'We do possess texts which refer to a human sacrifice in the Indian traditions, but such a practice may never have actually occurred, existing only as an ideal or possibility.[8]

The last statement is factually wrong. Early on, William Crooke, in addition to providing numerous textual references to human sacrifice, especially to the goddess Durgā and her multiforms as well as to demoniac village godlings in the Indian narrative literature, found

---

[5] Weber, 'Ueber Menschenopfer bei den Indern der vedischen Zeit'. One part of Weber's material, the myth of Manu's sacrifice of his wife, has now been explored in an absorbing book by Stephanie Jamison, *Sacrificed Wife / Sacrificer's Wife: Women, Ritual, and Hospitality in Ancient India* (New York, 1996).

[6] R. Mitra, 'On Human Sacrifices in Ancient India', *Journal of the Asiatic Society of Bengal* 45, Part I (1876) 76-118, reprinted in Mitra's book *Indo-Aryans: Contributions Towards the Elucidation of Their Ancient and Mediaeval History*, 2 vols (London and Calcutta, 1882) 2.49-113.

[7] W. Caland, 'Eine dritte/vierte Mitteilung über das Vādhūlasūtra', *Acta Orientalia* 4 (1926) 1-41 and 161-213 and 6 (1928) 97-241, reprinted in Caland's *Kleine Schriften*, ed. M. Witzel (Stuttgart 1990) 303-96 and 397-541.

[8] G. Flood, *An Introduction to Hinduism* (Cambridge, 1996) 41, 184, 218, respectively.

copious evidence of actual human sacrifices available in ethno-
graphic records and official documents.[9]

One important reason for statements like the ones quoted above
is probably the criticism leveled by such an authority as Hermann
Oldenberg in his very influential handbook of Vedic religion in 1894
and its revised edition in 1917. Oldenberg states that to his knowledge there is no sure evidence for the existence in Vedic India of a
genuine human sacrifice. However, Oldenberg had his own narrow
definition for this term and other reservations.[10]

A short summary of the practice of human sacrifice in the Veda
was offered in 1960 by one of the best twentieth-century experts of
Vedic and Hindu religion, Jan Gonda, who underlined its being a
debated issue. And in any case, as he noted, human sacrifice is no
longer topical in the Śrauta ritual. This being the only treatment of
the subject in his handbook, one gets the impression that Gonda did
not consider it a matter of great importance.[11]

Lack of space does not allow me to cover many points in this
chapter. Most of the debate has centered on isolated text passages,

---

[9] W. Crooke, *An Introduction to the Popular Religion and Folklore of Northern India*
(Allahabad, 1894) 294-301 and *The Popular Religion and Folk-Lore of Northern India*, II
(Westminster, 1896²) 166-79.

[10] H. Oldenberg, *Die Religion des Veda*², 361-4. After discussing the ritual of the fire
altar *(agnicayana)*, Oldenberg states: 'So erkennen wir hier den über die Erde verbrei-
teten Glauben wieder, dass ein Bau Festigkeit durch ein Bauopfer, insonderheit ein
Menschenopfer erlangt. Doch trifft offenbar die gebräuchliche Benennung dieses
Ritus als Opfer, sofern man "Opfer" im gewöhnlichen Sinn des Wortes versteht,
seine eigentliche Bedeutung nicht... Also ein mit der Tötung eines Menschen
getriebener Zauber, aber kein Menschenopfer im gewöhnlichen Sinn... Was sonst für
die Existenz vedischer Menschenopfer angeführt wird, scheint mir nicht jeden
Zweifel auszuschliessen. Wenn die alten Ritualbücher in einem eigenen Abschnitt
nach dem Rossopfer das "Menschenopfer" *(puruṣamedha)* mit allem Detail schildern,
so sieht das ganz nach einem Phantasieprodukt aus, dem Rossopfer nachgebildet
und aus dessen kolossalen Verhältnissen ins noch Kolossalere gesteigert. Sollte selbst
dies Prunkstück der grossen priesterlichen Modellsammlung irgend einmal die
Frömmigkeit eines Fürsten zur Ausführung begeistert haben, bliebe das doch ein für
die Betrachtung des wirklichen vedischen Kultus unerheblicher Zufall. Von echten
Menschenopfern aber, die entweder auf den Kultus von Kannibalen zurückgehen
oder als Sühnopfer die Hingabe eines Menschenlebens für verwirkte oder gefährdete
andere Menschenleben, als Erstlingsopfer einen Zauber für Mehrung der men-
schlichen Fruchtbarkeit darstellen, sind, soviel ich gegenwärtig sehe, im vedischen
Indien sichere Spuren nicht zu entdecken. Welches Gewicht den von solchen Opfern
berichtenden mehr oder weniger alten Legenden zukommt, bleibt zweifelhaft. An
sich ist es freilich durchaus möglich, dass die so weit verbreitete Praxis auch in
diesem Kulturbereich heimisch gewesen ist.'

[11] J. Gonda, *Die Religionen Indiens*, 2 vols (Stuttgart, 1960) I.173.

and concrete textual evidence might indeed be of great interest. I therefore discuss first a few important textual references and their interpretation, hoping to establish beyond reasonable doubt that Vedic texts do indeed attest to real human sacrifices performed within the memory preserved by the authors, and that by the time of the Brāhmaṇa texts, the actual practice of bloody offering had already begun to diminish. Then I underline the direct association of human sacrifice with some pivotal concepts of Brahmanical religion – cosmic man and his sacrifice. I conclude with a few words on the wider context of human sacrifice in the Veda and my own views in this regard. The alleged archaeological evidence of Vedic fire altars is not taken up here, as it is ably discussed and criticized by Hans Bakker in the next chapter of this volume.

1. The Śunaḥśepa legend

In 1852 Horace Hayman Wilson published an article 'On the Sacrifice of Human Beings as an Element of the Ancient Religion of India.'[12] In this paper Wilson translated the Vedic variant of the Śunaḥśepa legend as preserved in the then unedited *Aitareya-Brāhmaṇa*, which he sagaciously placed around 700-600 BC, in between the *Ṛgveda* and the later epic *Rāmāyaṇa*. For the benefit of the readers of this book who may not be acquainted with this text, some excerpts from Wilson's translation follow:[13]

> Harischandra [Hariścandra] the son of Vedhas, was a prince of the race of Ikshwáku [Ikṣvāku]: he had a hundred wives, but no son. ... [Sage] Nárada [Nārada] advised Harischandra to pray to Varuṇa for a son, promising to present him as an offering to that divinity. 'So be it,' said the prince; and repairing to Varuṇa he said: 'Let a son be born unto me, and with him, I will sacrifice to you.' – 'So be it,' said Varuṇa, and a son was born to the king, who was named Rohita. 'A son has been born to you,' said Varuṇa, 'sacrifice with him to me.' – 'An animal,' replied the king, 'is fit for sacrifice only after ten days from birth. When the term of purification has passed, I will sacrifice to you.' – 'Very well,' said Varuṇa. The ten days

---

[12] H.H. Wilson, 'On the Sacrifice of Human Beings as an Element of the Ancient Religion of India', *J. Roy. Asiatic Soc.* 13 (1852) 96-107.

[13] Wilson's antiquated spelling of the Sanskrit names and words is retained, except that ñ is replaced with ṇ, but the current spelling is given in square brackets at the first occurrence.

expired, and Varuṇa said, 'Now sacrifice with him to me.' … [Four more times the king asks for, and is granted, a postponement.] The youth grew, and was invested with arms; and Varuṇa said, 'now sacrifice to me with him.' The king replied, 'Be it so.' But he called his son, and said, 'My child, Varuṇa gave you to me, and I have also promised to sacrifice with you to him.' – 'By no means,' said the youth; and taking his bow, he set off to the forest, where he wandered for a twelvemonth.

Upon Rohita's disappearance, Varuṇa inflicted the descendant of Ikshwáku with dropsy; which when Rohita heard he set off to return home. On the way he was met by Indra in the shape of a Brahman [who urged him to wander on. This happened four more times, so that eventually] Rohita returned for the sixth year to the forests. Whilst wandering thus in the woods he encountered the Rishi [Ṛṣi, Sage] Ajigartta [Ajīgarta], the son of Suyavasa, who was distressed through want of food. He had three sons, Śunahpuchcha [Śunaḥpuccha], Śunahśephas [Śunaḥśepa], and Śunalángula [Śunolāṅgūla]. Rohita said to him, 'Rishi, I will give thee a hundred cows for one of these thy sons, that by him I may redeem myself.' But the Rishi, taking hold of the eldest, said, 'Not this one;' 'No, nor this one,' said the mother, securing the youngest; but they both agreed to sell the middle son Śunahśephas, and Rohita, having paid the hundred cows, took the youth and departed from the woods. He proceeded to his father and said, 'Rejoice, father, for with this youth shall I redeem myself.' So Hariśchandra had recourse to the royal Varuṇa, and said, 'With this youth will I sacrifice to you.' And Varuṇa replied, 'Be it so – a Brahman is better than a Kshatriya [Kṣatriya];' and thence directed the king to perform the sacrificial ceremony termed the Rájasúya [Rājasūya, the royal consecration]; and he, on the day of initiation, appointed Śunahśephas to be the human victim.

At that sacrifice of Hariśchandra, Viswámitra [Viśvāmitra] was the Hotri [Hotṛ] or reciter of the Rich [Ṛc]; Jamadagni, the Adhwaryu [Adhvaryu], or repeater of the Yajus …; but they had no one who was competent to perform the office of binding the victim, when consecrated, to the stake, whereupon Ajigartta said, 'If you give me another hundred cows I will perform the duty;' and they gave him the cows, and he bound the victim. But for the victim thus consecrated and bound, sanctified by the divinities of sacrifice, and thrice circumambulated by the priests bearing burning brands of sacred grass, no immolater could be found, when Ajigartta again offered himself, saying, 'Give me another hundred cows and I will immolate him;' accordingly they gave him the cows, and he went forth to sharpen his knife. In this interval Śunahśephas reflected,

'These [people] will put me to death as if I were not a man but an animal; my only hope is the aid of some of the gods, to whom I will have recourse.' [Śunahśepa now prays to various gods with Ṛgvedic verses quoted here by their initial words. While he was repeating the three concluding stanzas,] his bonds fell off, and he was set free; and the king, the father of Rohita, was cured of his complaint ... [The legend ends with Ajīgarta's claim to have his son back, the rejection of Ajīgarta by Śunahśepa, and Śunahśepa's eventual adoption by Viśvāmitra, who curses the eldest 50 of his 100 sons who refused to acknowledge Śunahśepa's primogeniture, so that these rejected sons became the ancestors of various despised tribes.]

The legend had been known from a later version in the first book of the *Rāmāyaṇa*, but that version 'leaves it doubtful whether an actual sacrifice of the victim, or one only typical [= symbolical], is intended,' while 'there is no question of its purport as it is found in the *Aitareya Brāhmaṇa*' and 'it may be received as authority to a qualified extent for ... the sacrifice, on particular occasions, of human victims.' In 1859, Max Müller published a new translation of the legend and edited its text with the variant readings of the *Śāṅkhāyana-Śrautasūtra*.[14] In his opinion, the legend 'shows that, at that early time, the Brāhmans were familiar with the idea of human sacrifices, and that ... Brāhmans were ready to sell their sons for that purpose.'[15]

Wilson compared Hariścandra's vow with Abraham's readiness to offer up his son,[16] noting that the purport of the divine command could hardly have been wholly unfamiliar to him, as a similar sort of sacrifice occurs in later Jewish history in the vow of Jephtha (*Judges* 11). The Jews borrowed 'the offering of children to Moloch ... from their idolatrous neighbours.'[17] Müller retorted: 'it does not necessarily follow from this legend that the Rishis, the authors of the Vedic hymns, offered human sacrifices' for 'no one would conclude from the willingness of Abraham to sacrifice his own son in obedience to a supposed command from Jehovah, that the Jews had been in the habit of offering their sons as victims.'[18]

---

[14] M. Müller, *A History of Ancient Sanskrit Literature* (London, 1859) 408-19 and 573-88.

[15] Müller, *Sanskrit Literature*, 408.

[16] See Noort, this volume, Ch. V.

[17] Wilson, 'Sacrifice of Human Beings', 105 f.

[18] Müller, *Sanskrit Literature*, 419. D. Shulman, *The hungry god: Hindu tales of filicide and devotion* (Chicago, 1993), has sensitively compared the similarities and differences

The older version of the *Aitareya Brāhmaṇa* explicitly quotes the seven hymns attributed to Śunaḥśepa in the *Ṛgveda* (1,24-30); the later version of the *Rāmāyaṇa* refers to 'sacred verses'. However, to Friedrich Rosen, who edited the first book of the *Ṛgveda* in 1838, the Śunaḥśepa hymns, 'except in one or two doubtful passages, bore no relation to the legend of the Rámáyaña, and offered no indication of a human victim deprecating death.'[19] A similar opinion was expressed by Rudolf Roth, who also published on the Śunaḥśepa legend of the *Aitareya-Brāhmaṇa*. Roth concluded that the features central to the legend came into being only after the *Ṛgveda*, and that they are of a didactic nature. The story is ethical and directed against the gruesomeness of human sacrifice.[20] According to A.B. Keith too, 'the whole story reveals the slaying as proposed as something utterly monstrous ... it is enough to show that human sacrifice was for the Brāhmaṇa period a horror beyond words.'[21] Rājendralāla Mitra, however, does find indications of human sacrifices in the *Ṛgveda*, and regards these as pointing to a real and not a merely symbolical sacrifice.[22] According to Julius Eggeling, the *Ṛgvedic* verses 1,24,11-13 and 5,2,7 contain the earliest reference to the story of Śunaḥśepa. The verse in the fifth book, addressed to Agni, says: 'Even Śunaḥśepa, who had been bound for the sake of a thousand (cows), didst thou let loose from the stake, for he had already been prepared (namely, for the sacrifice).' 'This legend, so far from bearing witness to the existence of human sacrifices as a generally recognized practice at the time when it originated, would rather seem to mark this particular case as an exceptional one.'[23]

Weber thought that the royal consecration (*rājasūya*), where Śunaḥśepa was supposed to be sacrificed, originally contained such a sacrifice, but the ritualized recital of the legend during the *rājasūya*

in the Biblical story of Abraham's *aqedah* (this Hebrew term for the sacrifice based on a divine command comes from the root *'qd* 'to bind to an altar') and its Indian counterparts, besides the Śunaḥśepa legend especially the Tamil and Telugu stories of a devotee's slaughter of his own son as a meal to Śiva disguised as a Bhairava ascetic who demands this ultimate sacrifice.

[19] Wilson, 'Sacrifice of Human Beings', 97.

[20] R. Roth, 'Die Sage von Çunaḥçepa', *Indische Studien* 1 (1850) 457-64 and 2 (1853) 112-23 at 115-8, 120.

[21] A.B. Keith (transl.), *The Veda of the Black Yajus School entitled Taittirīya Sanhitā* I (Cambridge, Mass., 1914) cxl.

[22] Mitra, 'Human Sacrifices', 89-95, 118.

[23] J. Eggeling, *The Śatapatha-Brāhmaṇa* V (Oxford, 1900) xxxv-vi.

is its only reminiscence.[24] Interesting proposals about the meaning and function of the legend at the royal consecration have been proposed by Jan Heesterman,[25] and we shall return to them presently. Unfortunately, space forbids following the discussion of the Śunaḥśepa legend further.[26] Yet the principal arguments for and against the legend's value as evidence for human sacrifice should be apparent from the early studies quoted above.

2. From human and bloody sacrifice to vegetable offerings

Wilson found vicarous sacrifice evidenced by the Śunaḥśepa story, in which 'one human victim is substituted for another, whilst in the parallel cases of antiquity the substitutes were animals.'[27]

Although he was sceptical about persistence from the Ṛgveda, Max Müller saw no reason to doubt the previous existence of human sacrifice suggested by the Śunaḥśepa legend. In his opinion the *Aitareya Brāhmaṇa* offers a striking confirmation of this.

> It is said there (*Ait.-br.* 6.8) that the gods took man for their victim. "As he was taken, *medha* ... went out of him. It entered the horse. Therefore the horse became the sacrificial animal. Then the gods took the horse, but as it was taken, the *medha* went out of him. It entered the ox. Therefore the ox became the sacrificial animal. The same happened with the ox. Afterwards the sheep, then the goat, and at last the earth became the victim. From the earth rice was produced and rice was offered in the form of *puroḍāśa*, in lieu of the sacrificial animal. The other beings, which had formerly been offered and then been dismissed, are supposed to have become changed into animals unfit for sacrifice; man into a savage, the

---

[24] A. Weber, 'Über die Königsweihe, den Rājasūya', in *Abh. Kön. Preuss. Ak. Wiss. Berlin 1893, Philosophisch-historische Klasse*, II.1-158 at 108-10.

[25] J.C. Heesterman, *The Ancient Indian Royal Consecration* (The Hague, 1957) 158-61.

[26] The interested reader may turn to the studies of F. Weller, *Die Legende von Śunaḥśepa im Aitareyabrāhmaṇa und Śāṅkhāyanaśrautasūtra* (Berlin, 1956); H. Lommel, 'Die Śunaḥśepa-Legende', *Zs. Deutschen Morgenl. Ges.* 114 (1964) 122-61; H. Falk, 'Die Legende von Śunaḥśepa vor ihren rituellen Hintergrund', *ibidem* 134 (1984) 115-35; D.G. White, 'Śunaḥśepa unbound', *Revue de l'Histoire des Religions* 203 (1986) 227-62; D.G. White, *Myths of the Dog-Man* (Chicago, 1991); Shulman, *The Hungry God*; A. Parpola, 'Sāvitrī and resurrection', in A. Parpola and S. Tenhunen (eds), *Changing Patterns of Family and Kinship in South Asia* (Helsinki, 1998) 167-312 at 287-300; and V. Hämeen-Anttila, 'Back to Śunaḥśepa: Remarks on the Gestation of the Indian Literary Narrative', in K. Karttunen and P. Koskikallio (eds), *Vidyārṇavavandanam: Essays in Honour of Asko Parpola* (Helsinki, 2001) 181-213.

[27] Wilson, 'Sacrifice of Human Beings', 106f.

horse into a *Bos Gaurus,* the ox into a Gayal ox, the sheep into a camel *(ushṭra),* the goat into a *śarabha.* All these animals are *amedhya* or unclean, and should not be eaten."

Müller comments:

The drift of this story is most likely that in former times all these victims had been offered. We know it for certain in the case of horses and oxen, though afterwards these sacrifices were discontinued. As to sheep and goats, they were considered proper victims to a still later time. When vegetable offerings took the place of bloody victims, it was clearly the wish of the author of our passage to show that, for certain sacrifices, these rice-cakes were as efficient as the flesh of animals. He carries out his argument still further, and tries to show that in the rice the beard corresponds to the hair of the animal: the husk to the skin; the *phalikaraṇas* to blood; the meal to the flesh; the straw to the bones.[28]

Jan Houben has recently discussed in detail the embarassment about violence in sacrifice to which the texts of the Middle and Late Vedic period attest, finding it to agree with the general trend towards nonviolence and vegetarianism that can be observed from these times onward in Indian culture.[29]

This *ahiṃsā* tendency was underlined already by Auguste Barth in 1879: 'Originally [Vedic sacrifices] were ... feasts ... in token of which the participants, priests and *yajamāna,* consume each a small portion of the different offerings.'[30] The necessity to eat the *iḍā* portion of each victim is implied in the reason given in *Śatapatha-Brāhmaṇa* 13,6,2,12-13 for the release of the human victims at the *puruṣamedha:* 'Now, the victims had had the fire carried round them, but they were not yet slaughtered, – Then a [bodiless] voice said to him, "Puruṣa, do not consummate (these human victims): if thou wert to consummate them, man *(puruṣa)* would eat man." Accordingly, as soon as fire had been carried round them, he set them free, and offered oblations to the same divinities, and thereby gratified those divinities,

---

[28] Müller, *Sanskrit Literature,* 419f.

[29] J.E.M. Houben, 'To Kill or Not to Kill the Sacrificial Animal *(yajña-paśu)*? Arguments and Perspectives in Brahmanical Ethical Philosophy', in J.E.M. Houben and K.R. van Kooij (eds), *Violence Denied* (Leiden, 1999) 105-83.

[30] A. Barth, *Les religions de l'Inde* (Paris, 1879), quoted from the English version, *The Religions of India,* transl. J. Wood (London, 1882) 56. Cf. also S. Lévi, *La doctrine du sacrifice dans les Brāhmaṇas* (Paris, 1898) 138.

and, thus gratified, they gratified him with all objects of desire.'[31] Repugnance against cannibalism is evidenced likewise by the following legend of the *Vādhūla-Sūtra* on the piling of the fire altar: 'Previously they used to immolate a man as a victim to Prajāpati. Karṇājāya piled his fire altar with this (sacrifice). But as the gods were retreating, Dhārtakratava Jātūkarṇi did not want to eat the *iḍā* portion of this (human victim). Then they made the horse the victim. But as the gods were retreating even further, Rahahkṣita Jātūkarṇi did not want to eat its *iḍā* portion. ... [Finally] they made a hornless goat the victim, saying: "The hornless all-coloured goat is Prajāpati's sacrificial victim".[32]

However, this sort of historical development is not necessarily the only explanation for the formation of the set of these five victims, since 'cows, horses, men, sheep and goats' are mentioned as sacrificial animals *(paśú)* belonging to Rudra as early as Atharvaveda 11,2,9.

3. The five animals and the fire altar

In the ritual piling of the fire altar *(agnicayana)*, all these five victims are bound to the stake, appeased, have fire carried around them, and are slain.[33] According to the *Śatapatha-Brāhmaṇa* (6, 2, 2, 18), the slaughter takes place on the first night of the year. The man who is bound to the stake with the longest rope is sacrificed first for Viśvakarman, then the horse for Varuṇa, the bull for Indra, the ram for Tvaṣṭṛ, and the he-goat for Agni. The *Kātyāyana-Śrautasūtra* (16, 1, 14) adds that the man is to be slain in a screened shed. The head of each of the five victims is cut off, and the trunks are thrown into water at a place where mud is later fetched for baking the bricks of which the fire altar is built. Mixed with the mud, the bodies become the five layers of the altar. The body of the goat, however, is prepared and partly eaten according to the normal rules of an animal sacrifice. According to another opinion, this is done with all five bodies. The heads are skinned and the brain removed – or neither skin nor brain is removed – and the skull is smeared with melted butter and deposited for later use. The heads will be placed (the human head in

---

[31] Eggeling, *The Śatapatha-Brāhmaṇa* V, 410-1.
[32] Cf. Caland, 'Eine vierte Mitteilung', 229-32.
[33] For the following, see Weber, 'Menschenopfer', 263ff., (1868) 55ff.

the middle and the others around it) in a newly made fire-pot *(ukhā)*, and the heads and the pot are consecrated and laid down as six bricks in the lowest layer of the fire altar. The *Śatapatha-Brāhmaṇa* (6, 2, 1, 37) criticizes those who procure the heads of the five victims without sacrificing them, for such sacrificers will become mortal carcasses, like Aṣāḍhi Sauśromateya, who died quickly after such heads had been put into his fire altar.[34] The same text also does not approve of golden or earthen replicas (38-39), but recommends the slaughter of the five victims, as was first done by Prajāpati and then by others up to Śyāparṇa Sāyakāyana. The text admits, however, that Śyāparṇa Sāyakāyana was the last to do so and that 'nowadays only these two (animals) are slaughtered, (a he-goat) for Prajāpati, and (a he-goat) for Vāyu' (39).

In the sequel (6, 2, 2, 1 ff.) the *Śatapatha-Brāhmaṇa* ascribes the sacrifice of a he-goat to Prajāpati to the Carakas, a rivalling school of the Black Yajurveda. Indeed, according to the *Kaṭha-Saṃhitā* (19, 8; 20, 8) and the *Taittirīya-Saṃhitā* (5, 1, 8, 1 ff.; 5, 2, 9, 1 ff.), the human head is obtained by buying it for 21 beans, the other (unspecified) sacrificial animals are set free after the fire has been carried around them, and only a he-goat for Prajāpati is sacrificed; a he-goat for Vāyu is also mentioned. These texts mention specifically a human head and the heads of a horse and a bull, the *Taittirīya-Saṃhitā* also the head of a snake, among the animal heads to be placed in the *ukhā* pot. The *mantras* of both the White and Black Yajurveda, however, are practically identical and mention the five victims as man or two-footer, horse, bull, sheep and goat.[35]

---

[34] J. McDaniel, 'Interviews with a Tantric Kālī priest: Feeding skulls in the Town of Sacrifice', in D.G. White (ed.), *Tantra in Practice* (Princeton, 2000) 72-80, has interviewed a Bengali Tantric priest, who feeds the skulls of his ancestral Kālī temple. 'Under the altar *(vedi)* of this temple there are 108 skulls buried. Some altars have 1,008 skulls. Skulls awaken the Goddess, and make her present here. Male gods have stones *(śilas)* or lingas [of Śiva], but goddesses have skulls' and 'The skulls in this temple mostly come from people who died in epidemics, especially cholera epidemics. Large numbers of people used to die, and there was no effective system of cremation at that time. Corpses would lie on the roadside or in the forests' (p. 77). I should like to point out that the numbers of the skulls (108 or 1,008) represent sacred numbers that ultimately seem to come from the number of bricks in the Vedic fire altar (10,800): they represent the 360 x 30 'moments' of the year.

[35] Could the 'five-skull seat' of the Bengali Tantrics ultimately be related to the five skulls of the Vedic fire altar? According to McDaniel, 'Interviews', 77 for the five-skull seat 'people use the skulls of a low-caste man, a jackal, a tiger, a snake, and a virgin girl *(kumārī)*. They must be young, and die suddenly by violence. Nobody wants the skulls of people who died of disease or old age. Some tāntrikas have a

The *Vādhūla-Sūtra*, which belongs to the Taittirīya school, states:

> Previously they used to immolate these five animal victims: a man for Prajāpati, for Agni; a horse for Agni *kṣatravat;*[36] a bull for Agni *kṣatrabhṛt;* a sheep for Agni *brahmaṇvat;* and a goat for Agni *puṣṭimat.* After a firebrand has been taken around them and the hornless goat for Prajāpati, these five are set free and the sacrifice concluded with the hornless goat for Prajāpati. – He should make these five animals out of rice and barley.

The *Vādhūla-Sūtra* further tells that Agni had revealed to the king of the Kurus the (secret) knowledge concerning the heads of the sacrificial victims *(paśuśīrṣavidyā)*. The learned Brahmins of the Kurus and Pañcālas wanted to have it, but the king did not reveal it to anybody until Śuddhojas Māṇḍavya sent his student Māriṣābhagi to the king. The king asked Māriṣābhagi's group to perform the sacrifice on his behalf according to that knowledge. The sacrificer whose priests do not have this knowledge will die.[37]

Even Oldenberg accepts that human beings had been killed during the construction of the fire altar not too long before the *Brāhmaṇa* texts were composed, though he denies that this killing had a sacrificial character. In his opinion, it was a charm purporting to give firmness to the construction, an example of a custom widely attested in India and elsewhere.[38] Indeed, according to the commentator Karka, the bodies make the bricks firm; Weber further compares this with Roman, German and Slavonic traditions of embodying a human or animal victim in a wall in order to make it firm, and thinks that a Proto-Indo-European origin is possible. But the *Śatapatha-Brāhmaṇa* insists on the real heads of the victims, because only if the heads of

---

special relationship with the Ḍoms... who work in hospitals. These Ḍoms notify them of appropriate deaths'. McDaniel's informant Tapan says that 'his grandfather's spirit has chosen to dwell in his favorite meditation place, his ritual seat, which is placed over five buried skulls at the foot of a large tree in the woods near the temple. His grandfather created this "five-skull seat" *(pañcamuṇḍī āsana)* and spent much time there during his life. When Tapan wishes to communicate with his grandfather's spirit, he sits on this ritual seat and meditates there' (p. 75).

[36] This and the following attributes specify forms of the Fire-God Agni related to different social groups.

[37] Cf. Caland, 'Eine vierte Mitteilung', 229-32.

[38] Oldenberg, *Die Religion des Veda*², 361-2, see above, note 13. Pirart, 'Le sacrifice humain', 8, too, concedes that the conception of a symbolic human sacrifice 'peut supposer l'existence, à une époque préhistorique, d'un sacrifice humain comportant l'immolation effective d'un homme.'

living animals are united with their bodies (represented by the five layers of the altar) do they become alive again.[39]

4. The Fire Altar and Cosmic Man

The 10,800 bricks of the fire altar represent the 30 x 360 moments of the year, and the body of the exhausted Creator God Prajāpati is conceived of as the year:[40]

> In building the great fireplace one restores and reintegrates Prajāp-ati, whose dismemberment had been the creation of the universe, and makes him whole and complete. At the same time and by means of the same ritual acts the sacrificer, who is identified with Prajāpati (cf. [Śatapatha-Brāhmaṇa] 7.4.1.15), constructs himself a new sacral personality and secures the continuance of his existence (amṛtam).'[41]

In 1883, Monier Williams wrote:

> The most preposterous of all the ideas connected with the sacrificial act was that of making it the first act of creation. In the Purusha hymn of the Ṛig-veda (X. 90) the gods are represented as cutting up and sacrificing Purusha, the primeval Male, and then forming the whole Universe from his head and limbs... The Tāṇḍya-Brāhmaṇa makes the lord of creatures offer himself up as a sacrifice. Even Sacrifice (Yajña) itself was sometimes personified as a god ...Indeed it is evident that human sacrifice was once part of the Brāhmanical system.[42]

It was early pointed out that the sacrifice of the primeval Puruṣa is likely to go back to Proto-Indo-European times, as it has a parallel in the Nordic myth of the Giant Ymir, out of whose body the gods built the heaven and earth, sea and mountains, and so on.[43] Other Indo-European peoples, too, have preserved comparable ideas,

---

[39] Cf. Weber, 'Menschenopfer', 263ff., (1868) 55ff.

[40] On the technicalities of the agnicayana ritual, see A. Weber, Indische Studien 13 (1873) 217-92, and Staal, Agni; on the agnicayana and Prajāpati, see J. Gonda, Prajāpati and the Year (Amsterdam, 1984) and Gonda, Prajāpati's Rise to Higher Rank (Leiden, 1986) 16, 166-75, 193f.

[41] Gonda, Prajāpati's Rise, 16f.

[42] M. [Monier-]Williams, Religious thought and life in India: Vedism, Brahmanism and Hinduism (London, 1883) 23f.

[43] Cf. L. von Schroeder, Indiens Literatur und Cultur in historischer Entwicklung (Leipzig, 1887) 217.

including the Slavonic (with Adam in Old Russian literature),[44] the Romans (with Romulus), and the Iranians (with Gayōmart in the *Bundahišn*).[45]

Sylvain Lévi, in his pioneering study of the sacrifice in the light of the *Brāhmaṇa* texts, briefly discussed human sacrifice. He observed that the only authentic sacrifice would be suicide, which has been known and practised in India at all times, probably also in Vedic times. In the sacrificial system of the *Brāhmaṇa* texts, however, it is represented by its closest counterpart, human sacrifice, in which man redeems himself by sacrificing man. The legend of the Śunaḥśepa is an important monument of this cruel practice.[46]

In his article 'Self-Sacrifice in Vedic Ritual', Jan Heesterman writes:

> The vedic ritual texts abound in statements equating the sacrificer with the sacrificial victim and, generally, with substances offered in the fire ... Generally, when fasting in preparation for sacrifice, the sacrificer becomes himself the oblational substance. Self-sacrifice, then, is a commonplace notion in the ritualistic discussions of the *Brāhmaṇa* texts. The sacrificer's prototype is Prajāpati, the Lord of Creatures, who is both sacrificer and victim. Holding both ends together in his person, Prajāpati is himself the sacrifice, as the texts never tire of stating. ... [T]he Prajāpati-sacrifice identification harks back to the celebrated Puruṣa hymn (*Ṛgveda* 10.90). By immolating the puruṣa, the primordial being, the gods break up the unchecked expansiveness of his vitality and turn it into the articulated order of life and universe. Life and order must be won out of their opposites, sacrificial death and destruction. Fittingly, this paradox is expressed in the enigmatically involuted phrases that conclude the hymn: "With sacrifice the gods sacrificed sacrifice, these were the first ordinances." The riddle is the more critical since the puruṣa is not just a mythic figure. The word simply means 'man'. The enigmatic phrase is the riddle of man's life and death.[47]

---

[44] The Old Russian 'Poem on the Dove Book', *Stikh o golubinoj knigě* (the title *Golubinaya kniga* here is a folk-etymological transformation of *Glubinnaya kniga* 'The Book of Profound Mysteries', designation of apocryphal works current in the Middle Ages), and its variants speak of the emergence of the boyar princes from the head of Adam, of the peasants from his knee; and of the sun from God's face, of the moon from his breast, the dawn from his eyes, the stars from his vestments, the winds from the Holy Ghost, and so on, cf. S. Schayer, 'A note on the Old Russian variant of the purushasūkta', *Archiv Orientální* 7 (1935) 319-23.

[45] References in Oberlies, *Die Religion des Ṛgveda* II, 381 n. 214 and Pirart, 'Le sacrifice humain'.

[46] Lévi, *La doctrine du sacrifice*, 133-8.

[47] J.C. Heesterman, 'Self-Sacrifice in Vedic Ritual', in S. Shaked *et al.* (eds), *Gilgul* (Leiden, 1987) 91-106 at 91f.

Heesterman has rightly questioned Friedrich Weller's conclusion that the Śunaḥśepa legend originally had nothing to do with royal rites.[48] In his opinion, the *rājasūya* is originally not an investiture of the king, but a yearly recurring festival by which the regeneration of the powers of fertility and the renewal of the universe are effected. The festival centres round the king, whose rebirth is equivalent with the universal regeneration and renewal. Now the chief interest of the legend lies in the birth of a son, conceived of as a real rebirth of the father [...] Hariścandra and Śunaḥśepa are ritually reborn through the sacrifice, through the brahman power extant in the *ṛc* stanzas [i.e. verses of the *Ṛgveda*] recited by Śunaḥśepa. Against this background it becomes clear why a brahmin should act as the sacrificial victim: he represents the brahman sacrifice out of which the sacrificer is reborn. [...] In the last resort it is, however, not the brahmin, who is immolated, but the sacrificer himself, who is in the case of Hariścandra doubled by his son and the brahmin Śunaḥśepa. He himself must pass through death in order to be reborn. Out of himself he is reborn, *ātmā hi jajña ātmanaḥ*, as Nārada teaches [...] The idea of the rebirth of the sacrificer out of himself is not in opposition to the idea of rebirth out of brahman sacrifice. The equation of the sacrificer with the sacrifice is well established; Prajāpati, the first sacrificer, is at the same time the sacrificial victim while he is also interchangeable with brahman.[49]

5. The wider context: Connections with Sakta Tantrism, the Near East and the Eurasian steppes

The theme of the severed head and its restoration, involving resurrection by means of a cultic drink (possessed by the victim), is pivotal in the 'Pre-Vedic, Asuric' religion sketched by Kasten Rönnow in 1929.[50] The theme is important also in the 'preclassical' phase of development that, according to Heesterman, preceded the 'classical' Vedic ritual of the *Brāhmaṇa* and *Sūtra* texts.[51] During the past forty years Heesterman has built up an impressive model of an 'agonistic'

---

[48] F. Weller, *Die Legende von Śunaḥśepa* (Berlin, 1956).

[49] Heesterman, *Royal Consecration*, 158-61.

[50] K. Rönnow, 'Zur Erklärung des Pravargya, des Agnicayana und der Sautrāmaṇī', *Le Monde Oriental* 23 (1929) 69-173.

[51] Cf. J.C. Heesterman, 'The Case of the Severed Head', *Wiener Zs. f. Kunde Süd- und Ostasiens* 11 (1967) 22-43.

and 'cyclical' system, in which violence, sexuality, feasting and changes of purity and impurity between two competing parties played central roles.[52] Developing studies of J.W. Hauer,[53] Samarendranath Biswas[54] and others, Heesterman has shown that sodalities of warring young men called *vrātya* were important agents in this ritual, and that their rites, the *vrātyastomas*, and other rites that share with the *vrātyastomas* some unusual components (such as ritual copulation)[55] are fossilized remnants of the archaic preclassical ritual.[56] In 1966, Paul Horsch was able to connect the *vrātyas* with the proto-epic *gāthā* and *śloka* verses of the Middle Vedic texts – and with the Śunaḥśepa legend in which such verses figure prominently.[57] At one point, however, that is, when the *Brāhmaṇa* texts were codified, the Vedic ritual was fundamentally changed, and the violent and sexual elements were mostly reduced to symbols. Heesterman has argued that this internal development of the Vedic ritual was the result of social and economic changes.

But there were outside influences, too. The human sacrifice of the Veda and the change in the ritual can and must be studied in a wider perspective as well. I conclude by mentioning some of my own endeavours in this regard. I am convinced that the 'preclassical' Vedic ritual prevailed in northern India before the arrival of the main wave of Ṛgvedic Aryans around 1350 BC, and continued to do so outside the Vedic realm and for some time even inside the Vedic area.[58] The concept of 'cosmic man' *(puruṣa)* and his sacrifice becomes suddenly important in the youngest hymns of the *Ṛgveda*, soon after the Ṛgvedic Aryans had settled in India and been in contact with its previous occupants, largely an earlier wave of Aryans

---

[52] Cf. J.C. Heesterman, *The Inner Conflict of Tradition: Essays in Indian Ritual, Kingship, and Society* (Chicago, 1985) and *The Broken World of Sacrifice: An Essay in Ancient Indian Ritual* (Chicago, 1993).

[53] J.W. Hauer, *Der Vrātya: Untersuchungen über die nichtbrahmanische Religion Altindiens* I (Stuttgart, 1927).

[54] S. N. Biswas, *Die Vrātyas und die Vrātyastomas* (unpublished Ph. D. thesis, Berlin, 1955).

[55] Foremost among the rites connected with the *vrātyastomas* are the new year rite *mahāvrata*, the horse/human sacrifice, and the construction of the fire altar *(agnicayana)*.

[56] J.C. Heesterman, 'Vrātya and Sacrifice', *Indo-Iranian Journal* 6 (1962) 1-37.

[57] P. Horsch, *Die vedische Gāthā- und Śloka-Literatur* (Bern, 1966).

[58] On the *vrātyas* as part of the Vedic tradition, see H. Falk, *Bruderschaft und Würfelspiel: Untersuchungen zur Entwicklungsgeschichte des vedischen Opfers* (Freiburg, 1986).

whose traditions seem to be continued in the *Atharvaveda*.[59] Previous research has strictly denied any genetic connection between the human sacrifices of the Vedic and Śākta Tantric traditions,[60] and this is understandable for chronological reasons alone. Unfortunately, the earliest texts on Śākta cults are rather late (from the fifth or sixth century AD onwards, starting with the Buddhist adaptations of Hindu Tantras),[61] and bridging the gap admittedly requires some act of faith, but there is an inclination to see an Atharvavedic background to many of the 'magical' practices of Śākta Tantrism.[62] As I do not want to leave my claim for a direct connection between the Vedic and Śākta Tantric human sacrifice entirely in the air, I would like to mention some of the principal arguments, also in order to point to different sources of origin. I have discussed these topics at length elsewhere, and limit myself here to little more than an enumeration.

There is evidence of human sacrifice in the iconography of the Harappan alias Indus Civilization that flourished c. 2500-1900 BC. On a seal from Mohenjo-daro, a severed human head (of a warrior, to judge from its 'double-bun' headdress) is placed on an altar in front of a sacred fig tree inhabited by an anthropomorphic deity, attended by a kneeling worshipper whose hands are raised high in adoration or prayer.[63] One Harappan seal also depicts a 'sacred marriage' between a bison bull and a prostrate human priestess, reminding one of the 'sacred marriage' of the Vedic horse sacrifice and the Lamaist thangkas depicting Yama's buffalo mating with a female corpse.[64] There is clear Near Eastern influence in other Harappan art motifs,

---

[59] See A. Parpola, 'From the Dialects of Old Indo-Aryan to Proto-Indo-Aryan and Proto-Iranian', in N. Sims-Williams (ed.), *Indo-Iranian Languages and Peoples* (London, 2002) 43-102.

[60] Cf. e.g. Wilson, 'Sacrifice of Human Beings', 107; Barth, *Religions of India*, 59: 'The Purushamedha of the old Brahmanism must be carefully distinguished from the human sacrifice... in the cultus connected with Durgā.'

[61] Cf. D. Snellgrove, *Indo-Tibetan Buddhism: The Indian Buddhists and Their Tibetan Successors* (London, 1987) 126ff.; T. Goudriaan and S. Gupta, *Hindu Tantric and Śākta Literature* (Wiesbaden, 1981) 20ff.

[62] Cf. e.g. T. Goudriaan, *Māyā Divine and Human* (Delhi, 1978).

[63] See A. Parpola, *Deciphering the Indus Script* (Cambridge, 1994) 256ff. with fig. 14.35.

[64] Cf. A. Parpola, 'The Pre-Vedic Indian Background of the Śrauta Ritual', in Staal, *Agni* II, 41-75; F.R. Allchin, 'The Interpretation of a Seal from Chanhudaro and its Significance for the Religion of the Indus Civilization', in J. Schotsmans and M. Taddei (eds), *South Asian Archaeology 1983* (Naples, 1985) 369-84; Parpola, *Indus Script*, 256f.

such as the 'contest' theme.[65] The Harappans are therefore likely to have had 'sacred marriage' rituals in which the male partner was put to death, as in the royal Inanna-Dumuzi cult of Mesopotamia. Willibald Kirfel in fact suggested in 1951 that this element of the Vedic horse sacrifice and the parallel human sacrifice might have been inherited by the Vedic Aryans from the agriculturalists of the Indus Valley.[66]

The water buffalo plays a dominant role in the Early and Mature Harappan religion, which included a buffalo sacrifice. The water buffalo bull, in Sanskrit *mahiṣa*, may therefore in earlier Indian rituals have occupied the place taken by the horse after it was imported by the Aryans as their ritually most important animal. The female partner in the 'sacred marriage' of the horse sacrifice, the chief queen, has the title *mahiṣ I*, which also denotes 'water buffalo cow'. Hundreds of buffaloes were offered to Indra before battle to increase his warring strength according to the *Ṛgveda* (5,29,8; 6,17,11; 8,12,8; 8,77,10), but there is only a single reference (*Maitrāyaṇī Saṃhitā* 3,14,10 = *Vājasaneyi-Saṃhitā* 24,28) to a water buffalo sacrifice (to Varuṇa) in the extensive Middle Vedic texts; this suggests a conscious suppression of buffalo sacrifice in Vedic religion.[67] In later South Asian religions, buffalo sacrifice is almost exclusively part of the goddess Durgā cult.[68] Hundreds of buffaloes used to be decapitated on the *vijayadaśamī*, the 'tenth day *(daśamī)* of victory *(vijaya)*' that concludes Durgā's *navarātri* festival 'lasting nine *(nava)* nights *(rātri)*' and celebrates her victory over the Buffalo demon.[69] Traditionally, war expeditions were started on the *vijayadaśamī* day, and in Karnataka a human victim used to be offered to the Goddess on this day by the warring bands until British times.[70]

[65] Cf. A. Parpola, 'New Correspondences between Harappan and Near Eastern Glyptic Art', in B. Allchin (ed.), *South Asian Archaeology 1981* (Cambridge, 1984) 176-95; Parpola, *Indus Script*, 246ff.

[66] W. Kirfel, 'Der Aśvamedha und der Puruṣamedha', in *Beiträge zur indischen Philologie und Altertumskunde Walther Schubring zum 70. Geburtstag dargebracht* (Hamburg, 1951) 39-50.

[67] Cf. A. Parpola, 'The Metamorphoses of Mahiṣa Asura and Prajāpati', in A.W. van den Hoek *et al.* (eds), *Ritual, State and History in South Asia: Essays in Honour of J. C. Heesterman* (Leiden, 1992) 275-308.

[68] Cf. M. Biardeau, *Histoire de poteaux: Variations védiques autour de la Déesse hindoue* (Paris, 1989) 1ff.

[69] See C.J. Fuller, *The Camphor Flame: Popular Hinduism and Society in India* (Princeton, 1992), 108-27; Parpola, 'Metamorphoses'.

[70] Cf. S. Silva, 'Traces of Human Sacrifice in Kanara', *Anthropos* 50 (1955) 577-92.

A lion-escorted martial goddess imported from the Near East is depicted on the seals of the 'Bactria and Margiana Archaeo–logical Complex' (= BMAC) of the Bronze Age (c. 2500-1500 BC) in Afghanistan and Turkmenistan; she apparently kept her Sumerian name Nana(ya) for two millennia, as her counterpart worshipped in Afghanistan in Kuṣāṇa times was so called, and is worshipped in Afghanistan even nowadays as 'Bibi Nanni'.[71] This BMAC culture interacted with the Indus Civilization, and may be a principal source of the 'Gangetic Copper Hoards'.[72] A BMAC-type cylinder seal from the Harappan site Kalibangan bears an Indus inscription and a tiger-escorted goddess in the midst of two warriors spearing each other. Vedic texts know Vāc ('Voice, Speech') as a goddess of war identified with the lioness and con-nected with the Vrātyas.[73] The Vedic vrātyastomas were performed before and after raiding expeditions, and closely resemble the later Hindu navarātri festivals of Goddess Durgā, which involve sexual licence and feasting with the meat of many different sacri-ficial animals.[74] The Vedic lists of 'unclean' animal victims (to be released) agree with Purāṇic lists of victims pleasing the goddess; in both cases, a human victim as the most appreciated offering heads the list.[75]

Excavations at the BMAC site Dashly-3 in northern Afghanistan brought to light a palace with the layout of a Tantric maṇḍala and a temple-fortress surrounded by a moat and three concentric circu-lar walls. In Afghanistan and Pakistan, the Ṛgvedic Aryans encountered an inimical people, called Dāsa, whose chief Śambara had in the mountains 'autumnal forts' (śāradī pur), possibly venues of the autumnal navarātri festival, like the fortress called Śār(a)dī in Kashmir. Many of the goddess's names (Durgā, Koṭṭavī, Tripura-sundarī) designate her as the guardian of the fortress (durga, koṭṭa, tripura).[76] Śambara has survived as the name of a fierce divinity of

[71] Cf. D.T. Potts, 'Nana in Bactria', Silk Road Art and Archaeology 7 (2001) 23-35.

[72] Cf. A. Parpola, 'The Coming of the Aryans to India and Iran and the Cultural and Ethnic Identity of the Dāsas', Studia Orientalia 64 (1988) 195-302.

[73] See A. Parpola, 'Vāc as Goddess of Victory in the Veda and Her Relation to Durgā', in Zinbun: Annals of the Institute for Research in Humanities, Kyoto University 34 (1999) 101-43.

[74] See Parpola, 'Vāc', 109ff.

[75] See Parpola, 'Metamorphoses'.

[76] See Parpola, 'Coming of the Aryans', 208ff., 258ff.

Śaiva origin in Tantric Buddhism, and, like Dāsa, appears to be Irano-Aryan in etymology.[77] The ethnicon Dāsa is cognate with Khotanese and Wakhi words meaning 'man, hero', which along with the linguistic peculiarities of Nūristānī and Māgadhī, suggests that the Dāsas were distant ancestors of the later Scythians or Sakas, who introduced headhunting and the skull cult to Afghanistan (Nuristan). As the acculturated rulers of the BMAC culture, the Dāsas then took these gruesome cults to the Indus and Ganges Valleys by the end of the third millennium BC.[78]

Human sacrifice and skull cults have survived to the present day especially in eastern India, in the Śākta Tantric worship of Durgā, Kālī and related goddesses. This Śākta tradition appears to be a direct continuation of the cultic practices involving human sacrifice that prevailed in South Asia before the coming of the Ṛgvedic Aryans. In the millennia older testimonia preserved to us in the Vedic texts, on the other hand, this pre-Vedic form of human sacrifice has a somewhat modified form, as it was first incorporated into a different religious tradition in an early phase of syncretism, only to be eradicated from the Vedic religion during a later phase of this process.

---

[77] See Parpola, 'Coming of the Aryans', 261f.; Parpola, 'Pre-Proto-Iranians of Afghanistan as Initiators of Śākta Tantrism: On the Scythian/Saka Affiliation of the Dāsas, Nuristanis and Magadhans', *Iranica Antiqua* 37 (2002) 233-324 at 273ff.

[78] See Parpola, 'Coming of the Aryans' and 'Pre-Proto-Iranians'.

IX. HUMAN SACRIFICE (PURUṢAMEDHA) CONSTRUCTION SACRIFICE AND THE ORIGIN OF THE IDEA OF THE 'MAN OF THE HOMESTEAD' (VĀSTUPURUṢA)

Hans T. Bakker

William Crooke, one of the great connoisseurs of the living traditions of India of his time and reporter of many a crooked thing,
notes in his delightful book *Things Indian* (first published in London
1906) under the heading 'House',

> Very similar to these [scil. houses] was the earliest Indo-Aryan
> house, the form of which has been handed down in the marriage
> shed of our days. The materials were wood, basket-work, and clay.
> The main feature was the corner-posts, which were fixed in the
> ground with rites, sometimes including human sacrifice, intended
> to conciliate the earth-spirits, and were always regarded as, in some
> sense, sacrosanct.[1]

Sub voce 'Human Sacrifice; Cannibalism' Crooke adds to this,

> All through the later course of history we meet occasional instances
> of the custom [i.e. of human sacrifice]. First we find the foundation
> sacrifice, either, as some believe, intended to appease the earth-
> deities of the place, or as a deliberate piece of god-making, to create
> a divine protector of the building. Many a fort and tank, as legend
> tells us, were guarded in this way. [...] Whenever we [i.e. the
> British] build a great bridge or harbour mole, our engineers are sus-
> pected of being on the look-out for victims, and people are careful
> not to wander abroad at night during the time the foundation is
> being laid.[2]

---

[1] W. Crooke, *Things Indian, being discursive notes on various subjects connected with India* (London, 1906; repr. Delhi 1972) 258.

[2] Crooke, *Things Indian*, 262f. Cf. M. Winternitz, 'Einige Bemerkungen über das Bauopfer bei den Inder', *Mittheilungen der Antropologischer Gesellschaft in Wien* 17 (1887) 37-40 at 39-40; C. Malamoud, 'Modèle et réplique. Remarques sur le paradigme

It is evident that all this 'information' is merely based on hear-say, but the fact that it was said and heard may be an indication that at least the notion of killing a human victim in the context of a construction sacrifice or *Bauopfer* was well-known. That the practice was actually wide-spread in the rest of Asia is well attested, as the articles by Barrett and Harimoto in this volume confirm.[3]

With regard to South Asia, however, the evidence is apparently more problematic, as already indicated by the title of a recent article by Jordaan and Wessing calqued on the title of an article by Paul Mus – *Construction Sacrifice in India 'seen from the East'*.[4] The reason why it is 'seen from the East' is that, on the one hand, the two anthropologists find abundant (archaeological) evidence for the practice in Southeast Asia, especially in Indonesia; this leads them to infer *(op. cit.* p. 229) that this violent custom may actually have received impulses from South Asia, the cradle of the Indianized cultures and religions of Southeast Asia. In South Asia itself, on the other hand, the two anthropologists have 'seen' comparatively little hard evidence that could support their inference. They suspect, however, that this is not so much due to the absence of the practice itself, than to prejudice on the part of indologists – after all South and Southeast Asia share, according to them, 'common prehistoric origins in Mus' monsoon Asia' *(op. cit.* p. 229), a dubious argument on which the two anthropologists set great store. Hence their exhortation: 'Further archaeological research is obviously needed into various aspects of (human) sacrifice, without dismissing possible indicators out of hand as has been done in the past' *(op. cit.* pp. 228f.).

Jordaan and Wessing make a distinction into two types, which partly overlap,

> namely appeasement sacrifice, aimed at gaining title to the land to be used from the spirits that are believed to own it, and animation sacrifice used to give the structure strength and protection by

---

du sacrifice humain dans l'Inde védique', *Arch. f. Religionsgeschichte* 1 (1999) 27-40 at 27f.

[3] See *i.a.* Winternitz, 'Einige Bemerkungen', 40; R. Jordaan and R. Wessing, 'Construction Sacrifice in India, "Seen from the East",' in J.E.M. Houben and K. R. van Kooij (eds), *Violence Denied* (Leiden, 1999) 211-47. I take 'construction sacrifice' as synonymous with 'foundation sacrifice'.

[4] P. Mus, *India seen from the East: Indian and indigenous cults in Champa*, Centre of Southeast Asian Studies, Monash University = *Monash Papers on Southeast Asia* 3 (1975).

animating it with the spirit of the sacrificial victim ('Construction Sacrifice', 219).

In the Indian context the former type of rites could be subsumed under the category of *Vāstuśānti* or *Vāstuśamana* ('Appeasement of the House') rituals. These rituals, to be performed whenever one begins the construction of and/or enters a newly built house are summarized by Kane in his *History* of *Dharmaśāstra*, Volume V, 790f. They derive from prescripts in various texts pertaining to the Vedic tradition dealing with domestic sacrifices – the *Gṛhyasūtras* – and develop in later digests to 'a very elaborate affair', which we, like Kane, pass over here, not 'for reasons of space', though, but because human sacrifice is not touched upon in this context.

The second type of sacrifice may be subsumed under the category of *Vāstupratiṣṭha* ('Installation of the House'), which is described by Kane *(op. cit.)* in Volume II, 833-36 (conflated with *Vāstuśānti* rites). This type of ritual also reaches back to Vedic times and is canonized in the same *Gṛhyasūtra* literature.

A central role in these rituals is reserved for the 'Lord of the Homestead', Vāstoṣpati, already hymned in *Ṛgveda* 7.54.1-3, a power who is represented by a firm post. Kane gives the following description of this House Sacrifice (Vāstuyajña).

> On an auspicious day and moment, the stone should be laid over jewels and all seeds; similarly the post is to be worshipped at the hands of four brāhmaṇas; the priest who should wear white garments, should be master of the Veda and should be accompanied by the artizans, should fix the post that is washed with water mixed with all herbs and covered with many whole rice and decked with clothes and ornaments to the accompaniment of Vedic mantras and the tunes of auspicious music; he should perform a homa with honey and clarified butter and should repeat the mantra *'vāstoṣpate prati'* (ṚV 7.54.1); then the owner should feed brāhmaṇas with a dish of rice-milk.[5]

[5] P.V. Kane, *History of Dharmaśāstra (Ancient and Medieval Religious and Civil Law in India)*, 5 vols (Poona, 1930-62) 2.834f. J. Gonda, *Vedic Ritual. The Non-solemn Rites* (Leiden, 1980) 154: 'an offering *(sthālīpāka* cooked in milk) is made to Vāstoṣpati with the formula "drive away evil; make our wealth increase; protect us always etc.".' Cf. H.W. Bodewitz, 'Atharvaveda Saṃhitā 3, 12: the Building of a House', *Annals of the BORI* 58-59 (1977-78) (= Diamond Jubilee Volume edit. by R.N. Dandekar), 59-68; A. Ray, 'House-Building Rituals in Ancient India', in *J.N. Banerjea Volume* (Calcutta, 1960) 298-312 at 311.

All this appears to give us little more than the usual harmless Brahminical ritualism, and seems remote from the gruesome practices in which animals or humans are slaughtered to lend their strength to the construction, as reported by Crooke and surmised by Jordaan and Wessing. Yet, appearances may be deceptive, especially in India.

The two anthropologists have recourse to an authority, Stella Kramrisch, who refers to *Śatapathabrāhmaṇa* 1.2.3.6-7, in order to underpin the homology of, on the one hand, the seeds placed underneath the foundation-stone and the rice offered to the Vāstoṣpati, and, on the other, the sacrificial animal *(paśu)*. This homology is believed to exist, because the grain 'has the nature of the sacrificial victim; this essence passed to sacrificial animals, it entered into the horse, ox, sheep and goat, and lastly into the earth with its rice and barley, etc.'[6] This at first sight curious doctrine goes back to early Brahminical speculation regarding the life-sustaining substance *(medha)* embodied in the sacrificial victim and transmitted in the sacrificial act. The primordial cosmic Puruṣa is the fountain-head of the *medha*. By his being sacrificed in the cosmic Puruṣamedha *(Ṛgveda* 10.90) the *medha* of the Puruṣa passed on to the horse, empowering the horse-sacrifice (Aśvamedha) etc., a lineage that finally makes the seeds of the earth fit for sacrifice *(medhya)*.[7]

Charles Malamoud warns against misinterpretation, observing that, rather than with a historical development, we are here concerned with a peculiarity of brahmanical thought, in which each part of a structure is at the same time equivalent of and comprising the whole.[8] All the same, it seems possible, if we take an orthodox brahmanical view, to see in the innocent *vāstuyajña*, House Sacrifice, its link with a less gentle, more bloody prototype, which, however, as far as house and temple building are concerned, is not attested in the texts, unless perhaps wrapped up in highly symbolic language that can be decoded only by learned brahmins and well-trained indologists. To deduce from this the unhistoric nature of such a bloody prototype may be a fallacy, though.

---

[6] S. Kramrisch, *The Hindu Temple*, 2 vols (Calcutta, 1946; repr. Delhi etc., 1977) I.16; Jordaan and Wessing, 'Construction Sacrifice', 222.

[7] Malamoud, 'Modèle et réplique', 29-31, rendering *Aitareya Brāhmaṇa* II.8.

[8] Malamoud, 'Modèle et réplique', 30: 'Le lecteur moderne peut même être tenté d'y voir le récit d'une évolution historique: du sacrifice humain à l'offrande végétale, le progrès de la civilisation suit le déplacement du *medha*. En fait, les événements... portent sur les pièces d'une structure qui a cette particularité... de comporter un élément qui est aussi l'équivalent et le contenant du tout.'

The Vedic text corpus knows of an 'animation sacrifice', to use Jordaan and Wessing's terminology, not to install a house or other permanent building, but to build a make-shift sacrificial fire-altar in the Agnicayana ceremony. Archaeological evidence confirms the historic reality of this type of fire-altar in ancient India.[9]

The building of the fire (*agnicayana*) and its altar is an elaborate and complicated affair, which is comparatively well researched. Asko Parpola discusses it again in his contribution to this volume and I, therefore, shall give here only the briefest possible outline, focussing on the blood-sacrifices that its construction requires.

After preparing the ground of the fire-altar, a knobbed, gold disk or plate is laid on a lotus-leaf; on this (plate) a man of gold is laid, directed towards the East, stretched out on his back. Then the *Puruṣasāman* should be sung. Thereupon the laying of the bricks is begun, the first one being the *svayamātṛṇṇā* ('the naturally pierced one') placed on the gold man to allow him to breathe. Within the altar also a living tortoise is built.

After a square mortar (*ulūkhalaka*) made of udumbara wood is installed at the 'northern shoulder' of the fire-altar, the fire-pot (*ukhā*) is placed in the middle and the heads of the five sacrificial victims (*paśus*) are installed, the human head in the middle of the fire-pot, the head of a horse towards the west, of a bull towards the east, of a ram towards the south, and of a goat towards the north, while seven gold pieces are laid in the seven orifices of the human head.

Hereafter the author Āpastamba prescribes, *Āpastambaśrautasūtra* (ĀŚS) 16.27.22,[10] that a snake head should be put on the right shoulder of the fire-altar, which is turned away from the other sacrificial heads lest, the *Taittirīya Saṃhitā* (5.2.9.5) remarks, it should bite these domesticated animals instead of wild ones. After the snake, Āpastamba enjoins (ĀŚS 16.27.23) that a human figure (*puruṣākṛti*) should be assembled (*cinoti*) by means of twelve 'turns' (*paryāya*), each spoken thrice, a (virtual?) body stretching from east to west, the head of which coincides with the head of the golden man. The

[9] *Indian Archaeology – A Review* [IAR] 1953-54, 10f. Plates XIII-XV; T.N. Ramachandran, 'Aśvamedha Site near Kalsi', *J. Oriental Research Madras* (Kuppuswami Sastri Research Institute, Mylapore) 21 (1951-52) 1-31 at 28-31. Cf. R. Thapar, 'The Archaeological Background to the Agnicayana Ritual', in F. Staal (ed.), *Agni. The Vedic Ritual of the Fire Altar*, 2 vols (Berkeley, 1983) I.2-40.

[10] *The Śrauta Sūtra of Āpastamba belonging to the Taittirīya Saṃhitā with the commentary of Rudradatta*, ed. Richard Garbe. With new appendix containing corrections and emendations to the text by C.G. Kashikar (Delhi, 1983²).

sacrificer gives praise to this construction by the Ṛgvedic Puruṣa Hymn (ṚV X.90).

It is clear that the central role of the human head (and the four animal heads) in the piling up of the fire-altar presupposes sacrificial slaughter of some sort. According to the Śrautasūtras of the Black Yajurveda, the human head should be cut off of a kṣatriya or vaiśya killed by an arrow or lightning,[11] after which it has to be covered with clay and set aside. The tradition of the White Yajurveda is more explicit that this ritual requires a human sacrifice. The Śatapatha-brāhmaṇa (6.2.1.18) unambiguously declares that 'a man (puruṣa) should be sacrificed first, for man is the first of the sacrificial animals (paśu).' The Kātyāyana Śrautasūtra (16.1.17) states that the victim, a vaiśya or rājanya, should be suffocated in a special secluded place,[12] after which his head is taken, though it allows the option that a head of gold or clay is used as a substitute (ibid. 16.1.18). The bodies of the four animal victims are thrown into the water from where the clay is taken to make the bricks.

In total the altar consists of five layers of brick, which may have the shape of a bird, especially the śyena (hawk). Although the obvious interpretation takes the layers as a substitute of the trunks, it cannot be excluded that, in particular in the case of the human paśu, the body of the victim was, occasionally perhaps, interred into the altar, to the effect that the puruṣa, i.e. 1) the Demiurge Prajāpati, 2) the sacrificial victim, and 3) the sacrificer (yajamāna), became reintegrated in the sacrificial sphere, a reintegration that is the alpha and the omega of the Agnicayana.

The remains of the three Agnicayana altars, found in Jagatgram (Dehra Dun District, UP) and warranted as such by third-century inscriptions, do have the shape of a hawk, but whether they include human and animal bones remains as yet unknown (Plate I).[13]

---

[11] ĀŚS 16.6.2-3; cf. Vārāha Śrautasūtra [VŚS] belonging to the Maitrāyaṇīya recension of Kṛṣṇa Yajurveda. Crit. edit. by C.G. Kashikar (Pune, 1988) at VŚS 2.1.1.50 and The Mānava Śrautasūtra [MŚS] belonging to the Maitrāyaṇī Saṃhitā, ed. J.M. van Gelder (New Delhi, 1961) at MŚS 6.1.2.23: vaiśya and rājanyabandhu. According to Baudhāyana Śrautasūtra (BŚS) 10.9, it should be the head of a vaiśya killed in battle (Baudhāyana Śrautasūtra [X] on the Agnicayana. Text by W. Caland, transl. Yasuke Ikari and H.F. Arnold, in Staal, Agni 2.478-675 at 499).

[12] The Śrautasūtra of Kātyāyana [KŚS], with extracts from the commentaries of Karka and Yājñikadeva, ed. A. Weber (Reprint, Varanasi 1972) at KŚS 16.1.14: parivṛte puruṣasaṃjñapanam.

[13] See note 9 above.

Plate I Agnicayana altar found in Jagatram. Taken from *IAR* 1953-54, Plate XIII A. Courtesy of the Archaeological Survey of India.

To sum up so far. From their inception the Indian higher, i.e. liter-ate, religions (I am limiting myself here to Vedism and Hinduism) know of and prescribe construction sacrifices, mostly of a highly symbolic nature. To judge by the texts, human sacrifice seems to have played a role only in the construction of a make-shift fire-altar, not in that of permanent constructions. Theoretically, it is quite possible to conceive of an Indian construction sacrifice, including human vic-tims, that evolved from ideas and practices developed in the context of the building of the Agnicayana altar, but if such an evolution took place, it did not find expression in Sanskrit texts dating from before the sixth century AD. It is remarkable, for instance, that the classical Indian book of the state, the *Arthaśāstra*, though elaborately describ-ing the lay-out and building of cities and fortifications (2.3), does not spend one word on construction sacrifices. It is of course perfectly conceivable that blood-sacrifices of this sort belonged to a realm less well represented by brahmanical and Hindu scriptures, but if this were the case on the scale suggested by Jordaan and Wessing, this would have become obvious long time ago through archaeology. Of course, we subscribe to their exhortation to do more unbiased archae-ological research, but much of this type of research has been done, and its outcome seems to be that human remains as part of the foun-dations of stone buildings in India occur only rarely. Not all indolo-gists are blind.

Yet, unnoticed instances do occur, and I wish to draw attention to two of them here. Both of them have so far not been seen as examples of construction sacrifices, but I would like to argue that their evidence is best explained by interpreting them as such. And both could be seen as 'construction variants' of the Agnicayana altar, the intellectual feasibility of which was postulated above.

In his report of the excavations in Kausambi, G.R. Sharma claims to have uncovered the remains of a genuine Agnicayana altar, outside of the eastern gate, within an enclosure-wall, sandwiched between the ramparts and the moat of this ancient town. This structure is assigned to the 2nd century BC (Plate II). Within the alleged five layers of the altar 'a large number of human skulls and bones of animals of different species, meticulously arranged' were found.[14] In layer one the excavators found, inter alia, a 'human skull', 'the shell of a tortoise' and 'the iron model of a snake' (Plate III).[15] Layer three 'yielded the largest number of bones with a preponderance of human bone': 'three complete human skulls, ten skull pieces and other skeletal material (Plate IV).[16] Summarizing, Sharma states that 'there is sufficient evidence to conclude that this fire-altar was piled up for the performance of the Puruṣamedha' (op. cit. p. 126).

Sharma's conclusions have been challenged by Schlingloff, whose criticism is in particular directed against the alleged historicity of the human sacrifice (puruṣamedha).[17] The criticism of Romila Thapar takes a different route. She not so much doubts the historicity of the puruṣamedha, but calls the 'fire-altar' itself into question.

> The identification of the site as a fire-altar does raise some problems. The location of the altar so close to the ramparts of the city seems unusual. [...] The shape of the bird as presently reconstructed appears to be rather curvilinear, whereas the bricks used for the altar would indicate a more rectilinear form. The interpretation of the objects found is also not convincing. [...] The frequency of human skulls and bones would also seem to suggest a ritual different from that described in the texts and it certainly is in excess of what is required. [...] there can be little doubt that the structure did represent some kind of sacrificial or funerary site.[18]

---

[14] G.R. Sharma, *The Excavations at Kauśāmbī (1957-59). The defences and the Śyenaciti of the Puruṣamedha* (Allahabad, 1960) 118.

[15] Sharma, *The Excavations at Kauśāmbī*, 122f. See Plates 33, 43 No. 38.

[16] Sharma, *The Excavations at Kauśāmbī*, 125. See Plates 36-38.

[17] D. Schlingloff, 'Menschenopfer in Kauśāmbī?', *Indo-Iranian Journal* 11 (1968/69) 175-89 at 188.

[18] Thapar, 'The Archaeological Background to the Agnicayana Ritual', 27.

Plate II Putative Agnicayana altar found in Kausambi.
Taken from Sharma, *Excavations at Kauśāmbī*, Plate 12.
Courtesy of the Archaeological Survey of India.

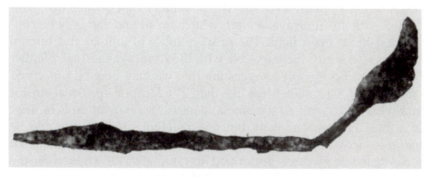

Plate III Iron snake found in Kausambi.
Taken from Sharma, *Excavations at Kauśāmbī*, Plate 43 No. 38.
Courtesy of the Archaeological Survey of India.

Plate IV Human skull found in Kausambi.
Taken from Sharma, *Excavations at Kauśāmbī*, Plate 33 B.
Courtesy of the Archaeological Survey of India.

Comparison of the Kausambi brick structure with the fire-altar remains in Jagatgram makes it clear at a single glance that the two are completely different. Thapar is right when she notes that the location where this brick construction was found, at the foot of the ramparts, is unusual and I would like to go one step further, saying that this location virtually excludes the possibility that we are here concerned with an Agnicayana altar, which has to and can only be constructed in an open field. The great number of animal and human remains also seems incompatible with the Agnicayana ritual. Neither can I accept Schlingloff's suggestion that we may here be concerned with a ritual 'Grabstätte' just like that. The location speaks against it and what to do with all the animal bones? The excavation is in need of a thorough reassessment, but my tentative suggestion would be that the uncovered brick structure represents the material remains of a construction sacrifice performed to 'animate', i.e. strengthen the defence constructions of the town. Taking its clue from the paradigmatic Agnicayana, this sacrifice entailed that animals and humans were slaughtered and bricked into an altar-like structure, yielding a

'Grabstätte' of a very peculiar kind. And what remains valid of Sharma's conclusions, against Schlingloff, is that the site does indeed testify to the practice of a Puruṣamedha, human sacrifice.

My other example is taken from the excavations in Mansar, 5 km west of the Rāmagiri/Ramtek, Maharashtra. I have dealt with this excavation extensively in other publications.[19] Here I shall focus on the 'two sacrificial altars, one in the shape of a śyena-citi [hawk] and the other a kūrma-citi [turtle], made of bricks', exposed by the excavators A.K. Sharma and J.P. Joshi in excavations carried out between 1998 and 2000.[20]

These two putative 'altars' have been found half-way up a natural hill that is completely covered by brick constructions, the nature of which is controversial, but the most plausible interpretation of which takes them as the remains of a large Hindu temple complex. The 'altar' layer is assigned to the third century AD by the excavators, but may be one or two centuries later. As in the case of Kausambi, the location – on a hillock, at the foot of, or underneath a Hindu temple – makes it a priori very unlikely that we have to do with a Vedic Agnicayana altar, as suggested by the excavators. No animal or human bones have been found in connection with these 'altars', but the area has yielded a most extraordinary and unique find (Plate V):

> In the śyenaciti, [a more than life-size] figure of a Puruṣa made of lime has been found sacrificed with his head smashed. The head of the figure is oriented towards west, whereas the legs are put towards east. A vedi in the chest portion with a hole for fixing a yaṣṭi over it was made and an earthen lamp was found kept nearby. Two pots have also been kept near the knee region of the figure which lies on his right side with an iron snake kept near his left toe, looking towards the human figure.[21]

When we collect all the unearthed evidence carefully and compare this with the ritual of the building of an Agnicayana altar as described in the literature, only one conclusion is possible: the

---

[19] H.T. Bakker, 'Religion and Politics in the Eastern Vākāṭaka Kingdom', *South Asian Studies* 18 (2002) 1-24; H.T. Bakker, 'Mansar', in H.T. Bakker (ed.), *The Vākāṭakas Heritage. Indian Culture at the Crossroads* (Groningen, 2004) 71-85.

[20] J.P. Joshi and A.K. Sharma, 'Excavation at Mansar, Distt. Nagpur, Maharashtra-1997-2000', *Purātattva* 30 (1999-2000) 127-31 at 128.

[21] Joshi and Sharma, 'Excavation at Mansar', 128.

Plate V The Man of Mansar. Photograph by the author.
Courtesy of the Archaeological Survey of India.

Mansar site is not an Agnicayana location. The most serious objec-
tion against such an identification is perhaps that the 'altars', though
fantastic constructions, do not consist of five layers of bricks. All the
same, like in Kausambi, much of the evidence seems to reflect an
Agnicayana paradigm. One of the conspicuous points in common
with Kausambi is the discovery of a little iron snake (Plate VI).
Whereas in Kausambi in the second century BC the foundation
structures may still have been reinforced by real animal and human
victims, 600 years later, in the heyday of India's classical culture
when the doctrine of no-injury, *ahiṃsā,* was fully developed, the
same effect may have been thought obtainable by an effigy, the Man
of Mansar. To cut a long story short, I believe that the excavators of
Mansar have hit upon the remains of a construction sacrifice.

The meaning and function of the Man of Mansar, the ceremony
with which he was installed, and the purport of his makers may
have comprised elements from the interpretation schemes that we
have discussed: 1) the reintegration of man and God through the
sacrificial insertion of a (substitute) human figure into the brick fun-
dament of an altar or a sacred building, and 2) the idea of a (human)

Plate VI Iron snake found in Mansar. Photograph by the author.
Courtesy of the Archaeological Survey of India.

sacrifice to safeguard the building, by warding off *genii loci,* on the one hand, and by embedding it in a recreated micro-macrocosmic unity, on the other.

The Lord of the Homestead, Vāstoṣpati, who was subsequently installed and worshipped, may have been represented by a firm wooden post that was placed in the hole in the breast of the clay figure (Plate VII).

Earlier we envisaged the theoretical possibility that a new concept of a construction sacrifice could have evolved from ideas and practices developed in the context of the Agnicayana altar, but added that, if such an evolution took place, it did not find expression in Sanskrit texts that date from before the sixth century AD. We have seen next that the evidence of at least two archaeological sites is indicative of such an evolution. The restrictive clause limiting our search to texts from before the sixth century AD is deliberate. This is, because I am of the opinion that from that century onwards we see a new concept

Plate VII Hole for the Vāstoṣpati post in the breast of
the Man of Mansar. Photograph by the author.
Courtesy of the Archaeological Survey of India.

gradually taking shape in the religious literature, an idea which
raises the Kausambi-Mansar progression that we tentatively elaborated to a higher level of doctrinal abstraction, so characteristic of
medieval Hinduism. I mean the idea of the Vāstupuruṣa, the 'Man
of the Homestead'.[22]

The author Varāhamihira (mid sixth century) begins his chapter
on 'Architecture' with the following two verses, after having said

---

[22] Phyllis Granoff, commenting on a draft of this article, made a significant observation, which I would like to quote from her letter (d.d. 13-2-03). She refers to Jain
stories, 'in which people have to undergo tremendous troubles in order to build a
temple. In fact, they often have to die. I think this may also be a reworking or memory trace of a construction sacrifice. Sometimes the donor or yajamāna has to die; in
a few cases he has to give up the possibility of having children, which is also a kind
of death.' See Ph. Granoff, 'The Householder as Shaman. Jaina Biographies of Temple Builders', *East and West* 42 (1992) 301-17 at 315. On the other hand, Granoff *op. cit.*
p. 316, refers to the 'common belief that a temple built over bones of a dead person
was doomed to collapse.' This belief may reflect the historical process, in which
blood sacrifice gradually became tabu and was replaced by symbolic representations
as described here.

that the science of house-building *(vāstujñāna)* came down from Brahmā.

> To be more precise, there was a being that by his body obstructed the earth and the sky; that being was forcibly seized by the immortals, who felled him, head-down. And wherever a god held it, there that god became established; the Creator ordained that the House Man *(vāstunara)* was to consist of those immortals.[23]

This myth, which still shows the marks of the Vedic concept of the Cosmic Man (Puruṣa), became the basis of an ideology that we find in nearly all Sanskrit texts dealing with the Hindu temple, be they sectarian religious scriptures *(Āgamas)*, or technical treatises concerned with architecture and the like, *Śilpaśāstra*. The central idea is that underneath the Hindu temple lies a diagram, a *maṇḍala*, that embodies the cosmic Puruṣa and houses all divinities. The temple, thus founded in a macrocosmic grid, is a junction of this world and the other, of micro- and macrocosm, a direct pathway to God and his paradise. Seen in this way, the ideology of the temple continues that of the Agnicayana altar.[24] However, the idea of the Vāstupuruṣamaṇḍala is first and foremost a theoretical concept, which had hardly, if at all, demonstrable effects on the actual architecture of the temple, or its archaeology for that matter.[25] It is one more ingenuous product of brahmanical speculation and carries its hallmark: abstraction. Taking its origin from the construction sacrifice, and ultimately from the Puruṣamedha in the context of the make-shift fire-altar, the sacrificial man is

---

[23] *Bṛhatsaṃhitā* of Varāhamihira. With English Translation, Exhaustive Notes and Literary Comments by Ramakrishna Bhat (Delhi 1981-82) 53.2-3: *kim api kila bhūtam abhavad rundhānaṃ rodasī śarīreṇa | tad amaragaṇena sahasā vinigṛhyādhomukhaṃ nyastam | |2| | yatra ca yena gṛhītaṃ vibudhenādhiṣṭhitaḥ sa tatraiva | tadamaramayaṃ vidhātā vāstunaraṃ kalpayāmāsa | |3| |*.

[24] Kramrisch, *The Hindu Temple* I, 95.

[25] N.R. Bhatt, 'Śaiva Āgamas', *Agama and Śilpa* (Bombay, 1984) 10-28, dealing with Āgamas and Śilpa, notes: 'The performer of the installation ceremony then draws a diagram called Vāstumaṇḍala on the site made even and clean and performs a fire ritual to please the deities of the lords of this maṇḍala. Vāstu means a site for dwelling. Vāstupuruṣa is a deity who governs the site and is lying on the site, and his limbs are occupied by different deities. Before construction, these deities are to be pleased and permission to use the site is to be obtained. This ritual is named *vāstupūjā*' (Bhatt, 'Śaiva Āgamas', 15). Occasionally a human-shaped figure may be found, though. Such a stone structure has been found at Kandhar (Dist. Nanded, Maharashtra) in excavations conducted by M.K. Dhavalikar and A.P. Jamkhedkar in *Indian Archaeology-A Review* 1983-84, 58f. Plate 45.

thus preserved in an idea understood only by visionaries and priests. For those in search of the nitty-gritty of human sacrifice the doctrine of the Vāstupuruṣa has little to offer, unless perhaps the insight that even the most gruesome of human practices can be viewed under the perspective of the sublime.

X. HUMAN SACRIFICE AMONG THE KONDS

Lourens van den Bosch

1. Introduction

The discovery of human sacrifice among the Konds of Eastern India is closely connected with British colonial rule in the first half of the nineteenth century. Forced imposition of taxes brought officials of the East India Company to the remote territories of the Bengal and Madras presidencies with their tribal traditions.[1] There they met with the practice of human sacrifice that was then current among the Konds in the region. These tribal people inhabited the mountainous regions of the Eastern Ghats of Orissa and its adjacent territories in Eastern India.[2] The immediate cause for a visit by the British to the region was the unwillingness of the Hindu *rajah* of Ghumsur to pay the required rates to the Collector for the Board of Revenues. The ruler's evasive reaction led to an expedition and a warrant for his arrest, but the *rajah* fled to the inaccessible mountains of the Phulbani district. Konds of this region regarded him as their *rajah* and offered shelter to him. During military campaigns that followed in 1836 and 1837 (also known as the Ghumsur wars) colonial officers made it clear that they did not appreciate the lack of cooperation in the extradition of the *rajah* and punished the aboriginals sternly: 'numbers of Konds were shot like wild animals. Some were seized and hung up

---

[1] F. Padel, *The Sacrifice of Human Being. British Rule and the Konds of Orissa* (Delhi, 1995); see also B. Das, prefatory introduction to the new edition of J. Campbell, *A Personal Narrative of Thirteen Years' Service among the Wild Tribes of Khondistan, for the Suppression of Human Sacrifice* (London 1865), newly edited under the title: *Human Sacrifices in India*, (Delhi, 1986) 20-2.

[2] For a general description of the Konds see B.M. Boal, *The Konds, Humans Sacrifice and Religious Change*, (Warminster, 1982), to which I refer in this article. Boal published afterwards an extended version of the book under the title *Human Sacrifice and Religious Change: The Konds* (New Delhi, 1997); R.N. Patnaik, *History and Culture of the Khond Tribes* (New Delhi, 1992).

on trees. Their villages were everywhere laid in ashes'.[3] Thus, the British established their authority in the region and started to map out the tribal traditions of the Konds.

In his first report about the situation (written in 1836), Mr. G.E. Russell, member of the Madras Board of Revenue, gave a few general traits of the Konds: their love for tobacco and liquor, the feuding between the clans, and last but not least, the practice of human sacrifice.[4] A first detailed account of the practice appeared from the hand of Mr. Stevenson, a civil administrator of the Ghumsur district, in the *Madras Journal* of 1837.[5] The author confronted the reader with 'the astounding discovery that we include among our fellow subjects a whole people who practice human sacrifice and female infanticide on a scale and with a cruelty, which has never been surpassed by the most savage nations'.[6] The situation made the British authorities aware of the fact that they had a civilising mission in the region. They could not tolerate that these 'savages' immolated innocent victims in the name of religion, and it will come as no surprise that they got the support of Christian missionaries.[7]

After the discovery of human sacrifice among the Konds, a number of articles and reports appeared that provided additional information, but they dealt in particular with the question of how the colonial authorities might suppress the barbarous custom. Some writers pleaded for force and intimidation, while others argued for mutual consultations and appealed to reason. John Campbell (1801-78), who worked among the Konds as Assistant Collector of the Ghumsur District and later became one of the Agents in charge of the fight against human sacrifice, argued that the utmost amount of persuasion and conciliation might go very well with firmness and resolution.[8] In a

---

[3] A. Duff, 'Goomsur; the late war there – the Khonds or Hill tribes', *Calcutta Review* 6 (1846, Jan-March) 1-85 (with extracts from the official reports), quoted by Boal, *Konds*, 38. See also Padel, *Sacrifice of Human Being*, 35-62.

[4] A. Duff, 'The first series of Government measures for the abolition of human sacrifice among the Khonds', *Calcutta Review* 6 (1846, July-September) 45-108, with the quote on p. 45. The passage is cited by Boal, *Konds*, 38.

[5] Duff, 'First series of Government measures', 49-50, Stevenson's description was incorporated in the second report of Russell of 1837; for parts of this description see also Boal, *The Konds*, 39; Campbell, *Human Sacrifices in India*, 54-6 and Padel, *Sacrifice of Human Being*, 37-40.

[6] The formulation is from the (colonial) ethnographer E.T. Dalton, *Descriptive Ethnology of Bengal* (Calcutta, 1872) 285.

[7] See Padel, *Sacrifice of Human Being*, 142-84 (government officials), 185-241 (missions) and 242-87 (ethnologists and anthropologists).

personal narrative, he related his service of thirteen years among the Konds and described the practice of human sacrifice in various districts of the region.[9]

In 1841, Lord John Elphinstone, Governor of the Madras Presidency, observed how little real progress the British had made in the suppression of human sacrifice, also denoted by the expression *meriah* sacrifice: neither force nor consultation had provided a lasting change in the Kond practice. He proposed therefore 'a policy of gradual and cautious measures... without any attacks upon national customs or religious prejudices'. These included the opening of routes and passes through the wild tracts, the encouraging of commerce between the hills and the plains, and the raising of a military police force from among the hill-men.[10] In addition to these measures, he appointed a special officer for the communication with the Konds, the Governor's Agent in Ganjam.

The first to be assigned to this position was Lieutenant Samuel Charteris Macpherson (1806-60), who was already well acquainted with the Konds in the Bengal territories. His new function enabled him to map out the customs of the Konds in the Ganjam district, which fell under the Madras Presidency.[11] He carefully described in which territories the Konds used to practice human sacrifice, and in which female infanticide.[12] His work paved the way for the institution of a special Agency for the Suppression of Meriah Sacrifice and Female Infanticide in the Hill-Tracts of Orissa in 1845, of which he became the first head.[13] The British officers were successful in their efforts and rescued many victims with the result that human sacrifice became virtually extinct among the Konds in the sixties of the nineteenth century.[14] In the place of human victims, buffalos were

[8] For Campbell's views see Duff, 'First series of Government measures', 70 summarised by Boal, *Konds*, 43. See also Padel, *Sacrifice of Human Being*, 252. He argues that Campbell's descriptions were coloured by his rationalistic and evolutionistic views.

[9] See Campbell, *Human Sacrifices in India*, 108f.

[10] Boal, *Konds*, 44f with the quote on 45.

[11] S.C. Macpherson, *Report upon the Khonds of the Districts of Ganjam and Cuttack* (Calcutta, 1842).

[12] A Duff, 'Captain Macpherson and the Khonds of Orissa', *Calcutta Review* 1847, VIII (July-September) 1-51, particularly on p. 12. See also Padel, *Sacrifice of Human Being*, 109-17.

[13] Boal, *Konds*, 70ff; Padel, *Sacrifice of Human Being*, 75-108. The agency was abolished in 1861 after the campaign was successfully ended.

[14] For Macpherson's harsh methods see Padel, *Sacrifice of Human Being*, 85ff. Burning and plundering villages formed a regular returning theme in Macpherson's

now sacrificed and the ritual became gradually adapted to the changed political situation.

Macpherson's reports and papers about the Konds are valuable, because they contain detailed descriptions of the Konds' way of life and their religious traditions. It is therefore unfortunate that he was unable to publish a more comprehensive study of their religion after the loss of his diaries, but he presented a succinct report of their religious beliefs and practices before the Royal Asiatic Society in 1852.[15] Barbara Boal, who lived for nearly twenty years as a missionary among the Konds in the Phulbani district and who was well acquainted with the Kui language, collected Macpherson's materials and those of other colonial officers about the Konds. She made a detailed study of the *meriah* sacrifice and its religious change over one hundred and fifty years.[16] Her detailed book contributes to a better, though far from complete, understanding of this ritual and offers a good compensation for the one-sided views of James George Frazer (1854-1941) and Mircea Eliade (1907-1986).[17] In addition to

narrative. For the transformation of human sacrifice into the buffalo sacrifice see Boal, *Konds*, 124-55, 238-61.

[15] See S.C. Macpherson, 'An account of the religious opinions and observances of the Kondhs of Goomsur and Boad', *Journal of the Royal Asiatic Society* 7 (1843) 172-99; *idem*, 'An account of the religion of the Kondhs in Orissa', *ibidem* 13 (1852) 216-74. See further William Macpherson who collected the materials of his brother on religion in chapter 6 of his *Memorials of Service in India: from the Correspondence of the late Major Samuels Charteris Macpherson, C.B. political agent at Gwalior during the Mutiny, and formerly employed in the Suppression of Human Sacrifice in Orissa* (London, 1865); see also Padel, *Sacrifice of Human Being*, 249f.

[16] See note 2. For a critical note on Boal's work, see Padel, *Sacrifice of Human Being*, 35.

[17] Nonetheless, German anthropologists (see below) have criticised Boal because she focused too much on the performance of the human sacrifice without giving due regard to the broader sociological and economic contexts in which it functioned. Moreover, she would not have paid enough attention to the theoretical aspects of the concepts of sacrifice and gift, discussed in anthropological, ethnological and sociological debates. Finally, she did not always reflect on the objectives of her research and the methods of investigations. For this reason more adequate approaches are required; cf. also Padel, *Sacrifice of Human Being*, 135-6, 278f. William Sachs (South Asian Institute of the University of Heidelberg) initiated a research program entitled: 'Das Meriah Opfer: Rituelle Konstruktion sozio-kultureller Identitäten der Dongria Kond in dem Nyamgiri-Bergen Orissas' (2001), which intends to supplement the historical studies on the *meriah* sacrifice with contemporary studies on the Dongriah Konds and to incorporate the recent anthropological theories and perspectives. The project is an extension of earlier research by German anthropologists and Indologists in Orissa; cf. e.g. H. Niggemeier, *Kuttiah Kond: Meriah Büffelopfer. Forschungsfilm E. 179 der Encyclopedia Cinematographica* (Göttingen, 1958); *idem*, *Kuttiah Kund: Dschungelbauern in Orissa* (Frankfurt am Main, 1964).

Boal's study, Padel dealt in his book with human sacrifice among
the Konds within the context of colonial and post-colonial debates
and elucidated the roles of the colonial administrators, missionaries
and anthropologists and their negative representation of Kond culture, in which human sacrifice functioned as a shibboleth of 'sav-
agery'.[18]

Frazer dealt in chapter 47 (Lityerses) of the *Golden Bough* with
human sacrifices for the crops. Central in his view was the idea that
one should connect the myth of the annual death and resurrection of
a god as found in ancient Greek and Oriental traditions with the
vegetation of the crops. The harvest rituals in many cultures
expressed similar ideas. People re-enacted the death and the future
rebirth of the god of fertility (or the corn-spirit) by killing a human
victim as his substitute. Yet Frazer did not only content himself with
circumstantial evidence, in which mimicry of the killing took place.
He thought it desirable to show that 'in rude society human beings
have been commonly killed as an agricultural ceremony to promote
the fertility of the fields'.[19] He devoted therefore a special section to
this type of rituals and focused particularly on the *meriah* sacrifices
of the Konds. The description of this rite, which he derived from
British colonial officers (in this case from Campbell and Macpherson), occupies nearly half of the section. In spite of this, one may ask
whether his interpretation of the ritual is adequate, because he based
it not so much on the mythological traditions of the Konds and their
interpretations as on his own reconstruction of the religious past of
humankind, in which he also relied on ideas of Wilhelm Manhardt
(1831-80).[20] Frazer warned his readers of the misinterpretations
made by early European writers. They were so much 'habituated to
the later idea of sacrifice as an offering made to a god for the purpose of conciliating his favour' that they therefore 'suppose that
whenever a slaughter takes place, there must necessarily be a deity
to whom the carnage is believed to be acceptable'. He concluded
with the observation: 'thus the preconceived ideas may be unconsciously colour and warp their description of savage rites'.[21] Boal

---

[18] For the title of the book see note 1.

[19] J.G. Frazer, *Golden Bough* (1922; reprint New York, 1994) 431-38 at 431.

[20] See also H.G.Kippenberg, *Discovering Religious History in the Modern Age* (Princeton
and Oxford, 2002) 81f.

[21] Frazer, *Golden Bough*, 437f.

aptly remarked that Frazer allowed himself to be carried away by the warning he wished to make.[22]

In his *Patterns in Comparative Religion* Eliade also dealt with human sacrifice in the broader context of agriculture and fertility rites. He based his views particularly on the materials collected by Frazer and argued that the seasonal regeneration of the forces of the sacred was the best clue to find a meaning in these human sacrifices.[23] The regeneration sacrifice was, according to Eliade, a ritual 'repetition' of the creation. The myth of creation included the death of a mythical being at the beginning of time, from whose body the worlds were made and the plants grew. 'The object in sacrificing a human victim for the regeneration of force expressed in the harvest is to repeat the act of creation that first made grain to live'.[24] To corroborate his views, Eliade referred to the human sacrifices of the Konds, which functioned (with those among the Aztecs) as important sources for the construction of his theories. Yet also in his approach, the model for the interpretation of human sacrifices is not primarily derived from the specific contexts within which these rituals functioned, but from the reconstructed archaic world-view at the basis of ancient agricultural societies. Eliade seems to have been influenced in this view by the German anthropologist Adolf Ellegard Jensen (1899-1965), whose studies about *dema*-gods proved to be highly stimulating.[25] Yet in his search for general patterns, Eliade also seems to have been carried away by preconceived ideas, which sometimes led to misinterpretations.

---

[22] Cf. Boal, *Konds*, 154. See also Padel, *Sacrifice of Human Being*, 135-40.

[23] M. Eliade, *Patterns in Comparative Religion* (Cleveland and New York, 1958) 330-66 at 341-5; for the references to the literature see 362-6, with a remark on the indispensability of the materials collected by Frazer as a source for primitive religion on p.362.

[24] Eliade, *Patterns*, 346.

[25] Eliade refers to A.E. Jensen, *Das religiöse Weltbild einer frühen Kultur* (Stuttgart, 1948), who paid attention to the mythology of the so-called *dema*-gods and to the rituals in which an incarnated god was sacrificed at the beginning of time in order to promote the fertility of the crops, the so-called 'Tötungsritual'. See also A.E. Jensen, *Mythos und Kult bei Naturvölkern. Religionswissenschaftliche Betrachtungen* (Wiesbaden, 1960) 191ff and T.P. van Baaren, *Het Offer. Inleiding tot een complex religious verschijnsel* (Utrecht, 1975) 88ff. Van Baaren did not pay any attention to the human sacrifice among the Konds, probably because the original sources were not available to him, while also recent anthropological studies on the Konds were lacking at the time, so that he could not check Frazer's ideas.

In her study of the Konds, Boal did not follow the pattern set by Frazer and Eliade, but tried to find an interpretation of the human sacrifice by referring to the religious traditions of the Konds, in which specific myths functioned as a charter for the practice. In the following paragraphs, I shall follow her example and show that the complexity of the human sacrifice among the Konds allows for various interpretations. First, I shall give some background information on the Konds and their subdivisions, territories, natural resources, village organisation and rituals. Subsequently I shall deal with some mythological themes. Thirdly, I shall focus on the human sacrifices and its various participants, and I conclude with some observations that may give us a better understanding of human sacrifice among the Konds.

2. The Konds and their background

British colonial officials used the word Kond not only for a tribe that inhabited the hilly regions of the state Orissa and its adjacent districts, but also for the hills in which they lived. The Konds referred to themselves as Kuwinga or Kondho, and the last name is to all probability related to the Telugu word for hill, *kond*. The Konds regarded themselves thus as people of the hills or mountains.[26] They can be divided in subgroups, among which are the Kui Konds of the Phulbani district, a district in which the first British officers collected their materials on the Konds and in which also Boal worked for a long time. These Konds refer to themselves as Kui people and to their hills as Kui country, but the word *kui* also refers to their language, a language that belongs to Dravidian linguistic stock.[27] The Konds are thus Dravidians in origin.

According to a census report of 1965, the Konds are the seventh largest tribal group in India, which comprises nearly 850.000 members.[28] They are sometimes also subdivided in the *Sasi* Konds, who mainly live in the plains, and the *Malliah* Konds, who inhabit the inaccessible mountainous regions. The *Sasi* Konds came under the influence of Hinduism, but the *Malliah* Konds kept their relative

---

[26] Padel, *Sacrifice of Human Being*, 12.

[27] *Ibidem*, 12-14 with the distinction between Kui Konds, Kuttia Konds, Kuvi Konds and Dongria Konds and two related dialects, namely Kuvi and Kui with a map on p. 13.

[28] Cf. Boal, *Konds*, 5.

independence and held on to their traditional religion. One may further subdivide between the Konds who performed human sacrifice,
also called the Meriah Konds,[29] and those who did not perform this
type of sacrifice, but practised female infanticide by exposing the
baby in the jungle. The descriptions by Campbell and Macpherson
about human sacrifice and infanticide refer to these two subgroups
of Kui Konds who remained outside the main stream of Hinduism,
although small groups of low caste Hindus resided in their territories. The most important among them were the Pams or Doms, who
functioned as intermediaries and traders.[30] The Pams provided
human victims for the sacrifice, acted as messengers, played music
at religious ceremonies and supplied the villagers with cloths, but
they had no voice in public meetings, and the Konds certainly did
not regard them as equals.

The hilly regions of the *Malliah* Konds form part of the Eastern
Ghats of Orissa and Andhra Pradesh. The central territory consists
of a plateau of about 2000 feet above sea level, but with mountains
rising up to 3500 unto 4000 feet. Dense mixed forests (inhabited by
tigers, jackals, hyenas, wild boars, and other animals) cover the eastern slopes of these hills, but in the populated valleys some agriculture takes place, mainly the cultivation of wet rice. The growing of
dry rice, maize, pulses and millet on plots of lands extracted from
the jungle with the help of slash and burn clearing supplements the
diet.[31] However, the harvest of these crops is not always enough to
feed the people and this leads to famine, particularly in times of
drought. The Konds therefore also complement their diet with products of the forest, namely with the hunting of game and with roots
and fruits gathered in the season. Macpherson relates that in his
time some exchange of forest products (tamarind, arrow word,
turmeric, ginger etc.) took place through the agency of Pam intermediaries who brought products from the lowlands in return.[32] The
Kond villages were thus not wholly self-contained communities in
the nineteenth century, but they had nonetheless to rely mainly on
their own natural food resources. These resources did not easily

[29] Eliade, for instance, calls these Konds, in imitation of Macpherson, Meriah
Konds.
[30] Boal, *Konds*, 1-4; Padel, *Sacrifice of Human Being*, 133-5.
[31] Boal, *Konds*, 26.
[32] *Ibidem*, 25 with a reference to Macpherson; see also Padel, *Sacrifice of Human
Being*, 134.

yield food, but required hard work and the results were often uncertain because of the poor condition of the soil and the capricious climate.[33] Moreover, the fauna proved also to be a liability for the people in the region. The dangerous anopheles mosquito was not only fatal for many people in the past but remains so to this day, and the Konds are still chronic sufferers from malaria. Briefly, the natural conditions in the Kond hills are far from friendly for the people living there; that is the main reason why the natural environment thoroughly dominates the worldview of the Kond people.[34]

The Kui Konds are subdivided in clans (*gossi*), exogamous patrilineal groups, that are further subdivided in lineages that often live together in villages. The clan members believe that they are all descended from a common ancestor and they take their clan names from natural objects. Thus, there is a fish clan, a crab clan, an owl clan, and so on, and the clans have kept the emblems of these animals secret for a long time.[35] Yet apart from this division in clans, lineages and sub lineages, there is also a distinct organisation in every village with a Kond headman, a lay ritual officiant (*dharni*), a priest (*jani*), and a local council made up of the head of each family in the village. This organisation is, among others, responsible for the performance of the communal rituals in the year cycle that aim to promote fertility and to guarantee an ordered relationship between gods, man and land.[36]

According to early colonial descriptions, the most important ritual of the Konds was the human sacrifice offered to the earth goddess during the Tonki festival at full moon in the cool season, usually in January or February, after the harvest was completed. 'This and the other agricultural rites concerned with fertility indicate', in the opinion of Boal, 'both their outlook and their involvement in the land; for

---

[33] The northwest monsoon that plagues the region from mid-June until October may easily destroy the fields, and lead to subsequent famine, but a delay of the rains is fatal as well. The rivulets in the valleys, essential for the water supply, dry up during the hot season making the soil hard and toilsome, while they become dangerous torrents in the rainy season. The high temperatures in May and the cold temperatures in December do not attract the peoples from the plain, which is one of the reasons why the mountainous regions remain rather isolated unto this day.

[34] *Ibidem*, 9-10 with references to F.G. Baily, *Caste and Economic Frontier: A Village in Highland Orissa* (Manchester, 1957).

[35] Boal, *Konds*, 200ff (The significance of the Konds' Bronze Emblems); see also E. Fischer and D. Pathy, 'Metall', in E. Fischer *et al.* (eds), *Orissa, Kunst und Kultur in Nordost-Indien* (Zürich, 1980) 163-86 at 177ff.

[36] Boal, *Konds*, 156ff.

these rites not only incorporate petitions to the deities but also express a sense of dependency on the land itself, linking each family almost sacramentally with its own fields and hill-plots'.[37] However, the *meriah* sacrifice also served to cement the mutual ties between various Kond clans and those with other groups that lived together in the villages in a certain territory (called *muta*). Thus not only the rules of clan exogamy characterised by reciprocal social and economic responsibilities, but also the common allegiance to the earth goddess as well as her worship through these sacrifices functioned as an important vehicle in the realisation of the idea of a community between the Konds and the other persons living within that boundary.[38] The frequency of the rituals led to inter-village co-operation in which human sacrifices were performed by rotation. After the slaughter of the victim, the attending parties from the visiting villages received shreds of the sacrificial meat to be offered in their own villages, so that they also shared in the supposed benefits.[39] The performance of the sacrifice thus also contributed to the solidarity between the villages and lessened tensions between the clans in a certain territory.

3. The mythological foundation for human sacrifice among the Meriah Konds

According to early colonial descriptions of Kond mythology (mainly referring to the Kui Konds), the most important gods are the Supreme Being Bura, creator of the universe, and the earth goddess Tari or Tari Penu (sometimes also called Tana Penu or Dharni).[40] In the beginning, Bura created the earth goddess as his consort, and afterwards the earth as her domain, but husband and spouse did not get along very well, because Tari was jealous and lacked wifely attentions. In order to have a devoted service Bura decided to create man, but Tari intervened in the process of creation and delayed the formation of man. According to the generally accepted myth, Bura took each time a handful of earth and threw it behind himself without looking, but Tari caught it and cast it each time aside. Thus, with the first handful, the trees, herbs, flowers and vegetables came into

---

[37] *Ibidem*, 27; see also Padel, *Sacrifice of Human Being*, 125-7.
[38] Boal, *Konds*, 107f.
[39] *Ibidem*, 122f. with a short description of the three year cycle.

being. Bura went on with his creation and took a handful of earth for the second, for the third and for the fourth time, each time throwing it without looking back. Each time Tari interfered in the creative process and threw the earth in the water, just alongside, and in the air. Because of her interference, the fishes, all wild and tame animals and the birds came into being. Then Bura looked behind and saw what was happening. To prevent Tari from obstructing his actions further, Bura placed the fifth handful of earth on the ground. Thus, the human race came into being. In the process, Bura sweated profusely and all this sweat, falling to the earth, contained his energy, which allowed procreation of animals and humans.[41]

During the primeval period the created world was free from all evil; men and their creator were, according to Macpherson's version of the narrative, in free communication with each other. However, Tari could not stand this, and her jealousy led her to open rebellion against Bura. She introduced all kinds of moral and physical evil to man, and scattered diseases and other disorders into Bura's creation. Only a few individuals rejected her wickedness, and Bura made them tutelary deities. The rest of humankind fell into a state of disobedience with the result that they also fought against each other. Therefore, through Tari's wickedness, everyone committed sins and became subject to death.[42]

At the same time, Bura and Tari were in fierce conflict over the superiority of the earth. According to Macpherson, with respect to the highest power two different views were current among the Konds. One 'sect' claimed that Bura defeated Tari, the other that Tari reigned supreme. Anyhow, the theodicy underlying these two mythological traditions is essentially the same, namely dualistic: man was confronted with two opposing forces that governed his life

---

[40] *Ibidem*, 50-5. Macpherson's description forms part of chapter VI of W. Macpherson, *Memorials of Service in India*, in particular p. 85f. Campbell's references to Kond mythology are extremely few, because he regarded their religion as superstition without substance. For the name Tari Penu see also Padel, *Sacrifice of Human Being*, 357.

[41] See also Padel, *Sacrifice of Human Being*, 117-24, with a short description of the context of the Kond religion and a summary of the most important rites. He rightly remarks that Christian terminology infested the early colonial descriptions. In his short survey of the religion of the Konds, Padel refers to Verrier Elwin, whose unpublished field notes on the Konds he consulted, cf. V. Elwin, *Tribal Myths of Orissa* (Bombay, 1954) who admits in the introduction that he has difficulties with the interpretation of many myths.

[42] Boal, *Konds*, 50-1 with Macpherson's version.

and had to choose a position with respect to them. The followers of Bura insist that Bura was triumphant and that he imposed the cares of childbirth on Tari's sex. Tari is in this view under the control of Bura, but he allowed her to strike as an instrument of his moral rule in case humankind deserved punishment. Tari's followers, on the other hand, claim that Tari remained unconquered, but acknowledge Bura as Supreme Being and as source of good, but they also believe that Bura's power is insufficient when Tari wants to inflict injury upon man. Although they admit that Tari is the source of evil, they also believe that she has the power to support humankind by not stopping Bura in his good work. Because of these views, two different kinds of rituals arose among the Konds.

From the preceding description, it is clear that the earth goddess was not a very pleasant character. The Konds feared her greatly because she easily inflicted all kinds of injuries and diseases upon them, but at the same time they believed that they might propitiate her and win her sympathy. A number of myths from the Tari 'sect' inform us about her commitment to humankind. Tari's followers relate that she taught man about agriculture, hunting and warfare, three domains that are of central importance to the Konds. But she did this on the condition that she received their worship through human sacrifice, which was her proper food.

The Konds also related a certain myth, in which Tari made a revelation to humankind by taking the form of a woman, called Amali Baeli,[43] one of their first ancestors. Thus, they connected the earth goddess with one of their ancestors. The myth runs as follows. At the time when the earth was created, every place was simply a swamp and the whole countryside swayed and shook continually. At this primeval time there was a Kui house shaking in the morass; a woman and a man lived there and their names were Amali Baeli and Bumi Kuari. When the man was out one day, Amali-Baeli was peeling vegetables for the pot. She cut her little finger and the blood oozed out, not falling on the vegetables, but on the ground. Then the heaving earth solidified and became very fertile. Amali Baeli said, 'Look, what a good change! Cut up my body to complete it!', but the Konds refused. Thinking she was a Kond, they were unwilling to sacrifice her; instead, they resolved to purchase victims from other

---

[43] The descriptions of the names often vary. Sometimes the narratives speak about Ambali Baeli.

peoples. Believing that, 'without the falling of human blood on the ground there is no fertility', Kond's ancestors sought a way of burying human flesh; and so began the *mrimi* (*meriah*) sacrifice.[44]

According to the tradition of the Konds, men still complained to Tari that they were poor and troubled in many ways. The goddess therefore demanded an extension of the human sacrifice, which had to be performed on many more occasions, with new ceremonies and new arrangements for the provision of victims. In addition, she told them that she would no longer limit the value of human sacrifice to her worshippers, but would extend its benefits to all humankind. The Tari worshippers thus believed that they became responsible for the well-being of the whole world, with the result that they practised human sacrifices in great numbers, both for community and family reasons. The community observances were as follows: 1) Every household shared the blood of a human victim at the time when a) its principal crops was sown or planted, b) as a harvest oblation and c) when additional human offerings were needed throughout the growing season; 2) A human sacrifice was performed if the goddess affected the health of the community, or if the flocks or herds suffered from disease or wild beasts; 3) A human sacrifice was performed if the headman's health or fortunes deemed it advisable, because the Konds regarded the headman's personal well-being as a mirror of how well or ill disposed the goddess was towards their community. Any sign of coming wrath was therefore immediately countered by public atonement with a human sacrifice. Besides the community offerings, family ('private') ones sometimes took place, for instance, when an unusual calamity marked the fury of the goddess against a certain household and when a priest deemed it advisable to bring the *meriah* sacrifice.[45]

In an account of the myth recorded by Edward Thurston at the beginning of the twentieth century, various themes are connected.[46] In primeval times, according to this version, the ground was sodden and only two females existed on the earth, Karaboodi and Tharthaboodi.

---

[44] Boal, *Konds*, 52, who refers to Macpherson's description in his *Memorials of Service in India*, 96f.

[45] Boal, *Konds*, 53; cf. pp. 3-4, with a different version of the myth as recently told among the Konds. See also Campbell, *Human Sacrifice in India*, 52 for the distinction between communal and individual offerings.

[46] Boal, *Konds*, 126-8 with the account of E. Thurston (assisted by K. Ranghachari), *Castes and Tribes of Southern India* (Madras, 1909; repr. New York, 1965) 368-71. Thurston (1855-1935) was a colonial ethnologist.

Each had a single male child, Kasarodi and Singarodi. These individuals sprang from the interior of the earth together with two small plants, on which they depended for subsistence. One day Karaboodi prepared food from these plants cut herself in the little finger and blood dropped on the ground. Instantly, the wet earth on which it fell became dry and hard. However, something more happened: the prepared food tasted much sweeter than usual and the son asked his mother for the reason of this change. That night Karaboodi had a dream and received a message about the institution of human sacrifice. Subsequently, she told her son that if he followed her instructions he would prosper in this world. He should no longer think of her as his mother. He should cut away the flesh of her back, dig several holes in the ground, bury the flesh, and cover the holes with stones. This her son did and the rest of the body was cremated. The wet soil dried up, and all kinds of animals and trees came into existence. The two boys married, built houses, and got children.

Some years later, Karaboodi appeared in a dream to her son. She told him that if he and Singarodi would sacrifice another victim, their land would be very fertile and their cattle could flourish. In the absence of a suitable victim, they sacrificed a monkey, but Karaboodi was not happy with this substitute. She appeared again in a dream and required a human victim. For twelve years, the two men and their eight children searched for a victim and they finally found a poor couple with a son. They offered them food, clothing, and shelter for a year, but in return for their kindness they asked permission to sacrifice the small boy, and the father gave his assent. They fettered the boy and gave him good care. Liquor was prepared for a feast and a bamboo pool with a flag hoisted on it was planted in the ground. Next day they sacrificed a pig near this post, and gave a feast. At this occasion, they proclaimed that they would tie the boy to a sacrificial post on the following day and sacrifice him on the third day.

On the night before the sacrifice, the *janni* (priest) took a reed and poked into the ground in order to find the place where the earth goddess resided. The Konds arrived from various villages and indulged in drinking. They taunted the boy, telling him that his parents had sold him to them, that his sorrow would affect his parents only, and that they would sacrifice him for the prosperity of the people. They conducted him to the place of the earth goddess and tied him with ropes. Then they made him lie on his stomach on a wooden structure, and cut pieces of flesh from his back, arms and legs. Parts were buried at the Konds places of worship, and others were positioned near a well with drinking water, and placed around the villages. The remainder of the sacrificed corpse was cremated. On the following day, a buffalo was sacrificed, and a feast prepared. Next day the bamboo post was removed outside the village, and a fowl and eggs were offered to the deity.[47]

This is not the place to analyse the various versions of the myth in detail, but it is clear that those Konds who perform the *meriah* sacrifice see a close connection between Tari, the earth and man. Amali Baeli was, according to Macpherson's description, the first human being and ancestor of the Konds who discovered the powerful and beneficial effect of blood on fertility. The Konds regarded her as the institutor of human sacrifice, but at the same time they denied that they immolated her as the first victim. This corresponds with the custom that the Konds always purchased victims from outside and did not employ their own people as victims: 'if we spill our own blood we shall have no descendents. We will obtain victims elsewhere. Will not the Dombo (Pan) and the Gahi (Sweepers) sell their children in times of distress?'[48] However, according to Thurston's version, one of the first female ancestors (called Karaboodi) discovered the power of blood and instructed her son to sacrifice her for the well-being of this world.

How should both versions of the myth be interpreted? Narrative traditions regard the two female protagonists as powerful ancestors who instructed the Konds in the practice of human sacrifice. Although both versions do not explicitly describe them as divine beings, the Konds nonetheless identified them with the earth goddess in their interpretations of the myth. They regarded Amali Baeli as a manifestation of Tari, and one may ask therefore how she acquired this position.

Thurston's version of the myth clearly shows that notions relating to a sacrifice of a primeval female ancestor were still current among some Konds at the beginning of the twentieth century. These notions are also at the basis of the myth of Amali Baeli, because she offered to sacrifice herself voluntarily after having observed the beneficial

---

[47] *Ibidem*, 127f. I have omitted the stanza recited by the priest (*janni*) at the buffalo sacrifice, because it does not seem to form part of the legendary account.

[48] *Ibidem*, 117 with the myth of Amali Baeli.

effects of blood on the fertility of the earth. It seems therefore best to suggest that Amali Baeli, by offering her blood and flesh to the earth, fused with the earth goddess. She thus acquired after her death the status of a goddess who promoted the well-being of her people. The fact that Konds identify Amali Baeli with Tari corroborates this view.

Yet there is no denying that the Konds, according to Macpherson's version of the Amali Baeli myth, refused to sacrifice their own ancestor, although she offered herself voluntarily. This refusal is only understandable in the context of traditions that at least know of such a sacrifice and of sacrifices in which Konds offered their own offspring. It seems therefore the best to regard Macpherson's version of the myth with its 'rationalistic' foundation of the refusal to sacrifice relatives as a transformation of an older version in the light of changed circumstances, when the Konds could easily find victims from outside. There was no longer a need to sacrifice their own flesh and blood with an appeal to the voluntary immolation of Amali Baeli. This latter view is, according to the early colonial descriptions, also at the basis of the actual practice of human sacrifice among the Kui Konds.

An analysis of this actual practice shows that one cannot simply speak of a sacrifice in which Amali Baeli (or the earth goddess) immolated herself for the sake of fertility, a sacrifice that the Konds would have ritually repeated in order to re-enact this primeval act of creation, as Frazer and Eliade have suggested. Neither the present version of the myth nor the actual rituals based on them identify the victims with Amali Baeli or with the earth goddess. The earth goddess demands a victim for the sake of blood. For this reason, it is rather artificial to classify the actual *meriah* sacrifice of the Konds under the heading of 'creation by sacrifice of the deity' or 'Tötungsritual', and to connect it with ancient agrarian rituals with at their basis the idea of dying gods.[49]

---

[49] Van Baaren, *Het offer*, 92ff deals with the notion of the 'sacrifice of a god' that is at the basis of some religious rituals and is also denoted by the German expression 'Tötungsritual' (derived from Jensen, see below). He states that one cannot unqualifiedly regard this ritual as a sacrifice, unless the god is first incarnated in a material manifestation (usually a plant, animal or human being). In addition, it is often unclear to whom the sacrifice is offered and the notion of a gift is often absent. Cf. also Jensen, *Mythos und Kult bei Naturvölkern*, 192: 'Es zeigt sich.....das die eben erwähnten sogenannten Menschen- und Tieropfer bei den echten Vertretern dieser Kultur zunächst gar nichts mit der Bezeichnung 'Opfer' in dem Sinne zu tun haben,

Macpherson observed a clear distinction between Bura and Tari as divine creators on the one hand, and their creations on the other one, finally resulting in the creation of human beings. Human beings took therefore, at least initially, a position that was different from that of the gods. However, this did not prohibit the earth goddess from taking the shape of a human ancestor in order to sacrifice herself for the well-being of her progeny. In other words, the mythological traditions of the Konds express various religious views that are not always consistent, but the *meriah* sacrifices performed during the first half of the nineteenth century show that the Konds regarded the victim as an offering to the goddess to satisfy her wishes. Older descriptions of the ritual that testify explicitly to the idea of a primeval sacrifice of the deity are not available.

In any case, the offering of human blood certainly is the central theme in both versions of the myth. Blood is regarded as the food that strengthens the weak earth so that it becomes firm and fertile, but it is not clear how this result is realised. One version of the myth states simply that Tari demands this sacrifice and offers fertility. The other relates that Tari resides in the earth and that one should donate the blood of the victim (and shreds of its meat) in the earth. In this latter case, the worshippers also offer the human victim to Tari, because the earth in its life-giving and life-taking aspect is essentially a manifestation of the earth goddess. They therefore strengthen her with the *meriah* sacrifice at harvest time, which enables her to resume her activities with respect to fertility in the following year.[50]

In her book on the Konds, Boal also refers to other mythical traditions about the origin of human sacrifice, but these follow in the main the two versions of the myths I discussed above. However, they also differ occasionally and give additional information. In some, a close connection exists between the earth goddess and the first ancestor of the Konds. In them Amali Baeli is not only described as the first woman who discovered the power of human blood and

wie ihn spätere Kulturen mit dem Worte verbinden. Es ist bei ihnen nichts anders als die festlich gestaltete Wiederholung des Urzeitsvorganges selbst... Die Gottheit wird nicht 'sich selbst zum Opfer gebracht' – wie man gelegentlich gesagt hat. Es währe vielmehr vorsichtiger und richtiger, wenn im Hinblick auf ganz bestimmte Tötungsvorgänge bei echten alten Pflanzenvölkern die Bezeichnung 'Opfer' überhaupt vemieden würde'. For this reason he introduced the more neutral expression 'Tötungsritual'.

[50] See also Padel, *Sacrifice of Human Being*, 118-21.

argued for the *meriah* sacrifice, but she is also regarded as the symbolic founder of the entire Kond people and is even identified with the earth goddess. According to Boal, the belief in the lineal descent from the earth goddess would also account for the Konds' unshakeable conviction that they are the true owners of the earth, possessing not only rights, but also obligations.[51]

4. The ritual of human sacrifice

In his book on the Konds, Campbell stated that sacrifice was the foundation of their religion. With a few exceptions, Konds generally propitiated their deity, according to him always a malevolent being, with a human sacrifice. The term used in this connection was *meriah* sacrifice, the term *meriah* being applied to the human victim (later also to the buffalo animal) as well as to the ritual.[52] In the great majority of cases, the Konds offered blood to the earth goddess under the effigy of a bird or an elephant in the hope of obtaining abundant crops, averting calamity, and insuring general prosperity.[53] Campbell added that the motive might be different when private persons made special offerings on their own account in order to obtain particular wishes. In spite of these diverse motives, the sacrifice had to be celebrated in public before the assembled people.[54] He also observed that regional variations existed with respect to the method of killing. In some areas the victim was first suffocated before pieces of meat were cut off the body; elsewhere the victim was bound between two strong planks or bamboos, one being placed across the chest, the other across the shoulders, before he was squeezed to death.[55] While life was ebbing away, the Konds threw the victim on the ground and chopped him into pieces.[56] Variations also existed with respect to the place of sacrifice. Sometimes the sacrifice occurred in a sacred grove dedicated to the earth goddess just

[51] Boal, *Konds*, 91 and 108.

[52] After the prohibition of human sacrifices the buffalo functioned as a substitute; cf. Boal, *Konds*, 124ff. German anthropologists (amongst others, Dr. R. Hardenberg) are at present engaged in research of *meriah* (in this case the buffalo) sacrifices among the Dongriah Konds within the broader context of Kond society (see note 17).

[53] See Campbell, *Human Sacrifices in India*, 39, 51f.

[54] *Ibidem*, 52f.

[55] For the sake of convenience I refer to the victim as male, but I admit that victims could be male or female.

[56] *Ibidem*, 57f.

outside the village, but in others near the village idols in the centre of the village.[57] The priest offered shreds of meat near these idols, while he divided the rest of the meat among the participants, who in turn buried them in different plots of lands in order to promote the fertility in a greater region.[58]

The Konds never varied regarding two basic rules in the acquisition of their victims. Firstly, they bought their victims with the price paid in full, without bargaining, by the free will of the seller, the parents or the intermediary. Secondly, the victim should offer himself 'voluntarily', which implies that he should not offer any resistance.[59] In order to achieve this state of acquiescence, the Konds drugged their victims with great amounts of alcohol or opium, and they sometimes broke their legs and arms so that they could not make gestures of resistance. Victims might be children or adults, male or female, but adults were more appreciated 'because they were more costly, and therefore the most acceptable to the deity'.[60] While the Konds mostly purchased the children from their parents, it were the Pans, a low caste of Hindu traders, who had a central role in the delivery of adult victims, by selling them to the Konds. According to Campbell, the price paid for the *meriah* victim usually consisted of cattle, pigs, goats, ornaments, and similar items, but not money.[61] The Konds thus gave expression to the idea that the victim was their true property, and not acquired by robbery or another illegal act that would invalidate the sacrifice.

In addition, the same author stated that the Konds treated the *meriah* victims (before being sacrificed) always with marked kindness. This becomes comprehensible, when one understands the

[57] Cf. Boal, *Konds*, 108 with the hypothesis that a close relationship existed between the earth goddess and the founding goddess of the village, as is clear from the invocations of the Kuttiah Konds. These Konds address the Earth Goddess not only by her personal name, Bangu goddess, but balance this in their invocations by additional names referring to the founder goddess (*Jakeri* Goddess) of the village and the village gods (*Darni* Goddess): 'Bangu Goddess, Earth Goddess, *Jakeri* Goddess, *Darni* Goddess, wants a sacrifice'.

[58] *Ibidem*, 55 and 58 with the observation: 'for they acknowledge their belief, that, if the body were buried whole, the benefit of the sacrifice would not extend farther than the lands of the person who found the victim; where as, if more widely distributed, the benefit would be proportionally extended'.

[59] According to the report of Mr. Russell (see note 68), criminals or prisoners of wars were not regarded as fitting subjects.

[60] See Campbell, *Human Sacrifice in India*, 50 and 52f with additional prescriptions.

[61] *Ibidem*, 58.

incorporation of the victim into Kond society. The victim should return the consideration of the Konds by his willingness to offer himself voluntarily for their well-being. The idea of voluntariness may have ancient roots and may go back to archaic hunting practices, where hunters pretended that the sacrificial victim voluntarily had appeared to be killed. They thus washed their hands of it.[62]

The *meriah* sacrifice was an elaborate affair. During the preliminary stage, preparations took place and the neighbouring villages received invitations to participate.[63] The actual rituals lasted three days and climaxed in the slaughter of the victim, the stripping of flesh from his bones and the offering of meat to the earth goddess. Subsequently, the funeral rites took place during which the priest and headmen burned the remains on a funeral pyre and scattered the ashes over the fields. Then they organized a feast in which they offered a buffalo to the earth goddess, ate from it and offered the inedible portions as gratification to the spirit of the Meriah victim. Finally, they presented the father or the procurer of the victim with a buffalo.

In the month before the *meriah* sacrifice, the victim was prepared ('devoted') and they cut off his hair. According to some descriptions, he was adorned with garlands, allowed freedom of movement, and was given to eat and drink whatever he liked.[64] Information was communicated about the date of the sacrifice to the neighbouring villages. The representatives who intended to take part in the *meriah* sacrifice performed a ritual (called Bringa ritual) under the supervision of the village priest that should safeguard the village while they attended the sacrifice in a neighbouring village. The priest addressed the earth goddess with the words: 'We shall go forth on your service. Do save us from suffering evil while engaged in it! We go to perform your rites; and if anything shall befall us, men will hereafter distrust you, and say you care not for your votaries. We are not satisfied with our wealth; But what we

---

[62] K. Meuli, 'Griechische Opferbrauche', in his *Gesammelte Schriften*, 2 vols (Basel and Stuttgart, 1975) II.907-1021 at 982-3, 995-7 (with references to other literature).

[63] See Boal, *Konds,* 113f with a summary of S.C. Macpherson, 'An account of the religion of the Kondhs in Orissa', *J. Roy. Anthrop. Soc.* 13 (1852) 216-74. Macpherson based his reconstruction on various native informants, particularly on a certain Sundoro Singh, who had been raised by the Konds, had a fluent command of the Kui language and was well acquainted with their beliefs and practices.

[64] See for variations Boal, *Konds*, 112-4.

possess we owe to you, and for the future, we hope for the fulfilment of our desires. We intend to go on such and such day to such
a village, to bring human flesh for you. We trust to attain our
desires through this service. Forget not the oblation.'[65] Subsequently
the members of the delegation washed their clothes and went out of
the village to the place where the *meriah* sacrifice was to be performed. The village priest, though, remained in the village and
fasted alongside with the heads of the households who also stayed
at home.

The central part of the ceremonies usually took up to three days.[66]
Everybody was welcome, for the festival, with its frenzied dancing
and singing, was declared to be for all humankind. Inspired by Tari,
the guests on the first day imbibed huge quantities of alcohol 'leading to the most gross and brutal licentiousness'.[67] According to the
early descriptions of Russell, the Konds stupefied the victim with
alcohol (toddy), and made him to sit at the foot of the post near the
village idol, bearing the effigy of the earth goddess (a peacock). The
assembled crowd then danced to the music, and addressed the goddess with the words: 'O God we offer this sacrifice to you; give us
good crops, seasons and health'. Then they turned to the *meriah*, saying: 'We bought you with a price, and did not seize you; now we
sacrifice you according to custom, and no sin rests on us'.[68]

Macpherson states that from the evening of the first day the victim
had to fast. On the morning of the second day, they washed him
carefully and dressed him in a new garment, then led him out from
the village in a solemn procession with music and dancing. They
fixed a carved post in the centre of the *meriah* grove and the priest

[65] Cf. Boal, *Konds*, 113ff with references to Macpherson and the text of the prayer
to the Earth Goddess Tari Penu during this Bringi ritual. The expression 'on such
and such a day and to such a village' should be specified according to the concrete
data, but Mapherson gives the general rule incorporated in the prayer.

[66] The early descriptions are not always clear on this point and sometimes a
shorter period is mentioned; cf. Boal, *Konds*, 112f.

[67] Campbell, *Human Sacrifice*, 112.

[68] For the earliest description reported by Mr. Russell to the Madras Government,
see *Selections from the Records of the Government of India* (Home Department, No. 5:
'History of the Rise and the Progress of Operations for the Suppression of Human
Sacrifice and Female Infanticide in the Hill Tracts of Orissa' (Calcutta, 1854). J. Sims
(ed.) has republished this volume on microfiches (nr. 6 and 7) in his re-edition of
Selections from the Records of the Government of India, 1849-1937, Bibliotheca Asiatica
(London, 1987). I could not consult either publication, but refer to Campbell, *Human
Sacrifice*, 52-5 with extracts from the description.

seated the victim at the foot of the post with the effigy of the peacock and bound his back to it. Then the priest (or a small boy) anointed the victim with oil, ghee and turmeric paste and adorned him with flowers.[69] During the second day, all paid reverence to the victim and tried to obtain even the smallest relics from him. Women particularly were intent upon drops of spittle and turmeric paste, but there are no indications that they regarded the victim as a god. During the second night, the feast went on. Men inspected the ground around the village with sticks, used in order to find the spot appropriate for the sacrifice to the goddess, and marked it.

On the morning of the third day, drinking and feasting continued, and the victim was refreshed with milk and palm wine. The worshippers inserted a short post into the earth, four larger posts were set up round it, and they seated the victim in the midst. Then the feasting came to an end and all moved to the place of sacrifice. The victim was stupefied with opium (according to others with alcohol) and his arms and sometimes his legs were broken, because it went against the rules to bind him. They believed that the *meriah* by not protesting with his arms and legs consented to the sacrifice. After this, a long ritual of invocations took place, interlaced with references to ancient legends and with a dialogue between the headman, the priest, and an actor who represented the unconscious victim.[70]

After the concluding dialogue, the priest placed the *meriah* between the two planks or bamboos, as described earlier. Then he invoked the Goddess and made an incision in the victim with his axe.[71] Subsequently the crowd threw itself on the victim and stripped the flesh from his bones, shouting, 'We bought you with a price! No sin rests on us!' The head and the intestines were untouched and guards watched over the remains during the night. According to Macpherson, the representatives of the various villages attending the

---

[69] See Boals, *Konds*, 113; Campbell, *Human Sacrifice*, 54 with references to Russell, who states that the priest must perform the *puja* (the offering of flowers, the incense, etcetera) 'through the medium of the Zoomba, who must be a Kond boy under seven years of age, and who is fed and clothed at the public expense, eats alone, and is subjected to no act deemed impure'.

[70] See Boal, *Konds*, with a summary of the description of Macpherson on 113-4 and the text of the dialogue on pp. 117-21.

[71] The text of the prayer runs as follows: 'When we omitted to gratify you with your desired blood, you forgot kindness to us. We possess but little and uncertain wealth. Increase it and we shall be often able to repeat this rite… Give us increase of wealth and we will give you increase of worship'; see Boal, *Konds*, 115f.

human sacrifice brought a share of the flesh home and placed it on a cushion of grass in the place of the public meeting. The priest received the flesh and divided it into two equal halves. He divided one portion among the heads of the households who attended the meeting and prayed to Tari Penu. Then he seated himself on the ground and scraped a hole in it. With his back turned towards it and without looking backwards, he placed the other half portion of the flesh in the hole.[72] All households added a little earth to bury it, and subsequently the priest poured water on it. Each head of the house rolled his shred of flesh in leaves and subsequently buried this piece in his favourite field, placing it in the earth in the same way as the priest had done. All returned home to drink and eat.

Russell describes the slaughtering of the victim rather differently. According to him, the Konds brought the victim to the village idol that was represented by three stones. There they killed a hog and the blood flowed into a pit prepared for the purpose. The intoxicated victim was thrown with his face in the pit where he died by suffocation. The priest then cut a piece of flesh from his body and buried it near the village idol as an offering to the earth. All present followed his example and also cut pieces, carrying them back to their own villages. They buried a part of the flesh near the village idol and a part on the boundaries of the village.[73]

The concluding ceremonies, lasting three days, concerned the funeral rites. On the morning after the sacrifice, the priest and the headman made a funeral pyre and cremated the remains of the victim; in some villages these were interred in a hole in the earth. On the same day, they sacrificed a goat and threw it aside without eating it. During the three days of mourning, they observed a number of ritual prohibitions. No house was swept; no fire was allowed to be given; no wood was cut and no strangers were received. Subsequently, the participants in the *meriah* celebration went to the organizing village where they celebrated the funeral feast (called *mara*). The priest slaughtered a buffalo and invoked the earth goddess with the words, 'O Tari Penu, you have afflicted us greatly; you have brought death to our children and our bullocks, and failure to our corn. You have afflicted us in every way, but we do not complain of this. It is your desire only to compel us to perform your due rites,

---

[72] *Ibidem*, 117 with the prayer offered by the priest of the flesh taking villages.
[73] See Campbell, *Human Sacrifices in India*, 54-5 with the extracts of Russell.

and to raise us up and enrich us. We were anciently enriched by this rite; all around us are great from it. Therefore, by our cattle, our flocks, our pigs and our grain we procured a victim and offered a sacrifice. Do you now enrich us! Let our herds be so numerous that they cannot be housed ... You know what is good for us. Give it to us!'[74] Subsequently he had the buffalo prepared as a meal and all feasted on it. They left the inedible portions as a gratification to the spirit of the victim. Then the priest was sent away with a pig or a buffalo calf.

The organisers of human sacrifice had to fulfil two more formalities. They presented a buffalo to the agent or the father who had sold the *meriah* victim, the so-called *duli* buffalo. One year later, they had to sacrifice a pig to the earth goddess to complete the rite, and addressed her with the words: 'O Tari Penu! Up to this time, we have been engaged in your worship that we commenced a year ago. Now the rites are completed. Let us receive the benefit!'[75]

5. The dialogue between the headman, the priest and an actor who represents the victim

Immediately before the slaughtering of the *meriah* victim, a dialogue took place between the headman, priest and actor who impersonated the unconscious victim. Macpherson gave an example of such a dialogue, but stressed that the form admitted endless variation.[76] The dialogue started with an invocation to the earth goddess with an enumeration of wishes; then it proceeded to the foundation myth of Amali Baeli with the institution of human sacrifice. The myth also explained why the Konds did not offer Amali Baeli at her request: 'If we spill our own blood, we shall have no descendants. We will obtain victims elsewhere'.[77] Subsequently the priest summed up Tari's instructions for the performance of human sacrifice and eulogised *meriah* sacrifice as indispensable for the well-being of the world. In addition, he praised the Konds as the only people who worshipped Tari in the right manner. The

---

[74] Boal, *Konds*, 116 with the text of the prayer (collected by Macpherson).
[75] Boal, *Konds*, 53-5, 107-14.
[76] The text is in Macpherson, *Memorials of Service in India*, 119-27. See also Boal, *Konds*, 117-21.
[77] Boal, *Konds*, 117.

Meriah Konds thus regarded themselves as responsible for the prosperity of the world.[78]

The actual dialogue starts with the weeping of the victim child and the uttering of curses by him. The family who raised the child is overwhelmed with grief and asks the goddess, 'Why have you instituted this miserable heartrending rite?' The earth goddess replies by the mouth of the priest: 'Away with this grief! Your answer is, when the victim shall weep: "Blame not us, blame your parents who sold you; what fault is ours? The earth goddess demands a sacrifice. It is necessary for the world".' Subsequently, the victim questions the priest and asks why the people do not use a vile and useless child, or a coward who is fit for nothing, but the answer he gets is that these persons are not suitable for sacrifice and never can become gods. According to the priest, it is essential for the validity of the sacrifice that the victim should be bought with a price. The boy should therefore blame his parents who sold him. The victim replies to this: 'And did I share the price my parents received. Did I agree to the sale? ... When did you conceive this fraud, this wickedness to destroy me? ... O my Fathers, do not destroy me!' Subsequently, the headman, who kept the victim in his house, steps in and refers to ancient traditions and concludes with the saying, 'O child we must destroy you. Forgive us. You will become a god. We shall profit by your fate'. In line with this, he argues that the victim's parents are guilty of the victim's fate and that they should be cursed.[79]

The victim now turns to the priest and asks him why his terrible fate was concealed. He accuses the priest of being a fraud and ridicules him bitterly. The priest replies that he is the friend of the gods and that he did not persuade the parents to sell their child. He states that the headman bought the victim and had only consulted him as a priest about the question: 'how may this child become blessed?' He had only replied that the victim would become a god after his immolation. Subsequently the priest addresses the victim with the words: 'You, as a god, will gratefully approve and honour me'. The victim reacts saying that the priest does not understand the suffering imposed upon him and that he is only after his own profit.

---

[78] *Ibidem*, 118: 'The deity preferred the sacrifice at the hands of our forefathers, and thenceforward the whole worship of the world was laid upon us, and now we discharge of it.'

[79] *Ibidem*, 118-9 with the quotes.

The priest tries to explain the situation to the victim with the words:
'The deity created the world and everything that lives; and I am his
minister and representative. God made you, the Mullicko (headman)
bought you, and I sacrifice you. The virtue of your death is not
yours, but mine; but it will be attributed to you through me'. When
the victim curses the priest, the latter threatens him with the words:
'Dying creature, do you contend with me? I shall not allow you a
place among the gods'. Finally, the victim resigns in his fate, saying,
'In dying I shall become a god; then you will know whom you serve.
Now do your will on me'. After the conclusion of the dialogue, they
sacrifice the victim for the well-being of the world.[80]

One of the central features in the dialogue is the notion of guilt
that is connected with the immolation of the victim. Not all Konds
accepted the appeal to the institution of this sacrifice by the earth
goddess. The 'sect' of Bura strongly opposed it, and members
believed that some Konds adopted this rite because of monstrous
delusions concocted by Tari for the destruction of her followers.
Thus among the Konds themselves a criticism of religious beliefs
and practices existed. In answer to this criticism, the followers of the
earth goddess stressed the universal value of human sacrifice. They
were the only Konds who worshipped her in accordance with her
prescriptions. Nevertheless, the dialogue also clearly shows that the
Meriah Konds themselves did not feel wholly at ease with the practice. They explicitly excluded sacrifice of victims from their own ethnic group, as is shown in some myths. In addition, the ritual killing
of victims, whom they had purchased and often had raised as if they
were their own children, caused feelings of guilt. The ritual dialogue
testifies to the grief of the 'stepparents'; their attachment to the child
also explains the custom that he was usually not immolated in its
own village, but somewhere else. The dialogue also deals with the
notion of guilt more directly. The priest and the headman unani-
mously argue that the victim should blame the parents who sold
him. Both try to comfort the sufferer by stating that his sad fate will
finally result in a divine status: 'when you shall have given repose to
the world, you will become a god, by the will of the gods'.[81]

The second thread in the dialogue is the repeated statement that
the worshippers of the earth goddess perform human sacrifice for

[80] *Ibidem*, 119-21 with the quotes.
[81] *Ibidem*, 118.

the benefit of the world. The immolation of the victim served to strengthen the earth. According to the myth, the earth became firm by blood and material life flourished.[82] However, it is incorrect to suppose (with Frazer and Eliade) that the blood of the victim had this beneficial effect automatically, as the ritual was essentially a repetition of a primeval sacrifice exemplified by Amali Baeli. The mythical traditions about the *meriah* sacrifice recorded by Macpherson clearly show that the earth goddess instituted the sacrifice in its present form and that the Konds offered victims to her in order to propitiate her. They thus hoped to realise the fertility of their land, people and livestock, and whatever other wishes Tari could fulfil. Since the earth was her domain and one of her material manifestations, they offered the blood and the meat in the earth in order to strengthen her and to avoid her wrath. In other words, the goddess brought about the well-being of the world.[83]

6. Further analysis and conclusions

The interpretation of human sacrifice among the Kui Konds within the context of the existing religious traditions such as prayers, dialogues and songs has contributed to a better (though far from complete) understanding of this ritual than was possible in the time of Frazer and Eliade.[84] However, these traditions also show complex and even contradictory forms. This is evident when one focuses on the various mythical traditions at the basis of the *meriah* sacrifice. Where some traditions suggest that Amali Baeli is a manifestation of the earth goddess and that she instructed her people how to perform human sacrifice by immolating herself, other traditions reject this view. Sacrifices with victims from outside were current in the first half of the nineteenth century, and the myths related during the sacrificial performance supported this custom. An analysis of the various mythical traditions makes it plausible that the custom to take

---

[82] Macpherson's description evokes this in the following words: 'and there came into use cows, bullocks, and buffaloes, sheep and poultry. Then also came into use the trees and the hills and the valleys, and iron and ploughshares, and arrows and axes, and the juice of the palm tree, and love between the sons and daughters of the people, making new households. In this manner did the necessity of the sacrifice arise'; cf. Boal, *Sacrifice of Human Being*, 117-8, who refers to Macpherson, *Memorials of Service in India*, 119-27.

[83] *Ibidem*, 118.

[84] See note 17 for the criticism by anthropologists of Boal's work.

victims from outside was an innovation, as described earlier. Only then it becomes comprehensible why the myth contains references to the refusal of sacrificing own kin and offers as solution to purchase victims from neighbouring castes. Anyhow, all versions of the myths make it clear that the Konds had to sacrifice human victims, because only human blood appeased the earth goddess and brought about the desired fertility.

In this connection, one may ask whether the custom to take out-siders instead of insiders had implications with respect to the sacri-ficial theory underlying the *meriah* sacrifice. Mythical traditions, which describe Amali Baeli as the first ancestor to sacrifice herself, seem to support the sacrificing of own blood relations. As Tari had offered herself in primeval times, likewise she requested the Konds to repeat this sacrifice by taking a victim from their own stock to strengthen the earth and to secure its fertility. In this interpretation, the Kond's sacrifice would have been a re-enactment of the immola-tion of a primeval being and it would support Frazer's (and Eliade's) theory that the *meriah* sacrifice was primarily a repetition of a divine act of creation, and not the gift of a human victim to the earth god-dess. The consistent application of these ideas should also have led to Kond's identification of the victim with the first ancestor who had sacrificed herself.

On this point, the theory runs into trouble, because the Konds – at least during the first half of the nineteenth century – did not take victims from their own ethnic group, nor regarded them as symbolic incorporations of Amali Baeli. However, they regarded the victim, after being dedicated to the goddess, as sacred and in that capacity as worthy of veneration. Nevertheless, all statements by the Konds favour an interpretation of the *meriah* sacrifice as a gift that is demanded by the earth goddess. In return, she secured the fertility of the land and the well-being of the people. The position of the vic-tim was not that of a god, but that of a human being whose blood was needed to propitiate the goddess and to mollify her into good-ness. The Konds tried to relieve the fate of the victim by the promise that he would become a god after his death, but the funeral rites do not express this view. It is therefore inaccurate to regard the *meriah* rites Konds performed during early colonial contacts as exemplary of a 'sacrifice of a god' or, to use the expression of Jensen, as a 'Tötungsritual'. Because we have no data on the performance of *meriah* sacrifice in earlier times, reconstructions of its origins, based on the survival of incidental ideas and customs, are therefore inevitably speculative, although sometimes unavoidable in explaining certain aspects.

Various mythical traditions established the legitimacy of taking human victims from outside, provided two conditions were met. Firstly, the sacrificers should pay the full price for the victim, and secondly, the victim should offer himself voluntarily. The first condition stipulated that the Meriah Konds be only allowed to offer a victim that they bought freely and that was their legal possession. The priest clearly stated this in his dialogue with the boy, saying, 'we did not kidnap you on the road, nor while gathering sticks in the jungle, nor when at play'.[85] The Konds thus sacrificed a victim who was their own lawful property and who was therefore acceptable to the earth goddess.

Yet there is also another aspect to be analysed in this context. Though the victim was not an ethnic Kond, people regarded him nonetheless as a member of their village community.[86] The actor who played the victim in the dialogue made it clear that the boy had fully participated in village life; the same ritual dialogue testified to the grief of those in whose house he had dwelt. The notion that the victim belonged to the village community may also explain why the Konds performed mourning rites to commemorate his death. However, the victim had also polluted all participants in the *meriah* sacrifice by his death. For this reason, they had to observe a number of ritual prohibitions during the three days of mourning.

The funeral ceremonies concluded with a communal meal in which the priest invoked the earth goddess. These rites not only marked the return to normal life, but also testified to the sending away of the spirit of the victim, after he was satisfied with the inedible portions of the slaughtered buffalo. The idea of a transformation of the victim into a god did no longer occur in this stage, but it seems plausible that he became united with Tari after she consumed his flesh and blood. The victim thus participated in her divinity.

The second condition stressed the notion of free will and was meaningful in the context of the primeval sacrifice, in which Amali Baeli offered herself voluntarily. Only a voluntary sacrifice led,

---

[85] Boal, *Konds*, 119.

[86] *Ibidem*, 111 with Mr. Russell's observations of 1837: children are reared for years with the family of the person who ultimately devotes them to death.

according to Kond belief, to the desired effects. By fulfilling the
demands of the earth goddess, the victim supported the world in a
way that was similar to that of Amali Baeli in mythic times. In other
words, the two conditions are meaningful, if one assumes that they
refer to a ritual that re-enacts the voluntarily immolation of a
primeval victim.

However, this idea became blurred by other sacrificial practices of
the Konds, practices that stressed the notion of a human sacrifice to
the earth goddess in order to secure fertility and to avert her wrath.
Tari Penu manifested herself chiefly as a malevolent goddess who
demanded her share and who caused all kinds of afflictions and
death if she was not satisfied. She exerted her powers over her
domain, the earth, and punished the people by means of drought
and torrential rains, poor crops and famine, all kinds of diseases and
other misfortunes, but by pleasing her with human blood, the Konds
believed that might support life and fertility. In many ritual invocations, this *do ut des* idea had a central place. The idea of a benevolent
goddess who sacrificed herself for the well-being of the people was
virtually absent in these invocations. Her malevolent characteristics
may also explain why the Konds not only performed *meriah* sacrifices to procure a good harvest, but also on many other occasions,
when circumstances required propitiating the goddess with a
human sacrifice.

The uncertain environmental conditions in which the Konds lived
are evident from many invocations that express feelings of dependency on the earth goddess. The prayer prior to the slaughtering of
the human victim, for instance, begins with the words: 'When we
omitted to gratify you with your desired food, you forgot kindness
to us. We possess but little and uncertain wealth. Increase it and we
shall be able often to repeat this rite... Here we present to you your
food.' Then the priest invokes the goddess for support and concludes with the words: 'Give us increase of wealth and we will give
you increase of worship!'[87] The prayer clearly testifies to notions of a
specific gift that the receiver should return with an appropriate

---

[87] Boals, *Konds*, 116 with the text collected by Macpherson. The prayer continues
with a series of requests, of which a few phrases may suffice: 'let our houses be so
filled with the noise of children that our voices cannot be heard by those from outside... Let our cattle so crowd our pastures that no vacant spot shall be visible to
those who look at them from afar... Let our poultry be so numerous as to hide the
thatch of the houses!'

reward. The Konds asked Tari to contribute to their well-being and to meet the obligations set by the sacrifice.

As we have seen, the *meriah* sacrifice was clearly a public affair; everybody was welcome and could participate in the festivities. Besides, the participants paraded the victim with drums and songs through the village so that the whole community could see him. Then they led him to the *meriah* grove with its shady sacred trees outside the village, where the final slaughtering took place. This place was clearly associated with the earth goddess and the immolation of the first ancestor.[88] The wounding of the victim by the priest and the pouring of his blood into the earth was the consummation of the rite, because he thus fed the earth and made it fertile. However, the sacrifice was not complete until the other villages shared in the benefits. For this reason, additional rites were performed. Russell described how priests of the neighbouring villages buried one portion near their village idols, while the villagers did the same with the remaining parts at the boundaries of the village.[89] He thus suggested a close connection between the earth goddess and the founding deities of the village.

In addition, Boal observes that the Konds often associated the earth goddess with the founding goddess of the village.[90] Some traditions explicitly mentioned that the earth goddess had taken the human form of the first ancestor. She had become the founder and protector of the Konds, and enabled life for her people by her sacrificial death.[91] The distinction between the earth goddess, the founding goddess of the village and the first female ancestor (sometimes called Amali Baeli), seems therefore to have been rather fluid in the imagination of the Konds. This blurred distinction can also be found in the divergent traditions with respect to sacred places for ritual activities.

Macpherson relates that the *meriah* rites were spatially divided between two sacred centres, namely between the *meriah* grove just outside the village and the idols in the centre of the village. However, it seems incorrect to associate the sacrificial place outside the village (i.e. the *meriah* grove) with the uncanny characteristics of

---

[88] Cf. Campbell, *Humans Sacrifices in India*, 54. On the sacrificial place, the Konds erected wooden poles with the effigy of the earth goddess (e.g. the peacock) on top.

[89] *Ibidem*, 54-5 with the extracts of Russell.

[90] See note 58.

[91] Boal, *Konds*, 108f.

Tari, and the sacrificial place in the centre (i.e. village idols), with the life-sustaining features of the village goddess.[92] An analysis of the prayers shows that both sacred centres equally shared in the positive and negative aspects of the divine. Moreover, Russell showed in his description of a *meriah* sacrifice that the division of sacrificial activities over two places did not always occur and that all ritual activities were sometimes performed at one place, namely in the centre of the village.

In other words, a distinct allocation of the negative and the positive aspects of the divine in a sacred landscape did not take place, and the deities represented by the village idols participated in the dreaded features of the earth goddess as well. The way in which the priest offered the shreds of flesh to the earth goddess and to the village idols illustrates this. The priest had to sit with his back turned towards the hole in which he had to offer the meat, thus avoiding a direct confrontation with the divine. The head of the household had to offer a piece of meat in his favourite field in a similar manner. The Konds thus propitiated the dreaded goddess and her representatives, without looking into the hole in the earth where she was supposed to reside. It is significant that in the prayer accompanying the offering they even apologised for the small quantity of meat, because this might evoke her wrath and cause troubles.[93] The Meriah Konds thus always remained sensitive of Tari's highly unpredictable features, features that also testify to the uncertainty of their relationship with their natural environment.

I conclude with a last observation. Many colonial descriptions of the *meriah* sacrifice mention the extreme cruelty with which the Konds slaughtered their victims. Sometimes they refer to practices of ritual torture that aimed to extract as much cries and tears from the victim as are possible in order to please the earth goddess, so that she would send a supply of rain that is in proportion to the quantity of tears.[94] This cruelty sharply contrasts with the friendliness with which the Konds usually treat their victims before the sacrifice. The cruel immolation of the victim in the ritual context is justified by

[92] One might thus contrast notions of bush, wilderness and death on the one hand, with ideas relating to the ordered life in the village and to the fields on the other one, as is sometimes done.

[93] For the prayer accompanying the act see Boal, *Konds*, 117.

[94] Boal, *Konds*, 112-3 with on p.113 the reference to Macpherson's, *Memorials of Service in India*, 130.

saying: 'we bought you with a price, and no sin rests on us', thus indicating that the Konds only permitted the behaviour, which would otherwise have been a transgression, under specific conditions.

Yet from a different perspective, and on a deeper level, the sacrifice seems also to reflect notions of wrath, particularly when one focuses on the re-enactment of the sacrifice of a mythic mother, Amali Baeli, who in her goodness had given herself for the fertility of the earth and the future of her children. Although her immolation was noble, there is no denying that, according to belief of the Konds, she had changed into the powerful and demanding earth goddess. As a revengeful mother who ruled the earth, she often punished her children with drought, failure of crops, famine, diseases and the like, when they did not give to her a due share. The focus thus shifted towards the *meriah* sacrifice as a gift to the earth goddess in order to avoid her wrath, though notions reflecting the sacrifice of a primeval ancestor were not totally lost. The ritual re-enactment of the sacrifice of the good mother offered therefore also a good opportunity to settle scores with the bad mother, and that in a religiously blameless way. From this perspective, the cruel treatment of the victim, being the substitute of the mother, may have been an act of wrath against her. The ritual thus enabled the Kond to express their feelings of hatred against an unpredictable mother goddess upon whom they totally depended for their subsistence and whom they had to please. In the case of the Konds, human sacrifice therefore not only referred to a common ideology at the basis of (early) agrarian societies with their dying gods and goddesses as Frazer and Eliade suggested, but also to feelings of dependency, of desperation and of wrath, which become transparent within contextual explanations.

XI. HUMAN SACRIFICE IN JAPAN

Kengo Harimoto

First of all, I would like to strongly emphasize that I am not a japa-nologist, but an indologist, and I usually work with Sanskrit texts. I happen to have the advantage that I can read materials written in Japanese. So, I hope that I can complement this collection of studies by supplying some information about human sacrifice in Japan. Because of my background, I had to collect information from litera-ture written by folklorists, ethnologists, scholars in religious studies and historians, who often do cite from the primary sources. There have been some studies in this area conducted throughout the twen-tieth century, but not many.

We can classify the major types of human sacrifice into four types, although not all of them have been satisfactorily demonstrated as really practised in the past:

1. Offering human life as gift or food to deities (practised regularly).
2. Offering human life to pacify troubling deities (practised irregu-larly).
3. Deaths that follow the death of other people (practised irregu-larly).
4. Self-sacrifice (could include any of the above, but mostly the sec-ond and the third, thus practised irregularly).

There are overlaps in these areas, and many episodes are combina-tions of two or more of the above.

1. Offering someone's life as a gift or food to a deity

Of these types, I would like to describe the sacrifice in which some-one is offered to a deity or a super-human being. Such a human sac-rifice or sacrifice in general would be expressed by the Japanese word *ikenie*, which means 'live meal'. The word itself does not exclusively mean human flesh as food, but any animal (even fish) sacrifice, including humans, can be meant.

It appears that many a Shinto shrine has a human sacrifice legend as its foundation story. The following is a typical representative:

> There once was a mighty animal, a demon, living in a mountain, forest or in water near a village. Each year the village had to offer somebody (many times it was a young woman) to the animal/demon as a victim. One year, a family was elected to offer their daughter, but they did not want it to happen. There came a stranger (traveler, mendicant, holy person (Buddhist) or warrior) to the village. The family asked him if their trouble could be solved. The stranger suggested it could and devised a plan. Sometimes they tricked the visitor into becoming the substitute, but usually the visitor thwarted such devious plans. Either by masquerading as the young woman or by putting something else in the place of the young woman, the stranger confronted the animal/demon. By his piety, physical strength or tactical skill, the stranger killed or defeated the animal/demon. In order to commemorate the event, the village built a shrine.

Perhaps the most famous and the oldest surviving tale of this type is the one that involves the origin of the sword, one of the three treasures of the imperial family.[1] This is related in the *Kojiki*,[2] which records the following story:

> Susanoo, a younger brother of the goddess Amaterasu (the highest deity in Shinto mythology), was wandering after he was banished from the heaven *takamagahara* for his violent act. He found an old couple in a mountain, that was rather sad. When being asked, they answered that they had to offer their youngest daughter to a *yamata no orochi*, a creature that had one body, eight snake-like heads and eight snake-like tails. Its size was as big as eight hills and valleys, and its belly was always red from the blood flowing from it. Originally, the old couple had eight daughters, but in the past seven years they had had to offer one daughter a year to the monster, and this year they had to give up their youngest daughter. Susanoo proposed that the parents would give the youngest daughter to him as

---

[1] The other two are a mirror and a shaped jade stone.

[2] One of the two chronicles of the Japanese imperial family. They both tell the origin of the family as well as the origin of Japan starting from the mythical period. *The Kojiki* is written in old Japanese. The other chronicle, *the Nihon-shoki*, is written in old Chinese, which was the official language for Japanese documents for a long time.

a wife, if he successfully killed the monster. At the night of the sacrifice, Susanoo let the parents prepare eight barrels of liquor and
place them at the site where the monster would appear. The monster appeared and began to drink the liquor, each head from a bar-
rel. Then the monster fell asleep and Susanoo began cutting off its
heads. When he realized that his sword had tipped, he cut open one
of the monster's tails and found a sword. The sword would later be
called the sword of *kusanagi (kusanagi no tsurugi)*. Susanoo gave it to
his sister Amaterasu. The sword would later become one of the
three symbols of the imperial court.

Apparently, the myth is a version of the very common myth in
which a hero rescues a young princess from a monster, like Perseus
rescuing Andromeda. It is also apparent that there are many symbolic aspects to the myth, judging from the description of the monster and the frequent use of the number eight, and names that share
similar syllables. The name of the youngest daughter is *kushinada-
hime (hime* means a daughter or princess); the monster comes from a
country called *koshi (koshi no kuni)*, and the later name of the sword
is *kusanagi no tsurugi (tsurugi* means a sword). Interestingly, the
sword will reappear in the other myth I am going to introduce in
this contribution, namely in the episode where it is explained how
the sword received the name *kusanagi*. Because of these correspondences, the later episode was perhaps included to provide an etymology for the name of the sword.

One feature of these stories, or the practice behind them, is that
the practices are said to have been performed regularly, that is,
annually. These practices, if they really existed, may have even
implied the consumption of human flesh in a community, although
it is never mentioned as such. However, we also note that all these
stories, including the archetypal myth, relate how human sacrifice
was stopped. One might therefore argue that these stories do not
prove that the Japanese offered human life to a deity on a regular
basis and, hence, practised cannibalism.

On the other hand, starting from the widespread tales of a one-
eyed monster, the first Japanese folklorist, Yanagita,[3] proposed a
theory that there may have been a custom to choose a villager each
year and to sacrifice him/her at an annual festival. He thought that
the Japanese have so many tales of one-eyed monsters because they

---

[3] Kunio Yanagita, 'Hitotsume-kozou', *Teihon Yanagita Kunio Shuu*, vol. 5 (1962).

marked the victims by injuring one eye and sometimes breaking one leg so that they could not escape; at the same time, other villagers could spot the victims by their physical damage. As this practice involves not only human sacrifice, but possibly also cannibalism, Yanagita was very cautious when he presented this view.

2. Offering Human Life to Appease Troubling Deities

There are many tales (hundreds?) of human sacrifice that involve waters-seas, lakes, rivers, ponds, castles, etc. A typical story goes like this:

> Certain people began to build a bridge/dike/canal or sometimes a castle. Sometimes the water was said to have a god living there in the shape of a snake or a serpent. The construction was difficult and the bridge/dike/wall of the castle kept breaking. Someone (a villager, Shinto priest or a Buddhist monk) with high virtue proposed to drown a person to appeal to the god who was unsatisfied in one way or another. At this point, there are several versions of the stories. Many times a traveler (it seems that a young mother with a very young child was the favorite tourist) was randomly chosen as the victim. Yet many times the one who proposed to offer a sacrifice volunteered to be the victim, considering that it would be a bit hard to decide whom the victim should be. Other times (typically with Buddhist twist) a monk offered a virtuous *sūtra* as the victim instead of a living person. Yet in other tales the victim escaped, although actually sinking, using his/her wit.

Again, there is an archetype of these tales in mythology. The story involves another tragic prince, this time a younger prince of the twelfth emperor (but it is still in half mythological times: there is no evidence that this emperor really existed). The prince was despised because of his violent behaviour. As his father did not want him to be around, he ordered him to conquer many rebelling states, thus preventing the prince from staying in the capital for all too long.

> Yamato Takeru was ordered to conquer the states in the East. He was accompanied by his wife Ototachibana-hime. When his fleet was crossing the channel between two peninsulas, a fierce storm struck them. Ototachibana told Yamato Takeru that she was going to throw herself into the sea to appease the sea god and so she did.

Surprisingly, this story is told as a story about self-sacrifice. There would later be hundreds of stories that someone had to die at sea to successfully accomplish something and probably the oldest story in this motif is already a story of self-sacrifice.[4]

It would appear that later Japanese often confused the two myths (those of Yamato Takeru and of Susanoo) when they composed all those folk-tales that told the stories of offering someone when people wanted to build a dike or a bridge. The most recent of these folk-tales can be even dated to the eighteenth century. Often it is said that there lived a serpent god in the water, which required a human life in order to allow humans to successfully control the water. Apparently, the description of the monster in the tale of Susanoo gave the impression that it referred to rivers (eight heads and tails, emcompassing eight hills and valleys). I can testify to the confusing nature of these two stories, as I kept confusing these two heroes since the first time that I read these stories as a child: two troubled younger brothers, who had episodes that involved the sword that is the symbol of the imperial court.

It may have been a historical fact that someone had to die when a ship encountered a storm. There is a Chinese record of a similar practice. The oldest historical record about Japan was written in the third century in China by a chronologist who served the court of 'Wei'. It records, among other things, the Japanese practice of having an extra person on a ship when they embarked on a long distance voyage. This person would be thrown into the sea when a storm struck the ship and the crew felt in danger of sinking. Since this is not a myth or a folk-tale, and the author writes of it as a current affair, it seems credible. Furthermore, there are court records of punishing someone who threw someone overboard into the sea when the ship encountered a storm. We may be reasonably certain that the practice of throwing someone into the ocean when it was giving trouble existed, although we do not know how long it lasted.

Another type of human sacrifice to accomplish something difficult involves building and would certainly count as a foundation sacrifice.[5] The word *hito-bashira* (human column) that describes the victim

---

[4] For the type of story see L. Röhrich, 'Die Volksballade von "Herrn Peters Seefahrt" und die Menschenopfer-Sagen', in *Märchen, Mythos, Dichtung. Festschrift F. von der Leyen* (Munich, 1963) 177-212, reprinted in L. Röhrich, *Gesammelte Schriften zur Volkslied- und Volksballadenforschung* (Münster, 2002) 113-54; H. Henningsen, 'Jonas, profet og ulykkesfugl', *Handels- og Søfartsmuseets Årbog* (Helsinki, 1966) 105-22.

[5] See also Bakker, this volume, Ch. IX.

to appease a deity is best applied to this type of sacrifice. I did not find many folktales in this area, but there was one incident when skeletons were discovered under the foundation of a palace of an emperor in the beginning of the twentieth century. Also, I remember visiting the sites where castles used to be. I was listening to a guide who explained how many humans were buried when they constructed the buildings. Those stories typically ended up with strange voices being heard during the night or people seeing ghosts.

3. Funeral Sacrifice

There was a time in Japan (4th to 7th century AD) when many large-scale tombs were built. They were mounds of earth with varying shapes and sizes. Some can be quite large (280m across the long axis). And we do find clay figures of many things – houses, chariots, horses and men. There is no doubt that these clay figures were substitutes for real things or people to accompany the dead to the underworld. Also, there is no doubt that this practice was influenced by Chinese culture. As to whether they indeed used real things before substituting them with clay figures, things become a bit controversial. There does not seem to be any controversy with regard to the sacrifice of horses (mainly in the fifth century). However, when scholars examine if the Japanese did kill and bury real human beings with the dead, problems arise. The common view among historians used to be that there is no evidence of humans killed and buried when someone died. However, recent studies are inclined to think that the human bones found around the tombs were the result of people killed and buried to accompany the dead. There also are caskets that had two sets of skeletons in one. Two people dying at the same time usually does not occur naturally.

Apart from the archaeological findings, there are also records that pertain to the topic. The chronicle of Wei records that when the shamanic queen of Yamataikoku (controversial country) died in 248 AD, they built a big mound/tomb and buried 100 slaves.[6] The half mythological chronicles of Japan (the aforementioned Nihonshoki) describes the origin of human shaped clay figures.

---

[6] The location of Yamatai-koku and the identity of the shamanic queen Himiko have become the topic of an ongoing debate. One may even say that the debate has become a national passtime. Everyone seems to have an opinion as to where Yamatai-koku was, and each year several new theories pop up.

According to them, they were introduced when an emperor ordered to stop the custom of planting living people around a tomb. He could not stand listening to them crying for days until they died and seeing their bodies consumed by dogs and crows after their deaths. Some dispute the credibility of this story, but it is certainly interesting to see that the origin of clay figures is ascribed to a humanitarian reason. This does not necessarily mean that the emperor objected to burying people after they were killed, but at least he objected to half burying people while they are still alive.

As there also was a ban on killing oneself, others, and horses at the time of funeral issued in 646 AD, it seems hard to argue against the possibility that the practice existed. There was no reason for the Chinese to make up a story or for anybody to issue a ban on something that did not exist. Even after the ban, there are documents that record suicides of family members, subjects, after someone had died. There also is an interesting order issued by the court in 833, which strictly prohibited the custom of killing the widow after the husband's death. It seems that there has been a shift in the Japanese mentality to the extent that forcing someone to die was bad but voluntarily committing suicide was virtuous.

4. Self-sacrifice

This brings up the topic of self-sacrifice. As we saw already, all of the three types of human sacrifice above can take the form of self-sacrifice. Even tales about the end of regularly practised human sacrifice often have someone volunteering to substitute for the victim and to defeat the demon/beast. In the cases of offering someone's life to accomplish a difficult task and the deaths that follow someone else's death, it would even seem that self-sacrifice (cf. Ototachibana and many stories of subjects following the lord) was the origin of the practice.

In that sense, perhaps we can say that the idea of human sacrifice lived for a long time in Japan – even until recently. It was a well established custom among the Samurais (warrior class) to commit suicide (*harakiri/seppuku*), e.g., at the death of the lord, at the time of defeat, or when convicted of a crime. It was considered an honourable death compared to being killed by somebody else. Suicides were even rather widespread among generals at the end of World War II. Many of them may have been afraid of being prosecuted as war criminals, but some did think that they should die, as the nation (divine nation) was defeated. Banzai charges were feared among the American Marines.

At this point, I would have to mention kamikaze tactics. The word *kamikaze* comes from the time the Mongols under Khubilai tried to invade Japan twice in 1274 and 1281. Both times they failed. During both occasions their ships were completely wrecked by strong typhoons on the coast of western Japan while their army stayed on board. On the second attempt, it is said that the whole army of 100,000 soldiers disappeared overnight when a typhoon struck the area. For the Japanese side, it was nothing but a miracle. When the soldiers went out to fight the morning after the typhoon, they saw nothing but wrecks and drifting bodies. Where once had been many ships, there now was nothing. And that happened twice. The Japanese began to think that Japan was protected by divine force. They said that the divine wind (*kamikaze*) blew. That is where an officer of the imperial navy took the name from, when he devised a plan to make fighter planes into suicide bombers. When Japan was in danger of being invaded by a foreign country, they hoped the divine wind would blow once again. But behind this idea, I see the same pattern of thinking as the stories of throwing someone into the water. The water (the Pacific) was giving them a hard time. After all, the young pilots were thought to offer their lives to the emperor who was a god himself. There may have been a mental image of Ototachibana throwing herself into the sea to protect her husband (an emperor's prince) when they devised the kamikaze tactics, at least subconsciously.[7]

So, going back to the fundamental question – did the Japanese practice human sacrifice – I can at least say that the idea was nothing another-worldly or primitive, but lived for a long time. It evolved into the idea of self-sacrifice in the case of emergency.

[7] E. Ohnuki-Tierney, *Kamikaze, Cherry Blossoms, and Nationalists: The Militarization of Aesthetics in Japanese History* (Chicago, 2002).

XII. HUMAN SACRIFICE AND SELF-SACRIFICE IN CHINA: A CENTURY OF REVELATIONS

Tim H. Barrett

No collective study of human sacrifice in the Old World can afford to ignore China, for it raises disturbing questions for any researcher. A century ago references to human sacrifice there could probably be overlooked as betraying no more than the occasional lapses into barbarism that disfigure most civilisations. The image of China as, for all its modern troubles, a fundamentally rational and relatively humane society – the image that had so impressed Europe in the eighteenth century – remained then and indeed to some extent still remains surprisingly unquestioned.[1] Yet the science of archaeology has over the past one hundred years established beyond the shadow of a doubt the fact that if we are to talk of origins, the roots of Chinese culture go back to a society distinguished by the constant and widespread sacrifice of human victims, and in the light of this knowledge the whole subsequent history of the area potentially takes on new meanings. For we are not dealing with hints and possibilities, with echoes of long-forgotten barbarities which perhaps never happened, or happened only at the peripheries of the culture, but with a newly revealed distant past of routine slaughter that may prompt us to reconsider many aspects of Chinese life down to our own times, from popular reactions to drought to the highly ritualised executions carried out on prisoners.[2] For this reason the following remarks range widely, eschewing any attempt to narrow

---

[1] For a concise account of the violent aspects of Chinese culture and their effacement in most images of China, see B.J. ter Haar, 'Rethinking Violence' in Chinese Culture', in G. Aijmer and J. Abbink (eds), *Meanings of Violence: A Cross Cultural Perspective* (Oxford, 2000) 123-40.

[2] Some of the most interesting work on executions is in Japanese, but see V. Kit-yiu Ho, 'Butchering Fish and Executing Criminals: Public Executions and the Meanings of Violence in Late Imperial and Modern China', in Aijmer and Abbink, *Meanings of Violence*, 141-60.

down the meaning of human sacrifice to a certain 'ideal type' of sacrificial behaviour in favour of a broad approach covering an entire
continuum from the offering up of human sacrifices to gods,
through the submission under duress of human victims to execution
so that they might accompany the departed into their new existence
as ancestors (that is, beings worthy of worship), on to other forms of
ritualized but more voluntary self-sacrifice.

Rather than start in the distant past, however, let us emphasize
the way in which the entire issue is still with us by turning to a
book published in 1996, *The Real China: From Cannibalism to Karaoke*,
in which a well-known British writer on China revealed the dark
deeds of Cultural Revolution days in a remote part of south China.
Factional struggles there had become so bad that vicious infighting
culminated in two students leaders being 'hung on trees as 'sacrifices',' and then butchered and eaten.[3] The subsequent spread of
revenge cannibalism was only halted with difficulty by the inter-
vention of outside authority, and the whole incident hushed up
until a diligent Chinese journalist uncovered it almost a generation
later, in 1993. Today the basic reliability of that account would seem
to be generally accepted, even if its mode of presentation has been
placed within a larger literary context in one more recent study.[4]
Never the less, granted that by 1996 the Cultural Revolution had
entirely lost the sheen that it had once had in some Western circles,
this revelation seemed to jar with every image of China we had ever
believed in, as a society that had inherited for better or worse a
great weight of civilisation, culture, and Confucian learning. An
atavistic outbreak of human sacrifice in Communist Mongolia in
1932, while apparently not so widely known even now, might not
surprise us if it were, given the Western image of the Mongols.[5] Yet

---

[3] J. Gittings, *Real China: From Cannibalism to Karaoke* (London, 1996) 199.

[4] Gang Yue, *The Mouth That Begs: Hunger, Cannibalism, and the Politics of Eating in
Modern China* (Durham, NC, 1999) 228-52. The best review and analysis of these
events, as Professor Barend ter Haar of Leiden University has kindly pointed out to
me, may be found in D. Sutton, 'Consuming Counter-revolution: The Ritual and Culture of Cannibalism in Wuxuan, Guangxi, China, May to July 1968', *Comparative
Studies in Society and History* 37 (1996) 136-74. I have also been grateful for the bibliography on violence and other materials posted on Professor ter Haar's website,
www.let.leidenuniv.nl/bth/, and urge readers who wish to gain more than an introduction to the topic of human sacrifice in China to acquaint themselves with the full
range of his work, which is addressed to larger issues surrounding violence in
Chinese society, especially in recent centuries.

[5] C.R. Bawden, *The Modern History of Mongolia* (London, 1989) 33, 320.

the very concept of sacrifice probably still seems entirely out of place in China to many.

But in fact this would have said more concerning the manufacture of the image of Confucianism in Europe than about Chinese religion as practised in China. True, both Buddhism and Taoism, the great organised traditions within Chinese civilisation, are at one in rejecting blood sacrifice in favour of sparing the lives of animals, as has been pointed out in a recent study.[6] But even in the case of Taoism the relationship with the religion of the people has become so close that a Taoist priest supporting his village festival consecrates the very knife used to sacrifice pigs, even though the deed of slaughter is not carried out in his presence.[7] And in any case, it has recently been discovered too that the news that Confucius himself routinely received animal sacrifices was quite deliberately excised from the earliest Jesuit accounts of China, as inconsistent with their optimistic vision of a country suffused with the light of natural religion and ripe for rapid conversion.[8] The truth of the matter was, whether the first Jesuits cared to emphasize the matter or not, that religious observances in China regularly required the slaughter of large numbers of animals, from the carnage meted out on the Emperor's behalf at the Temple of Heaven to the quotidian killing of a chicken as an integral part of a whole host of minor ritual observances in every village in the land.[9] Like it or not, the notion of animal sacrifice was and indeed is by no means alien to Chinese civilisation.

One would have hoped that the sacrifice of human beings was another matter, and in fact there is no text known to me from any period of Chinese history that explicitly recommends the act, though as we shall see, the same is by no means true of cannibalism. But even one hundred years before 1996, the first academic attempts to describe the entirety of Chinese religion found ample room for a discussion of the topic. This was the celebrated *Religious System of China*, by J.J.M. de Groot, a massive but incomplete undertaking that

---

[6] T. Kleeman, 'Licentious Cults and Bloody Victuals: Sacrifice, Reciprocity, and Violence in Traditional China', *Asia Major*, Third Series, 7 (1994) 185-211.

[7] K. Dean, *Taoist Ritual and Popular Cults of South-east China* (Princeton, 1993) 101.

[8] L.M. Jensen, *Manufacturing Confucianism: Chinese Traditions and Universal Civilisation* (Durham, NC, 1997) 66-8.

[9] B.J. ter Haar, *Ritual & Mythology of the Chinese Triads: Creating an Identity* (Leiden, 1998) 151-79, for example, gives an excellent overview of the blood covenant in Chinese life and thought.

in the light of modern scholarship suffers from a number of faults.[10] A thorough exploitation of the textual materials available to him, however, is not amongst these, and De Groot is as a result able to give a reasonably full account of what the Chinese cultural tradition had preserved concerning human sacrifice in early China, to say nothing of some rather disturbing indications of the survival of similar practices into much more recent times.

Specifically, De Groot includes a discussion of human sacrifice in the ninth chapter of the part of his first 'Book', on 'Disposal of the Dead', that is devoted to 'Graves', since the clearest instances in transmitted sources of human sacrifice relate to the burial of live retainers in the graves of their superiors in pre-imperial times.[11] He also includes a few more recent examples, down to rumours concerning the burial of the predecessor of the famous Kangxi Emperor in the seventeenth century, but in every case these concern non-Chinese rulers from beyond the northern borders. He does note that the Manchu conquerors of China who still ruled in his day certainly had nothing on their statutes concerning human sacrifice at funerals, but a recent writer on the pre-conquest Manchu regime confirms that such was not originally the case, for before they were obliged to promulgate laws for the entire subject Chinese population they had already moved from royal funerals at which a number of women might be killed to regulations stating that only one wife should die.[12]

That the ruling house should have originally openly followed such practices explains why De Groot is then obliged to discuss the unregulated existence of similar customs among the Chinese population. For he devotes some space also to the question of suttee (he uses the Anglo-Indian term), which was certainly still very much in vogue in late imperial China, but which (with qualifications) requires consideration under the heading of self-sacrifice. A generation later a brilliant summary of what was known concerning ancient China in 1927 from one of the leaders of French sinology expands the range of De Groot's references somewhat, and includes an allusion to an ancient burial opened in later historical times that allegedly yielded up the

---

[10] For some strictures on De Groot's progress as a scholar, see M. Freedman, 'On the Sociological Study of Chinese Religion', in A. Wolf, *Religion and Ritual in Chinese Society* (Stanford, 1974) 19-41 at 24-31.

[11] J.J.M de Groot, *The Religious System of China*, Volume Two (Taipei, 1967, reprint of Leiden, 1892-1910) 721-35.

[12] P.K. Crossley, *The Manchus* (Oxford, 1997) 78.

horrific spectacle of human bones strewn all over the place.[13] But, as is pointed out in the introduction to the English translation of this work that appeared over half a century later, after this point more systematic archaeological investigations changed our understanding of early China as a whole quite radically. Thus today, if for example one reads *The Cambridge History of Ancient China*, published in 1999, one may find plenty of descriptions of unambiguous traces of human sacrifice unearthed by modern archaeologists. It is no longer possible to believe, as the philosopher Mencius claims to have done in the late fourth century BC, that human sacrifice was simply the result of sporadic over-literal interpretations of the custom of burying life-like figures with the deceased, rather than *vice versa*.[14]

Before turning in more detail to our current state of knowledge, however, we should trace several other intermediate stages in the development of our understanding. 1951, for example, saw an article published on 'Ritual Exposure in Ancient China', which as well as adding to our knowledge of ritual nudity in China and beyond, pointed out a number of functions for human sacrifice in China apart from simply providing companions for the dead. The main interest here was in rain-making rituals, which might involve the ritual exposure to the blazing sun of a shaman, in his role of servant of the god supplicated, as a way of bringing pressure to bear on the deity. But in a study rich in etymological research the author did establish that as an extreme measure ritual exposure might give way in early China to sacrifice.[15] He also identified some later cases in which self-sacrifice (or more commonly, the threat of it) on the part of a community leader such as a king or other authority figure achieved the same result. A subsequent American study added further examples in this category in a broader exploration of Chinese rainmaking in 1978.[16] In 1994 one of Britain's best-known experts on early China, too, provided some additional references of the same

---

[13] H. Maspero, trans. F.A. Kierman, Jr., with an introduction by D. Twitchett, *China in Antiquity* (Folkstone, Kent, 1978) 106. Some doubts are cast, however, on the historicity of this episode by T.F. Mumford, 'Death Do Us Unite: Xunzang and Joint Burial in Ancient China', *Papers on Far Eastern History* 27 (1983) 1-19 at 6.

[14] De Groot, *Religious System* II, 808.

[15] See E.H. Schafer, 'Ritual Exposure in Ancient China', *Harvard Journal of Asiatic Studies* 14 (1951) 130-84 at 131.

[16] See A. Cohen, 'Coercing the Rain Deities in Ancient China', *History of Religions* 17 (1978) 244-65 at 247, note 9.

sort in a study of rainmaking and dragon cults.[17] Chinese research had meanwhile established that the phenomena discussed in the 1951 article could also be well attested textually from the so-called 'oracle bones', sources retrieved by archaeologists during the twentieth century that have provided an unexpected picture of China in the late second millennium BC.[18]

But although this shows that Edward Schafer, the author of the 1951 work, allowed room for further research even on the topics he did explore, he also suggested in passing a detailed categorization drawn from the comparative study of human sacrifice for analysis of possible purposes of the deed, namely to avert plague, to end famine, to increase fertility, and to bring rain.[19] This list in itself is clearly constructed with a view to the possible apotropaic functions of human sacrifice only, excluding the service in death already identified by De Groot. But it did provide some avenues for further research, including topics touched upon in later publications by Schafer himself. His later descriptions of the culture of the Chinese South – a region which extended originally even north of the Yangtze, and which was for centuries much more similar to Southeast Asia than to the Chinese civilisation that eventually came to dominate the area – draw on the writings of modern Chinese scholars and others to emphasize, for example, the link between dragon boat racing and human sacrifices to river gods.[20] Even in historical times, he suggests, southerners might still practice human sacrifice to ensure fertility, but in this they were simply continuing what northerners had once done, but had later erased from their collective memories.[21] Such a view of the South as a backward version of the North echoes the earlier explorations of early China by French scholars in the light of their familiarity with Annam and its surrounding territories.[22]

---

[17] M. Loewe, *Divination, mythology and monarchy in Han China* (Cambridge, 1994) 149.

[18] See Qiu Xigui, translated by V. Fowler, 'On the burning of human victims and the fashioning of clay dragons in order to seek rain as seen in the Shang dynasty oracle bone inscriptions', *Early China* 9/10 (1983-85) 290-306.

[19] Schafer, 'Ritual Exposure', 183.

[20] E.H. Schafer, *The Vermilion Bird: T'ang Images of the South* (Berkeley and Los Angeles, 1967) 218; cf. also *The Divine Woman: Dragon Ladies and Rain Maidens* (San Francisco, 1980²) 31-34.

[21] Schafer, *Vermilion Bird*, 53, 58.

[22] Thus D.C. Twitchett, in his Introduction to Maspero, *China in Antiquity*, xvii.

A somewhat different account of human sacrifice in Southern culture may be found in the work of Schafer's German colleague, W. Eberhard, published in their fullest form in English in 1968. Though his remarks on the topic are somewhat scattered and not quite comprehensive, they nevertheless add up to the fullest treatment given especially to later Chinese sources in a Western language to date, and provide an authority reconsidered also, as it happens, in 1996 in *The Real China*, even if the latter work rejects the notion that the cannibalism which it reports was due to the recrudescence of the barbaric practices of a 'minority' people.[23] Eberhard is aware, for example, of a very detailed description of human sacrifice for the purpose of capturing a human soul, carried out by Mongols in China in the age of Marco Polo.[24] He notes that human sacrifices connected to water gods and the Dragon Boat festival persisted until the same epoch.[25] He further hypothesizes concerning the abandonment of human sacrifice from that period on of alternative fertility sacrifices in the south as the result of the increased introduction of the (water) buffalo in southern agriculture and the consequent rise of a cattle cult.[26] Indeed, the very bloodiness of these replacement rituals has subsequently been put forward as a reason for the reappearance of cannibalism in the Cultural Revolution, though not all commentators have been persuaded of this explanation.[27] But above all, he distinguishes completely a whole syndrome of southern observances based on human sacrifice in aid of fertility and directed towards trees, mountains and rivers from the northern habit of what he calls 'succession to death'.[28] And even the demise of the northern custom he sees as the outcome of a choice between local cultural practices.[29]

The bulk of his information, however, centres on the waylaying and sacrifice of strangers to fertility cults in the more 'backward'

[23] See note 3, above, and also see the remarks of Gang Yue on ethnicity and cannibalism, note 4, above.

[24] W. Eberhard, *The Local Cultures of South and East China* (Leiden, 1968) 314.

[25] Eberhard, *Local Cultures*, 396.

[26] Eberhard, *Local Cultures*, 342, cf. 185.

[27] Sutton, 'Consuming Counter-Revolution', 166, mentions this explanation, but on the following page he expresses doubts as to Zhuang cannibalism. Somewhat further north, among Yao groups, the festival does not seem to have been particularly horrific: see L. Rainey, 'The Secret Writing of Chinese Women: Religious Practices and beliefs', in A. Sharma and K.K. Young (eds), *Annual Review of Women in World Religions* 4 (Albany, 1996) 130-63 at 143.

[28] Eberhard, *Local Cultures*, 173.

[29] Eberhard, *Local Cultures*, 466.

parts of Central and Southern China, reports of which would seem
to cluster towards the immediately pre-Mongol period. Indeed, they
are so common at this time that one runs across them in the most
unlikely places: one account of a lucky escape overlooked by Eberhard has even been translated into English more recently as part of
a sort of handbook of Neo-Confucian terminology.[30] One way to
explain this clustering would be to suggest that it reflects a particular period of history, when the Chinese population in the South was
advancing rapidly into areas hitherto little touched by colonisation,
that marked a turning point between increased contact and eventual
assimilation – or more probably extinction through contagious diseases – for the original inhabitants. The eventual end of sacrifices to
river gods in late Mongol times, when plague and famine were ram-
pant, might also be taken to mark a similar stage in the same
process, though other explanations are also no doubt possible in
both cases: we shall return to the problem shortly.[31] It must, however, be said that though Eberhard's approach is entirely sinological
in terms of its sources, it would seem to make sense in terms of the
ethnography of South-East Asia even in modern times, where one of
the remoter hill peoples of Vietnam is said to have practiced human
sacrifice 'for a good harvest or for peace and happiness' into the
1950s.[32]

Any re-examination of his material, however, would have to take
into account subsequent research published in Japanese: one authority on religion in Chinese literature picks up the theme as early as
1964, though the fullest statement of his findings may now be found
in a survey of Chinese popular belief published in 1982.[33] Like Eberhard, his attention is in the first instance attracted by the glut of
material from the period leading up to the Mongol conquest, which
he supplements with copious cases from official records, and analyses from a number of different points of view, stressing for example

[30] Wing-tsit Chan, trans., *Neo-Confucian Terms Explained* (New York, 1986) 162-3.
This passage is, however, included in the survey by Sawada, described below,
though even he has come to it by rather circuitous means.

[31] For high mortality rates in the fourteenth century in China as elsewhere, which
must have struck particularly hard against marginal peoples in contact with the Chinese, see H. Franke and D. Twitchett (eds), *Cambridge History of China* VI (Cambridge, 1994) 585, 622.

[32] J. Schleisinger, *Hill Tribes of Vietnam, Volume Two: Profile of the Existing Hill Tribe
Groups* (Bangkok, 1998) 27, with reference to the Ca Tu; cf. the Gie-Trieng, 30

[33] Sawada Mizuho, *Chûgoku minkan shinkô no kenkyû* (Tokyo, 1982) 332-73.

the importance of the human liver in the sacrifices described; the evident connection with some sort of annual cycle; and so forth. His explanations are in some ways more cautious than those of Eberhard, and unfortunately he does not pick up some of the earlier materials, which include an interesting case of human sacrifice being eliminated by the representative of a 'higher' religion – in this case, Taoism, though another example has been noted where the eliminator of human sacrifice to a river became in his turn a rain deity.[34] But our Japanese author does by contrast follow through with an account of later imperial China, when the emphasis seems to have shifted away from sacrifice to some sort of chthonic deities towards tales of the mutilation or vivisection of living victims. Such later material, however, still awaits comprehensive treatment in a Western language, though one hopes that a study will not long be delayed.[35]

The initial Japanese research just described has itself been reconsidered, along with some other Japanese observations on human sacrifice during the early centuries of the last millennium, in recent work published in Japan by an expert on the popular religion of the period. Using some materials not hitherto available, he has published two studies that cast a certain amount of doubt on the hypothesis of increased contact with minority peoples put forward above in commenting on Eberhard's work. Rather than pinning any blame on outsiders himself (though he does not deny the possible existence of homicidal cults among ethnic minorities), he locates the upsurge in reports of human sacrifice in the fear of popular religion amongst the educated elite that had become particularly acute at a time of rapid and energetic religious development.[36] This type of explanation is reminiscent of those interpreters of the Indian phenomenon of thuggery who would see it as no more than a product of the fears of the British rulers of the day.[37] On this alternative

---

[34] This is the reference to the *Taiping guangji* at the foot of Eberhard, *Local Cultures*, 174; cf. Cohen, 'Coercing the rain deities', 249.

[35] In due course this material will no doubt be covered by the ongoing research of Barend ter Haar, from whom we may expect a further monograph – doubtless of great value – in the near future.

[36] Kanai Noriyuki, 'Sôdai Kei, Konan hokuro ni okeru oni no shinkô ni tsuite'', *Komazawa daigaku Zen kenkyûjo nempô* 5 (1994) 49-64 and 'Sôdai ni okeru yôshin shinkô to 'kessai jima', 'satsujin saiki' saikô', *Risshô daigaku tôyôshi ronshû* 8 (1995) 1-14.

[37] Such scholarship is somewhat undermined by the apparently incontrovertible data on the Gonds considered here by Lourens van den Bosch (this volume, Ch. X);

hypothesis, the subsequent decline in fear of ending up as a human sacrifice at the hands of strangers might be a function of the success of the government in bringing popular religion under a greater degree of control, or at least of the educated elite learning not to worry about popular religion over the course of time.[38] The possibilities are, in any case, not mutually exclusive.

Meanwhile, one topic touched upon by Eberhard that has already had a bearing on our survey, even if it is normally a somewhat tangential one, is that of cannibalism. Here Eberhard's treatment again expands the single category into various distinct varieties – survival cannibalism, revenge cannibalism, and so forth. Amongst these 'ritual cannibalism' is indeed recognised as a practice requiring a form of human sacrifice, but only amongst one southern minority culture.[39] The considerable literature on cannibalism in China – an all too frequent occurrence in a heavily populated country subject to recurrent famines – culminated in 1990 in an entire monograph, though as reviewers did not fail to point out, even this did not incorporate all the findings of earlier scholars.[40] Its author, like Eberhard, evidently does not regard ritual cannibalism as a Chinese practice, stating that 'learned cannibalism in China has little to do with ritual and superstition, while in many parts of the world it has much to do with them'.[41] This does seem to me to need a little qualification, since there was certainly one Tantric text in the Chinese Buddhist canon that, as recent research has found, against all earlier expectations, enjoined the lavish consumption of human flesh in a ritual situation.[42] True, the work in question was translated from a Sanskrit original in 985, and even

---

see also his 'Criminal Religion? An Essay on the Thugs of India', in B. Luchesi and K. von Stuckrad (eds), *Religion im kulturellen Diskurs. Festschrift für Hans G. Kippenberg zu seinem 65. Geburtstag / Religion in Cultural Discourse. Essays in Honor of Hans G. Kippenberg on Occasion of His 65th Birthday* (Berlin and New York, 2004) 615-42. But in historical terms it does in some respects fit well with unpublished research by Dr. Anne Gerritsen of Warwick University suggesting that the socially well-rooted and well-accepted form of local religion familiar from recent centuries in China was the outcome of a more volatile period of development.

[38] On this understanding, studies such as V. Hansen, *Changing Gods in Medieval China, 1127-1276* (Princeton, 1990), would reflect a deliberate government policy of using its powers of patronage (or at least recognition) to bring popular religion more securely within its sphere of influence; state support of Buddhism might also reflect a desire to promote amenable forms of religion over threatening ones.

[39] Eberhard, *Local Cultures*, 449f.

[40] The most detailed review was that by R. Kolb, 'Kannibalismus im vormodernen China', *Monumenta Serica* 44 (1996) 393-403.

[41] Key Rey Chong, *Cannibalism in China* (Lakewood, New Hampshire, 1990) 171.

[42] M. Strickmann, *Mantras et Mandarins* (Paris, 1996) 261-5.

then it was kept out of the first, imperial edition of the canon. But it did slip past the censors thereafter, and has appeared (with what we must take to be implicit imperial endorsement in many instances) in every subsequent edition to this day.

Admittedly though a recent monograph shows that some forms of Tantrism did affect popular Chinese religious practice, as far as I am aware there is so far nothing to show that this text condoning cannibalism played any part in actual ritual conduct in China.[43] The main sources challenging the blanket denial just referred to come not from the age of Tantrism but from earlier in the first millennium AD, a period not much discussed in relation to human sacrifice. During this era memories of funerary human sacrifice had evidently faded in North China, and when allegations are made that rebels against the state in the second century of the era sacrificed a human being to try to secure the success of their enterprise, modern scholars have taken this to be no more than an early example of the phenomenon suggested by our second Japanese expert, a deliberate or perhaps unpremeditated denigration of an alien (though not necessarily ethnically distinct) threat.[44] We have already noted in discussing our first Japanese authority that this period already shows evidence of 'outsiders' deemed originally homicidal being brought into the fold of civilization by their conversion to superior forms of religion, and for the most part the pattern distinguishing a civilised 'we-group' eschewing human sacrifice is during this period consistently contrasted with 'Others', even if at least one historian of medicine has suggested that the mainstream knowledge of anatomy at this time derived in part from (one presumes) earlier human sacrifice.[45] There is, however, one striking exception to this pattern that turns up sporadically in the latter half of the first millennium, and that concerns charges laid against the rulers of China, the Chinese emperors themselves, of human sacrifice to astral powers and of cannibalism in the pursuit of immortality. This phenomenon I have made the topic of a separate study which has appeared in 2004 in a specialist publication.[46]

[43] E.L. Davis, *Society and the Supernatural in Song China* (Honolulu, 2001).

[44] See the remarks of B. Hendrischke, in L. Kohn (ed.), *Daoism Handbook* (Leiden, 2000) 158.

[45] S. Yoshimoto, 'The Anatomy and Carnivarism (*sic*) in China', *Nihon ishigaku zasshi* 25.1 (1979), 14-31 (in Japanese).

[46] T.H. Barrett, 'The Madness of Emperor Wuzong', *Cahiers d'Extrême-Asie* 14 (2004) 173-86.

My study suggests that while one cannot rule out the possibility of unspeakable imperial evil behind the well-guarded walls of the palace – and Schafer, perhaps in the light of his earlier researchers, certainly seems to have entertained the possibility that one emperor was quietly securing the ritual dismemberment of his subjects – the rumours recorded in our sources must also be seen in the light of Buddhist propaganda directed against monarchs who expressed hostility to the religion.[47] As the Chinese probably perceived it, human sacrifice was routine in India, the alien civilization best known to them, for it was mentioned casually in didactic materials translated into Chinese, and was also encountered by one famous Chinese visitor.[48] Chinese sources of information about India in particular suggested through stories like the Sutasoma legend, well known throughout Buddhist literature, that cannibalism and human sacrifice were vices all too typical of wicked rulers. Thus fears normally directed against outsiders to Chinese society were in this case projected by a substantial portion of the population – or at least, the highly placed clerics and lay supporters who sought to influence imperial policy – deliberately or unconsciously onto the figure at the very heart of the Chinese polity, in what might be construed as a remarkable testimony to the strains inherent in the medieval Chinese state. That is not to say that there are no pieces of evidence that might indicate actual imperial wrongdoing, especially in the matter of cannibalism, but our author who prefers to deny any instance of religious cannibalism may perhaps be right at best – as one would hope – in terms of actual practice, as opposed to Chinese theory as to the possible functions of cannibalism.

For even he, while doing his best to portray Chinese cannibalism as a somewhat banal affair, and human sacrifice as not just a Chinese preoccupation, freely admits that the most horrendous rituals are described in literature, going no further than a single source – 'It is said that if one eats children, he will have a long life. Elsewhere it says that to extend life one has to eat a child's heart and liver after they have been boiled in hot water. One will then remain young for

---

[47] E.H. Schafer, *Pacing the Void: T'ang Approaches to the Stars* (Berkeley and Los Angeles, 1977) 93, 95. See also Hou Ching-lang, on 223-4 of 'The Chinese Belief in Baleful Stars', in H. Welch and A. Seidel (eds), *Facets of Taoism* (New Haven, 1979) 193-228, and De Groot, *Religious System* V, 574f.

[48] See E. Chavannes, *Cinq cent contes et apologues bouddhiques extraits du Tripitaka chinois* II (Paris, 1911) 165; A. Waley, *The Real Tripitaka* (London, 1952) 38-40.

a thousand years. If one eats 1111 hearts of children for medicine, then one's life can be extended to tens of thousands of years. We might add here that Chinese preferred to sacrifice a little boy and then a young virgin instead of a pig or sheep when they prayed to heaven for rain in times of drought. Generally, the Chinese used young boys and girls as a kind of sacrificial lamb, and then ate them at various official functions. Boys, especially their heads, were more desirable than girls for those occasions'.[49] My problem with this is not simply that the worst that can be imagined may eventually – if mercifully only very occasionally – be carried out, but rather that such wild fantasies would seem to retain unpleasant echoes of practices which fit in all too neatly with what we know of much earlier religious history. And elsewhere it is clear, in the context of drought-ending immolations of the sort described by Schafer, that practices recorded in literature in the language of myth now seem quite easy to interpret in terms of real events through correlation with descriptions still surviving from earlier times in historical materials, even without the assistance of archaeology.[50]

And it should further be admitted that a limited form of human flesh consumption was widely (though not officially) promoted in late imperial China. This was the provision of a portion of one's own flesh by a filial child in order to provide a restorative tonic for an elderly parent. Scattered references may be found already in De Groot's work, though a more systematic treatment may be found in the study on cannibalism I have just cited.[51] Regrettably, however, a particularly fine technical study of the use of a number of human body parts in Chinese medicine is based on a source that disapproved of the use of human flesh.[52] But most recently a paper published at a British university, drawing in part on important research by a Chinese historical anthropologist, has illuminated the significance of the theme in popular literature, especially in the *Xingshi*

---

[49] Chong, *Cannibalism*, 143-4, drawing all his examples from the fantastical novel *Journey to the West*.

[50] Note C.E. Reed, *Chinese Chronicles of the Strange* (New York, 2001) 37, entry 547, and note 93, 72.

[51] De Groot, *Religious System* II, 458, 747, 752, 775, 793 and IV, 386-7; Chong, *Cannibalism*, 93-102.

[52] W.C. Cooper and N. Sivin, 'Man as medicine: Pharmacological and Ritual Aspects of Traditional Therapy Using Drugs Derived from the Human Body', in Nakayama Shigeru and N. Sivin (eds), *Chinese Science* (Cambridge, Mass., 1973) 203-72.

yinyuan, a composition of the mid-seventeenth century, in which its use is far more than merely incidental.[53] Here we are clearly talking not of human sacrifice, but at best of a form of self-sacrifice that was normally less than fatal. Even so, for reasons that will eventually become apparent, the category of self-sacrifice, as I have already suggested at the outset, is worth including in this survey. One practical reason that might be mentioned at this point is that while the chances of any of us ending up as victims of human sacrifice at present are infinitesimally small, there is an extremely slight but still not quite negligible chance in the modern world of suffering from someone else's act of self-sacrifice, through a hijacking, a suicide bombing, or whatever.

On the other hand, there seems little point in dwelling on the best-known examples of what has been called Confucian martyrdom, simply because in most cases it conspicuously lacked formal, structured elements comparable to the famous practice of *seppuku* (more vulgarly, *hara-kiri*) in the Japanese tradition. Those who preferred death to dishonour in China, as in the West, died in a variety of ways, by no means all of their own choosing. It is merely conventional to speak of some individual deaths, such that of a famous calligrapher and imperial loyalist of Tang times, as martyrdoms.[54] More collective fatal acts of defiance at the end of the Song dynasty and the Ming dynasty likewise may have much to teach us about martyrdom in its broadest meaning, but less about sacrifice in any literal sense.[55] At best later loyalist resistance to the death carries echoes of the ritual slaughter attending the burial of China's earliest rulers. Indeed, rather than explore any further for the moment developments in later Chinese history, it is time to revert to the narrative of our unfolding knowledge of early China. For it is there that patterns first emerge that make sense not only of these loyalist episodes but also of a number of subsequent phenomena.

Perhaps the most significant monograph bearing on human sacrifice in early China in recent years has been a well-wrought and highly influential treatment of sanctioned violence as a whole during this stage of Chinese civilization by the contemporary American

[53] D. Berg, *Perceptions of Lay Healers in Late Imperial China* (Durham, 2000) 18-26.

[54] Thus A. McNair, *The Upright Brush: Yan Zhenqing's Calligraphy and Song Literati Politics* (Honolulu, 1998) 87, 139.

[55] On the Song, see R.L. Davis, *Wind against the Mountain* (Cambridge, Mass., 1996), and on the Ming, J. Dennerline, *The Chia-ting loyalists* (New Haven, 1981).

scholar Mark Edward Lewis. This attention to the overall context clarifies the originally very close relationship that existed between hunting, warfare, and the sacrifice of animals and humans in the service of gods and ancestors.[56] Eventually during the first millennium BC, despite in some ways an intensification of the culture of violence, the conception of sacrifice changed to one in which moral considerations now played a part, even though the notion of loyalty might entail suicide, or inflicting death on others, for one's lord.[57] Where a problem still occurred was with the killing of an overlord. Here, drawing on work first done by another leading light of early twentieth century Paris sinology, and on an important article published in 1984, Lewis demonstrates how a situation of regicide as routine as that in the *Golden Bough* gives way to one in which it became necessary to expiate the crime through self-sacrifice, or the offer of it.[58] Elsewhere, too, loyalty and self-sacrifice are seen as the key to replacing the old, amoral order of human sacrifice with one in which the requisite blood is shed but morality is sustained.[59]

This account of a process of change reflected in new myths later in the millennium compares intriguingly with the brute facts on the history of human sacrifice as narrated on the basis of archaeology throughout the *Cambridge History of Ancient China*. In this work a sequence of passing references starts with the revelation of human sacrifice as already a distinctive feature of Chinese burials well before the age of written evidence.[60] It dwells next on the Mesoamerican levels of slaughter that accompanied most important burials in the late second millennium BC.[61] So staggering has been the scale of sacrifice now unearthed by archaeologists from burial sites of the period that it is easy to overlook the presence in the same society of another form of human sacrifice, also very familiar from elsewhere, namely the burial of a human victim to secure the foundations of a

---

[56] M.E. Lewis, *Sanctioned Violence in Early China* (Albany, 1990) 26-28.

[57] Lewis, *Violence*, 77f.

[58] Lewis, *Violence*, 205-10.

[59] Lewis, *Violence*, 79f.

[60] R. Bagley, in M. Loewe and E.L. Shaughnessy (eds), *The Cambridge History of Ancient China* (Cambridge, 1999) 159.

[61] Note for example Bagley, in *Cambridge History of Ancient China*, 192-4, on the last page of which he is moved to make comparison with the Mesoamerican parallels, though in fact the comparison is already made by P. Wheatley, *The Pivot of the Four Quarters* (Edinburgh, 1971) 316, a generation earlier.

building.[62] Eventually the *Cambridge History* traces the decline in human sacrifice and the emergence of alternatives.[63] One might add parenthetically that most recently, research on animals in Early China has suggested why dogs were particularly favoured in funerary sacrifices, while one leading art historian has advanced a good reason why statues might have been preferred by some to slaughtered humans or animals, in that they are not subject to decay.[64]

But it also becomes apparent that throughout the evidence touched upon in the *Cambridge History of China* there is a tension reflected in the archaeological evidence between two types of human sacrificial victim, those to whom violence was done, often through decapitation – typically placed at some distance from the main figure buried – and those in closer attendance who appear to have been treated with some dignity. All are agreed that the massive burials of the early period show clear signs of the prevailing social hierarchy, with captured prisoners of war probably providing the lowest ranks of the victims. [65] But even in the later stages of the practice archaeologists in China have distinguished between 'companions in death' and 'human offerings'.[66] In short, the apparently differing degrees of compulsion exercised would seem to suggest that both sacrifice and self-sacrifice were involved together from the start.

True, the mute evidence of human remains cannot reveal the extent to which victims were subjected to social pressures. We may well feel that the spread of moral suasion as a substitute for physical

---

[62] Note the passing references in Bagley, *Cambridge History of Ancient China*, 178, 184. This practice is more amply described at an earlier stage of scholarship in Wheatley, *Pivot of the Four Quarters*, 41-6, who cites Cheng Te-k'un on the likelihood that housing for both living and the dead was consecrated in the same fashion at this time. For the non-Chinese parallels, note the learned commentary by I. and P. Opie, *The Oxford Dictionary of Nursery Rhymes* (Oxford, 1980) 275f.

[63] Lothar von Falkenhausen notes as many as 166 victims in one Qin burial from the sixth century; where Mark Lewis records the abolition of human sacrifice only in 384 B.C., *Cambridge History of Ancient China*, 486, 602, respectively.

[64] R. Sterckx, *The Animal and the Daemon in Early China* (Albany, 2002), 232; L. Ledderose, *Ten Thousand Things* (Princeton, 2000) 65-8.

[65] Thus D.N. Keightley, *Cambridge History of Ancient China*, 266-7, 286; cf. Bagley, *ibid.*, 192, for the distinction between those victims buried with care, and those who were decapitated or mutilated. Cf. also Wheatley, *Pivot of the Four Quarters*, 66, for the use of live prisoners of war in an emaciated condition in the foundations of buildings.

[66] Thus Wu Hung, in discussion of a case when tomb images were already partially replacing some of the human victims, *Cambridge History of Ancient China*, 733f.

coercion or straight decapitation made little difference in the long run – especially if we put ourselves in the constricted shoes of a nineteenth century Chinese widow expected, as De Groot describes all too graphically, to join her spouse in death.[67] Unfortunately I am aware of no general treatment of the theme of the voluntary victim in early China, surely something of a lack, especially in view of the long-term influence of the classical heritage. For it is worth pointing out that one version of the paradigm of self-sacrifice first identified in 1984 – one, that is, in which the problem of succession is left entirely tacit – ended up in a very influential place indeed, even as that version of the paradigm which made more explicit the notions of regicide and consequent guilt was effectively marginalised and almost lost to the tradition.[68]

In the former case, however, a chapter in one of the Confucian canonical texts, the *Shang Shu*, purportedly describing events at the start of the dynasty under which Confucius lived, but actually a later composition, records an episode highly commended by its Christian missionary translator.[69] No mention is made here of the bloody deeds that, as we know from other sources that the tradition was to marginalise in time, were believed to have attended the seizure of power by the new order. Rather, we are presented with a touching domestic scene. The young king appears to be mortally ill, and his uncle directs a prayer to be written imploring the gods to take him instead, on the grounds that he can serve them better, which he then has placed in a chest. The king recovers, but others try to poison his mind against his uncle as a potential usurper. Providentially, he happens to open the chest and discovers the prayer, so that the uncle's good intentions are revealed.[70]

What influence this canonical passage on the substitution of one life for another may have played over the centuries no one seems so far to have asked. But if we pass from a Confucian to a Buddhist context, many issues surrounding the practice of self-sacrifice in

---

[67] De Groot, *Religious System* II, 747-50.

[68] S. Allan, 'Drought, Human Sacrifice and the Mandate of Heaven in a Lost Text from the *Shang Shu*', *Bulletin of the School of Oriental and African Studies* 47 (1984) 523-39.

[69] Sarah Allan sees this source as probably early. For another view on the dating of this *Jin teng* chapter in the work, see the remarks of E.L. Shaughnessy, in M. Loewe (ed.), *Early Chinese Texts: A Bibliographical Guide* (Berkeley, 1993) 379.

[70] J. Legge, *The Shoo King* (Volume Three in *The Confucian Classics*, Oxford, 1893-4) 351-61.

later times will no doubt be clarified shortly, with the publication of
a doctorate already awarded in 2001 at the University of California,
Los Angeles. In this pioneering work the author takes up the case of
self-immolation as practised by Chinese Buddhist monks, mostly as
it would seem as free agents engaged in public rituals which they
felt to be sanctioned by Buddhist texts, albeit ones that were probably composed in China.[71] Earlier patterns of self-sacrifice, such as
drought prevention, appear to have played a part in some cases, as
the author, who is familiar with most of the literature reviewed here,
does not fail to point out. Yet he is equally chary of reducing a complex and much more important phenomenon than we previously
thought to simple pre-existing Chinese cultural causes. The role of
Buddhist rhetoric, for example in praising the self-sacrifice of the
Buddha to be, the bodhisattva, whom we may recall donated his
body to a hungry tigress, is also acknowledged. In fact, these fabulous acts of self-destruction in earlier lives gave rise to devotional
cults that spread out across Asia from their supposed original sites
via pilgrim routes, and that not simply in textual or oral form, but
also via the material culture of devotional objects that such routes
carried.[72] In this connection it is also perhaps worth observing that
the serving up of one's own flesh to ailing parents, already described
above, cannot be safely identified in Chinese culture before the
introduction of Buddhism, and others have certainly drawn attention to a famous popular religious text concerning the self-sacrifice
of one's own body for the ingestion of a parent that is of clear Buddhist derivation.[73] But the misreading of unfamiliar rhetoric, too, is
not assigned a place of undue importance in this remarkable study.
Rather, counter-examples, such as the existence of Taoist parallels,
all caution us against too simplistic an approach to a rich and varied
tradition.

---

[71] J.A. Benn, 'Burning for the Buddha: Self-immolation in Chinese Buddhism'
(Ph.D. dissertation, University of California, Los Angeles, 2001). See already J.A.
Benn, 'Where Text Meets Flesh: Burning the Body as an 'Apocryphal Practice' in Chi-
nese Buddhism', *History of Religions* 37 (1998) 295-322.

[72] Note the example given on 245-6 of T. H. Barrett, 'The origin of the term *pien-
wen*: an alternative hypothesis', *J. Roy. Asiatic Soc.* III 2 (1991) 241-46.

[73] See S. Sangren, *Chinese Sociologics: An Anthropological Account of the Role of Alien-
ation in Social Reproduction* (London, 2000) 292, note 294, but note also note 293 on the
'Chineseness' of the situation. Sangren's observations, in any case, are not addressed
to the overall phenomenon of flesh sacrifice and filial piety, but to the specific case
of unmarried daughters.

That such a note of caution should be sounded in a monographic account of one aspect of human sacrifice should not, on reflection, surprise us. So far we have primarily been concerned to review the appearance of themes related to human sacrifice in general accounts of Chinese religion and history, and even then, with an eye to the interests of the broader study of human sacrifice, our discussion has primarily been limited to material in Western languages, though an exception has been made in the case of the most important contributions of Japanese scholarship. But if we return once more to early China, and look at one or two of the contributions in English exclusively devoted to problems in understanding human sacrifice, similar warnings concerning complexity to those we have seen made in relation to self-immolation soon become apparent. For example, a re-examination of the evidence for funerary human sacrifice in the first millennium BC in 1983 cautions that the propensity for Chinese archaeologists to use the same traditional term, *xunzang*, to describe all burials where additional deaths seem to have been incurred may well have obscured a shift from multiple human sacrifice to something more like 'sati' (again, as once with De Groot, the Anglo-Indian term appears) as the nuclear family rose in importance over the course of time, though even this suggestion is hedged about with qualifications concerning the regional diversity even within North China of funerary custom as revealed by recent archaeology.[74]

Even more sobering is the latest contribution on human sacrifice in the second millennium BC known to me, an essay published in 1996 that unusually displays a wide comparative knowledge of human sacrifice, including the main Mesoamerican examples.[75] This draws on the rich textual documentation of the aforementioned 'oracle bones' (which apparently mention a sum total of 14,197 human sacrifices) as well as archaeology to suggest yet another interpretation of human sacrifice, not considered by scholars working on later periods, that quite reverses the stereotypical fear of outsiders betrayed in later sources. In the author's view it seems quite possible that the Shang state, traditionally viewed in China as the ancestor of their own polity, deliberately undertook the hunting and ritual killing of the neighbouring population outside its political control in

---

[74] Mumford. 'Death Do Us Unite', 13, 19.
[75] G. Shelach, 'The Qiang and the Question of Human Sacrifice in the Late Shang Period', *Asian Perspectives* 35 (1996) 1-26.

order to create a sharp division of loyalties that would ensure that its own subjects were in no position to decamp elsewhere but were forced to sustain their adherence to their overlords. This adds an intriguing political dimension to any religious interpretations of early Chinese sacrifice, and needless to say it is a dimension of which we find not a hint in later Chinese history.

True, the supposedly civilised Chinese in their interaction with what they deemed to be lesser races, like the representatives of any imperial system, tended not infrequently to act in ways that entirely subverted their theoretical distinctions between civilization and barbarity.[76] One may even find occasional gossip about Chinese officials making it their habit to eat the livers of their supposedly inferior neighbours, as well as of criminals.[77] But, as we have seen, the Chinese in historical times usually preferred to think of themselves as the victims of human sacrifice. The mute discoveries of archaeology will always need interpretation, but as soon as we turn to written sources in Chinese, even those from the first millennium BCE originally employed by De Groot and later reconsidered by Schafer, Mark Lewis and others, we are not dealing with simple and naïve reportage but with implicit beliefs about the meaning of human sacrifice. These beliefs, moreover, certainly changed over time and space, so that it becomes difficult to treat 'Chinese civilization' as any sort of unity. Indeed, the principle function of this survey has not been to summarize our state of knowledge in any comprehensive way, but rather to demonstrate something of the range of issues that a consideration of human sacrifice in China raises.

At the same time, I trust that enough will have been said to suggest that both comparatively and within the context of studying China the apparently marginal topic of human sacrifice in this cultural zone in fact leads us into areas of considerable importance, worthy of full-length monographic study or even several studies in the future. Were our sources for other cultures as forthcoming as the archaeological evidence has proved to be for China, would some of the other contributions in this volume also have been obliged to

---

[76] For some examples of this from the first millennium AD, see C. Holcombe, *The Genesis of East Asia, 221 B.C. – A.D. 907* (Honolulu, 2001) 28f.

[77] See Ding Chuanjing, ed., *Songren yishi huibian* 4 (Beijing, 1981) 169 – unfortunately, I have not had the English translation of this compendium of anecdotes from the late tenth to the thirteenth centuries to hand.

cast an equally rapid glance over an equally perplexing mixture of problems? One day, perhaps, new evidence may lead us to new considerations of other cases. By that time, one might hope, the Chinese case will have received more careful and detailed attention. Until then, these few unsystematic observations may even so serve for the time being as a starting point for better work.

INDEX OF NAMES, SUBJECTS AND PASSAGES

Jan N. Bremmer

PRINTED ON PERMANENT PAPER • IMPRIME SUR PAPIER PERMANENT • GEDRUKT OP DUURZAAM PAPIER - ISO 9706

N.V. PEETERS S.A., WAROTSTRAAT 50, B-3020 HERENT